## Michael Bloch

Born in 1953, Michael Bloch read law at St John's College, Cambridge, and was called to the bar by the Inner Temple. He worked for Maître Suzanne Blum, the Parisian lawyer of the Duke and Duchess of Windsor, and wrote six books about the couple. His other subjects include Hitler's foreign minister Ribbentrop, F. M. Alexander (founder of the Alexander Technique) and the politician Jeremy Thorpe. He met James Lees-Milne in 1979, became his literary executor on his death in 1997, edited the last five original volumes of his diary and has written his biography.

*The Diaries of James Lees-Milne were originally published as follows*

Ancestral Voices, 1942–3 (Chatto & Windus, 1975)
Prophesying Peace, 1944–5 (Chatto & Windus, 1977)
Caves of Ice, 1946–7 (Chatto & Windus, 1983)
Midway on the Waves, 1948–9 (Faber & Faber, 1985)
A Mingled Measure, 1953–72 (John Murray, 1994)
Ancient as the Hills, 1973–4 (John Murray, 1997)
Through Wood and Dale, 1975–8 (John Murray, 1998)
Deep Romantic Chasm, 1979–81 (John Murray, 2000)
Holy Dread, 1982–4 (John Murray, 2001)
Beneath a Waning Moon, 1985–7 (John Murray, 2003)
Ceaseless Turmoil, 1988–92 (John Murray, 2004)
The Milk of Paradise, 1993–7 (John Murray, 2005)

*Also by James Lees-Milne*

The National Trust (ed.), 1945
The Age of Adam, 1947
The National Trust Guide, 1948
Tudor Renaissance, 1951
The Age of Inigo Jones, 1953
Roman Mornings, 1956 (Heinemann Award)
Baroque in Italy, 1959
Baroque in Spain and Portugal, 1960
Earls of Creation, 1962
The Shell Guide to Worcestershire, 1964
St Peter's, 1967
Baroque English Country Houses, 1970
Another Self, 1970
Heretics in Love, 1973
William Beckford, 1976
Round the Clock, 1978
Harold Nicolson, 1980–1 (Heinemann Award)
Images of Bath, 1982
The Country House: An Anthology, 1982
The Last Stuarts, 1983
The Enigmatic Edwardian, 1986
Some Cotswold Country Houses, 1987
Venetian Evenings, 1988
The Fool of Love, 1990
The Bachelor Duke, 1991
People & Places, 1992
Fourteen Friends, 1996

# Diaries, 1942–1954

*Abridged and Introduced*
*by Michael Bloch*

## JAMES LEES-MILNE

JOHN MURRAY

First published in Great Britain in 2006 by John Murray (Publishers)
An Hachette UK Company

First published in paperback in 2007

4



A CIP catalogue record for this title is available from the British Library

ISBN 978-0-7195-6681-3
Ebook ISBN 978-1-84854-709-4

Typeset in Monotype Bembo by Servis Filmsetting Ltd

Printed and bound by Clays Ltd, St Ives plc

John Murray policy is to use papers that are natural, renewable and recyclable products and made from wood grown in sustainable forests. The logging and manufacturing processes are expected to conform to the environmental regulations of the country of origin.

John Murray (Publishers)
338 Euston Road
London NW1 3BH

www.johnmurray.co.uk

# *Contents*

# *Introduction*

James Lees-Milne was born in 1908 and died in 1997 in his ninetieth year. Until he was in his early sixties, he was unknown to the reading public except as the author of a dozen stylish, middle-brow works of architectural history, and as an occasional contributor of articles on country houses to *Country Life*. Those interested in architectural conservation were also aware that, during thirty years (1936–66) on the staff of the National Trust, he had helped save for the nation some of England's most important country houses. A bachelor until his forties, he had in 1951 married a general's daughter, Alvilde Chaplin. Both had an emotional preference for their own sex and the marriage was often stormy, but by the late 1960s they had settled down to a fairly harmonious existence at their house in the Cotswolds, Alderley Grange. Jim (as he was known) had numerous devoted friends of both sexes, who admired him for his many engaging qualities, but few of whom seem to have regarded him as especially clever. He regarded himself as a dreadful failure, and was obsessed by the thought that he was going to die soon and become forgotten.

Then, in 1970, he created a minor sensation with a book entitled *Another Self*, which was autobiographical in nature but written in the style of a novel. In it, he portrays himself as a bewildered simpleton who, throughout the first third-century of life, faces a series of bizarre and frightening confrontations with ogre-like figures – an irascible father, a bombastic employer, crusty colonels, and so on. Though he fails to distinguish himself in any of these encounters, he somehow muddles through thanks to a combination of survival instinct and good luck. The book is hilariously funny (in a way that recalls the silent movies), and some of the situations it describes are so preposterous that readers have often wondered how far they are true. *Another Self* established Jim's reputation as an Englishman of letters: in the thirty-six years since its appearance, it has rarely been out of print.*

*Another Self* takes Jim's life up to the end of 1941, when he was invalided out of the army and returned to work for the National Trust; and there was some speculation as to whether he had a sequel in mind. In a sense, he had. For at the beginning of 1942 he had started to keep a diary; and, encouraged by the success of *Another Self*, he set about editing this for publication. The first volume, covering 1942 and 1943, was published by Chatto & Windus in 1975, and fascinated readers with its accounts of wartime visits to eccentric country house owners, of London social life during the Blitz, and of the diarist's romantic feelings for both sexes. Critics discerned in it a unique, original flavour: Jim had a sharp eye, and an ability to depict both people and places in a few vivid words; he captured the spirit of the times; he was both waspish about others and critical of himself; his tone alternated between the comic and the poignant. A second volume, covering 1944 and 1945, followed two years later. During the 1980s, two further volumes were published, covering the years 1946 to 1949: these dealt with the rather grim world of post-war Britain, but nevertheless aroused admiration for the same qualities of candour, wit and sharp observation.

In 1949 (as described in the diary), Jim fell in love with the woman he was to marry, and at the end of that year he discontinued his diary, having kept it regularly for eight years. He resumed it from early 1953 to mid 1954, then stopped again. During the next seventeen years, he recommenced it sporadically, but most of these fragments he later destroyed as they touched upon difficulties in his marriage of which he did not afterwards wish to be reminded. However, in the summer of 1971, doubtless inspired by the fact that he had begun to contemplate the publication of his earlier diaries, he resumed a regular journal; and this time he continued faithfully for the remaining twenty-six and a half years of his life. In his last years, Jim began to edit this later series of diaries for publication by John Murray, covering the years 1971 to 1978

* It is currently available from Michael Russell as a Clocktower Paperback.

in three volumes; and since his death in 1997, I as his literary executor have completed the series with a further five volumes, bringing the total to twelve.

This compilation brings together, in abridged form, the first four original volumes, covering 1942–9, together with part of the fifth, covering 1953–4. These volumes were all given semi-ironic titles derived from Coleridge's 'Kubla Khan' – *Ancestral Voices* (1975), *Prophesying Peace* (1977), *Caves of Ice* (1983), *Midway on the Waves* (1985) and *A Mingled Measure* (1994). They have had an interesting publishing history. The first three volumes were published by Chatto & Windus; the fourth was published by Faber & Faber, who reprinted the first three; the fifth was published by John Murray, who reprinted the first four. The first four titles have recently been reprinted again by Michael Russell, who at the time of writing is about to follow suit with the fifth.

It may be useful to review Jim's life up to the time he began his diary at the age of thirty-three. He was born at Wickhamford Manor, Worcestershire, on 6 August 1908, the second of three children of George Crompton Lees-Milne and Helen, *née* Bailey. Three facts may be noted about his parents. First, although they lived the life of the country gentry, they hailed not from old county families but from 'trade': their money derived from a cotton mill in Lancashire, from where they had moved to Worcestershire only a couple of years before Jim's birth. Secondly, although they led a leisured Edwardian existence, their wealth was running out, so that Jim, unlike most of his contemporaries from similar backgrounds, began adult life with no money or the prospect of it and faced with the necessity of earning a living. Thirdly, they were philistines who were mainly interested in field sports and had little time for art, literature or religion: Jim's aesthetic, literary and spiritual interests were therefore not the result of his upbringing, but discovered for himself.

In *Another Self* Jim writes that, as a child, he was terrified of his stern and irascible father, and worshipped his beautiful, vain and rather dotty mother. Unlike his sturdy younger brother Dick, he was a daydreamer, and rather a cissy who until adolescence secretly longed to be a girl. The happiest period of his childhood seems to have been the First World War, when he saw little of his parents and lived with his widowed grandmother in a romantic Elizabethan house set in a huge estate. At prep school and Eton he did not shine at either work or games, and was regarded as dim and backward. He did, however, form passionate friendships, notably with Tom Mitford, brother of the later famous Mitford sisters (all of whom Jim got to know), and Desmond Parsons, younger brother of Michael, 6th Earl of Rosse. (Characteristically, Jim later fell in love with sisters of these boys – Diana Mitford and Bridget Parsons.)

After Eton, Jim endured the strange experience of being sent by his father to a London secretarial school where he was the only man. He longed to go to Oxford, however, and with support from his mother he managed to enter Magdalen College at the age of twenty. He read history, and scraped a third-class degree: much of his time was spent idling with his main friend of the period, the artist undergraduate Johnnie Churchill. It was during these otherwise unproductive university years that his interest in architecture was awakened, as he marvelled at the glories of Oxford and made the most of opportunities to visit nearby country houses. In *Another Self* he writes of a dinner party at one such house at which the drunken tenant, cheered on by rowdy undergraduates, defaced the portraits and committed other acts of vandalism: the horror of the occasion filled him with a desire 'to devote my energies and abilities, such as they were, to preserving the country houses of England'. Around this time he made several friends who were knowledgeable about architecture and encouraged him in such ambitions, notably John Betjeman, Robert Byron and Osbert Lancaster.

For the moment, the job Jim sought did not exist; and he came down from Oxford in 1931 without prospects or any idea of what to do. Fortunately his handsome looks, pleasing manners and soulful personality soon won him influential friends. Foremost among these were two eminent men (both married homosexuals) who became father-figures to him and helped complete his education – the ex-proconsul and statesman Lord Lloyd and the ex-diplomat and man of letters Harold Nicolson. Lloyd employed Jim as his private secretary from 1931 to 1935, and taught him to work hard; Nicolson – in whose London flat he went to live in 1934 –

encouraged his interest in literature and introduced him to a set of brilliant young writers including Raymond Mortimer and Eddy Sackville-West. Nicolson also kept a subsequently famous diary, intended for eventual publication, and probably inspired Jim to think of expressing himself in this form.

In 1934 Jim was received into the Roman Catholic Church, to which (like many of his contemporaries) he had been drawn by a longing for spiritual authority, a fascination with sumptuous rituals and a love of Italy – as well as possibly by a subconscious desire to shock his parents. They were indeed scandalised, and for a year he was unwelcome at Wickhamford – though he found himself 'adopted' by a number of prominent Catholic matrons such as the novelist Marie Belloc Lowndes and the courtier 'Puss' Milnes-Gaskell. Other (non-Catholic) women who took him under their maternal wing included Jean Hamilton, wife of the famous soldier Sir Ian Hamilton, and Kathleen Kennet, formidable widow of Scott of the Antarctic.

A lusty youth, Jim had many casual affairs with both men and women during his twenties. In 1935 he fell in love with Lady Anne Gathorne-Hardy, sister of the 4th Earl of Cranbrook, a lively young woman with literary interests whose cousin had married Johnnie Churchill. They announced their engagement, but felt unable to marry until they had overcome their poverty. Hoping for a career in journalism, Jim left Lloyd's service and joined the staff of Reuters; but he detested his bombastic employer Sir Roderick Jones, and resigned after only a few months. Soon afterwards, in a fit of depression, he called off the engagement, causing some distress to Anne (who went on to marry one of Jim's former lovers, the bookseller Heywood Hill).

It was at this moment of near-despair (March 1936), when he was penniless, jobless, and in disgrace for jilting his *fiancée*, that Jim suddenly landed the job of his dreams as Secretary to the newly created Country Houses Committee of the National Trust – a job which he largely owed to Harold Nicolson, whose wife Vita Sackville-West knew the sister of the Trust's senior official, Donald Matheson. A charity founded in the 1890s to preserve the English landscape, the Trust (which then had fewer than five thousand members, and a staff of five) had only recently adopted the conservation of country houses as one of its purposes. Jim's main duties were to help prepare a list of the houses deemed most worthy of preservation, to discuss this (with a view to obtaining tax concessions) with the government's Department of Works, and to visit those owners who were potentially interested in future arrangements with the National Trust. He threw himself into his work (which carried an annual salary of £300) with almost religious fervour, and soon became adept at both assessing the merits of houses and charming their owners. Although few properties came into the Trust's ownership at this period, Jim got to know such future donors as the Sackvilles of Knole, the Hoares of Stourhead, the Lucys of Charlecote and the Berwicks of Attingham. Together with his friends Robert Byron and Michael Rosse, he was also involved in founding the Georgian Group in 1937.

Jim adored literary society and longed to establish himself as a writer, but his literary talents, like other aspects of his personality, matured slowly. Before the war he worked on several books, including a novel and a biography of the poet Gerard Manley Hopkins, but none of these got into print and little trace of them survives. When his diary begins in 1942, he seems to have been contemplating a study of the historian Thomas Carlyle and his wife Jane (whose London house had become a National Trust property) – but this too came to nothing, and it was not until 1947, when he was almost forty, that he published an original work, *The Age of Adam.*

In March 1938 Jim fell in love with Rick Stewart-Jones, a young conservationist working for the Society for the Protection of Ancient Buildings. For the next eighteen months, they lived together (along with a bohemian collection of lodgers) in a large house in Cheyne Walk, Chelsea, which Stewart-Jones had bought and was attempting to restore. During these months, Jim was also beguiled by two handsome young protégés of Harold Nicolson – James Pope-Hennessy, and the American Stuart Preston. And there were at least two further women he considered marrying, including Gabriel Herbert whose sister married Evelyn Waugh.

The outbreak of war in 1939 – which he regarded as a disaster for civilisation – brought a temporary end to Jim's work for the National

Trust, which suspended most of its activities. During the Phoney War he trained as an ambulance driver for the Red Cross. In the spring of 1940, when he was about to be called up for army service, Michael Rosse arranged for him to be commissioned into the Irish Guards, a largely Catholic regiment. Jim proved a ludicrously inept soldier: in *Another Self*, he claims to have marched a platoon over the White Cliffs during a bombing raid on Dover. Fortunately his competence in action was never tested, for in October 1940, while on leave from his training battalion, he was caught in a London bomb blast, sustaining injuries which rendered him unfit for service.

Jim spent the next year in military hospitals, suffering from a condition eventually diagnosed as Jacksonian epilepsy. As he returned to health the National Trust was returning to life, as desperate country house owners began to look to it for the future salvation of their currently requisitioned properties. Through the influence of his former boss Oliver, Viscount Esher, he was discharged from the army in October 1941 and returned to work for the Trust, now based at West Wycombe Park, Sir John Dashwood's Palladian mansion in Buckinghamshire famous for its associations with the Hell Fire Club. It was there that Jim began his diary in January 1942.

These diaries speak abundantly for themselves; but one should bear in mind what they do *not* contain. With an eye on the future reader, Jim naturally concentrates on the more amusing aspects of life, such as visits to country houses and social gatherings, whereas his existence was largely taken up with the tedious grind of his job and the daily struggle against difficult wartime and post-war conditions, which are mentioned in passing. We seldom see him at his desk, though it was there that he probably spent most of his time, drafting letters and memoranda and, later, writing his books. He makes us aware of his romantic feelings for people of both sexes, but (in keeping with the conventions of the time) he hardly ever alludes to a sexual encounter, though there were undoubtedly many before his marriage. He says relatively little about either his health or his finances, although it is clear that both were a constant preoccupation.

It has sometimes been suggested (even by its admirers) that Jim's diary reveals him to have been a snob, a socialite and a reactionary. How far are such claims justified? He was emphatically not a snob in the sense of looking up at the great and down on the humble. He admired the noble only when they behaved nobly; and he had been brought up to treat everyone the same, and show sympathy with the unfortunate. On the other hand, it is certainly true (and is indeed among the diary's chief glories) that he was intrigued to meet the eminent, had a keen sense of social distinctions, and was quick to notice middle-class pretensions. In his own social life, he liked small gatherings of friends, but did not much enjoy large parties of strangers; diffident by nature, he tended on such occasions to be a quiet observer in the corner of the room. As for his political views, these come across as absurdly blimpish at some moments, surprisingly egalitarian at others. During the war, he joined a movement dedicated to promoting the ideal of world government; after 1945, his attitude towards Labour Britain was ambivalent. He writes much about the menace of socialism; yet in a typical entry of February 1948 he lambasts his own class and generation as 'cliquey, dated, prejudiced, out of touch with the new world and preposterously exclusive – arrogant, arrogant, with few redeeming qualities of any kind'.

Having edited the four volumes of his 1940s diary, Jim destroyed the original manuscripts: all that survive are four handwritten foolscap pages from the summer of 1947, which (by kind permission of the Beinecke Library at Yale, where the bulk of his papers now reside) were used as endpapers to the original hardback edition of this volume. However, for the years 1946–9, a typescript exists which represents an intermediate stage between manuscript and publication; and the manuscript of 1953–4 is in the Beinecke. This material discloses various passages which Jim removed in order to spare the feelings of people who were then still alive. With a few exceptions, these people are now long dead; and where the excisions are interesting, I have restored them. This in particular alters the complexion of 1949, a year which ends with his decision to marry Alvilde. At her own request, passages were taken out which showed that, in love with her as he was, he had doubts about marriage. She predeceased him in 1994; and in the interests of a true record, I have put these passages back in. It was probably also for his wife's sake that he removed the poignant account of his infatuation for a man met on a train on 10 April 1953, which fans will recognise as characteristic.

My main editorial task, however, apart from the drafting of footnotes (with which the original volumes were sparing), has been to reduce the diaries to less than a third of their original published length. In doing so I have not only made a selection of entries, but pruned and trimmed many of the individual entries themselves. I have allowed myself every liberty; but I conceal nothing, for the original volumes remain in print with Michael Russell, and may be consulted by scholars and indeed by all who feel inspired to read more.

For assistance of various kinds I am grateful to Mark Brockbank, Patric Dickinson, Sue Fox, Bruce Hunter, Jonathan Kooperstein, R. B. McDowell, Hugh Massingberd, Roland Philipps, the late Stuart Preston, Liz Robinson, Nick Robinson, John Russell, John Saumarez Smith, Tony Scotland, Caroline Westmore, and the staffs of the Beinecke Library, the London Library and the Oxford & Cambridge Club.

Michael Bloch
mab@jamesleesmilne.com
March 2006

For further information about James Lees-Milne's life and work, visit the Official James Lees-Milne Website at www.jamesleesmilne.com

# 1942

# 1942

*Thursday, 1st January*

West Wycombe Park [Buckinghamshire] is a singularly beautiful eighteenth-century house with one shortcoming. Its principal living-rooms face due north. The south front is overshadowed by a long, double colonnade which induces a total eclipse of the sun from January to December. Consequently we are very cold in the winter, for the radiators work fitfully these days. Our offices are in the Brown Drawing Room and Johnny Dashwood's* small study beyond it. Matheson,† the Secretary, Miss Paterson,‡ Eardley Knollys§ and I work in the latter room; Miss Ballachey, a typist and 'the junior' (aged 15) in the bigger room with all the filing cabinets.

*Monday, 5th January*

Early this morning I set out on a short tour in the very old National Trust Austin. Before I reached Princes Risborough the car practically stopped, and a rather delicious smell of rice pudding, accompanied by a curious knocking sound, came from inside. I drew up at a garage and asked what could possibly be the matter. The garage man at once said, 'You've got no water in your radiator.' I was humiliated. I am constantly being humiliated.

---

* Sir John Dashwood, 10th Bt (1896–1966); owner of West Wycombe Park, which he donated to N.T., 1943; m. 1922 Helen Eaton (d. 1989).

† Donald MacLeod Matheson (b. 1896); Secretary of N.T., 1932–45.

‡ Miss Florence Paterson, head of N.T. clerical staff, described by J.L.-M. as 'a saintly nanny figure' (*People & Places*).

§ Artist and aesthete (1902–91); on staff of N.T. from 1941.

I arrived at Althorp [Northamptonshire] more than half an hour late. Lord Spencer* was huffy at first because of my lateness, and because of the depreciation of Althorp by the agent whom the Trust had employed to make a report on the property. He understandably associated the Trust with the agent's ignorance and lack of taste. In the end I liked Lord Spencer for not being crosser than he was. He said I was the first National Trust person who had talked sense. Certainly I appreciated Althorp. But the difficulties will be infinite before we get it. I stayed to luncheon – poached eggs with maize and cabbage – which we ate in a little panelled room. Lady Spencer, like a goddess, distilled charm and gentleness around her.

I continued to Haselbech for the night, where I found Aunt Con† in her new cottage, which is too technological for words. You press one button beside the bed, and a metal arm offers you a cigarette in a cardboard holder; another, and tea spouts from a tap into a cup; yet another and the mattress becomes as hot as St Lawrence's gridiron. The whole room was a tangle of wires inadequately insulated. I was in terror of being electrocuted.

*Tuesday, 6th January*

Passing through Hitchin, I noticed St Ippolitt's Church dominating a hill on my left, and got out to search for George Lloyd's‡ grave. On his deathbed he asked to be buried here. I found the grave huddled amongst ordinary parishioners', which I don't suppose he would have liked. I stood over it thinking of him for

---

* Albert Edward John ('Jack'), 7th Earl Spencer (1892–1975); m. 1919 Lady Cynthia Hamilton, dau. of 3rd Duke of Abercorn.

† Constance Shieffelin of New York (1872–1963); m. 1900 Charles Bower Ismay (1874–1924), partner of White Star Shipping Line; châtelaine of Haselbech Hall, Northamptonshire; wealthy widow who was a mother figure to J.L.-M. during the 1930s.

‡ George, 1st Baron Lloyd (1879–1941); imperial proconsul and Conservative politician, Secretary of State for the Colonies 1940–1, whom J.L.-M. had served as private secretary, 1931–5; lived at Clouds Hill near Hitchin, Hertfordshire.

a quick moment, and left in a hurry, because it was bitter cold. Then I turned for a second and thought, how odd that that well-groomed body which I had known so well in its dapper Savile Row suits was rotting within a few yards of me, in this intense northern cold which he hated. Robert Byron* used to say he never thought of his dead friends in connection with their decomposing bodies, but I cannot help it. I suppose this signifies that I have too little faith in the immortality of the spirit.

*Wednesday, 7th January*

Back at West Wycombe I found troops occupying the village and manoeuvres in progress. My bedroom commandeered for a brigadier. The Irish Guards are among the armoured brigade, for Kennedy, once my servant at Dover, saw me cross the road in the village and asked the estate office to ring me up. I went and talked to him and gave him 10 shillings. Was pleased he should wish to see me.

*Sunday, 11th January*

Found Eddy [Sackville-West]† at tea and Lady Colefax‡ who is staying. Lady Colefax dressed in thick blue tweed. She must have been pretty once. Her face is now like an intelligent pug's, or a dolphin's. I felt she might snub me if I said something ingenuous, whereas she would not snub Eddy, whatever he might say.

*Monday, 12th January*

It is freezing hard and the park is covered with rime. Helen [Dashwood] elects to come to London for the free lift, and plumps

* Traveller, art critic and writer (1905–41), who had been lost at sea some months earlier.

† Hon. Edward Sackville-West (1901–65); music critic; s. father 1962 as 5th Baron Sackville; a paying guest at West Wycombe.

‡ Sibyl Halsey (1874–1950); society hostess; founder, 1933, of London decorating firm (later Colefax & Fowler); m. 1901 Sir Arthur Colefax, QC (1866–1936).

herself in the front seat by me so that poor Miss Paterson is obliged to sit in the back seat in the cold. All goes well and the two committees pass uneventfully. Lord Zetland,* the Trust's chairman, is wry, starchy and pedagogic; Lord Esher,† like a dormouse, small, hunched, quizzical, sharp and cynical; Ronnie Norman,‡ the eternal handsome schoolboy, noisily loquacious until he finds the conclusion to an argument, when he stops like an unwound clock; Nigel Bond,§ dry, earthy, sound, unimaginative; Sir Edgar Bonham Carter,¶ twisted by arthritis, fair, impartial, but too subdued to be heeded by the others; Mr Horne,** the old, sweet-sour yet genial solicitor, who has sat in attendance ever since, as an articled clerk, he helped draft the constitution of the National Trust in 1895, now beyond his prime, and havering.

*Friday, 16th January*

I set off for East Sheen to walk across Sheen Common. This is a worthwhile property for it rounds off one corner of Richmond Common. Though the ground is fairly deep under snow I pad across it between birch trees and over heath. I try to find a way into Richmond Park, but the military have commandeered the whole of it, and there is no ingress whatever. So I walk miles round by Mount Clare, which cannot be seen from the road, and across Putney Heath, today quite beautiful and shimmering under the snow. Before Wimbledon I take a bus into Ewell. There I inspect Hatch Furlong, a wretched property, now a cabbage patch on either side of an arterial road, and surrounded by ribbon

---

* Lawrence Dundas, 2nd Marquess of Zetland (1876–1961); Conservative politician, Secretary of State for India, 1935–40; Chairman of N.T., 1931–45.

† Oliver Brett, 3rd Viscount Esher (1881–1963); chairman of N.T. committees, and of Society for Protection of Ancient Buildings; m. 1912 Antoinette Heckscher.

‡ R.C. Norman (1873–1963); Vice-Chairman of N.T., 1924–48; former Chairman of London County Council and BBC.

§ Secretary of N.T., 1901–11, who later served on its committees (1877–1945).

¶ Lawyer and civil servant (1870–1956).

** Benjamin W. Horne of Horne & Birkett, solicitors.

development. I lunch with Midi* at Ashtead House where she is living with her mother-in-law Lady Gascoigne, who resembles a cow accustomed to all weathers, with the kindly, rough manners of one.

*Saturday, 17th January*

I arrive by bus at Leckhampton House which Mrs Stewart-Jones† has just bought on the Berkshire Downs. It is tea-time. The household is very cheerful, domestic and welcoming after the cold outside. The dove is cooing, the lamps are bright, the toast is thick and the tea steams.

Reginald Blunt‡ is living here. He is a dear old man, courteous and cultivated. He is 85, very independent, and with all his wits about him. I talked to him about the Carlyles. He even remembers Mrs Carlyle, who died in 1866. He used to take a jug of milk from the rectory cow to them each day, and in proper season mulberries from the rectory garden. One morning, Mrs Carlyle received the mulberries from him at the door of 24 Cheyne Row and said, 'Wait! Mr Carlyle has a present for you.' Presently Carlyle descended in his long dressing-gown, with a rosy apple on a plate. Reginald Blunt was terribly disappointed that the apple was made of china; but he has it to this day. He knew Rossetti, who used to play whist at the rectory. His language was appalling. The following day he would write a letter to the rector, Blunt's father, apologising for his swear words.

Blunt is in favour of absolutely rebuilding Chelsea Old Church, though not of absolutely rebuilding everything on principle. I agree.

---

* Hon. Mary O'Neill (1905–91); friend and confidante of J.L.-M. since 1930; m. 1934 Frederick ('Derick') Gascoigne, s. of Brig.-Gen. Sir Frederick Gascoigne (1873–1944) and Cicely, dau. of Gen. Edward Clive.

† Mother of 'Rick' Stewart-Jones (1914–57), architectural conservationist and J.L.-M's most intimate friend since March 1938.

‡ Chelsea historian (1857–1944).

*Saturday, 24th January*

Nancy [Mitford],* who is now living at West Wycombe, is mad about the Antarctic Expedition† and has collected every book about it she can lay her hands on.

I went up to London with Helen this morning for David Lloyd's‡ wedding. Met Midi at her new club, a fantastic institution of which all the members are MFHs and their wives. We at once decided we were too poor to eat there and must go to a pub. Could not find one, but instead found Claridge's. Midi directed me to the 'Causerie' where she said there was a lovely hors d'oeuvres with wine, as much as you liked for 4 shillings. There was chicken on the menu too and since it was thrown in with my Madeira, we ate it too. After all that the bill came to 18 shillings.

*Sunday, 25th January*

Went to Mass in Cheyne Row held in the vestry for its warmth. Afterwards to Carlyle's house and sat in the kitchen talking to the Strongs. The Strong family have now been caretaking for a period longer than Carlyle lived in the house; and Mrs Strong's mother worked for Carlyle. I then went to Brooks's. As I stood by the fire talking to Ran Antrim,§ we overheard Lord Trenchard¶ say to Lord Mottistone,** 'I don't see how the Japanese can hold out much

---

* Hon. Nancy Mitford (1904–73), eldest of the Mitford sisters, daughters of 2nd Baron Redesdale (all of whom J.L.-M. knew through his school friendship with their brother Tom); novelist; m. 1933–57 Hon. Peter Rodd (1904–68), yr s. of 1st Baron Rennell.

† The second expedition of Captain Robert Scott (1868–1912), which reached the South Pole on 17 January 1912, only to discover that the Norwegian Amundsen had got there before them, Scott dying on the return journey ten weeks later.

‡ 2nd Baron Lloyd (1912–85); o.c. of J.L.-M's sometime employer, 1st Baron; m. 1942 Lady Jean Ogilvy, dau. of 11th Earl of Airlie.

§ Randal McDonnell, 13th Earl of Antrim (1911–77); wartime RN officer; Chairman of N.T., 1965–77.

¶ Sir Hugh Trenchard (1873–1956); founding figure of RAF; cr. Viscount, 1936.

** Maj.-Gen. John Seely (1868–1947); soldier and Liberal politician; cr. Baron Mottistone, 1933.

longer now.' In the library, I read Reginald Blunt's short book on the Carlyle household. Eddie Marsh* sat reading beside me but did not talk to me. This is very civilised club behaviour.

*Wednesday, 28th January*

Went up to London to the dentist. Finished Cherry-Garrard's† book in the train. His terrible descriptions of the cold affected me physically, so that I shivered all through luncheon at Brooks's, and by the time I arrived at the dentist's, felt sick. After he had finished with me, I was sick. On recovery, I walked to Heywood Hill's‡ bookshop. A strange bearded man wearing a brown fustian cape§ was dictating a letter to Heywood at his typewriter. Anne whispered myseriously, 'He is the claimant to the throne of Poland.' But there hasn't been a Polish throne since the eighteenth century.

Walked across St James's Park to Westminster and looked at Archer's¶ Baroque church in Smith Square, completely gutted by fire. I recollect dragging a reluctant Jamesey Pope-Hennessy** into it in the first winter of the war on the plea that it would probably be destroyed. The shell is intact and with a little trained ivy would make a fine Piranesi†† ruin. Had tea with Lady Colefax at her cosy little house in Lord North Street. She was sitting on a stool right in

---

* (Sir) Edward Marsh (1872–1953); civil servant and man of letters, friend of writers and poets including Rupert Brooke and Siegfried Sassoon.

† Apsley Cherry-Garrard (1886–1959); youngest member and survivor of Scott's expedition, about which he wrote in *The Worst Journey in the World* (1922).

‡ Eton contemporary of J.L.-M. (1906–86), and founder of bookshop in Curzon Street, 1936; m. 1938 Lady Anne Gathorne-Hardy (1911–2006), o. dau. of 3rd Earl of Cranbrook, to whom J.L.-M. had been engaged in 1935.

§ Probably the Austrian-Polish aristocrat Prince Lichnowsky.

¶ Thomas Archer (1668–1743); gentleman architect favouring continental rather than English Baroque; worked at Chatsworth.

** James Pope-Hennessy (1916–74); yr son of Dame Una (1876–1949) and General Richard Pope-Hennessy (1875–1942); writer and bohemian, who was eventually killed by 'rough trade'.

†† Giovanni Battista Piranesi (1720–78); Italian etcher of fabulous imaginary architecture.

front of the fire so that the room was made distinctly chilly by her acting as a fire screen. Hers is a scientific sort of snobbery. She is evidently hell-bent on collecting scalps, and impatient with anything that may deflect her from the chase. Her friends ring her up about people as one might ring Selfridge's Information Bureau. Bogey Harris,* who came in soon after me, said, 'By the way, Sibyl, I have been meaning to ask you, who is Mrs Benthall, the mother of Sir Somebody Benthall?' 'Mrs Benthall, *Mrs* Benthall,' she repeated, with emphasis on the Mrs, 'I am afraid I really can't help you there.'

*Sunday, 1st February*

I called on the Rosses† in Eaton Terrace. Michael looking very well and Anne most affectionate and sweet. They took me to Prince Vsevolode‡ and Mamie's for a drink. The Prince is very ugly and rather dull. She, still beautiful, is called Princess Romanovsky-Pavlovsky (a stage joke name) because she is a morganatic wife. Had gin and peppermint to drink, not very nice. Mamie does all her own housework. He is fifth in succession to the throne of Russia, and his succession is as likely as the uncrowned King of Poland's.

To bed early, worn out, because I sat with Rick Stewart-Jones until 2.30 last night after he suddenly turned up. Although I forget his very existence during prolonged absences, I find after ten minutes' talk he is the only person to whom I can say just everything.

---

* Edwardian society figure; 'an old crony of Lady Cunard, noted for his wit, when he deigned to give an exhibition of it'.

† Michael Parsons, 6th Earl of Rosse (1906–1979); landowner and architectural conservationist, whose brother, Hon. Desmond Parsons, had been a schoolfriend of J.L.-M.; m. 1935 (as her 2nd husband) Anne Armstrong-Jones (*née* Messel; 1902–92).

‡ Prince Vsevolode (1914–73), grandson of Grand Duke Constantin, younger brother of Tsar Alexander II; m. (1st) 1939–56 Lady Mary Lygon (1910–82), 3rd dau. of 7th Earl Beauchamp of Madresfield Court, Worcestershire.

*Thursday, 5th February*

A horrid day in London. Cold intense, and a bitter wind blowing nasty wet snow in one's face. The SPAB* office in Great Ormond Street is almost the only building left standing in this devastated area. All round, where whole squares and streets of houses existed a short time ago, are now empty blankets of snow. The meeting had already begun, with Lord Esher in the chair. They were discussing an official invitation to send representatives to list old buildings in London which they consider should not at any cost be sacrificed to post-war improvements – for instance, the Mansion House's future is threatened. The chief item on the agenda was Holland House. It appears that the whole interior is gutted, and the staircase is rotting in the rain and snow. Everything else has gone except the walls, which in my opinion are no longer Jacobean, for the windows, copings, etc. were largely Victorianised. I submitted that the chief point about Holland House was its historical associations, which have now gone for ever. Anyway, the Ilchesters† will never live in it again, and I feel sure that the £37,000 needed to rebuild it will not be forthcoming after the war. The prospect of a twentieth-century Jacobean fake is surely worse than a Victorian Jacobean fake.‡

*Sunday, 8th February*

Still freezing hard and the drive desperately dangerous and slippery. Eddy is here again, and Cecil Beaton§ came last night. He is quite grey, and darts like a bird. He is flagrantly Twentyish. He must be very successful if money-making is an indication. I do not mean to be critical for he is an artist, and I find him very sympathetic though a little alarming. This morning on my return from Mass at High Wycombe

* Society for the Protection of Ancient Buildings, founded by William Morris in 1877; its current Chairman was 3rd Viscount Esher, also Chairman of Country Houses Committee of N.T.

† Giles Fox-Strangways, 6th Earl of Ilchester (1879–1959); m. 1902 Lady Helen Stewart (1876–1956), e. dau. of 6th Marquess of Londonderry.

‡ See entry for 28 April 1942.

§ Artist and society photographer (1904–80).

I gave him an hour's typewriting lesson. Towards the end we started gossiping, and then I saw how entertaining and sharp he is.

Yesterday's luncheon revealed Helen in a new light, for the curate and his old mother came. H. said to us just before they arrived that there must be no witticisms and no house-party talk, just the sort of thing Mama would say. They were indeed an eminently 'bedint'* couple, and H. said so poor that they undoubtedly didn't have enough to eat. The mother was sadly dressed for the terrible cold, and most humble and pathetic. He a facetious young man in a long black cutaway coat, with black dusty hair badly cut and a blue blotchy face. Yet the two were proud in their reciprocal love. Helen made great efforts to entertain them, and induce them to have a square meal. Alas, they were far too genteel to be pressed to second helpings. After dinner I took up my knitting – 'the true sock' Clementine [Beit]† calls it, which on St Milne's day, instead of liquefying, will unravel if there is to be a good harvest. Cecil had hiccoughs he laughed so much. Eddy took up his knitting, an endless khaki scarf. We must have looked an odd spectacle. Still, I wish Helen would not call us the two old bombed houses.

We talked about beautiful women, and it was interesting to listen to Cecil on the subject. He deprecated Tilly Losch,‡ and said Diana Cooper§ was probably the most beautiful woman he had photographed. Of Sarah Churchill,¶ Vic Oliver's wife, 'Perhaps

---

* Word from the private language of Harold Nicolson and Vita Sackville-West, meaning 'common'.

† Clementine Mitford (1915–2005); cousin of the Mitford sisters; m. 1939 Sir Alfred Beit, MP, 2nd Bt (1903–94); she was lodging at West Wycombe to be near her husband, serving nearby with the RAF.

‡ Ottilie Ethel Losch (1907–75); Austrian dancer and actress; pre-war lover of J.L.-M's schoolfriend Tom Mitford; m. 1939–47 (as his 2nd wife) 6th Earl of Carnarvon.

§ Lady Diana Manners (1892–1986); officially yst dau. of 8th Duke of Rutland (though she supposed her father to have been the journalist and politician Harry Cust [1861–1917]); actress; m. 1919 Alfred Duff Cooper (1890–1954; cr. Viscount Norwich, 1953), diplomatist, politician and writer.

¶ Actress (1914–82); dau. of Winston Churchill; m. 1st 1936–45 Vic Oliver, Austrian-born entertainer (1896–1964), 2nd 1949–57 Anthony Beauchamp, 3rd 1962–3, 23rd Baron Audley (1913–63).

I should not tell tales out of school, but if her nose were only her own.' 'Well, whose is it?' Nancy asked. 'Gillies's,'* he said.

*Saturday, 14th February*

Wickhamford [Manor, Worcestershire, J.L.-M's family home]. Walk with Deenie† in the afternoon to the Sandys Arms and talk with Maggie in her back room which smells of dusty plush and stale cheese, and a knot of hair on the top of her hair like the shiny crust of a cottage loaf. She is big with the child to be born in April and heartily disgruntled by the prospect. 'Oh, Master Jim, I could kill that there Bert [husband] for what he's done to me – and at such a time too.' I could also readily kill Bert for taking Maggie away from us in the first place.

*Monday, 16th February*

Taking Mama and Deenie with me, I went to Dowles Manor near Bewdley, where I went in and talked to Mr Elliott. Very frail and ill with rheumatism, he spoke of dying shortly and wants the National Trust to have the house and twenty acres of the valley as soon as he can get the consent of his elder daughter now in Ceylon. This may take six months or more. A complete picture postcard house, olde worlde black and white, the outside almost ridiculous. Mama at once said, 'What a dream!' Certainly the stencilling inside is remarkable. It is of the date of the house, *circa* 1570, and covers both beams and plaster panels. On this account alone the building is important. Walked by the trout brook to our [the N.T's] adjoining Knowles Mill property and talked to the woodman's wife. Lovely rustling walk beside the water under trees.

---

* An eminent surgeon.

† J.L.-M's widowed aunt Doreen Cunninghame (d. 1952); lived at Stow-on-the-Wold, Oxfordshire.

*Tuesday, 17th February*

Dined with Harold Nicolson* and Jamesey at Rules. We talked about Byron's sex life. Lady Byron† is said to have recorded in her diary that when she once told Byron that she could not sleep with him because she had 'the curse', he replied, 'Oh, that's all right, I can sleep with Augusta.'‡ Sounds improbable to me – I mean Lady Byron recording it. In Hobhouse's§ copy of Moore's *Life of Byron* [1835], which Harold possesses, Hobhouse has pencilled in the margin that Lord Holland told him the reason why Lady Byron left her husband was that Byron attempted to bugger her; that Augusta was not the cause. Harold attributes the incest-boasting to Byron's subconscious getting-his-own-back on Augusta, who when he was a boy was much his senior in social sophistication. For it was Augusta who taught him correct manners which Byron was supremely backward in acquiring, if he ever properly acquired them, owing to Mrs Byron's slipshod and provincial upbringing of her son. Again in Hobhouse's copy, where Moore gives a high-falutin poetical reason for Byron's desire for Hobhouse to leave him alone in Greece, a caustic marginal note gives the true reason. It was quite simply that Byron did not want another English gentleman, even his best friend, to witness his sexual aberrations, which were – in Hobhouse's words – a disgrace to his class and country.

---

* Hon. (Sir) Harold Nicolson (1886–1968); yst s. of 1st Baron Carnock; diplomatist, writer and politician; National Labour MP for West Leicester, 1935–45; friend and mentor of J.L.-M. since 1933; m. 1913 Hon. Vita Sackville-West, novelist and poet, o.c. of 2nd Baron Sackville; they had restored Sissinghurst Castle, Kent, and created its garden.

† Annabella Milbanke (1792–1860); heiress and mathematician; m. 1814 George Gordon, 6th Baron Byron (1788–1824), from whom she separated before the birth of their daughter, 1815.

‡ Hon. Augusta Byron (1783–1851); half-sister of 6th Baron Byron; m. Colonel George Leigh; her 3rd dau. Medora (b. 1814) was rumoured to be from an incestuous liaison with her brother.

§ John Cam Hobhouse (1786–1869); friend of Byron, who accompanied him on his travels to the Iberian Peninsula and Near East, 1812–14; later a Whig MP and minister; cr. Baron Broughton.

*Thursday, 19th February*

Walked to the Epstein* exhibition at the Leicester Galleries. Jacob and the Angel in alabaster. Strong, ugly and vastly arresting. One is awed and repelled by the Jew. I was struck by the number and variety of people wrapt in contemplation. There is undoubtedly a growing interest in works of art among all sections. I would give my soul to be busted by Epstein, and would then probably be sick at the sight of the thing.

I took the 4.30 from Euston to Manchester and arrived at 10, worn out by the journey. At the Midland Hotel ordered supper, very expensive, about 10 shillings, of chill soup, golden plover with wet swimmy veg presented on one plate, and coffee. Extraordinary people in the hotel, peroxide blondes decked with false gems, and middle-aged men with their ears sunk into the fat of their necks and the wire bridges of their specs into their noses. Rolls of skin over their collars.

*Friday, 20th February*

Accompanied by two bank managers, a surveyor and a solicitor, I went to inspect Hen Cote Cottage and Daisy Nook. Had been considerably put off by the names, but lo! the property was immensely worth while. Surrounded by Manchester, Oldham, Ashton, it is a blessed oasis. A deep gully of some thirteen acres with a rushing yellow-backed burn through it. Much frequented by the inhabitants of these towns. There are wildish moors nearby, and I decide it is just the sort of land the Trust should hold. My companions charming. Lancashire people are like children, friendly and warm, but inferiority-complexy about people from the south. They are always talking of Lancashire qualities, and seemed pleased when I told them that I myself derived from these parts. Worcestershire people never go on about Worcestershire qualities, I notice. Bitterly cold day, a film of ice practically covering the burn.

---

* (Sir) Jacob Epstein (1880–1959); sculptor.

Took express train back to London in order to dine with Jamesey. He joined me at Brooks's at 9, too late to get dinner there, and had no money. I was extremely tired by then, and cross. Walked to the Barcelona Restaurant where we had to wait half an hour before we were served. Testily I tell J. he is becoming spoilt and too reliant on his youthful charm. At once realise I make the mistake of admitting that he still has these qualities, not that he isn't perfectly well aware of them.

*Saturday, 21st February*

To Moss Bros in the morning where I bought a maroon velvet smoking jacket for 8½ guineas and thirteen coupons. I still have a few coupons left till June.

*Sunday, 22nd February*

From High Wycombe I bussed to Bray Wick [Berkshire] and from there walked to Ockwells Manor. I was last here in 1936. My host, Sir Edward Barry,* now eighty-four, is as lively as ever. He has one servant. Sir Edward himself stokes the boiler every morning. The house is sadly dusty. We had a delicious English roast beef luncheon with Yorkshire pudding, rhubarb tart to follow. A gin and vermouth warmed me first of all, for it is still bitterly cold. Sir Edward wants to sell. He owns 600 acres with a rental of £1,200 and is asking £75,000 because an American millionaire offered him that figure ten or more years ago. He spurned Cook's† offer of £40,000. I fear I cannot help him unless he changes his tune. He took me round the house again. Although it is most important, yet it does not please. Sir E. is 2nd Baronet and Baron du Barry in Portugal, which is strange.

---

* Sir Edward Barry, 2nd Bt (1858–1949). Thirty years later, J.L.-M. described Ockwells Manor as a property which had once been regarded as 'a fifteenth-century manor house . . . of the first importance', but was by then considered 'an over-restored fake' (*Ancient as the Hills*, 5 April 1973).

† Ernest Cook; grandson and co-heir of the travel agent Thomas Cook; rich, eccentric recluse and benefactor of the N.T., to whom he gave Montacute House and the Bath Assembly Rooms (see entry for 28 June 1946).

*Tuesday, 24th February*

Packed all the relevant papers into my old black bag and caught the 9.06 from West Wycombe station to London for the Country Houses Committee meeting which I had to take myself since Matheson is away ill, with a temperature of 104. Rather nervous how I was going to acquit myself this first time I have ever taken a meeting alone. But as a matter of fact all went fairly well. The old gentlemen are so fearfully ignorant of the intricacies of most items on the agenda that one need have little fear of them. Besides, they one and all are *so* nice.

*Saturday, 28th February*

Nancy often shocks me, accustomed as I am to think of her running contrary to conventions in her girlish, mocking manner. For example she said to me today, looking at me very seriously in the way people do when they know what they are about to say will meet with disagreement, 'It is clearly our duty to remain in England after the war, whatever the temptations to get out. The upper classes have derived more fun from living in this country since the last war than any other stratum of society in any other country of the world. No more foreign parts for *us*,' with a hiss on the last sibilant.*

*Sunday, 1st March*

Before luncheon, Nancy said, 'I must just dash to the Beardmore.' 'The what?' Helen asked. 'Don't you know', we said, 'that the upstairs lavatory is called after the Beardmore Glacier.† It faces due north, the window is permanently propped open so that it can't be shut, and the floor is under a drift of snow.' Helen doesn't find this

* As soon as the war was over, Nancy Mitford moved to France and never lived in England again.

† Glacier in Antarctica, the world's largest, discovered by Captain Scott in 1911 and named after one of his expedition's sponsors.

a funny joke. After luncheon, Eddy, Nancy and I huddle over a few green logs in the fireplace, Eddy trying to read *The Mill on the Floss*, I Jane Carlyle's letters. We turn to discussing H's extraordinarily unadult character, her terror of being left out of anything that may be going on, her pique over preconceived plans going wrong, and a certain resentment over others enjoying something she fears she may be missing.

I motored to Eton in time to take Francis [Dashwood]* out to tea in the Cock Pit, where we ate the familiar bap rolls with jelly jam and whipped cream, and Austrian chocolate cake. Only the cream was ersatz, and the cake tasted of straw rolled in dung. Then to Evensong in College Chapel where the traditional ceremonial is invariable. The 'ram'† marches in the same deliberate, self-conscious manner. The same scrubby little boys sit demurely on the knife boards. In how short a time is contact with the younger generation completely lost. How can I be sure about what I believe these boys to be thinking about the service and each other, for I could never ask one, and no one would venture to tell me? Yet there they are, very well-mannered it is true, but flashing across the nave confidential smiles that mean so much, ogling and making assignations without a word being spoken. Oh the squalid thoughts and the romance of it all at the time, I remember!

*Monday, 2nd March*

Eardley and I motored to Princes Risborough to look at a wall at the bottom of the manor garden which is falling down. Afterwards Mrs Vaughan, our tenant, showed us over the house. She is the widow of Dr Vaughan, late headmaster of Rugby, a distinguished lady who has 'let herself go'. Very countrified, untidy and dressed in subfusc. She has the thinnest nose bridge I ever did see, like the edge of a pocket knife. I could not take my eyes off it.

---

* Son (1925–2000) of Sir John Dashwood, whom he succeeded as 11th Bt, 1966.

† The 'ram' is a procession of Fifth Form boys, led by the head of the school up the nave before services begin; 'knife boards' are narrow benches.

*Saturday, 7th March*

There is a great stir in Brooks's about the member who has been asked to resign, and won't go. He doggedly makes use of the library every day and even insists on privileges which the most hardened old members would not dare demand after half a century's membership. He has been so rude to the servants that in a body they informed the Secretary they would leave unless he did. Now there is to be an extraordinary meeting in order formally to expel him. Such a thing has never been known in the whole history of Brooks's. The offender is a vulgar, sinister-looking fellow, who prowls around the club. When he leaves a room the older gentlemen break into muffled whispers.

I went to tea at the Kinnairds'* house in Lennox Gardens [Kensington]. Tea was on a table in front of the fire and Lady Kinnaird on her knees with the toasting fork. Very friendly, but offered the butter half-heartedly, and when I said, 'I don't eat butter', also half-heartedly, she did not press. I refused the sugar offered, taking out my saccharine, and again was not pressed. I was asked to take the honey from the comb with my knife to save dirtying a spoon. Lord K. wanted to know all about the National Trust and the country houses scheme. He lamented the servant scarcity and said it was a scandal elderly people should not be allowed a full quota of servants. Lamented education of the lower orders. I was a good deal entertained, and couldn't help liking them. All so unrealistic and old-fashioned.

*Sunday, 8th March*

In the afternoon, Rick [Stewart-Jones] and I walked in the sun. He wanted to look at the slum parts of Chelsea around Lots Road power station. It is remarkable what vast areas there have been destroyed, and yet the power station is unharmed. R. is fascinated by the problem of reconstructing these devastated areas when the

* Kenneth FitzGerald, 12th Baron Kinnaird (1880–1972); m. 1903 Frances Victoria Clifton.

war is over. It is slums in which he is most interested. I am not at all. We looked at the Moravian Cemetery at the back of Lindsey Palace.* There is a nice little cottage, and an old chapel, now a studio. Half-hidden by the long grass of a lawn are round and square stones on the ground, with inscriptions on them. The Moravians were buried standing up, the easier to scamper away at the sounding of the last trump.

*Monday, 9th March*

The sun was shining and the air almost balmy as I walked through Belgravia. For the first time this year I inhaled that familiar scent of London, which ought to be so full of promise and happy days. But alas, now it augurs despair, inevitable misery, and destruction. For the spring is a season one has come to dread. Yet the birds in Green Park were singing oblivious of the future; and in spite of my awareness of it I found my feet skimming over the grass.

I once firmly believed in the permanency of human relationships. I suppose I read about their impermanency in books, but could not bring myself to acknowledge it. Now I know it to be a fact, just as every physical creation is transitory. The realisation ought doubtless to strengthen my divine love, but I do not think it does.

*Saturday, 14th March*

I walked round St Paul's Cathedral. It was full of little brown men, Burmese or Siamese, herded by kind English drago-ladies. The ambulatory and the transepts are closed to the public, and there is a great chasm where the bomb fell in the north transept. The inner screen whereon used to be '*Si monumentum requiris, circumspice*' is totally destroyed. The Duke of Wellington's ornate monument is

* Extensive property in Cheyne Walk, Chelsea, rebuilt *c.* 1750 by Baron Zinzendorf as a headquarters for the Moravian Church, and subsequently broken up into several houses. It was Rick Stewart-Jones's ambition (briefly realised to a limited extent) to buy up its various components and restore its unity.

bricked up with iron stays from one side to the other. All the sculpture covered with dust and dirt.

I walked through the devastated area to the north of the Cathedral. It was like wandering in Pompeii. The sun was shining warm and bright. There was not a breath stirring, only the seagulls wheeling and skirling over the ruins. Not a sound of traffic when I was in the midst of the isolation. From one spot there is waste land visible as far as the eye can roam. It was most moving. Unfortunately the ruins are not beautiful, too like scarred flesh, and as yet untoned by time. I do pray they will at all costs keep the Wren spires, even if they must clear away the shells of the naves. I walked past the ruins of Christchurch Newgate, St Giles's Cripplegate, St Vedast, St Lawrence Jewry, St Benet's, St Mary-le-Bow (when I last saw this church it still had a roof on it though badly damaged; a subsequent raid has evidently finished it off), and so on. Walked to Finsbury Circus via the Guildhall, past Liverpool Street, back via St Botolph, little St Ethelburga the Virgin, St Helen's (these three unharmed), up Queen Victoria Street and back to St Paul's, where I took a bus to Brooks's, exhaustion and tea.

*Wednesday, 18th March*

I went to the National Gallery and met Clarissa Churchill* walking down the steps. She said she had failed to get in, having been told that only ticket holders would be admitted. In fact she had gone to the wrong door. We bought tickets (1 shilling each) and just squeezed in. We had very bad seats right at the back behind the performers. Elena Gerhardt† sang Schubert and Brahms, and Myra Hess‡ played Schumann. No wonder it was a popular day. We ate sandwiches and drank coffee in the canteen.

---

* Niece (b. 1920) of Winston Churchill, and sister of J.L.-M's Oxford friend, the artist J. G. 'Johnnie' Churchill (1909–92); m. 1953 Sir Anthony Eden (1897–1977; Foreign Secretary, 1940–5, 1951–5; Prime Minister, 1955–7; cr. Earl of Avon, 1961).

† German mezzo-soprano (1883–1961), resident in London since 1933.

‡ English concert pianist (1890–1965; DBE 1941).

Clarissa walked with me as far as Brooks's. She told me that Randolph [Churchill]'s* wife had no intention of sticking to him, and that Mr Churchill would be very sad if the marriage broke up. She said that General Pope-Hennessy's death was brought on by a stroke. A Colonel Someone was having tea with him and put him into a rage by remarking that Russian tanks were bad. When the visitor left the General went to Dame Una's room, very upset, had a seizure and died four hours later. Cecil Beaton observed, 'Careless talk costs lives.'

A special meeting was held at Brooks's this afternoon formally to expel the member who has been rude to the servants and has used bad language. The Chairman announced that he had just received a letter from the member announcing his resignation after all, and promising never to cross the threshold of the club again. Great relief was expressed by everybody at this end to their embarrassment. Later in the day, I passed the man, looking unconcerned and truculent under the arcade of the Ritz. Instantly I felt sorry for him and wondered why he had behaved like this. I can quite understand how, if one senses that one is disliked, one is impelled to make oneself detested.

*Tuesday, 24th March*

I arrived at Brede [Sussex] at 7.30 in time for dinner with Clare Sheridan,† whom I had not seen for years. She looks a little older, is stout but magnificent. She was wearing corduroy trousers which did not suit her, but the next morning she wore a terracotta skirt with flowing shawl to match. She kept flinging the shawl about her in Isadora Duncan‡ fashion. Clare is a pacifist, and we spoke of the

---

* Journalist and politician (1911–68), Conservative MP for Preston, 1940–5; o.s. of Winston Churchill; m. 1st 1939–46 Hon. Pamela Digby (1920–97; she m. 3rd Averell Harriman), 2nd 1948–61 June Osborne.

† Clara Frewen (1885–1970); sculptor; first cousin of Winston Churchill, their mothers having been sisters; m. 1910 William Sheridan, descendant of Irish playwright.

‡ American dancer (1877–1927), strangled when her long scarf became enmeshed in the wheel of the Bugatti motor car in which she was being driven.

war, and of spiritual values. I found that I agreed with her fundamentally. She is a big woman and has the bigness to remain detached from the war. I remember once thinking that in the event of war most of my friends would have the bigness to remain so detached, but no, none of them seem to be, not even myself. Clare is. It is true that now Dick [her son] is dead, she can afford to be. Clare has woven a spiritual seclusion and wrapped herself in it like a cocoon. She thinks her cousin Winston ought to go. She praises the contrasting virtues of Stafford Cripps,* who neither smokes nor drinks, and is impressed by the love of the people in his own village for him.

*Thursday, 26th March*

After breakfast, at which I was offered a goose egg and, like an ass, refused it for fear of appearing greedy, we went down to the park to look at Brede Place, now occupied by soldiers. It is a wonderful house and to my surprise not large. Nothing, save Dick Sheridan's five bathrooms and heating plant, has been added to the house since Henry VIII's reign. A very perfect late medieval house, with a wide view, yet remote. It has several panelled rooms. Clare would sell Brede for £7,000, but there is little land and no other form of endowment. Yet it would let if the Trust held it, I feel sure.

Left for Smallhythe [Place, Kent]. Miss Edith Craig† was in bed, but the two other odd old ladies were about, Christopher St John and 'Tony' (really Clare) Atwood. They were dressed in corduroy trousers and men's jackets, one homespun, the other curry tweed. Their grey locks were hacked short and both wore tam-o'shanters. They were charming to me and gave me a huge two-handled mug of coffee. In Ellen Terry's little house one feels that she might walk past one at any minute, and in her bedroom that she might appear sitting before her dressing-table brushing her hair.

* Sir Stafford Cripps (1889–1952); Labour politician, then in War Cabinet as Lord President of the Council.

† Daughter (d. 1947) of the actress Ellen Terry (1847–1928), who had donated her mother's house, Smallhythe Place near Tenterden, to the N.T. in 1939, continuing to live there with two women friends.

*Saturday, 28th March*

The coffee room at Brooks's was full. I was just going to withdraw when Professor Richardson* hailed me and told me to sit with him. He is a dear man, and a little dotty. I don't always understand his esoteric jokes and insinuations. He is always punning. He spoke disparagingly of Groping Ass and Meddlesome,† his two *bêtes noires*. He says all great architecture is derivative when it is not deliberately imitative. He claims to have discovered Wren's own working notebooks, but will not reveal or publish them, for there is no one alive worthy to profit from them. He only reads eighteenth-century newspapers, of which he has an enormous stock, for he says the news is just the same in them as it is today. You merely need to substitute the names of countries occasionally, and not invariably.

At 2.15 I joined the Hills at Miss Jourdain's‡ and Miss Compton-Burnett's§ where they were lunching. A great occasion. Margaret Jourdain is patently jealous of Ivy Compton-Burnett, whom she keeps unapproachable except through herself. The two have lived together for years and are never parted. They are an Edwardian and remarkably acidulated pair. The coiffures of both look like wigs. Miss C.-B., whom I consider to be the greatest living English novelist, is upright, starchy and forthright. There is a bubbling undercurrent of humour in every observation that she makes, and she makes a good many, apparently hackneyed and usually sharp, in a rapid, choppy, rather old-fashioned upper-middle-class manner, clipping her breathless words. She enunciates clearly and faultlessly, saying slightly shocking things in a matter-of-fact tone, following up her sentences with a lot of 'dontcherknows', and then smiling perceptibly. She has a low, breasty chuckle. She has not unpleasing, sharp features, and her profile is almost beautiful. But she is not the kind of woman who cares tuppence for appearances, and wears a simple, unrememberable black dress which she smoothes down

---

* (Sir) Albert Richardson (1880–1964); Professor of Architecture, London University, 1919–46.

† Walter Gropius and Erich Mendelsohn, German modernist architects.

‡ Author of books on furniture and decoration (d. 1951).

§ Novelist (1884–1969; DBE, 1967).

with long fingers. We talked chiefly of country houses. Miss Jourdain looks rather wicked and frightening when she peers through her quizzing-glass. Miss C.-B. says that Miss J. has too little occasion to use it these days, now that there are so few houses available with furniture to be debunked.

*Thursday, 2nd April*

I drove with Eardley [Knollys] to Avebury. He took me round the Circle. He is madly keen on Avebury and rather peevish about my lack of enthusiasm for the ugly stones which Keiller* has dragged from the ground into the light of day. I cannot approve of the proposal to destroy the old village inside the Circle. I admit that the empty sections of the Circle are impressive where the terraces have been cleaned of scrub and are neatly cropped by sheep; but to remove medieval cottages and clear away all traces of human habitation subsequent to the Iron Age seems to be pedantic and a distortion of historical perspective. We walked round the manor garden. Eardley was bored by the house because it is not classical but romantic. Today's fashionable distaste for the romantic in English country houses is as overemphasised as was the Edwardians' for the classical and regular.

*Saturday, 4th April*

Two young men to luncheon, one called Eric Knight who is half German, having a German mother and German wife, the other in the Air Force and reeking of cheap scent. Knight with long, golden hair, a large nose and thick, ugly Yiddish lips, was unprepossessing but interesting about Russia which he visited in 1935. His impressions in that year were that the Soviet system was a laughable and total failure. Nothing worked. Everything was tawdry and drab. The people were corrupt and ready to commit any treason for money, which all lacked. He spoke to many beggars, some of them educated old ladies who complained to him of their miseries in

* Alexander Keiller (1889–1955); archaeologist.

frightened undertones. My convictions regarding the Russian campaign are that the Germans are not yet in earnest. I foresee a renewal of the German onslaught when the mud has gone, and a terrible Russian defeat.

*Tuesday, 7th April*

Talked with Mama in her bedroom this morning. She is full of complaints as usual. Papa has let the large cottage for only £2 although it is fully furnished; there are endless parties of people in the house; the garden boy is leaving, and the gardener, who is forty-three, may be called up; and Gertrude is to be married in a fortnight. She is the only servant in the house now, and Colonel Riley, who is billeted on them, has to be waited on, hand and foot. Mama is very distressed because Gertrude is due to have the curse the very day of the wedding, which could not be arranged otherwise because her young man has to take his leave when he is given it.

*Wednesday, 8th April*

This afternoon Sarah* ran into the office at West Wycombe calling for Miss Paterson. The tapestry room chimney was on fire. I dashed upstairs and with Helen went on to the flat roof. Smoke was pouring from the chimney stack. I got a stirrup pump and soaked the stack with water. Within five minutes of the fire being extinguished the fire brigade arrived. I secretly enjoyed the incident. Helen was very scared, which was only natural, looked very white and issued and counter-issued orders in a snappish way.

*J.L.-M. was invited to stay at Cumberland Lodge, Windsor Great Park, by the elder statesman and leading Roman Catholic layman Lord FitzAlan.*†

---

* Sarah Dashwood; o. d. of Sir John and Lady Dashwood; m. 1946 4th Baron Aberdare.

† Lord Edmund FitzAlan-Howard (1855–1947), yr s. of 14th Duke of Norfolk; cr. Viscount FitzAlan of Derwent, 1921; Lord-Lieutenant of Ireland, 1921–2; m. 1879 Lady Mary Bertie (d. 1938).

*Thursday, 16th April*

A tedious 2½-hour journey by a series of buses to Englefield Green. Mediterranean sky, and the chestnuts having burst their buds are in the fan-unfolding stage. All the trees along the Thames valley are shooting buds noisily.

I walked through Bishop's Gate into Windsor Park and was overtaken by Alathea FitzAlan-Howard on her bicycle. She is the FitzAlans' pretty granddaughter aged eighteen, frail and freckled. I arrived just in time for dinner for which there is no changing these days. Lord FitzAlan's son staying.* It is the first time I have seen him, a tiny, rather wizened, insignificant man with a wooden leg. Magdalen† sad as ever, with heavy folds of tumbling, wispy hair parted in the middle of her head and looped behind anyhow. Two Grenadier officers came to dinner. They are guarding the King and Queen who are present at Royal Lodge next door. One is called Lascelles and is Blanche Lloyd's nephew,‡ very good-looking and fair-haired, tall and 'the flower of English youth', a plant that always makes me stare and rub my eyes in admiration and envy. Both are on guard for a week, may not leave the locality, and sleep only half-undressed in the royal stables. Yet they look uncrumpled, immaculate. They seldom see the King.

Lord FitzAlan talked to me after dinner in his study about the Stanley Baldwins.§ S.B. is by no means a fool; is on the contrary extremely astute, and far from obstinate as is often supposed. His besetting fault is indolence. He confided in Lord F. that his reason for not rearming was that the country would not stand for it at the time.

* Hon. Henry FitzAlan-Howard (1883–1962); father of Alathea (b. 1923); s. father 1947 as 2nd Viscount.

† Lord FitzAlan's unmarried daughter (1880–1974).

‡ John Frederick Lascelles (1922–51); o.s. of (Sir) Alan ('Tommy') Lascelles, courtier (whose sister Blanche m. 1911 George Lloyd, later 1st Baron).

§ Conservative statesman (1867–1947); Prime Minister 1923–4, 1924–9 and 1935–7; cr. Earl, 1937; a friend of J.L.-M's paternal grandparents, his neighbours in Worcestershire where he was the local MP; J.L.-M. (as related in *Another Self*) had met him staying at Cumberland Lodge in 1935.

*Friday, 17th April*

I was given the Chapel Room, a stuffy, old-fashioned bedroom, with a huge, made-up oak bed, very comfortable with two fat rich linen pillows.

Mass in the Chapel at 9. One of the Jesuits from Beaumont comes three times a week to say Mass. The Blessed Sacrament is kept in this Chapel which is well arranged and furnished, unlike the usual makeshift type found in country houses. The ceremony was somehow extraordinary. There were Magdalen, Alathea, a lady's maid and one very old woman from I don't know where, all under veils. Lord FitzAlan served in spite of his eighty-seven years, shuffling about genuflecting like a two-year-old. The priest, Father Day, son of the judge in the Parnell case, is a cripple with arthritis and can barely move. He crawls at snail's pace, leaning heavily on his stick. I was in agonies lest he or Lord F. should collapse, but each supported himself on the other. Yet the scene was impressive and the recollection of it fills me with pleasure. I went to Confession and as usual had to rack my brains to extract the worst sins since I last confessed, which was at Dover I believe. I find it hard to decide which are my sins. I was given 3 Paters, 3 Aves and 3 Reginas. Only Lord F. and I communicated. Lord F. handed me a clean napkin and I trembled lest the priest, who was creaking and groaning, should drop the wafer. The wafer dissolves so foamlike in my mouth, always adhering to the roof of the mouth first of all.

I drove to Egham station with Father Day, who is an inquisitive old man, wanting to be told everything, who I am (who am I?), how I spell my name, how long I have known Cumberland Lodge and what is my age. Not an agreeable priest, and his false teeth do not fit.

*Thursday, 23rd April*

Today at Bradbourne [Kent], that once most romantic, untouched, primitive Queen Anne house of the Twisdens, I was reminded of a meeting in a House of Commons committee room just before the war. A few of us were assembled to discuss how the East Malling Horticultural Research station could buy and establish itself in that place. For some reason Lloyd George* joined us. He swept into the room like a whirlwind. When he settled down I observed him. He resembled a red turkey cock with a crest of white feathers. He gobbled and spluttered, was opinionated and rude. When this plethoric old bird announced that he did not care a damn about the beautiful Bradbourne, or for any country house for that matter, I hated him. Of course I was too insignificant for him to address a word to me. But I cast such intensive looks of hatred and indignation at him that he was obliged to notice them. He merely gave a frown of irritation as though I were a tiresome fly.

My reception at the Wool House at Loose was just as Eardley foretold. The house has been divided into two since the war. Miss Hunt lives in one part; some people called Beeson in the other. The house is a hideous, pretentious, genteel over-restored fake, just like its inhabitants. A horrible property. I hope it gets bombed. Miss Hunt shouted a catalogue of grievances against the Trust for not carrying out repairs to the bogus half-timber which she has been obliged to attend to at her expense. The Beesons came out of their part and shouted abuse at Miss Hunt, and then at me. I could not bear it and fled, without seeing the museum of African flints and trophies.

Drove down Watling Street, by Gravesend and Deptford. This unconfined Thames estuary is rather exciting, sprinkled as it is with drifting pylons, factory chimneys and distant gasometers gleaming in the sunshine across the river, with squadrons of bombers flying overhead.

*Tuesday, 28th April*

Miss P. told me in the office that the Bath Assembly Rooms† had been gutted by fire in the raid on Saturday night. It has upset me dreadfully that so beautiful a building, hallowed by Jane Austen and Dickens, should disappear like this in a single night. Eardley, who was staying the weekend with his mother, came in for the full brunt. He says the Circus has a crater in the middle of the grass,

---

* Liberal statesman (1863–1945); Prime Minister, 1916–22; cr. Earl, 1945.

† Acquired by the N.T. before the war through the generosity of Mr Ernest Cook.

and all the windows are blown out. Two houses in Royal Crescent are burned out, the Abbey windows are gone, and the fires and destruction have been devastating. This is a reprisal raid for ours over Lübeck. Both raids are sheer barbaric bloody-mindedness, anti-culture and anti-all that life stands for. I positively want not to survive the war when things like this can happen.

At 11 Ted Lister* called for me and I took him to Holland House. We walked in at the gates and right up to the house where we talked to the caretaker, who had been on the spot when the house had burnt about a year ago. It is a shell. The only part remaining, though badly damaged, is oddly enough the Jacobean staircase, with one of the Jacobean doorways leading to it. The Spanish leather under the stairs still hanging in festoons from the walls. A sedan chair and a small lacquer chest, half-burnt, are left. The painted panelled room for Charles I which I remember Lord Ilchester once showing me is gone. We could just distinguish where it had been, for I saw traces of one painted pilaster. The library and everything else irretrievably gone. I am glad I once visited this house, and danced in it, in its heyday. Ted and I walked along the terraces, through the old walled garden and northwards through the park, and down a long lime avenue. The grass was long and unmown, but the trees were fresh and re-budding, quite indifferent to the terrible indignities of last year. The tranquillity made it difficult for us to realise we were in the centre of London. How important it is to preserve what remains of this sanctuary.

I was an usher at Peter Scott's wedding† but did precious little work. Kissed K. [Kennet] at the reception but only had a quick word with her. Peter shook hands warmly, and thanked, and God-blessed, which I thought nice of him, considering that I had not given him a present – yet.

---

* Edward Graham Lister (1873–1956), of Westwood Manor, Wiltshire; diplomatist and art collector; bachelor admirer of J.L.-M.

† (Sir) Peter Scott (1909–89); o.c. of 'Scott of the Antarctic' and J.L.-M's friend Kathleen *née* Bruce, sculptor (1878–1947; she m. 2nd Edward Hilton Young [1879–1960], Liberal politician, cr. Baron Kennet, 1935); naval officer, sportsman, artist, naturalist and writer; m. 1st 1942–51 Elizabeth Jane Howard, 2nd 1951 Philippa Talbot-Ponsonby.

*Thursday, 30th April*

In King's Bench Walk I was joined at 10.30 by Harold [Nicolson] and Jamesey who had been dining together. Jamesey was bright, affectionate and entertaining. He was furious about our senseless destruction of the old town of Lübeck, where he said there were no military or factory objectives of any kind. The 'Baedeker' reprisal bombing was consequently brought on by our foolish philistinism. Even Harold could not deny that the Lübeck raid was a mistake on our part. Jamesey said we were worse philistines than the Germans, who do at least care for their own monuments whereas the British are bored to tears with theirs. Harold agreed. Then J. and I became provocative. Jamesey, backed up by me, asserted that all civilised people desired a compromise peace. Harold hastened to contradict him with a vehemence which suggested to me he was in secret agreement. He admitted to me later that Singapore was a bad business; also Hong Kong; that our people were demoralised, and did not fight.

*Friday, 1st May*

In bed at night I thought – for I could not get to sleep – that my mind is like a ravine with dense patches of fog. I get along all right until suddenly I become muddled, fuddled, at a loss for words, and quite inconsistent and irrational; often silly and at times almost hysterical. At breakfast Harold said, 'Jamesey asks me, "Did you realise in September 1939 that this war would mean the end of the world?" Of course I realised that it meant the end of the world for us, but not for the vast majority.' I replied that as I did not belong to the vast majority his argument had no appeal for me.

*Saturday, 2nd May*

After inspecting our mill at Burnham Staithe I walked to Burnham Market [Norfolk]. No food at the Hoste Arms, but at the Nelson I got beer and hot meat rolls. There were evacuees at the bar recounting their bomb experiences in London. 'The wife said to me, she said, did you ever? Me and my kiddies', etc. Slightly drunk on a pint of bitter, I joined in the conversation and found myself recounting my (non-existent) experiences of the Germans and their atrocities. 'Would you believe it,' I said, 'they cut out the heart and began . . .' 'Well I never,' they said in a chorus of delight. Cockneys are good-hearted people. These particularly deplored warfare against women and children. Yes, I said, and put in a plea against the deliberate bombing of our cathedrals and churches, to test their reaction. Reaction: 'One in a hundred may care for such old-fashioned places. They are all right to see now and then. It's flesh and blood what matters. For myself, the whole lot can go.' All most good-natured and honestly meant. Philistines!

The old cottages in this part of the world are faced with smooth flints, or large pebbles picked from the shore and washed smooth by the sea. They give a cream to the strawberry brick walls. Sometimes they look like Easter eggs stacked by children. All along the coast to Cromer there is a great structure of iron barricading, covered with barbed wire in defence against the invaders, if they should come this way.

*Saturday, 9th May*

Over a cup of tea at Brooks's I opened the *New Statesman* and began an article by Raymond Mortimer* on the Royal Academy exhibition. I read there was one gallery devoted entirely to pictures by Wilson Steer† and Sickert,‡ that there was a Vanessa Bell§ of the Queen and princesses, someone else of the Prime Minister and a Moynihan¶ of Eddy Sackville-West. I was so excited that I did not even finish the article or my tea, and rushed to the Academy before it shut, bought a catalogue and went the rounds. Nowhere could I find any of the sixty or so pictures by the most

* Literary reviewer (1895–1980); lover of Harold Nicolson.
† Philip Wilson Steer (1860–1942); English artist.
‡ Walter Sickert (1860–1942); German-born Danish artist.
§ Vanessa Stephen (1879–1961); English artist, member of Bloomsbury Group; m. 1907 Clive Bell.
¶ Rodrigo Moynihan (1910–90); Spanish-born English artist.

eminent contemporary artists mentioned by Raymond. The beast had, by way of skit, written a mock review of all those artists' works which he would have liked to see exhibited. I was furious with him.

*Thursday, 14th May*

Mr Forsyth* the architect drove me in his respectable Austin saloon to Norfolk. Mr Forsyth is so scrupulously correct, polite and imperturbable that I feel ill at ease. He clears his throat continually and speaks in a low voice for fear of appearing assertive. Never looking to left or right he drives straight ahead hour after hour. I shift uneasily in my seat. I long to let out an expletive like 'Fuck!', just to see how Mr Forsyth would react. Instead I say, 'Mr Forsyth?' He inclines his granite profile one inch, and says, 'Yes, Mr Lees-Milne?', with Uriah Heep-like humility. I say, 'If you don't stop this instant and let me get out, I shall burst my bladder.' He is absolutely appalled. He stops the car in silence. As I get out I say in a jolly way, 'Don't you want to pee too?' He scowls, and replies, 'Well, I wouldn't put it quite like that', yet gets out himself. Long after I am relieved, and back in my seat, I see him through the mirror still at it at the rear wheel. Quite clearly he was in the same straits as I was. Silly ass.

On arrival at Blickling [Hall]† we are greeted by a sea of Nissen huts in the park in front of the Orangery, and a brick NAAFI construction opposite the entry to the house. The sudden view of the south front takes the breath away. We walk round the outside. Then Lord Lothian's secretary, now our housekeeper-caretaker, conducts me round those staterooms on the first floor that are not occupied by the RAF. The furniture has now been removed to Henley Hall for safety; the best pictures removed too. The RAF are in Miss O'Sullivan's‡ bad books for they have needlessly broken several windows, and smashed the old crown glass. They have forced the

---

* W. A. Forsyth; SPAB architect, who did work for the N.T.

† Palatial Jacobean house bequeathed to N.T. by Philip Kerr, 11th Marquess of Lothian (1882–1940).

‡ The said housekeeper-caretaker.

locks of the doors into the staterooms, out of devilry. This sort of thing is inevitable.

*Friday, 15th May*

At Melton Constable [Norfolk] we were welcomed most kindly by Lord Hastings,* who is living in the stable wing, lateral to the main block. He is a sort of Edwardian stage peer with a purple visage. He is vastly proud of the place and has recently celebrated his family's 700th anniversary of their lordship of Melton Constable, unbroken from father to son, which is remarkable. He prefaced his reception of us with a resumé of his family honours and connections. His ignorance of the house's architecture was however startling. He kept dogmatising pompously, and wrongly, about this and that feature. The house is ruined to my mind by the 1880s additions. They could easily be pulled down so as to leave the lovely 'Wren' block intact. But Lord Hastings prefers them to the original house. A pity that it has lost its roof balustrade and cupola. We looked at the church in the park. It contains a Caroline family pew hugely out of proportion to the nave, and an ugly war memorial to the men of Melton Constable, headed by the name in large letters of The Hon. —— Astley, followed underneath by the names in smaller letters of the humble privates and gunners of the village.

*Thursday, 28th May*

I lunched in Cornwall Gardens with Margaret Jourdain and Ivy Compton-Burnett. Ernest Thesiger† was the fourth person. He is an old pansy, affected, meticulous, garrulous and entertaining. We sat in a high-ceilinged, pitch-dark dining-room, and ate lentil soup, white fish with sauce and steamed potatoes, a rhubarb and ginger tart, Morecambe shrimps and biscuits. Margaret Jourdain opened

* Albert Edward Delaval Astley, 21st Baron Hastings (1882–1956).

† Actor (1879–1961); first cousin once removed of (Sir) Wilfred Thesiger (1910–2003), explorer, who was in J.L.-M's house at Eton.

a large bottle of Cidrax, poured out Thesiger's and my glasses and was about to pour her own, when Miss C.-B. shouted, 'Margaret! Remember at breakfast it was decided that you were to finish the opened bottle of flat Cidrax.'

We talked about servants. She agreed that today fewer servants managed to get through double the work. They are better fed and housed, she said. Her parents took care to have excellent food themselves, whereas their children were thrown the scraps. Miss Jourdain gave us cherry brandy, but did not offer any to Miss C.-B., who took some for herself. She swigged it in one gulp, declaring that it was excellent and she would have some more. Miss J. intervened and would not allow it. Miss Jourdain said of Freya Stark,* who is at present broadcasting from Cairo under the direction of the Foreign Secretary, that hers 'is a voice that breathed o'er Eden'.

*Saturday, 30th May*

I picked flowers to take to Mrs Stewart-Jones in London. When I reached Cheyne Walk after tea, I learned that she was dying and not expected to last many hours. All the family were wonderfully calm and resigned. Di† took in my flowers and about 7.30 came to tell me I could now go in to see her, for she was having a lucid moment. I went in. She lay in a bed in the window at the far corner of the room. Rick was at one side of the bed, offering her a drink of water from a spoon. Edward holding her hand at the other side, and Di sitting by the window smiling at me. I went to the end of the bed and blew her a kiss, to which she replied by raising her hand to her lips very feebly. I was struck by the change in her appearance, particularly by her sunken eyes and the sharp, thin line of her jaw. She was propped against raised pillows. Di said to her, 'Jim has brought you these flowers', and to me, 'Tell her you have brought them for her.' So I said rather foolishly, 'I hope you like them. They came from the garden today.' Edward raised the bowl of roses and

* Travel writer (1893–1993; DBE 1972).

† Rick Stewart-Jones's sister Dione (d. 1975); m. Patrick Murray.

honeysuckle and handed her a rose to smell. She understood perfectly and looking at it, said, 'Lovely', in a slow, painful way. This was, I believe, the last word she spoke. She looked at me a little and smiled, then closed her eyes and remained so quiet for a few seconds that I thought she must have died. Then she took a deep breath and held her hand to her breast. I noticed how swollen her hands were, and blue. Rick gave me a chair to sit on, but I felt embarrassed by seeming to be curious in just watching her die. So I quietly slipped away.

*Saturday, 13th June*

I took a bus to Knebworth [Hertfordshire] where I was met by the agent and motored to Knebworth Manor. Lord Lytton* pompous, courteous in a keep-your-distance manner, patrician and vice-regal. He was wearing rather precious country clothes, a too-immaculate tweed suit, a yellow-green shirt of large checks loose at the collar, and a gold chain round his neck. He has truly beautiful blue eyes. If one did not know otherwise one would suppose him to be what my father calls 'effeminate' by the well cut yet long silver hair deliberately curled round the nape of his neck.

We walked through the gardens of Knebworth House. It is undeniably hideous. The old house was rebuilt by Bulwer Lytton in 1847, and if only Lord Lytton had not recently removed the gargoyles from the absurd turrets and the heraldic animals from the terrace, it would be a perfect specimen of a Disraelian Gothic mansion. The whole outside is stuccoed in a base way. The Jacobean grand staircase and the Presence Chamber are terribly shoddy. The only room I liked was the Palladianised great hall. Lord Lytton has had the paint stripped off the wainscote. He said it was the first stripping to be undertaken in England. At present the Froebel Girls' College is installed in the house, which becomes them. Lord Lytton

* Victor, 2nd Earl of Lytton (1876–1947); imperial proconsul and Conservative statesman; grandson of the novelist and politician Bulwer Lytton, 1st Baron (1803–73).

is determined to return to the house after the war. I insisted on going round the estate for he offers the whole 3,000 acres in endowment. My view is that the estate is more worth holding, because of its nearness to London, than the house, for all its historic associations.

I got back to London in time for dinner to find Jamesey waiting. We dined at Brooks's over claret and returned to his flat in Chester Square where I stayed the night. Jamesey said he wanted to sleep with a woman, and expressed misgivings. I said it was as easy as falling off a log. The moment these words were out of my mouth I realised how discouraging they must have sounded.

*Saturday, 20th June*

At the White Hart in Lincoln I met Lord Brocket* who motored over from Burghley. He drove me in his blue two-seater Rolls-Bentley up the Roman road to Norton Place. Here we met Major Hoult, his agent, and his nephew, a Colonel Trevor (younger than me), in the Commandos. We motored round the whole property, Lord Brocket going conscientiously into every cottage and over every farm building.

At 5.30 we left for Culverthorpe,† giving lifts on our way to RAFs and WAAFs. Brocket is breezy and good-natured, although he does 'buck' a bit. He has a slightly tiresome seeing-the-sunny-side-of-everything manner. He is amusingly convinced of his nobility, and explained at great length his Irish descent from the O'Cains, whoever they may be. His crest of a cat rampant figures prominently on the radiator of his car. However, he is condescending enough to include me among the well-bred. He did not care much for Culverthorpe. I think it is lovely although in a deplorable condition owing to troops stationed in the house. The splendid hall has been partitioned into an orderly room and officers' mess with passage between. The

* Arthur Roland Nall-Cain, 2nd Baron Brocket (1904–67); inheritor of brewing fortune.

† See entry for 15 April 1943.

capitals of the columns have been boarded up, and the Wootton panels shrouded under canvas. I noticed a great crack in the Hauderoy painted ceiling over the stairs. Many glass panes are broken and the surrounds of one window are blackened by a projecting stove pipe.

We reached Ayot St Lawrence [Hertfordshire] at 11 p.m. The whole village, olde worlde and rather horrifying, particularly the Brocket Arms, belongs to him. Much to my surprise he banged on the inn door. I saw he had been leading up to something. It was to be a pretty piece of patronage. The publican opened the door and there was a great deal of 'Oh, your lord-shape! You must come in. My friends would be honoured to see your lord-shape', for it was after closing time. We were ushered into the saloon bar, I keeping well to the rear like a bad smell. The publican clapped his hands, and announced in an awful voice, 'This is Lord Brocket.' B., still wearing his cap at a jaunty angle, beamed, bowed and received the homage of a dozen demi-mondaines and flash-alfs during an impressive hush. Trying to be inconspicuous I was pushed forward. I must say B's friendliness is unfeigned. He introduced me to all and sundry, and shook hands with them in a hearty fashion. The peer charmingly condescending. We were supplied with 'gin and It' and cheese rolls. There was much forced hilarity, B. nudging me and laughing a bit too much. With more ushering, the other way round, and 'Good night, Lord Brocket! Good night, your lord-shape', we swept out, having caused a stir, and left them all astounded.

We got to Brocket [Hall] at midnight. The big house is filled with expectant and parturiating [*sic*] mothers from the East End, so Brocket keeps a room at Warren House across the lake, a little seventeenth-century bailiff's house. Here we drank tea and ate sausage rolls. I asked him outright how closely associated he had really been with Hitler. He said he had only met Hitler three times through H.* (whose name I forget), his link with the Nazis.

* Possibly the anglophile Walther Hewel, Hitler's former prison mate and court entertainer.

He knew Ribbentrop quite well, and liked Goering, who was 'the only gent of the party'. In fact Brocket has faint hopes even now that at some future date terms might be reached through Goering. I asked him if he had believed Hitler to be honest. He said, 'No, not exactly.' From the first he thought him repellent and abnormal. The democratic press was Hitler's bugbear, and he told Brocket that Chamberlain ought to put the English press lords in a concentration camp. Brocket replied, 'I agree. Only you will have to put your press controllers in camps likewise, and we shall all be happier.' And Hitler added, 'I will put them in the same camp.'

Brocket greatly liked and admired Chamberlain. The truth is that although Brocket is a fundamentally nice man, he is stupid. Chamberlain ought not to have been intimate with a man of his calibre. One infers that the fleshpots of Brocket and Bramshill were a bait. At any rate Chamberlain made a confidant of Brocket who found himself in an exalted position undeservedly. Then he was made a scapegoat. B. told me that because he went so frequently to Germany and was so closely connected with the leading Nazis, Halifax used him as a channel through which to communicate to Hitler and Ribbentrop the views of the Government. He assured me that he constantly warned the Nazi leaders that Britain would fight, if only with her fists, were the Germans to march into Poland. The Nazis just would not believe this. Hitler never relinquished the belief that Chamberlain had bluffed him at Munich by pretending that Britain was in a position to fight, if sufficiently provoked, nor his subsequent conviction that such action was quite impossible. Hitler harboured a grievance against Chamberlain ever after.

Brocket's nervous breakdown at the beginning of the war was brought about by the aspersions thrown at him from all quarters. He confesses that he has not yet recovered, and cannot walk any distance, and is suffering from a weak heart. At all events he was graded Class 4 and rejected for military service. At the end of these confidences he said we must be on christian name terms; but I don't for the life of me know what his name is. I feel rather sorry for him. He is by no means dislikeable.

*Saturday, 27th June*

I dine with Johnnie Churchill and his new little wife.* Pam and Derek Jackson† join us in the neat little flat. Derek is positively pro-Nazi. What a catching disease Mitfordism is! There is Derek, a gallant man older than me, a rear-gunner in air-force blue, awarded a DFC, in private life a brilliant scientist, saying that we can't win the war, that he loathes the British lower classes who have forced him into this unnecessary war (absolute tosh!), and that the Germans know the best way of treating them, which is to crush them under heel. We argued. I think he cannot be absolutely in earnest, but is probably more so than a stranger might suppose possible.

Before the Jacksons came, Johnnie told me of his experiences at Dunkirk. He said it was hell, but not such hell as an ordinary air-raid on London. He did not see many of our people die, but he did see Belgian civilians cutting off the heads of German parachutists; and he watched unmoved German airmen burning to death in their planes. He felt very savage, yet exalted. Although only a camouflage major he was put in charge of a whole company of men whose captain, a Highland officer, had been removed for cutting off the fingers of German prisoners for their rings.

*Sunday, 28th June*

I walked from the station to Clandon [Park, Surrey] where Noël and Giana Blakiston‡ are living among the stored documents from Noël's Record Office. Otherwise they and the two children have

---

* J. G. Spencer Churchill (1909–92); nephew of Winston Churchill; artist, with whom J.L.-M. had crammed for Oxford in 1928; m. 1st 1934–8 Angela Culme-Seymour, 2nd 1941–53 Mary Cookson, 3rd 1953 Kathlyn Tandy (d. 1957), 4th 1958–72 Anna Boston.

† Hon. Pamela Mitford (1907–94), 2nd of the Mitford sisters; m. 1936 (as the 2nd of his 6 wives) Professor Derek Jackson, inventor (d. 1982).

‡ Assistant Keeper of Public Records (1905–84); m. 1929 Georgiana Russell (1903–95).

this enormous house to themselves. They live in the small room on the right of the hall, and dine in the servants' quarters in the basement. The house is dirty and in decay. We went on to the roof. One chimney stack had a name and the date 1790 carved on the brick. The lead on the roof is thin in places and needs recasting, and relaying. The hall and most of the downstairs rooms are stuffed with records. After tea Noël and the children gave a play in a toy theatre, with scenery of Clandon made by themselves. The words were written by Noël in Pope* couplets, very cleverly. The Blakistons are sweet people.

*Wednesday, 1st July*

To London for an SPAB meeting to discuss the Society's policy about the rebuilding of churches and other monuments after the war. Lord Esher was clearly not in favour of any form of rebuilding, it seemed to me. I do not go as far as this myself and think that each case must be judged according to its own merits and the state of its damage; that certain churches like St James's Piccadilly, where more than the outside walls survive and detailed and measured drawings exist, should be rebuilt as they were. John Macgregor† said that the original moulds for the plaster cornices at the Assembly Rooms, Bath, were known to exist, which favours the argument for those wishing to rebuild the Rooms.

*Friday, 3rd July*

At the Jardin des Gourmets we had a modest dinner, with only lager to drink, and the bill was £1 11*s.* 6*d.* for two. It is monstrous! You pay 7/6 table cover, for the mere privilege of sitting down. In fact the new limit of 5 shillings for every meal seems to be evaded and the price of meals to be increasing if anything.

---

* Alexander Pope (1688–1744); poet and satirist, master of the 'heroic couplet'.

† Expert on staff of SPAB.

*Friday, 10th July*

Matheson, Eardley and I attended an absurd Trust meeting at Watlington,* absurd because there was not a single committee member apart from the chairman. When it was over Esher sent Eardley and me out of the room in order to discuss with Matheson the staff reorganisation. Eardley and I stood in the hall straining our ears to catch what Matheson was shouting at Esher, who is a little deaf. I crept down the passage as far as I dared. I nearly reached the keyhole but Eardley made me giggle so much that I had to come away for fear of betraying myself.

*J.L.-M. spent a weekend with 'Midi' Gascoigne, then living at Buscot, Oxfordshire.*

*Saturday, 11th July*

After tea, we bicycled over the fields and across the river to Kelmscott [Manor]. The old, grey stone gables are first seen through the trees. The house is surrounded by a dovecote and farm buildings which are still used by a farmer. The romantic group must look exactly as it did when William Morris† found it lying in the low water meadows, quiet and dreaming. It is like an etching by F. L. Griggs.‡ The garden is divine, crammed with flowers wild and tangled, an enchanted orchard garden for there are fruit trees and a mulberry planted by Morris. All the flowers are as Pre-Raphaelite as the house, being rosemary, orange-smelling lilies, lemon-scented verbena. The windows outside have small pediments over them. Inside there are Charles II chimney pieces, countryfied by rude Renaissance scrolls at the base of the jambs. The interior is redolent of Morris and Rossetti, yet not the least nineteenth-century, which speaks loudly for their taste. Most of the rooms have Morris

* Watlington Park, Oxfordshire, Lord Esher's country house.

† Writer, artist, designer and political radical (1834–96).

‡ Etcher (1876–1938).

wallpapers, and contain many framed drawings by them both, of Mrs Morris and the children. The room in which Morris worked has a great four-poster. Rossetti's room is lined with the tapestries which, when the wind blew them about, worried him and induced nightmares. I like bad old tapestries to be chopped about and treated as wallpaper. They make a superb background to the pictures. I leant out of the casement window, unlike the Lady of Shalott, and gazed across the flat, meadowy landscape and the winding river which looked so comfortable and serene. I do not remember experiencing such sweet peace and happiness as during these two hours.

*Sunday, 12th July*

Midi and I went for a long walk through hayfields, talking chiefly about her circle of women friends. She says there is nothing they will not discuss with her and each other unashamedly. They tell her how often they sleep with their husbands, what they do in bed, and whether it brings on palpitations. One of them says her husband, although little over forty, cannot sleep with her more than once a month because all his life he has had too much sex. I just don't believe this reason is the true one. There can't be any man of that age incapable of sex at least once every night in the year. What I do know is that husbands do not talk together about their wives in this fashion.

*Wednesday, 15th July*

At Brooks's I ran into Eddy [Sackville-West], Raymond [Mortimer] and Roger Senhouse,* who on seeing me said, 'What a svelte figure he still has!' Eddy said, 'I should think so too at his age. But I must tell you he's blind as a bat and out of vanity won't wear his spectacles.'

---

* Roger Pocklington Senhouse (1900–70); bibliophile, translator, and co-founder of the publishers Secker & Warburg; sometime lover of Lytton Strachey.

Q.* dined with me at the Mirabelle in Curzon Street. Together we drank a couple of bottles of *vin rosé* at 18/6 a bottle, the whole dinner costing £4. It was an absurd evening. We both got rather tipsy. On leaving the restaurant at midnight we had to walk down Curzon Street to sober ourselves. Linking arms we swayed. I told her Lord Brocket had written me a letter saying, 'Stop brocketting me'. Q. said, 'And don't start brocketting me either.' In the taxi I thought what is happening now must have happened a hundred, no a thousand, no a million times. How bored taxi drivers must get at nights. Or are they merely revolted? And I also thought, women have legs, and tongues like conger eels.

*Saturday, 18th July*

From Warwick station I was driven to Charlecote Park. It is the second time that I have been there; the first was in 1936, which shows how long negotiations have been dragging on. On that occasion I was sent to consider and report upon the merits of the house. Sir Henry Fairfax-Lucy,† military, dapper and arrogant, walked me quickly round the park and garden. It was a rainy day, I remember. On returning to the porch, whence we had set out immediately on my arrival, Sir Henry stretched out his hand and bade me good-bye. In those days I was shy. Nervously I asked if I might see inside. The reply was, 'There is absolutely no need. Charlecote is known to be one of the great, the greatest houses of England. Good morning.' So without disputing I went off with my tail between my legs. On my return to the office I was told I had been a fool.

Now, as for Sir Henry Fairfax-Lucy, today I have found out about him. He may be a pompous ass like Justice Shallow (who was supposed to be Sir Thomas Lucy), but underneath the strutting,

* Mystery lover of J.L.-M., a married society woman.

† Sir Henry Cameron-Ramsay-Fairfax, 3rd Bt (1870–1944); m. 1st 1892 Ada Lucy (d. 1943) of Charlecote Park (adding 'Lucy' to his surname), 2nd 1944 Norah Mackenzie.

the peppery, the arrogant surface, a kindly old man lurks.* In fact I am rather sorry for him, because I think he is a little odd. He is obstinate and muddle-headed because of his oddness. I believe he struggles to be reasonable, and just cannot manage to be. His ideas do not co-ordinate. His lisp is like that of a peevish child eating pap.

We went inside the house this time; and then round the park, again in the rain. He showed me the complicated boundaries of the land he proposes to make over. But he kept contradicting himself so that neither he nor I knew at the end of my visit what his intentions were. Although most indefinite he was most exacting. He was also very cheese-paring, reducing the total income the Trust should receive to shillings and pence as well as pounds. I thought he was rather touching when he urged haste – how is this to be achieved with him? – if we wanted the transaction to go through. 'I don't want to say anything unseemly, but Lady Lucy is very seriously ill.' The place is of course hers, not his.

*Monday. 27th July*

The committee today raised my salary from £400 to £500. Eardley's to his, and my, disgust was raised a mere £25. He is going to write to the committee refusing it.

*Sunday, 2nd August*

Jamesey says that if knowing famous men and keeping diaries is all that is necessary to acquire fame, he wonders more people do not keep them. Cecil Beaton, he says, keeps such a diary, and J. has read parts of it.

*Thursday, 6th August*

My birthday. I am thirty-four, though I pretend to be thirty-three.

* It didn't – see entry for 13 June 1945.

*Friday, 7th August*

I had a late tea with Kathleen [Kennet] at Fritton [Norfolk], for I am to stay with the Kennets for the weekend. Lord Kennet arrived shortly after me. We dined off rabbit, claret, nectarines and raspberries. I am already getting a few spots from all this fruit. Lord K. showed me his books. Evidently I said something disparaging. His old bound editions are as great treasures to him as houses are to me. I must concede this. But I do resent Lord Kennet's superciliousness. He is so morose too.

*Saturday, 8th August*

I stroll about with K. in the morning after being given breakfast in bed. I find myself strangely tired and long to be left alone with the book I have picked up here, Geikie Cobb's on the Ductless Glands, instead of embarking upon intense conversations with K. so early in the day. I give up, for one must pull one's weight a bit in other people's houses when one has been such a fool as to visit them. So I pick raspberries with K. and converse. A Major Jack Abbey comes to luncheon. He is gossipy and wet. In the afternoon I feel really ill and heavy, owing to my Epanutin [drug], I suppose. I sleep hard until tea-time. Peter Scott and his new wife Jane come unexpectedly after tea for two nights' leave. At dinner I feel horribly shy with them and hardly speak. This family makes one feel inferior and excluded. I admire their prowess, and at the same time despise their intellects. They are more intelligent, less intellectual than I am. In fact they are thorough middle-brows. K's great failing is to blow the trumpet of her family until one is deafened and wants to run away from the din. It's true they always do the decent, and the right thing. But they appear priggish and self-righteous.

We drank champagne for dinner to celebrate Peter [Scott]'s arrival, so surreptitiously, so ostentatiously produced by Lord K. Peter showed us his latest drawings of Jane, also some photographs of earlier drawings of his, including the one of me, which I must say looks better in photograph than in the original. Kathleen was enraptured at the drawings and cried, 'Look, Augustus [John] could not have produced anything finer than these!' None of them has any understanding of art whatever. Then Peter talked of his sea exploits; and I marvelled. He explained how bomb effects are greater on sea than on land. He has certainly done gallant things. His adoring wife is only nineteen. She is a little too skinny and lanky to be really beautiful yet. Beauty may come. I am not surprised that she worships Pete, for this philistines' ideal of manhood, no, this god, is of course attractive. He is stocky, sturdy and square to be sure with a small bright face and a turned-up nose. There is something great about the sweep of his brow. He is untidy in his dress. His blue eyes twinkle and when he smiles he can be fascinating; and his short, deep laugh is unforced.

*Tuesday, 11th August*

While I was walking through the Ritz an umbrella hooked my arm from behind, and there was Peter Derwent* – my first sight of him since the war. He was looking far thinner, younger and more handsome than formerly. I commented on his thinness and he replied, 'It would be difficult to be otherwise these days.' He has returned from Berne and hopes to join the RAF. He said how sorry he was about Robert [Byron]'s death, adding, 'But then we have all had our private troubles', his only reference to his wife's death in Switzerland. He said what a long time ago it seemed when we four – the other two being Robert and Michael [Rosse] – founded the Georgian Group. Yet it was only five years ago. He seemed unhappy, lost and hopeless.

*Saturday, 15th August*

During the last few days I have been reading Byron's *Don Juan* for the third time. I remember the first was in 1927 during Mama's and my voyage to Genoa, when I was confined to my cabin in the Bay of Biscay, feeling wretched. Even then I was able to perceive the wit of it. Now I still find myself gasping aloud in admiration. There

* George Harcourt Vanden-Bempde-Johnstone, 3rd Baron Derwent (1899–1949); diplomatist and man of letters.

is nothing like it. I am also in the middle of Symons' life of Baron Corvo,* a most nauseating figure. Even reading the book makes my flesh creep. It is the aroma of the soiled priestly habit that makes me feel sick, the very vicious creature masquerading as deeply devout. I must take warning. I met Symons at Lady Cranbrook's† in the Thirties. He was a horrid, sinister character too.

*Friday, 28th August*

Mama and I have been sorting out old trunks in the loft above the motor-house. We came across some drawings of mine done at the Ashmolean where Albert Rutherston‡ was teaching. To my surprise a few of them were not too bad. The discovery has inspired me to sketch again. This evening I drew the house across the pond, and recaptured the immense joy of using my eyes as hard as I could. Eyes get wasted, like muscles, for lack of intensive exercise.

*Saturday, 29th August*

I had a row with Papa after dinner. He expressed idiotic views about the Duke of Kent.§ Said that he was a worthless fellow and 'no better than a pansy', a phrase I abominate. I could not tolerate this silly imputation by someone who knew nothing whatever about the prince. I blew up. Words flew, as of old. I cannot, alas,

---

* Pseudonym of Frederick Rolfe (1860–1913), scoundrel and novelist; *The Quest for Corvo* (1934) by A. J. A. Symons (1900–41), though unfinished, began a trend of quasi-biographical works piecing together the lives of mystery men.

† Lady Dorothy Boyle (1879–1968), dau. of 7th Earl of Glasgow; m. 1899 Gathorne Gathorne-Hardy, 3rd Earl of Cranbrook (1870–1915); J.L.-M. often visited her house at Snape in Suffolk in 1935, when he was engaged to her daughter Anne (later Lady Anne Hill).

‡ Artist (1881–1953; *né* Rothenstein); founded Ruskin School of Drawing.

§ The Duke (1902–42), yr bro. of King George VI, had been killed four days earlier when the RAF aircraft in which he was travelling to Iceland crashed into a Scottish mountainside. J.L.-M. had once encountered him 'when he made a nervous speech at an SPAB dinner' and been struck by his 'boyish figure and complexion' (*Ancestral Voices*, 26 August 1942).

stay here more than two nights without allowing myself to be provoked beyond endurance.

*Friday, 11th September*

Mr Fortescue and his wife came to luncheon at West Wycombe. He is an Eton master and I was up to him for German during one half. He is now Francis's classical tutor. He is a tall, dirty, uncouth creature, very intelligent and a good linguist. He visits Iceland for the Government because he speaks Icelandic. He surprised us by saying that after the war the custom of wearing Eton clothes and top hats would be discontinued. It is curious how today people want to abolish uniforms as though they are something to be ashamed of, or are emblems of servility. But we are all servants, whether we are generals, bishops, cooks or Etonians. Helen and all of us, Francis, indeed, fell upon Mr Fortescue at once. Francis claimed that it was more economic to wear Eton clothes for, being black, they don't show the spots, and last longer. The seats of the trousers can be patched *ad nauseam*, since they are concealed by the tails.

*Tuesday, 15th September*

Lady Throckmorton* asked me to Coughton [Court, Warwickshire] for the night, to go through the list of family heirlooms with her. She is living in the south wing only. The rest of the house is empty, in expectation of American officers, or nuns.

Lady Throckmorton is delightful: plain, unfashionable, intelligent and downright. *Très grande dame.* She has worked in Coughton's interests for thirty years, upholding the Catholic tradition, without becoming a Catholic herself. It is entirely owing to her that Coughton is to become Trust property, in the face of seemingly insuperable obstacles raised by the entail and the hostility of the Throckmorton family.

---

* Lilian Brooke (d. 1955); m. 1905 Lt-Col Richard Throckmorton (1866–1916); granted the style and precedence of a baronet's widow when her son, Sir Robert Throckmorton (1908–89), succeeded his grandfather as 11th Bt, 1927.

Coughton is a thoroughly romantic house, though I must say the late Georgian front is gloomy. There is something unconvincing and drab about thin rendering which peels. The central Perpendicular tower and the half-timbered wings are beautiful, as well as picturesque. The family associations – the papistry, recusancy, Gunpowder Plot and intermarriages with other ancient Catholic families – are thrilling.

*Friday, 25th September*

I took a bus from Newcastle, standing all the way, and arrived at Wallington at 7.30 in the rain and dark. Matheson and John Dower* met me by the stables and carried my bag. I was tired and depressed all day, and found the Trevelyan family† overpowering in spite of the kind welcome they gave me. Lady Trevelyan came out of the drawing-room in a sweeping, stately rush, shaking my hands warmly and exuding cordiality. When I went into the dining-room Sir Charles rose and shook hands in the same hospitable way. I don't quite know why, because they are dyed-in-the-wood socialists, this should have surprised me. A newly married daughter Patricia, big with child, is living here; so is another daughter Pauline (Mrs Dower). Her husband, the aforementioned John Dower, is working on post-war National Park schemes, is very left-wing, and from his connections and position is, according to Matheson, important.

Lady Trevelyan speaks succinctly, carefully and measuredly, using the north country clipped 'a', and is distinctly 'clever'. Gertrude Bell‡ was her sister. Lady T. is handsome in a 'no

---

* Architect and town planner (d. 1947); m. 1929 Pauline Trevelyan (b. 1905), e. dau. of Sir Charles, Dep. Chm. National Parks Commission, 1956–66; their son Michael (b. 1933) was Dir. Gen. Countryside Commission, 1997–2002.

† Sir Charles Trevelyan, 3rd Bt (1870–1958); politician, since 1920s supporting the Labour Party (in whose governments he had served as President of the Board of Education); m. 1904 Molly, dau. of Sir Hugh Bell, 2nd Bt.

‡ Intrepid English traveller in the Middle East (1868–1926), who was instrumental in founding the Kingdom of Iraq (1921).

nonsense about appearances' manner, and looks as though she may have been the first woman chairman of the L[ondon] C[ounty] C[ouncil]. She is authoritarian, slightly deaf, and wears pince-nez. The two daughters are abrupt and rather terrifying. After dinner I am worn out, and long for bed. But no. We have general knowledge questions. Lady T. puts the questions one after the other with lightning rapidity. I am amazed and impressed by her mental agility, and indeed by that of the daughters, who with pursed lips shoot forth unhesitating answers like a spray of machine-gun bullets. All most alarming to a tired stranger. At the end of the 'game', for that is what they call this preparatory school examination, they allot marks. Every single member of the family gets 100 out of 100. The son-in-law gets 80, Matheson (who is a clever man) gets 30. I get 0. But then I am a half-wit. Deeply humiliated I receive condolences from the Trevelyans and assurances that I shall no doubt do better next time. I make an inward vow that there will never be a next time.

*Friday, 2nd October*

A[nne] H[ill] said this afternoon that Charles Fry* swore to her he had slept, at different times, with three of her cousins, two sisters and a brother – a good record. This reminds me that Randolph [Churchill] once told me O[swald] M[osley]† boasted to him of having what he called 'stretched the cock over three generations', *i.e.*, slept over a period of years with a grandmother, her daughter and her granddaughter. I don't know who they were. Jan, Angela Kinross's‡ mother, came to tea with the Hills, where I am staying.

---

* Partner of B. T. Batsford, publishers.

† Sir Oswald Mosley, 6th Bt (1896–1980); politician, founder of British Union of Fascists, 1932; interned under Defence Regulation 18B, 1940–3; m. 1st 1920 Lady Cynthia Curzon, 2nd 1936 Hon. Diana Guinness (*née* Mitford, 1910–2003, with whom J.L.-M. had been in love aged eighteen, and who was also now interned); his mother's sister, Dorothy *née* Heathcote-Edwards (1884–1965), was the widow of J.L.-M's uncle Alec Lees-Milne (1878–1931).

‡ Angela Culme-Seymour (b. 1913); m. 1st 1934–8 Johnnie Churchill, 2nd 1938–42 Hon. Patrick Balfour, writer, who s. 1939 as 3rd Baron Kinross (1904–76).

It appears that Angela has had her illegitimate child, a son, before her divorce from Patrick is through. She has entered his birth under the father's name, though he is still married. Legally speaking, however, the child could be the Hon. Something Balfour, and if Patrick were killed he would have a claim to be Lord Kinross unless the Balfour family disputed the title.

*Monday, 5th October*

At Englefield Green I called on Mrs Whitbread about her house, Burford, in Shropshire. She was unnecessarily modest about it, trying to rake up some Norman associations, whereas from the photograph it appears a decent George I house. It is extraordinary how quite intelligent people think that a house's site mentioned in Domesday is a better qualification than its architecture by Wren.

*Friday, 9th October*

At 2.30 I attended a meeting of Mrs Ronnie Greville's* executors – Lords Ilchester, Bruntisfield† and Dundonald,‡ and Terence Maxwell. A most interesting and complex subject, involving an estate of some £2 million. Mrs Greville has left Marie Antoinette's necklace to the Queen, £20,000 to Princess Margaret Rose, and £25,000 to the Queen of Spain. Everyone in London is agog to hear the terms of Mrs G's will. She was a lady who loved the great because they were great, and apparently had a tongue dipped in gall. I remember old Lady Leslie exclaiming, 'Maggie Greville! I would sooner have an open sewer in my drawing-room.'

---

* Margaret McEwan, heiress to brewing fortune; society hostess (noted for her malice) and art collector at Charles Street, London and Polesden Lacey, Surrey; m. 1891 Capt. the Hon. Ronald Greville (1864–1908); died September 1942, bequeathing bulk of her fortune to N.T.

† Victor Warrender (1899–1993); Conservative MP and office-holder, 1923–43; cr. Baron Bruntisfield, 1942.

‡ Thomas Cochrane, 13th Earl of Dundonald (1886–1958).

*Monday, 12th October*

By appointment with Sir Henry Hoare* [of Stourhead, Wiltshire], I was at the County Hotel, Salisbury, by 2 o'clock. I gave my name to the porter and sat in the dreary lounge to wait. A young RAF sergeant came in and sat down. I looked up and saw a face of ineffable beauty which smiled in a most beseeching manner. The sergeant took out a cigarette, offered me one, and was about to introduce himself when, damn it! Sir Henry Hoare was announced.

Sir Henry is an astonishing nineteenth-century John Bull, hobbling on two sticks. He was wearing a pepper-and-salt suit and a frayed grey billycock over his purple face. He had a very bronchial cough and kept hoiking and spitting into an enormous carrot-coloured handkerchief. He talked about his bad knee, and told me he had lost a kneecap. I found myself shouting, for he is rather deaf, 'Do you find it much of a handicap having no kneecap?' After the third repetition I decided that my question was inept.

Lady Hoare is an absolute treasure, and unique. She is tall, ugly and eighty-two; dressed in a long black skirt, belled from a wasp waist and trailing over her ankles. She has a thick net blouse over a rigidly upholstered bosom, complete with stiff, whaleboned high collar round the throat. Over this a black and white check jacket, evidently reinforced with stays, for it ends in tight points over her thighs. The sleeves are exaggeratedly mutton-chop. She has a protruding square coif of frizzly grey hair in the style of the late Nineties, black eyebrows and the thickest spectacle lenses I have ever seen. She adores the memory of George Lloyd and is quite convinced that he was the greatest Englishman of this century.

The Hoares took me round the house, which is packed to the brim with good things, and some ghastly things like cheap bamboo cake stands and thin silver vases filled with peacock feathers. On the grand piano an impenetrable forest of silver photograph frames. The house

* Sir Henry Hoare, 6th Bt (1865–1947); head of banking family; m. 1887 Alda Weston; they donated Stourhead to the N.T. shortly before their deaths, which took place on the same day, 25 March 1947.

was gutted by fire in 1902 and rebuilt by Sir Aston Webb* from old photographs and records. There are some Rococo chimneypieces brought after the fire from another Hoare house in Northamptonshire. Only the Regency picture gallery and library in the projecting wings were spared. All the contents however were saved, including the wonderful suite of furniture by the younger Chippendale.

For dinner we had soup, whiting, pheasant, apple pie, dessert, a white Rhine wine and port. Lady Hoare has no housemaid, only a cook and butler. But she said with satisfaction, 'The Duchess of Somerset at Maiden Bradley has to do all her own cooking.' She kept up a lively, not entirely coherent prattle. She said to me, 'Don't you find the food better in this war than in the last?' I replied that I was rather young during the last war, but I certainly remembered the rancid margarine we were given at my preparatory school when I was eight. 'Oh!' she said. 'You were lucky. We were reduced to eating rats.' I was a little surprised, until Sir Henry looked up and said, 'No, no, Alda. You keep getting your wars wrong. That was when you were in Paris during the Commune.'

*Wednesday, 14th October*

I motored with Captain Hill† to Polesden Lacey. The house was built by Cubitt in 1818 and looks from a distance across the valley much as it did in Neale's view of that date. The interior was, I imagine, entirely refitted by Mrs Greville, in the expensive taste of an Edwardian millionairess. But it is not vulgar. It is filled with good things, and several museum pieces. The upstairs rooms are well-appointed, in six or seven self-contained suites with bathrooms attached. There is a grass courtyard in the middle of the house.

Mrs Greville has been buried in the rose garden to the west of the house, next to the dog cemetery in accordance with female country house owner tradition. The gardens are unostentatious and

* Stourhead was not in fact rebuilt by the great Sir Aston Webb (1845–1930), but by the local architect E. Doran Webb.

† Sir John Dashwood's land agent at West Wycombe, often asked by the N.T. to report on properties.

rather beautiful: the grounds very beautiful, with a splendid view across the vale from the south front to the wooded hill beyond. Queen Mary's Walk is a straight grass ride bordered with yew.

*Sunday, 1st November*

I called for Anne Rosse at her uncle's house in Stafford Terrace, a house bought by her grandfather Linley Sambourne,* the *Punch* cartoonist of the 1880s. It is a period piece, untouched. It is choc-a-bloc with art nouveau. The Morris-papered walls are plastered with old photographic groups and Sambourne drawings, the frames touching each other, weird clocks galore, stained-glass windows, Victorian walking sticks and parasols. Anne and I walked round the pretty back streets by Holland Park, and took a bus to the Ritz, where Michael joined us at 1 o'clock, and Oliver Messel† at 2 o'clock. We talked over the luncheon table until 4. Oliver is a camouflage major in Norwich. He has discovered Ivory's‡ disused Assembly Rooms, made them into his headquarters, and is redecorating them.

*Thursday, 12th November*

Helen [Dashwood] has taken the news of our departure manfully. I feel sorry for her, as she will have to look for other lodgers. She knows she may do worse than have us. Yesterday the odious butler walked out of the house at 9.30 without warning because Helen asked him, quite nicely, to fetch her some marmalade for breakfast.

*Sunday, 15th November*

I walked to 1 Hyde Park Gardens to tea with Sir Ian Hamilton.§ This house, which in 1910 was decorated by Roger Fry in sombre

* Artist and illustrator (1844–1910).

† Theatrical producer, designer and artist (1904–78); brother of Anne Rosse.

‡ Thomas Ivory (1709–79); leading builder and architect in Norwich.

§ British general (1853–1947), distant family connection of J.L.-M., whose formidable wife, Jean *née* Muir (1861–1941), had been an 'honorary aunt' to him in London during the 1930s.

black and green for Aunt Jean, is redolent of memories of her and her lovely luncheon parties. There used to be a smell of joss-sticks burning in the hall. Sir Ian was in the dining-room which he now uses as a living-room. It is panelled and has Scotch ancestors on the walls above. He was lying on a sofa with a rug over his knees. Mrs Leeper at the tea-table. He will be ninety in February, and is thinner and less frisky than formerly. In fact when I arrived he was quiet and listless. He appears to be asleep until something rouses his interest. Then he is full of fire. Mrs Leeper talked to me about the Royal Academy plans for the rebuilding of London, and the war in North Africa. Suddenly Sir Ian woke up, and launched into a long, irrelevant story about his talking very confidentially with Marshal Lyautey,* who was stone deaf, at a Foreign Office reception, and realising that the other guests were drinking in every word. He said he was in the house last year when a bomb destroyed the house opposite. He swears his house moved a foot out of place, hesitated for an awful second, and fell back into place. He can prove the truth of the statement by some marks made by a supporting girder in the basement. Sir Ian is always courteous and cheerful. He said that we were third cousins, once or twice or thrice removed – I forget which – through the Menteiths of Cranley. I have always liked this old warrior, and I dearly loved Aunt Jean. When on leaving I shook his hand, with its bony protuberance from the wrist, he said, with much earnestness, 'Thank you, my dear boy.'

*Monday, 16th November*

Rick and John Russell† organised a concert tonight at Whistler's House, 96 [Cheyne Walk], in which Eddy and young Benjamin Britten‡ played on two pianos Schubert and Chopin, and a tenor,

* French soldier and imperialist (1854–1934).

† Writer and future art critic (1919–2008) who resembled the young Shelley; then doing war work at the Admiralty and planning to write a book on Henry James; friend and lodger of Rick Stewart-Jones.

‡ Composer (1913–76).

Peter Pears,* sang extremely competently the *Dichterliebe* of Schumann as well as *Seven Sonnets of Michelangelo*, composed by Britten himself. Everyone said what a good concert this was. I am so ignorant I can only judge music emotionally, not intellectually. The concert was to raise funds to procure railings for the protection of Chelsea Old Church. Rick in his usual generous way had paid for them in advance. Cecil Beaton on leaving thanked me profusely for the lovely party. I did not disabuse him by saying it was nothing to do with me. Actually I was in such pain with my leg during the concert that I could not sit. I stood outside the door of the ballroom with K. Clark,† who I could see was cold and bored.

*Wednesday, 25th November*

In the Travellers Club Harold was dressed in tails and white waistcoat, the first time I had seen anyone so dressed since the war began. He said he had been told to put on these clothes by the Camroses,‡ with whom he was to dine, and suspected the presence of royalty, the King of Greece most probably. Harold was looking sleek, smarmed and bald; and was in fact feeling very shaken and stiff, poor thing, having been run down by a taxi on his way to Buckingham Palace to see a diary of Nigel's in the hands of a brother Grenadier officer on guard there. Another taxi had picked him up, put him into his cab and asked where he should take him. Harold said, determinedly but rather unconvincingly, 'Buckingham Palace'. 'No, no, sir! Come, come! St George's Hospital or the Westminster?'

Harold talked of Mrs Greville, a common, waspish woman who got where she did through persistence and money. She was her father's illegitimate child, her mother being unknown. She married

* Tenor and organist (1910–86); domestic as well as professional partner of Benjamin Britten.

† Kenneth Clark (1903–83); art historian, Surveyor of the King's Pictures, 1934–44; cr. life peer, 1969.

‡ William Berry (1879–1954); proprietor of *Daily Telegraph*; cr. Baron Camrose, 1929, and Viscount Camrose, 1941; m. 1905 Mary Agnes Corns.

reputable, dull Captain Ronnie Greville, and jumped off from this safe spring-board. She built herself a fictitious reputation for cleverness, and was not even witty. But she had the ambition to cultivate ambassadors and entertain them at Polesden Lacey, so that in her constant travels she could demand return favours in special trains and red carpets, to the chagrin of foreign officials.

Jamesey said he would dine with me at Brooks's, for he had no money. Actually he is far richer than I am. I told him I had already invited John Gielgud* to supper, if he were free. Nevertheless, Jamesey insisted on eating immediately for he was ravenous. So I ordered dinner and we began on pheasant. Then a message came that John Gielgud would have supper at 9.15 with me at the Ivy. It was then 8.15 and we were already surfeited. But we finished our dinner, and Jamesey decided he would come to the Ivy too. I made him promise me he would behave, even if he disliked John. We walked to the Ivy in the blackout and James told me Harold had come upon a passage in *Thraliana*† in which Mrs Thrale lamented the fashionable vice among young men, especially prevalent in Scotland. This she attributed to the kilt.

Jamesey immensely liked John Gielgud who is charming, but inattentive. In conversation sophisticated remarks patter off him like undirected raindrops. He kept nodding to left and right to his friends coming and going. He is about to fly in a bomber to Gibraltar for four weeks' performances of sketches. He says if there is no rival show of legs, the troops will come. He was very scandalous about M.B.‡ who decoyed a young man into his Eaton Square house, and made him strip M.B. and beat him. The young man laid on with such violence that M.B. screamed in agony, and

---

* (Sir) John Gielgud (1904–2000); actor, with whom J.L.-M., then an Oxford undergraduate, had had a six-week affair in 1931.

† Recollections by Mrs Hester Thrale (1741–1821) of her friendship with Dr Samuel Johnson (1709–84), of which an annotated edition incorporating new material had been published in 1942.

‡ It has been speculated that 'M.B.' may have been Lord Louis Mountbatten (1900–79; cr. Earl, 1947), at this time Chief of Combined Operations: he was known to have these tastes.

the butler appeared. When confronted with the scene all the butler remarked was, 'I thought you rang, sir.'

*Thursday, 26th November*

On leaving the club at 8.45 I saw workmen tearing out a large chunk of the William IV railings which flank the doorway. I was livid with rage, and told the porter to allow no more to go. At Waterloo Station I sent the club Secretary a furious telegram; another to Lord Ilchester, and another to Professor Richardson.

*Friday, 27th November*

To Owletts [Kent]. Sir Herbert Baker,* who has had a stroke, is eighty, kind, Christian-like and cultivated. He was reading French poetry when I arrived. He insists on accompanying one, dragging his legs in a manner which pains one as it must pain him. We lunched and discussed which pieces of furniture ought to stay permanently in the house. Lady Baker is no less delightful. She was an Edmeades of Nurstead Court, two miles away. They call themselves, with justifiable pride, yeomen of Kent. The Bakers have lived at Owletts since 1780. Both are of stalwart stock, integrity written in their faces. Lady Baker said to her husband, 'I wonder if future generations will attribute all decent buildings of these times to Lutyens or Baker?' I feel that in spite of his detractors – and he is not popular today – there is something great about him when he is being creative and not merely imitative.

*Wednesday, 2nd December*

I met the builder at 104 Cheyne Walk who thinks he may be able to do the necessary work by mid January, but I am still rather worried by having no furniture, not to mention money for the expense of moving in.

---

* Architect (1862–1946); designer with Sir Edwin Lutyens of New Delhi; m. Florence Edmeades.

This morning I had a letter from Lord Ilchester, thanking me for having drawn his attention to the railings at Brooks's. He at once took up the matter with Lord Portal at the Ministry of Works. Apparently it was just a stupid mistake, and the pieces of railing taken away would be replaced. If these railings really are saved it will be owing to one of those rare chance interventions, my happening to stay the night at Brooks's while the demolition men were beginning their beastly work.

*Thursday, 24th December*

I went home for Christmas, or rather I stayed with Midi in the village, having half my meals with her and half with the family. Midi's younger child Veronica* is undeniably beautiful with copper-coloured hair and fair skin, but she tries to be funny, and is strikingly unfunny. Bamber† is a sensitive, delicate and adventuresome little boy.

Mama told me how last week she was in the room while Papa and Colonel Riley were planning a Home Guard exercise to take place the following day. Rather brutally they intended to humiliate another officer, saying to each other, 'William, the damned fool, will never be able to capture the aerodrome. If he were the slightest use, of course he would, etc.' They then discussed how it ought to be done, tracing on a map the complicated route he should take, mentioning the names of bridges, roads, villages and the map numbers. Mama all the while was pretending to read *The Times*, but was actually jotting down on a pad all they said. When they left after an hour she rang up the damned fool William, and reported to him word for word what they had said, giving the exact map references. The result was that much to their surprise and disgust William captured the aerodrome with flying colours.

---

* Veronica Gascoigne (b. 1938); m. 1960 Hon. William Plowden.

† Arthur Bamber Gascoigne (b. 1935); writer, broadcaster and publisher; m. 1963 Christina Ditchburn.

*Thursday, 31st December*

In the office yesterday afternoon the telephone rang, and Eardley said to me, 'You are wanted. The name is Stuart Preston.'* I was amazed. Stuart flew from America yesterday. He is a GI. The last time I saw him was at dinner with Harold [Nicolson] at the House of Commons in the summer of 1939. I remember Harold saying, 'The next time we see Stuart over here, he will be in uniform.'

I 'saw' or rather 'slept' – and not alone – the New Year in. Could there be a happier augury for 1943?

* Anglophile New York bibliophile of independent means (1915–2005); protégé of Harold Nicolson and pre-war lover of J.L.-M.

# 1943

# 1943

*As 1943 began, J.L.-M. was busy sorting out the contents of the two houses which Mrs Greville had bequeathed to the National Trust – 16 Charles Street in Mayfair, and Polesden Lacey in Surrey. He was preparing for the National Trust's return from West Wycombe to its London offices at 7 Buckingham Palace Gardens, and his own move into 104 Cheyne Walk, Chelsea, a small house owned by Rick Stewart-Jones. For some months his social and romantic life was dominated by the slightly ridiculous figure of Stuart Preston, his American lover of the late 1930s who had arrived back in London with the US Army, and whose extraordinary success in the highest English social circles J.L.-M. regarded with a touch of irritation.*

*Saturday, 2nd January*

Stuart and I left to catch a train to High Wycombe. We chased it down the platform and the guard allowed us to jump into the van just in time. In the train he talked with rapture and awe of his dinner last night with the Duff Coopers. He finds her wondrous, incredibly flippant, brilliant and witty, but cruel and un-middle-class. He kept on repeating the last phrase, with wide open eyes. All I could find to say was, 'What else did you expect?' He says that in his billets in North Audley Street he sleeps on straw with one blanket.

*Friday, 8th January*

My temperature being sub-normal I decided to risk pleurisy, pneumonia, death and go to London to catch a glimpse of Q. even if I had to come straight back again. Waiting for the bus in the half light and the frost, my body felt sweaty hot, and my hands and feet like icicles. In Charles Street I gave the old caretaker,

Mrs Reid, a pork pie as a present. It was by way of throwing a sop to Cerberus. For when Q. breezed in she was quite polite to her. I find the attitude of humble women to well-dressed women invariably the same, suspicious and resentful. And when Q. breezed out after five minutes of ecstasy, Mrs Reid, though cordial, looked triumphant. Then Harold [Nicolson] called to leave a note for Stuart. He was bright and shabby, and Mrs Reid beamed upon him. Harold strode up and down the stone hall nostalgically but unregretfully recalling the awful parties he had attended in this house. Again the doorbell rang. Stuart walked in, and because he is under thirty Mrs Reid beamed on him. Over a huge fire in the dining-room Stuart and I crouched under the steel scaffolding and between the stacks of French furniture. I ate sandwiches and Stuart a plateful of ready-cooked American field rations of meat minced up with beans from a tin which Mrs Reid heated for him. Disgusting it looked too. Both of us drank whisky from a flask. I continued to work alone in this eerie house, and left after dark, purloining like a thief in the night a broom, a brush and a cake of scrubbing soap.

I dined with Q. at Prunier's off *homard à l'américaine* and a glass of champagne each. I was obliged to stay at Duke's Hotel, St James's Street.

*Saturday, 9th January*

At 104 Cheyne Walk I found Miss Paterson with the new char, Mrs Beckwith, a dear, gentle mouse from Battersea, sweeping and washing floors busily. Jamesey called and took me to lunch at the Good Intent. He is very happy at the moment. He talked of Stuart whom he had met last night dining with Harold. He thinks him personable, but in that Pope-Hennessy way was terrifyingly analytical. Asks me if he is sincere. I don't yet know, I tell him. We return to the house and this time I really get down to sweeping and clearing away the mess of two years' accumulation of air-raid detritus. Jamesey very immaculate with a calf-bound book under one arm follows me around, asking querulously if it is really necessary for me to sweep. He soon slopes off to call on Logan Pearsall

Smith.* When he has gone Miss P., Miss Beckwith and I drink tea in front of a huge fire in my room, sitting on the bed, the only piece of furniture that has yet arrived.

After dinner I went to 4 King's Bench Walk to spend the night at Harold's. Harold came in at 10.30 and we talked till after midnight. He makes me talk freely as though I am cleverer than I am, and feel happier than I am. He is still optimistic about the outcome of the war. The Czechoslovakian Prime Minister, with whom Harold lunched yesterday, had that morning been interviewing two Czech youths just arrived in England after walking across Germany. They reported that every German they met spoke of defeat as the inevitable outcome for them.

*Tuesday, 12th January*

By early train to London again to meet Kenneth Clark at Charles Street. He was extremely helpful and took much trouble examining all the pictures, of which he was to my contentment even more critical than Christie's, and recommended keeping even less than they did.

I joined Stuart at the Connaught Hotel but since we could not get a table we lunched at Brooks's. Stuart had spent the weekend at Panshanger. The only other guest was Lord Hugh Cecil.† He and the Desboroughs‡ spoke about Lord Rosebery and Queen Victoria not as legendary figures, but as friends whom they had all known. Lady Desborough is a step-granddaughter of Lord Palmerston and a great-granddaughter of Byron's Lady Melbourne. Stuart slept in a room the walls of which were hung with the heraldic achievements of a Lord Cowper, an eighteenth-century ancestor who was a Prince of the Roman Empire.

---

* American man of letters (1865–1946).

† Lord Hugh Cecil (1867–1956); yr s. of 3rd Marquess of Salisbury, Prime Minister; Conservative politician and Provost of Eton; cr. Baron Quickswood, 1941.

‡ William Grenfell (1855–1945; cr. Baron Desborough, 1905) and Ethel ('Ettie') *née* Fane (1867–1952) of Panshanger Park, Hertfordshire; leading members of 'the Souls'.

*Thursday, 14th January*

Today we leave West Wycombe for good, to return to our London office and life. Whiteley's only sent one van, and that an hour and a half late, instead of the two ordered. I drove Miss Paterson and Miss Ballachey in the National Trust car stacked with our own belongings. On the way we picked up my dachshund Pompey. He was sick, once over Miss Paterson's second-best coat and again out of an open window into a London street. Dreadful confusion on arrival at the office, but worse when Miss Paterson and I reached 104 Cheyne Walk after dark. The charwoman had not even lit a fire for us. There was no electric light because the company said the house was too damp to test the wiring. No stick of furniture yet save one bed each. The Ascot heater not working, and so no hot water. We had an uncomfortable night, Pompey sleeping on and falling off a chair beside me.

*Saturday, 16th January*

Some furniture arrived this morning. Miss P. and I worked like Trojans. I had to help haul my large sofa through the window on the first floor, since it had stuck on the staircase. After tea I changed and went to Ian Hamilton's ninetieth birthday party. He had invited ninety friends, mostly relations, and all the children from the neighbouring streets. He gave them a conjuring entertainment and a Punch and Judy show, with one marionette as Hitler. Mrs Churchill was leaving the door as I arrived. I talked to Shane Leslie* about his boy Jack,† now a prisoner of war since Boulogne. He often hears from him and says Jack laughed when the Germans manacled him. Dined with the Pope-Hennessys, Dame Una talking of Shane Leslie's new edition of Cardinal Vaughan's‡ love letters to Lady Herbert of Lea.

---

* Shane Leslie (1885–1971) of Castle Leslie, Co. Monaghan; Anglo-Irish landowner and writer; first cousin of Winston Churchill (their mothers being sisters); s. father as 3rd Bt 1944.

† John Leslie (b. 1916); s. father 1971 as 4th Bt.

‡ Herbert Vaughan (1832–1903); Cardinal Archbishop of Westminster 1892–1903; closely attached to Elizabeth Herbert (1822–1911), widow of the statesman Sidney

*Sunday, 17th January*

Rick turned up last night a Coldstream Guardsman, looking the picture of health, but in actual fact depressed and overcome by the whole experience. He said he could not cope and was so dispirited, with so little to say, that I, friend as I am, was bored. For the first time I have known him I made an excuse to leave, and slunk home to bed.

The siren went during dinner at Brooks's, and the noise of our gunfire was worse than I have ever known it. During the night there was a second raid. Miss P. was rather frightened by the din, so we sat under the stairs in our dressing-gowns. Pompey was quite unmoved. I did not like to ask Miss P. if she regretted our having left the country for this sort of thing.

*Wednesday, 20th January*

Went to tea with Jamesey in his flat to meet Rose Macaulay* and Lady Crewe.† Lady C. was there when I arrived, wrapped in expensive furs and wearing black gloves. She talked spicily to Jamesey in whispered asides, and they giggled a lot. This behaviour did not make for a comfortable trio. Then she talked to us both about Polesden Lacey. She told how Mrs Greville's mother was the wife of the day-porter at Mr McEwan's brewery. McEwan 'for convenience' put him on night duty. I brought some of my photographs of Manoeline architecture to show Rose Macaulay, who is shortly going to Portugal to write a book for the Ministry of Information. My first impression was of a thin, desiccated figure in a masculine tam-o'shanter, briskly entering the room. James says she is like Voltaire to look at. Actually her profile is less sharp than her full face, and is handsome. She talks too fast and too much.

---

Herbert, 1st Baron Herbert of Lea, from the time of her conversion to Catholicism in 1866.

* Novelist and travel writer (1881–1958; DBE 1958).

† Lady Margaret Primrose, yr dau. of 5th Earl of Rosebery (Liberal Prime Minister, 1894–5); m. 1899 (as his 2nd wife) Richard Monckton Milnes, 2nd Baron Houghton (1858–1945), Liberal statesman and HM Ambassador to Paris, 1922–8, cr. Marquess of Crewe, 1911.

*Saturday, 23th January*

My house is settling down. The room with three large and long windows on the front faces the river and the big barge moored alongside. A fourth window at the west end faces Lots Road power station and the bend in the river opposite Battersea and the next bridge upstream. The windows being so very dirty, since the cleaners have not yet come, make it all but impossible to see the views, but I know they are there. My glazed curtains have white sheaves of flowers on a cherry ground, and are torn and shabby. The floor is parquet. In one corner beside an Adam hob-grate is the Empire bureau with fall flap on which I write this diary. Other pieces are my unsightly bed with hideous servants'-pink cover; an upright winged armchair in crimson damask; a silk covered sofa of a different crimson; a mahogany half-circular-fronted commode; an anthracite stove always burning in the other fireplace; Persian rugs; a large painted tin tray of Margate, *circa* 1850, over one chimneypiece. The room is thoroughly unpretentious and on the whole pretty.

*Monday, 25th January*

Went to Warfield House, Sir George Leon's* near Bracknell [Berkshire], for luncheon, and stayed until 4. He considers making over his house and 400 acres, consisting of four small farms with pedigree herds. Rather an absurd, opinionated man, but public-spirited and pathetically patriotic like so many rich Jews on this side of the Channel. We parted fast friends. The red brick house is Queen Anne. He has had it colour-washed, and the thin windows and even the reveals painted dark blue. The interior was decorated sumptuously by Lenygons before the war. There are fawn pile carpets in every room and passage. His furniture is first-rate, chiefly late seventeenth- and early eighteenth-century walnut. He showed me a suite of Charles II armchairs from Holme Lacey with

* Sir George Leon, 2nd Bt (1875–1947). (His grandson, 4th Bt [b. 1934], is the actor John Standing.)

particularly delicate stretchers. His pictures are immaculately cleaned and varnished, and include Poussins, Richard Wilsons, Cuyps. A typical, safe, rich, decent man's collection.

Met Jamesey at Brooks's and he conducted me to Argyll House. Lady Crewe was curtseying to Hapsburg Archdukes. Straightaway Jamesey got off with Lady Cunard,* and was delighted with her and the party. I disliked her and it as I knew I should. Stuart drank too much and we had great difficulty in getting him to leave. James and I had some anxious moments with him in the bus. In the restaurant he ate no dinner and talked of lords and ladies in a loud American voice.

*Saturday, 30th January*

Margaret Jourdain and Ivy C.-B. came to tea. I had forgotten at what time to expect them. To my surprise and concern they turned up on the dot of 4. They are slightly prim and correct, and it evidently distressed them that I had to descend to the kitchen, make and fetch the tea, and lay the table in their presence. I was made to feel that I was not behaving quite as I should. It was a horrid tea in consequence, and this they clearly minded, without saying so. To make matters worse John Russell, whom I had bidden to meet them, did not turn up till after 5, having been to a concert. However they stayed till after 6. Ivy C.-B., talking of the ineffectual results of the Germans' last raid on London when they hit a school and killed thirty children, observed, 'It isn't as though they were even impeding the war effort. On the contrary, they are really helping it by making the milk ration go further.'

*Wednesday, 3rd February*

I had a horrible day with Colonel Pemberton at Pyrland Hall near Taunton. He is a fiendish old imbecile with a grotesque white moustache. When I first saw him he was pirouetting on his toes in

* Maud Burke of San Francisco (1872–1948); m. 1895 Sir Bache Cunard, 3rd Bt (1851–1925), owner of shipping line; hostess.

the road. He has an inordinate opinion of himself and his own judgement. He is absolutely convinced that Pyrland is the finest house in Somerset and he is doing the Trust a great service in bequeathing it. The truth is the property does not comprise land of outstanding natural beauty and is of insignificant size; moreover the house, though large, and basically eighteenth-century, has been thoroughly Victorianised as to windows and rendering. The army occupies it at present. It has a nice Georgian staircase and some plaster cornices and mahogany doors on the curve. I was drawn into several acrimonious arguments with the old man, whom I cordially disliked, for he insisted upon contradicting whatever I said. He gave me an exiguous lunch of bread and cheese, both hard as wood, a baked potato in its skin, dry as sawdust, and watery apple pie with Bird's custard. Ugh! He expected me to return and waste the following day in discussion. But I had already made up my mind after the first half-hour of my visit. I could not have borne him or Pyrland an hour longer. Having hated me like poison he was nevertheless furious when I left at 4. I conclude that he has to have some victim on whom he can vent his spleen. I got back to London in time to have a late supper of oysters and stout with Gabriel Herbert.*

*Sunday, 7th February*

Midi, Stuart and I went to Windsor by train. We walked to Eton and looked for our various boys in their houses. Then Stuart and I lunched with the Provost, Lord Quickswood. There were just the three of us. I was surprised to find Lord Q. such an old man. He was shy at first, though full of solicitude for Stuart, the American soldier ally, who seems to be treated by all society as a lion. But then Stuart is attentive to the old and throws off anecdotes and literary

* Gabriel Herbert (1911–87); eldest of the three daughters of Mary Herbert of Pixton Park, Somerset, a Catholic house often visited by J.L.-M.; m. 1943 Major Alexander ('Alick') Dru. J.L.-M. later wrote: 'There was a time in the mid Thirties when I thought I was a little in love with Gabriel, and she seemed a little in love with me' (*Beneath a Waning Moon*, 21 November 1987).

quotations like pearls before swine. Lord Q. warmed after a time, but has little charm, and is impersonal. An old-fashioned luncheon of roast turkey, brown potatoes and sprouts, 'shape' (that ghastly wobbly pudding) and bottled blackberries, accompanied by beer followed by sherry. Lord Q. showed us all the portraits in the Provost's Lodge from the Gheeraerts of Lord Essex to the Romneys and Beecheys of Old Boys. He also took us over Lower School, and Upper School, showing us the bombed bit. The Head Master's room has quite gone, all but the roadside wall. There is a deep crater where it was. Stuart fascinated by it all, and particularly by Lord Quickswood's use of 'ain't', his top hat and white bands. Stuart asked if we might see the College Library. Lord Q. thought for a moment, and said apologetically, 'I much fear I cannot do that. My man is out this afternoon, and I do not know where to switch on the lights.'

Tea at the Cockpit. Stuart took out Lady Desborough's grandson, and I Francis Dashwood, who is now in Pop.* After College Chapel Stuart and I called on Mrs Montgomery† who lives in a hideous corner house facing the entrance to Windsor Castle. She is the eighty-year-old daughter of Sir Henry Ponsonby. She has evidently had a stroke and it is not easy to understand what she says. She is wizened, sharp, and brimful of talk. She repeated to Stuart the most flattering things told her about him by Logan Pearsall Smith, who is a close friend. She spoke of Queen Victoria who was her godmother and whom she disliked. She said that during dinners at the castle no one was allowed to speak, and if they had to ask for something, not above a whisper. The Queen would address her family in German. The familiar phrase '*Das ist schrecklich!*' haunts her. She once witnessed the Queen greeting Mr Gladstone, who had been summoned to dine. Gladstone was nervous about what his reception would be, and fumbled with his walking-stick. He

* Colloquial term for the self-electing Eton Society, whose members, identified by their fancy waistcoats, enjoy various privileges and act as school prefects.

† Alberta Victoria Ponsonby (1862–1945), dau. of Queen Victoria's private secretary Sir Henry Ponsonby (1825–95); m. 1891 Maj.-Gen. W. E. Montgomery (d. 1927).

was then over eighty. But contrary to expectation, when the Queen appeared she went straight up to him, leaning on a stick herself, and said, 'Mr Gladstone, you and I have known days when neither of us was lame', and laughed very sympathetically.

*Thursday, 11th February*

I arrived in the full swing of Cecil Beaton's party in Pelham Place. Cecil's house is sophistically [*sic*] decorated. It is Nineties-ish, with red flock walls and varnished aspidistras in tall pots, and tight little smart leather chairs. He was saying about his secretary, 'When I go away I leave her, not on heat, but on board wages, I mean.' While talking to Alice Harding* I felt something boring into my spine, which means that one is being talked about maliciously. True enough, on turning round I saw Eddy [Sackville-West] and Nancy sitting on a low sofa dissecting each guest one by one and hooting with laughter. I joined them. Nancy was telling how Lady Leconfield† had been certified for descending in the lift at Claridge's stark naked. The little lift boy was sharply reprimanded by the hall porter. In self-defence he protested that he could not see above the lady's knees, she was so tall.

*Thursday, 18th February*

Today I bought a new eye-glass on a black string. It is the greatest help in reading menus and bus numbers, instead of fumbling for spectacles.

At 6 o'clock I went to St George's Hospital where Stuart has been removed, for he is suffering from jaundice. He is happy there because he is in the centre of London and can see Apsley House from his window. He pulled up his bedclothes and showed me his stomach, which is bright lemon. I delivered chocolates, stamps and writing paper.

* Much-married Astor heiress.

† Beatrice Rawson; m. 1911 Charles Wyndham, 3rd Baron Leconfield (1872–1952) of Petworth Park, Sussex (see entry for 19 July 1945).

*Sunday, 21st February*

I had tea with Mrs Montgomery at Windsor. It was, I believe, a success. We found that we liked and disliked the same people. She was thrilled that I knew Ivy Compton-Burnett, whom she considers our greatest novelist. She has lent me one of her books that I have not read, as a hostage she explained, so that I should have to come back and return it to her. Alan Pryce-Jones* is her cousin. She loves Jamesey very much and the Sergeant [Stuart Preston] not so very much. She absolutely loathes Queen Victoria and Evelyn Waugh. She cannot feel dispassionately about anyone. We touched on Raymond [Mortimer], Eddy [Sackville-West], Basil Dufferin.† 'Now we have another,' she cried eagerly, as their names cropped up, 'we will put him here', indicating a place at the large empty tea table, 'and will come back to him when we have disposed of X. We will give him ten minutes', or 'quite twenty minutes', as the case may be. When I left she referred to me as being 'quite one of us'. 'I loathe low-brows' were her parting words. What will she think of me when she finds out?

*Monday, 1st March*

The whole of London congregates around the Sergeant's bed. Like Louis XIV he holds levées. Instead of meeting now in Heywood Hill's shop, the intelligentsia and society congregate in public ward no. 3 of St George's Hospital. When I arrived Stephen Spender,‡ looking worn out by his fireman's duties, was sprawled at the end of the bed. Raymond [Mortimer] came for a brief visit. Lady Cunard called when the entire ward were stripped to the waist and washing. She pronounced the procedure barbaric. Then a member of Stuart's unit came to announce baldly that he must expect to be in the front

* Eton contemporary of J.L.-M. (1908–2000), a brilliant charmer; editor *Times Literary Supplement*, 1948–59.

† Basil Blackwood, 4th Marquess of Dufferin and Ava (1909–45); friend of J.L.-M. at prep school, Eton and Oxford; Under Secretary for the Colonies, 1937–40.

‡ (Sir) Stephen Spender (1909–95); poet; co-founder with Cyril Connolly of *Horizon*, 1939.

line when the invasion starts. S., quite unconcerned, said he could not possibly be killed. I wonder, does every soldier feel as confident?

*Friday, 5th March*

Newton's house* in which he was born in 1642 is about twenty years older. It is Cotswoldy, with good steep pitched roof, stone corniced chimneys and mullioned windows. It has four large bedrooms, one of which was partitioned off in about 1666 with panelling of that date so as to form a study for Newton. Upstairs the L-shaped room is said to be the one whence Newton watched the apple fall. The original tree's descendant, now very aged, stands on the site of its forebear in the little apple orchard in front of the house. The secretary is going to find out what species of apple it is. Tenant farmers have lived for 200 years in the house. The present ones are leaving because all of the surrounding land has been exploited commercially for the limestone, and is now arid, blasted heath and hummocks of infertile slack. It is a scandal that good agricultural land is allowed to be so treated by commercial firms and left thoroughly wasted and useless. The little manor house has light, but no sanitation. There are earth closets in the garden.

*Monday, 8th March*

I arrived at the Dorchester at 8 and was wafted in the lift to an upper floor, then directed down airless, daylightless passages to Emerald Cunard's apartments. Her sitting room is sympathetically furnished with French things. Already assembled were Lady Moore, Garrett Moore's† lovely wife, and Lady Lamington,‡ a pretty woman. Garrett Moore followed me. I have known him more or less, less rather than more, since Eton days. He is tall, thin,

* Woolsthorpe Manor, Lincolnshire, given to the National Trust in 1943 through the Royal Society and the Pilgrim Trust.

† Garrett, Viscount Moore (1910–89); e.s. and heir of 10th Earl of Drogheda (whom he succeeded as 11th Earl, 1957); m. 1935 Joan Carr, pianist (d. 1989).

‡ Riette Neilson (d. 1968); m. 1922 3rd and last Baron Lamington (d. 1951).

willowy, sharp-featured, distinguished and patrician. A poetic and romantic-looking man if ever there was one. Lady Cunard darted like a bird of paradise into the room at 8.25; and we dined off expensive, pretentious food which lacked the refinements of good cooking. Our hostess kept complaining how at this stage of the war the country should have learnt to have adequate butter and milk distribution. I sat on her left, Lady Moore on my left. The latter is animated and bewitching. Her coif *à la* Queen Alexandra was most becoming. Lady C. was a little *distraite* throughout; and conversation was not sparkling in spite of a promising beginning.

At 10 we went below to a concert given for Sibyl Colefax's benefit by the Griller Quartet and Denis Matthews* at the piano. Unmusical though I am, I enjoyed it immensely. Lady Cunard introduced me to all and sundry, some of them the friends of a lifetime, as though I were a visitor from Mars. And so I suppose I am to her. I walked all the way home from the Dorchester, cogitating the evening's experience, and thinking myself a fool for being so buttoned up, and suspicious – of what? Some friendly and decorative and sophisticated people in a circle to which I do not belong.

*Tuesday, 9th March*

At 6 to St George's, arriving simultaneously with Logan Pearsall Smith. I wanted to retire but Stuart earnestly begged me to stay. Pearsall Smith is an old, frail man of heavy, ungainly build. He may be a bore for he tells long stories 'at' one, in a laborious, monotonous tone, laughing all the while and salivating a good deal. But he was quite funny with his story of a practical joke he played on Virginia Woolf in pretending to be the outraged person whose name she had in *Jacob's Room* 'taken in vain' from a tombstone in Scarborough churchyard. This delightful blackmailing story was interrupted by tiresome Lady H. arriving. Again Stuart implored me not to leave, so I did my best by talking to her to allow him to have some conversation with the old man. When he had left I helped get rid of Lady H. Stuart got back into bed, looking tired,

* Pianist and writer on music (1919–89).

and promptly began eating a lobster. Whereupon Harold arrived. I got up to go, not without promising to return tomorrow, for there was apparently something very important S. had to tell me alone. But S. is never alone.

*Wednesday, 10th March*

I picked up the Eshers in the National Trust car and motored them from the Lansdowne Club to Polesden Lacey. Lady E. sat in front with me, Lord E. behind. He behaved like a schoolboy, calling out for me to stop at intervals so he could buy cakes, she rebuking him. Referring to the cold of West Wycombe in winter and Helen's apparent indifference to it, he remarked, 'People are never cold in their own houses. They derive warmth from satisfaction with the economies they are making.' At Polesden they went round every room, and looked into every corner, cupboard and drawer. They commented on every object; they liked the outside of the house and the grounds, and distant view. Esher said he had no quarrel to make with my plans and schemes. Yet he teased me unmercifully, and joked about Matheson's dislike of comfort and terror of beauty.

I dropped the Eshers at Paddington station, and went to see Jamesey. He was lying in bed with the curtains drawn. Under the shaded lamp his pallid face looked like old ivory. With his glowing coal eyes and glossy hair he resembles a Florentine prince. Then I called on the Sergeant and gave him Lady Esher's violets with her love. He was better, but there was no opportunity to hear those important words.

*Monday, 15th March*

After breakfast, I carried out what I had resolved. That is to say I took Pompey's basket, hid it away, burned his two bones, his cotton reel, his blanket and cushion in the incinerator in the yard. I threw his chain as far as I could into the river. I got a taxi, and told the driver to take me to the vet. I held the little dog on my knees without looking at him, without (thank God) seeing his eyes. I told the vet to destroy him, and walked out, and away. All this

I did without a qualm, for his cough was getting worse, and his fits persisted. For five or ten minutes I felt almost jubilant. Had I not done the right thing? Would someone ever do the same service to me? In walking rapidly along the embankment I felt, at first with surprise, then shame, the tears coursing down my cheeks. By the time I reached the door I felt nothing but unmitigated grief. I had been no better than a murderer.

I dined with Puss Gaskell* at the Berkeley. Douglas Woodruff† and his wife, to both of whom I felt antagonistic and was provocative, Carmen Wiggin and Hubert Howard‡ were there. Mrs Woodruff told me that Alick Dru and Evelyn Waugh§ were her two best men friends. I said that Evelyn represented the English Catholicism which was anathema to me. It was sectarian, superior, exclusive and smug. Besides, Evelyn was the nastiest-tempered man in England, Catholic or Protestant. His review of Raymond [Mortimer]'s book was personal vituperation. Having delivered myself of these ill-mannered phrases, I felt better and enjoyed the party. I talked to Puss about Queen Mary's gifts to Mrs Greville. She promised to find out which they exactly were, so I can identify them. She said there was nothing the Queen would like more than to visit Polesden and 'play around'. Thank God, she can't.

*Thursday, 18th March*

At 2 o'clock to Martin's Bank at which were present Colonel Robin Buxton, Lord Sackville,¶ his solicitor, and Lord Willingdon** – the

---

* Lady Constance Knox (1885–1964); dau. of 5th Earl of Ranfurly; m. 1905 Evelyn Milnes Gaskell; Lady-in-Waiting to HM Queen Mary, 1937–53; known to J.L.-M. as 'Aunt Puss'.

† Editor of *The Tablet*, 1936–67 (1897–1978); m. 1933 Hon. Marie Acton.

‡ Hon. H. J. E. Howard (1907–87), yr s. of 1st Baron Howard of Penrith; patrician Roman Catholic.

§ Novelist (1903–66); m. (2nd) Laura Herbert (sister of Gabriel, who m. Major Alick Dru, 1943).

¶ Major-General Charles Sackville-West, 4th Baron Sackville (1870–1962); father of Eddy S.-W.

** Inigo Brassey Freeman-Thomas, 2nd Marquess of Willingdon (1899–1979).

first and last Knole trustees. They had been lunching well, and I was given a glass of port. We discussed Knole. Lord Sackville could not have been more friendly or anxious to co-operate. I can't think why Eddy does not like him more. He is gentle and sympathetic and always treats me with paternal affection because I am a friend of Eddy. We left it that I was to send him Garrard the estate agent's figures for his comments, whereafter the trustees would decide how much endowment they could and would provide – the capital suggested is enough to yield £3,000 p.a. I am not sure how pleased the Trust will be with me for disclosing these figures, but I believe we must always be absolutely frank with decent donors like Lord Sackville. My sympathies are always with them. In fact my loyalties are first to the houses, second to the donors, and third to the National Trust. I put the Trust last because it is neither a work of art nor a human being but an abstract thing, a convenience.

*Friday, 19th March*

This afternoon I took the tube to Richmond, and thence a bus to Petersham. I walked down the long drive to Ham House. The grounds are indescribably overgrown and unkempt. I walked round the house, which appeared thoroughly deserted, searching for an entrance. The garden and front doors looked as though they had not been used for decades. So I returned to the back door and pulled a bell. Several seconds later a rusty tinkling echoed from distant subterranean regions. While waiting I recalled the grand ball given for Nefertiti Bethell* which I attended in this house some ten years ago or more. The door was roughly jerked open, the bottom grating against the stone floor. The noise was accompanied by heavy breathing from within. An elderly man of sixty stood before me. He had red hair and a red face, carrot and port wine. He wore a tail-coat and a starched shirt front which had

* Nefertari (*sic*) (b. 1917); dau. of Hon. Richard Bethell (an Egyptologist who was present with Howard Carter at opening of Tutankhamen's tomb in 1922 and d. mysteriously seven years later), e.s. of 3rd Baron Westbury and Lady Agatha Tollemache, dau. of 3rd Earl of Dysart; m. 1941 Lt-Col James Innes.

come apart from the waistcoat. 'The old alcoholic family butler,' I said to myself. Without asking my name or business, he said, 'Follow me.' Slowly he led me down a dark passage. His legs must be webbed, for he moved in painful jerks. At last he stopped outside a door, and knocked nervously. An ancient voice cried, 'Come in!' The seedy butler then said to me, 'Daddy is expecting you', and left me. I realised that he was the bachelor son of Sir Lyonel Tollemache, aged eighty-nine.* As I entered the ancient voice said, 'You can leave us alone, boy!'

Sir Lyonel was sitting on an upright chair. He was dressed, unlike his son, immaculately in a grey suit, beautifully pressed, and wore a stock tie with a large pearl pin. I think he had spats over black polished shoes. A decorative figure, and courteous. He asked me several questions about the National Trust's scheme for preserving country houses, before ringing the bell and handing me back to his son.

The son showed me hurriedly round the house, which is melancholy in the extreme. All the rooms are dirty and dusty. The furniture and pictures have been moved to the country for safety. There is no doubt whatever that, even without the contents, this house is worthy of acceptance because of the superlative interior treatment, the panelling, the exquisite parquetry floors, the extraordinary chimneypieces, the great staircase of pierced balusters, the velvet hangings, etc. It is a wonderful seventeenth-century house, and from the south windows the garden layout of symmetrical beds, stone gate plinths and ironwork is superb. Once we were away from the father, whom he clearly holds in mortal dread, the son became confidential. He said the family were worth £2 million and did not receive as much as sixpence in each pound; that they had two gardeners instead of twelve, and no indoor servants except a cook (and himself). He told me he was so distracted by looking after the Ham property and the Lincolnshire estate that at times he felt suicidal. I looked straight at him, and knew that the poor man meant it. When I waved goodbye, the faintest flicker of a smile crossed his bucolic face, and a tiny tear was on his cheek.

---

* Sir Lyonel Tollemache, 4th Bt (1854–1952); his son, 'young' Lyonel, later 5th Bt (1886–1969).

*Saturday, 20th March*

Dined with Q. at the Mirabelle. She offered me £1 towards the evening's expenses, which I accepted without demur. I do hope and believe she meant me to. I told her I hated the Mirabelle. Got home at 11.30 and sat over the fire for hours. Felt overcome with loneliness. It was too late to ring up Q. I have nothing to reproach her for, yet I keep thinking, 'Would I, if I were she, gratuitously go off to —— for ten days leaving Jim behind in London?' Obviously, yes, I ought to in the circumstances. But would I, that's the point? I am such a fool in these respects. She is obviously right. She has duties. Every day I have a letter, sometimes a postcard too. There can be no mistaking their underlying meaning – which is now, and not for ever.

*Monday, 22nd March*

Chips [Channon]* walked with me across the park. He tried to pump me about the Sergeant, so that I wondered at first whether he were in love with him. He asked me whether Stuart was really rich, or really very poor. Everyone was asking, for S. is extremely mean with money if he is not poor. I honestly did not know. Was S. an impostor, he wondered? I said such an idea had not occurred to me, but volunteered to observe it was rather a pity S. was undiscriminating in his choice of friends. He said, No, in that respect S. had not erred, he cared for distinguished people like Lady Desborough and myself. I could not help laughing. When we parted in Pont Street, he said, 'Do not worry yourself about the Sergeant. He is being well looked after by X.-B.†' I did not believe it.

---

* (Sir) Henry Channon (1897–1958); American-born Conservative MP, homosexual, socialite and diarist; m. 1933–45 Lady Honor Guinness, er dau. of 2nd Earl of Iveagh.

† X.-B. has been identified as Alan Lennox-Boyd (1904–83); Conservative MP, Parliamentary Secretary to Ministry of Aircraft Production, 1943–5; cr. Viscount Boyd of Merton, 1960; m. 1938 Lady Patricia Guinness (sister of Lady Honor Channon). J.L.-M. later wrote that 'I slept with him more than once, but they were not romantic occasions' (*Holy Dread*, 20 March 1983).

*Tuesday, 23rd March*

This conclusion was confirmed by what Stuart told me at dinner tonight. He said it took him some time to realise that X.-B. was madly in love with him in the teasing way that Robert Byron once was with me. When he was obliged to tell X.-B., who is one of Chips's best friends, that he could not return his affection, he received, much to his astonishment, a tremendous scolding from Chips. Chips was plaintive. He had meant to do S. a good turn by introducing him to a man who would ply him with champagne and load him with jewels. But, said S., 'I can buy my own champagne, and I don't like jewels. Thanks all the same.' Oh, the cynicism, the worldliness of these people!

*Thursday, 25th March*

When I told Eddy today that I was going this afternoon to stay at Gunby Hall in Lincolnshire, with Field Marshal Sir Archibald Montgomery-Massingberd,* he could not believe his ears. Could there possibly be such a man? Indeed the Field Marshal received me in his study. He is tall, large, a little ponderous, handsome and impressive; yet very gentle and kind. Lady Massingberd is slim, grey, jolly and also kind. They are Peter Montgomery's† uncle and aunt on both his father and mother's sides of the family and are very fond of him; but because he has not yet married they are leaving him out of any settlement of Gunby they may make. The house is 1700, symmetrical, of secondary size, and of deep-plum brick with stone dressings. Every room and passage within has simple contemporary panelling. It was built by the Massingberds and is full of their portraits, including three Reynoldses. Now the Air Ministry is threatening to fell all the trees in the park and demolish the house, both

---

* Field Marshal Sir Archibald Montgomery-Massingberd (1871–1947); Chief of the Imperial General Staff, 1933–6; m. 1896 Diana Langton (who assumed her mother's maiden name of Massingberd on inheriting Gunby, and d. 1963).

† Captain Peter Montgomery (1909–88) of Blessingbourne, Co. Tyrone; landowner and musician, with whom J.L.-M., as recounted in the last chapter of *Another Self*, had shared a hotel bedroom during an air raid in 1941.

in direct line of a runway which they have constructed without previously ascertaining the proximity of these obstacles. If these threats can be averted with our help, the Montgomery-Massingberds are ready to make the property over to the Trust straight away. They are such dear people that even if the house were worthless I would walk to the ends of the earth to help them.

A plain dinner with only water to drink. Wine and spirits are put away for patriotic motives. Hot water cut off for the same reason. Otherwise the house is full of servants, including a butler and pantry boy and four gardeners. Of course they revel in their imposed suffering. I wish I did.

*Saturday, 27th March*

Nancy came round at 3.30 and found me painting the stairs. I took her to Carlyle's House, after which we returned here and made toast. Eddy and Dame Una Pope-Hennessy joined us – a most enjoyable tea. The Dame, looking like a priestess, sat on an upright chair so as to see out of the window. She said the Cardinal's* Requiem Mass was wonderfully moving. All the bishops and abbots in the kingdom were present; also the Papal Nuncio and the Archbishop of New York.

John Russell came and talked after dinner. He is ambitious to become a recognised man of letters. At 2 o'clock in the morning I was woken by the telephone. It was Stuart to tell me he had been dining with Emerald Cunard, Rex Whistler† and Duff Cooper, and they had talked of love and kissing on the mouth. He was in ecstasy over the evening. Petulantly I asked why this astounding piece of information could not have been withheld until later in the morning.

*Monday, 5th April*

The Sergeant must be a very simple man. He said he had been obliged to tell X.-B. that he could not see him again. His conduct

* Arthur Hinsley (1865–1943); Archbishop of Westminster, 1935–43 (Cardinal, 1937).
† Artist (1905–44).

was spoiling a beautiful friendship, etc. X.-B. was suicidal, and quivered so on receiving this broadside that he could not hold his glass, and had to put it on a table. S. said, 'Do you know, he tried to embrace me in Chips's house, and Rex Whistler walked into the room.' He was very indignant at being exposed to such a false situation. I said, 'Couldn't you have laughed it off without being unkind?' 'Laugh?' he said, 'Laugh? But it is no laughing matter.' I said, 'But it seems to me that it is.' Then he said a Cabinet Minister was mad about X.-B. 'Marvellous!' I said. 'Not at all. X.-B. won't look at him.' I see no way out of the tangle.

*Thursday, 8th April*

Yesterday I was quite ill, and had to stay in bed. Terrible headache, and turned my head first to one side of the pillow, then the other, like the pendulum of a clock, seeking and never finding relief. Not since my hospital days have I been unable to read, when ill. And what did I think about? Nothing whatever. The mind can be a total blank and blackness, conscious only of that relentless, regular throb.

This evening I dragged myself out of bed, bathed, shaved and took a taxi to dine with the Osbert Lancasters.* Contrary to expectations I enjoyed myself. So often when one has a temperature and is feeling like death, one can be gay, and scintillate, knowing that when the festivity is over, one will collapse again.

*Saturday, 10th April*

Unless I write in my diary the events of the past day that evening, or at least the next morning, there is little point in keeping one. Is there anyway? A catalogue of names, places and engagements is stale and unprofitable. That is what a diary tends to become after a time. And I cannot stop. I would like this diary to entertain two or three generations ahead when I am under the sod. I cannot really believe that I ever shall be dead. The prospect is too squalid to dwell

* (Sir) Osbert Lancaster (1908–86); cartoonist, humorist, writer and dandy, then working in Foreign Office; m. 1st 1933 Karen Harris, 2nd 1967 Anne Scott-James.

upon. It is impossible to think that I and those I love, and our loves, can be snuffed out like a streak of wind over a wave. Surely some lingering vibration must be left behind, for ever?

The Sergeant said I credited no one with sensibility but myself – quite true; that I believed the world to revolve around me – quite true (who doesn't?); that I supposed only I knew the true meaning of love, and the mysteries of the universe – quite true. What about him, for instance? Well, the truth certainly is that he does lack sensibility, and has no inkling of the meaning of love or the mysteries. He is a feather on the stream of life. Feathers can be decorative but they are easily blown about. But he is a very clever feather all the same. He also quivers with sensitivity, if not sensibility.

He had a row this morning with Chips, who advised him to get a transfer out of London, anywhere so long as he leaves the capital. And the reason? He is unwittingly destroying X.-B. who is suffering from a breakdown, being odious to his old mother, cruel to his young wife, and about to commit suicide or else murder the Sergeant. It makes me indignant with the egoism of these people. I told S. he had made a mistake in seeing X.-B. again. He admits it, but says his intentions were 'strictly honourable'. They were idiotic. At all events he is moving his belongings from Chips's house and will not see him again.

*Thursday, 15th April*

I took a taxi to Ashwick [Somerset] to see Mr Frank Green* about Culverthorpe [Lincolnshire], which belongs to him. Nothing much came of our interview beyond threats. The old tyrant lay in a large four-poster, wearing a striped dressing-gown and a woollen night-cap with a bobble on the end of a string. The bobble bounced up and down his nose as he spoke. His face is that of a rugged, wicked John Bull, a Rowlandsonish face. He dismissed the subject of Culverthorpe, the purpose of my visit, and concentrated on the Treasurer's House, York. Was he to understand that someone had

* Donor of the Treasurer's House, York, to the N.T., 1930. He had recently offered Culverthorpe (see 20 June 1942), but on conditions which were difficult to accept.

dared, dared to shift the furniture in one of the rooms? Did I not realise that he had put studs in the floor to mark the precise spot where every single piece of furniture in the house was to stand? He looked me full in the eyes in an accusatory manner. I flinched under the awful gaze. 'There!' he cried out, '*you* are guilty! I knew it', and the bobble on the string flew around his cheeks. In actual fact I was not guilty. I hadn't been to the house for ages. 'Mark my words,' he went on. 'I am an old man. I may not have very long to live. But I warn you that, if ever you so much as move one chair leg again, I will haunt you till your dying day.' And he wagged a skinny finger under my face. I slunk off with my tail between my legs.

*Saturday, 17th April*

Jamesey came for the night, arriving at 11.45 when I was asleep on the sofa with *The Guermantes Way* open on my lap. He was in a state of hysterical bewilderment. He had been dining with M.A.B.* who told him he was 'beautiful as the dawn', and gave him a strong drug. He suspected she wanted to seduce him, and was repelled but fascinated. He fears the next time he will be lured into her bed. 'But isn't that just what you are wanting?' I said. 'Don't be so disgusting' was the retort.

*Wednesday, 28th April*

In an ambling country train in Norfolk, my thoughts turned to love. It seemed to me incredible that any human being could not fall in

* It has been possible to identify 'M.A.B.' as Bridget (Lady Victor) Paget (Hon. Bridget Colebrooke [1892–1975], yr dau. of 1st and last Baron Colebrooke; m. 1922–32, as 2nd of his 3 wives, Lord Victor Paget [1889–1952], yr bro. of 6th Marquess of Anglesey). She appears under her real name elsewhere in the original published diary – as does her daughter Ann Paget (b. 1923), with whom James Pope-Hennessy also claimed to be in love (and to whom, the diary tells us, he rashly considered proposing marriage on 10 December 1943). It was necessary to conceal Bridget's identity in some entries since – despite J.L.-M. describing her in 1943 as an alcoholic and 'dope fiend' – she was still alive in her eighties when the edited diary was typeset in 1974 (though she died in an accident soon afterwards, before publication).

love with woman and man and, furthermore, be in love with both simultaneously. It was just not true that one could not be in love with more than one person at the same time. All I do know is that 'in love' is damned and devilish, can only bring unhappiness and ought to be eradicated root and branch. Therefore one is left with unadulterated jolly old lust exclusively. And a good thing it is too. If only one had complete mastery of one's emotions! At this moment there was a jolt, the train which had stopped started, gathered speed, and flashed past the noticeboard with 'Dereham' written in large letters. I had failed to get out. Oh Lord! No doubt the Church would say this was a judgement for harbouring impure thoughts.

Arrived at Elsing Hall late. It is a 1740s house built in square knapped flints; and has square gables typical of these parts with heraldic finials and twisted chimney stacks. It has been unfortunately restored in the 1850s. Nearly all the mullion windows have been replaced with plate glass. A moat completely surrounds the house. There is an open roofed hall, and an intact 1470 chapel. Mrs Thackeray and her sister Miss Clarendon Hyde are the owners, and the last of their line since the reign of Egbert. Their line was Browne, their mother being the Browne heiress. They are impoverished. They have one indoor servant only. The house is incredibly shabby, dirty and primitive. It is pathetic how within three years country people, who are unable to travel, become blind to the squalor to which they have been reduced. In spite of the terrible *délabrement* among which they live, these ladies with their long Plantagenet pedigree, their courtesy and ease of manner, were enchanting.

*Sunday, 2nd May*

After lunching at a Polly's Pantry [in Marlborough], we [J.L.-M. and Stuart Preston] walked two miles down the Bath road to visit Miss Ethel Sands* and Miss Hudson who are living in a small, late-Georgian rectory at Fyfield. Miss Sands looks like a typical American spinster one meets in a seedy *pensione* in Florence. She has a round, smiling face and a gash of prominent teeth. She is rather like an ugly

* American artist (1873–1962).

horse, yet her mother was a famous beauty, as we witnessed from the drawings of her by Sargent. Miss Hudson is older and resembles old Lady FitzAlan. We did not like her much. Stuart said they belonged to the '*haute Lesbie*', and theirs was a romance of years. They looked to him like two old men wearing wigs. Stuart began by talking to Miss Sands, so I had Miss Hudson. My attention was distracted by what the other two were saying. Ethel Sands showed us her modern pictures, including Sargents and Sickerts of herself and Nan Hudson. They gave us toasted buns and chocolate cakes for tea. After tea I talked to Ethel Sands and Stuart to Miss Hudson, to whom he paid not the slightest attention, while politely answering Yes and No, and listening to our conversation about Proust and Lady Bessborough. In talking to Miss Sands you realise how very astute she is behind her simple manner and nervous giggle.

*Tuesday, 11th May*

Had several drinks of very neat whisky with Jamesey in his dolls' house flat. Then the objective of the visit, M.A.B., arrived. She is dark, thin, with the most beautiful legs; and has a dead white, slightly horsey face. She was dressed in black, very smart; had exotic scent, plenty of gold bracelets and bangles, and a suspicion of a blue bow somewhere at the back of her hair. She moved delicately as though she might dope, with the dope fiend's caution. She drank a lot, and seemed to admire James a lot. She was very entertaining in a dead-pan way which was disarming. Talked of Welbeck,* Wilton† and other habitual haunts, her relations, friends, enemies, anything that came into her head. I liked her up to a point.

*Saturday, 15th May*

While I was lunching at Rick's café next door, Ethel Walker‡ sat herself down at my table. For months I have watched her pass my

* Welbeck Abbey, Nottinghamshire, seat of the Dukes of Portland.

† Wilton House near Salisbury, seat of the Earls of Pembroke.

‡ Painter and sculptress (1861–1951; DBE 1943).

windows in a lost, painful stagger, with her fat old dog on a chain. She is an ancient woman with a face striated like the valleys of the moon, a face balanced on an overweight sack. Her voice is like the thunder of waters from a subterranean cavern. She told me she had just completed her masterpiece of two small children, very naughty, bad sitters. Miss Walker grumbled at the food and ate the lot.

I took the train to Windsor to have tea with Mrs Betty [Montgomery]. She lent me several books, including *Au Bal avec Marcel Proust* by Marthe Bibesco. Mrs Montgomery never met Proust. But he sent her his photograph which she showed me. It is of a sleek young waiter wearing a gardenia. Mrs Betty is irritated that Proust has 'come into fashion'. We put him on the 'block' for quite twenty minutes, and we pinned beside him Lord Alfred Douglas,* who as a young man, Mrs Betty said, was no Adonis but spotty and without colour. She claims that she is a 'Catholic atheist', and that Jamesey and I are the only other members of this sect. She said to me without forethought, 'Just hand me my spectacles, dear James II', and when I left, 'Tell Jamesey he is still James I.'

*Tuesday, 18th May*

After dinner I went, at Jamesey's request, to M.A.B's flat. Although it was a hot night, the curtains were drawn, and the two were crouching before an anthracite fire. M.A.B. tiny and huddled-up, much the worse for whiskies, mumbling in her attractive but incoherent manner, and hiccoughing. She intersperses every sentence with 'darling' and 'sweetheart'. Her language is stagey and Twentyish. Speaking of some family she said, 'They're nuts like us.' She said she had been the Prince of Wales's mistress. His hair, she said, was the most attractive part of him. She also had an affair with Lord Dudley† at the same time. Once, on the Riviera, she had a bedroom sandwiched between Lord Dudley's and the Prince's. Both kept wandering into hers all night so there was a great

* Poet (1870–1945); nemesis of Oscar Wilde.

† Eric, 3rd Earl of Dudley (1894–1969); friend of Edward, Prince of Wales (1894–1972; later King Edward VIII and Duke of Windsor).

mix-up. When Jamesey confided in her that some of his friends were homosexual she replied, 'Darling, now I'm going to say something which will make you cross. I never felt that way when I was young.'

*Saturday, 22nd May*

I dined with Marie Belloc Lowndes* in her charming small house in Barton Street. Just ourselves. She gave me an orange cocktail, iced, from a jug, and quaffed her glass like a medicine. She was wearing a flowing, flowered dress over her enormous wide frame down to her ankles. Her dinner was the best I have had since the war began – gulls' eggs (two each), fried salmon and rich sauce, poussin with red wine, a pudding, coffee, African brandy. How does she manage it? She talks volubly with a French intonation, rolls her 'r's, is excellent company, extremely knowledgeable on most subjects and very gossipy. There is no writer on the continent whom she does not seem to know. She is certain that the Prince Consort was a Jew.†

Mrs Belloc Lowndes has insatiable curiosity about people. She began dinner with, 'I am told there is a most charming, handsome and clever American over here, a Mr Sergeant. I am sure you must know him. Do tell me about him.' Oh lord, I thought, the same old subject. 'To begin with,' I said, 'he is called Mr Preston. He happens to be a sergeant in the American armed forces. It is true he is everything you say.' 'Oh I should so like to meet him. Will you introduce him to me?' 'Of course,' I said. 'That is easily arranged. He would simply love to know you.' At that moment the telephone rang. To my intense surprise, Chips Channon (how does he know the engagements of his acquaintances?) was on the line to tell me that Stuart's younger brother, a GI, was in London at a loose end, looking for Stuart. Where was Stuart? I said I thought he was

---

* Novelist (1868–1947); sister of the writer and Catholic publicist Hilaire Belloc (1870–1954).

† This rumour – that Albert was the son of Baron von Mayern, a Jewish chamberlain at the Coburg court – is taken seriously by A. N. Wilson in *The Victorians* (2002).

staying the night in the country. What was to be done with the brother? He was now at Chips's house. Chips could not possibly give him a bed for the night. Not in that enormous house in Belgrave Square? I thought that strange. So I said I would willingly put him up. I would call for him at 10.30. 'No, no,' said my hostess, 'send him *r-r*ound here at once.' What is he like, I asked Chips. 'Fascinating, the living spit of Stuart,' Chips said.

Marie Belloc Lowndes was full of excitement. She is always eager to make new friends, to be kind to the young and to show goodwill towards our American allies. After ten minutes the doorbell rang. I opened the door. Without saying a word, a short, sallow, oleaginous youth, wearing large square spectacles, stood on the mat, shaking my hand like a pump handle. He was surprisingly uncouth, answered 'yah' to our enquiries, and whistled when he was not grunting. My hostess's face fell a foot, and she threw me a beseeching glance which clearly meant 'Surely there must be some mistake.'

*Wednesday, 26th May*

I spent all day yesterday in the train from Euston to Windermere. This morning Bruce Thompson* motored me through heavy rain across the moors, to Kendal and Appleby. The intermittent sun and great plumes of black smoke made a sublime scene, sweeping and chasing each other across the moors. Yet, cockney that I have become, I find the mountains lonely and depressing. We moved on to Temple Sowerby [Manor], the McGrigor-Philips house. Mrs McGrigor-Philips is a tall, ungainly, exceedingly coy woman, and a low-brow writer under the pen-name of Dorothy Una Ratcliffe. He is a grubby, red-visaged, hirsute old teddy bear. They laid down a lot of nonsensical conditions in making over the house, intending to provide the minimum endowment although she is a millionairess, having inherited a fortune from her uncle, Lord Brotherton. Bruce Thompson was infinitely patient and polite, and only occasionally betrayed what he was thinking by pursing his lips.

* N.T. representative in the Lake District, 'where he knew everyone, rich and poor, exalted and humble' (*People & Places*).

The house, which I once saw in 1938, is of tawny orange sandstone. Although the core of the house is Jacobean, what one now sees is eighteenth-century. Temple Sowerby is at present occupied by the Railway Wagon Repairers and their families. The Philipses retain one small wing and a caravan for a bedroom. The walk above the flowing burn at the rear of the house is very romantic. From the front are distant views across green pastures of the mountains in the Lake District. It is a lovely setting.

*Friday, 28th May*

James and I, after draining the whisky in his flat, began walking to Chelsea. After nearly an hour we realised we had been walking in the opposite direction and were quite lost. This was brought about by earnest talk of our various perplexities. I warned James that he ought to be more reticent with his women friends who were incorrigible gossips; that by confiding everything in them he risked betraying his men friends, and there was a freemasonry among men friends that he ought not to abuse. He assured me he could not possibly have a friend without being honest to him or her. I could not agree with this policy and said surely it was better not to spill the truth before everyone who took one's fancy. One must have loyalties, and they necessitated reticence. But no, he immediately disclosed how M.A.B. had passionately kissed him in a taxi yesterday. Jamesey is so engaging that, maddened as I am by him at times, I forgive him all his trespasses.

*Saturday, 29th May*

I went to Herstmonceux to stay with Paul Latham.* This was an act of charity because I have never known him well. To my surprise, Eddy had told me he would be glad to see me, whereas he declined to see most of his closest friends. I got muddled with

* Sir Paul Latham, 2nd Bt (1905–55); Conservative MP, 1931–41, disgraced and sent to prison in 1941 after allegations of sexual assault by his batman; sometime sado-masochistic lover of Eddy Sackville-West.

my trains and was 1½ hours late. Paul was sitting in the window of the bothy where he lives. He left prison in January having been there for 1½ years. He was very thin but healthier and handsomer than I remember him. He still has a frightening look of craziness in the crimped gold hair, anthropoidal head, albino eyebrows and cold blue eyes. He talked incessantly of himself and prison. He is touched that everyone on the estate is nice to him. Paul has become incredibly sentimental, yet his conversation is more depraved than anyone's I have ever heard. He is obsessed by sex and haunts the most dangerous places, he told me. He also enjoys repeating disobliging things said about one. He is a sadistic man.

He had the grace to acknowledge Eddy's great kindness in helping him. He won't move from the estate or see any close friends from his old world, except Eddy; yet he is irritated by Eddy's devotion. We walked round the grounds and the outside of this fairy-tale castle. The Hearts of Oak Benefit Society have done great damage to the contents, which Paul foolishly left in the building. I am terribly sorry for him but would pity him far more if he were less wayward and less egocentric.

I got back only just in time to dine with Emerald Cunard, still wearing my brown country suit. Dinner was at 8.30 yet the blinds were all drawn, the windows firmly shut, and the room was stifling. I was in a muck sweat. There were Field Marshal Wavell,* Sir D'Arcy Osborne,† our Minister in the Vatican, a nineteen-year-old Paget girl,‡ Chips Channon, Jamesey and myself. I sat next to Jamesey and Chips, who is bear-leading Wavell, sitting in the background with a proud expression on his face and flipping the whip gently from time to time. Wavell is stocky, with a smiling rugged face and a wall eye. He is slow, distracted and shy. Emerald's prattle, sometimes very funny nonsense, flowed like a river. I think this embarrassed him at times. He was coaxed by Chips into reciting Browning and Ernest

* Field Marshal Sir Archibald Wavell (1883–1950); C.-in-C. Middle East, 1939–41, India, 1941–3; Viceroy of India, 1943–7; also a poet; cr. Viscount, 1943, Earl, 1947.

† Sir Francis D'Arcy Godolphin Osborne (1884–1964); diplomatist, British Minister to the Holy See, 1936–47; s. 1963 as 12th and last Duke of Leeds.

‡ Presumably Ann Paget: see note to 17 April 1943.

Dowson which he did in a muffled, inarticulate voice, incredibly badly. Much too much applause from Emerald and his prompter. It seems extraordinary that a man in his position should be staying with a flibbertigibbet like Chips. I found him cosy and cultivated. The other guests were disappointed with him. He is certainly an old man who seems finished.

*In June J.L.-M. fell ill, and recuperated at Wickhamford.*

*Thursday, 1st July*

I went to Wickhamford and was restored to health by Mama, who was angelic to me. Only Mrs Haines helps her in the mornings. Otherwise Mama does everything – housework, cooking, washing up, to which, because she is hopelessly disorganised, there is absolutely no end. She spends as much time in complaining and congratulating herself as in actually working. And what she does, she does indifferently. I am reminded of Dr Johnson's remark about a dog walking on its hind legs: 'It is not well done; but you are surprised to find it done at all.'

*Tuesday, 6th July*

Papa drove me to Hidcote [Gloucestershire] to tea with Laurie Johnston* who took us round his famous garden. It is not only beautiful but full of surprises. You are constantly led from one scene to another, into long vistas and little enclosures, which seem infinite. Yet the total area of this garden does not cover many acres. It is also full of rare plants brought from the most outlandish places in India and Asia. When my father and Laurie Johnston were absorbed in talk I was tremendously impressed by their profound knowledge of a subject which is closed to me, like hearing two people speak fluently a language of which I am totally ignorant.

---

* Major Lawrence Johnston (1871–1958); American horticulturist who created gardens at Hidcote, Gloucestershire and La Serre de la Madonne, Mentone.

*Wednesday, 7th July*

From Evesham to Shrewsbury by train, changing at Hartlebury to the Severn Valley line. What a beautiful valley it is, with gently sloping wooded banks and miniature scenery, even on a grey day. I stayed two nights with the Berwicks* at Attingham [Park, Shropshire]. They inhabit a fraction of the east wing. The WAAFs occupy the rest of the house. The Ministry of Works has at my instigation protected the principal rooms by boarding up the fireplaces and even dados. The uniform Pompeian red of the walls is I presume contemporary, that is to say late eighteenth-century. In my bathroom the walls were papered with Captain Cook scenery just like the upstairs bedroom at Laxton [Hall, Northamptonshire]. The first night we had champagne to celebrate Attingham's survival to date. After dinner I read through the 1827 Sale Catalogue of contents, many of which the 3rd Lord Berwick, then Minister to the Court at Naples, bought from his elder brother the 2nd Lord.

*Thursday, 8th July*

Lady Berwick and I went to tea at Cronkhill, one of the houses on the estate, built by John Nash† in 1810. It was designed in the romantic style of an Italian villa, and is the precursor of many similar Victorian villas. Lady Berwick behaves towards her neighbours with a studied affability, a queenly graciousness which must be a trifle intimidating to those upon whom it is dispensed.

After tea I walked with Lord Berwick in the deer park having been enjoined by his wife to talk seriously about Attingham's future, and press him for a decision on various points. I did not

* Thomas Noel-Hill, 8th (and penultimate) Baron Berwick (1877–1947); m. 1919 Edith Hulton (d. 1972), dau. of William Hulton, Anglo-Italian artist. J.L.-M. (as related in *People and Places*) had first visited them in August 1936 and been enchanted by them both (while aware that Lady Berwick took the decisions); having no children, they were eager from the first to donate the house and estate to the N.T., though this was only achieved on Lord Berwick's death in 1947.

† Architect (1752–1835).

make much progress in this respect. On the other hand, he expanded in a strangely endearing way. When alone he loosens up and is quite communicative. All the seeming silliness and nervousness vanish. He talked to me earnestly of the ghosts that have been seen at Attingham by the WAAFs. Lady Berwick would not have tolerated this nonsense, had she been present. He kept stopping and anxiously looking over his shoulder lest she might be overhearing him, but he did not stand stock still and revolve, which he does in the drawing room when she starts talking business. He told me that Lady Sibyl Grant,* his neighbour at Pitchford [Hall], constantly writes to him on the forbidden subject, passing on advice as to health which she has been given by her spiritual guides. She no longer dares telephone this information for fear, so Lord Berwick asserted, of the spirits hearing and taking offence, but more likely for fear of Lady Berwick overhearing and strongly disapproving. He is not the least boring about his psychical beliefs but is perplexed by the strange habits of ghosts. He asked me, did I think it possible that one could have been locked in the housemaid's cupboard? And why should another want to disguise itself as a vacuum cleaner? Really, he is a delicious man.

*Saturday, 17th July*

When I told Q. that I could not face tagging on to Emerald's party after dinner and going on to the Rutland ball, she asked me to 'dine with us', meaning herself and spouse. This infuriated me. I said I would think about it. When she said on the telephone this morning, 'I am not pressing you, but if you want to come, there is a place for you, and dinner is at 8', I still said nothing. She rang me up again at 7.15. I said I would not go. And I didn't. Miserably I dined by myself, and gratuitously chucked the only privately given ball since the war began. In fact I deliberately cut off my nose to spite my face, and derived only the tiniest bit of satisfaction thereby.

---

* Lady Sibyl Primrose (1879–1955), dau. of 5th Earl of Rosebery (and sister of Margaret, Marchioness of Crewe); m. 1903 Captain (later General Sir) Charles Grant (1877–1950). See entry for 17 March 1944.

*Monday, 19th July*

On returning in the bus I was put into a paroxysm of rage by reading in the evening paper that Rome had been bombed. I was to have seen Harold tonight. I did not dare go for I should have been hysterical and abused the Government. Instead I drank Pimm's with Jamesey at the Carlton Hotel. Together we vented our rage over the bombing. He said Churchill had sanctioned it, with 'I don't care a damn what buildings they destroy.'

*Thursday, 22rd July*

I dined with the Princesse de Polignac.* Clarissa [Churchill], John Pope-Hennessy† and David Horner were present. The last invited because apparently the Princess thought he was E. M. Forster.‡ He is a slightly epicene, elderly young man who lives with Osbert Sitwell.§ He has a soothing, low voice, but his manner is embarrassingly affected. After dinner we talked of the Rome bombing. John, who is cautious and sensible, advised that we must collate our facts before launching into protests. Then we talked about English novelists. This led to Proust. Our hostess evidently disliked him. She had known him since he was a handsome young man with melting brown eyes, until his death. It was impossible to endure his company for long at a time. He was touchy and took umbrage at every supposed slight. In fact he detected slights where they never were intended – in a tone of voice or look. As a result he would fire off thirty letters to you in rapid succession. In France before the war none but the Saint-Germain set recognised his gifts. When the Princess found that there was already a Proust Society in

* Winaretta Singer (1865–1943); heiress to sewing machine fortune; m. (2nd) Prince Edmond de Polignac (d. 1901); Paris society figure, patroness of artists and composers; her current companion, Alvilde Chaplin, was to become J.L.-M's wife in 1951 (though he had yet to meet her at this time).

† (Sir) John Pope-Hennessy (1913–95); elder brother of James P.-H.; art historian and museum curator, then serving in the Air Ministry.

‡ Novelist (1879–1970).

§ Sir Osbert Sitwell (1892–1969), 5th Bt; writer, brother of Sacheverell and Edith.

England, only *Chez Swann* having been published, she was amazed. Proust was either in the depths or the heights, when he would toss money to servants as though it were chicken feed. His life was studded with unfulfilled romantic attachments. He never ceased to correspond with the Princess, although their periods of intimacy were fitful. She supposes he enjoyed quarrelling with his friends. She dispelled the rumour I had heard that she was the origin of Madame Verdurin by telling us that when she entertained Proust lovers in her King's Road house before 1914, they called themselves, for fun, by the names of characters in *Chez Swann*. One was Cottard, another Brichot, and she was Madame Verdurin.

*Friday, 23rd July*

This evening I walked home – about three miles – across Hyde Park and Exhibition Road, listening to the voices of Czech, Polish and French soldiers. I love the present cosmopolitanism of London. Summer nights in London are soft and velvety even if the previous day has been grey. At nights the colourlessness disappears, and the savage emptiness of the black-out is filled with pools of violet, blue and yellow light. I am at last feeling well again and have a zest for living.

*Saturday, 24th July*

I had tea with Logan Pearsall Smith. I certainly should have visited him before. He has a splendid capacity for mockery and fun. And of course he has literary refinement; perhaps no other sort. He coughs and spits incessantly. Stuart seems to be his present preoccupation. He admitted that at first he thought Stuart too good to be true, endeavoured to catch him out, and failed. Having checked him up through mutual friends he pronounced him to be aristocratic (according to American social rules), rich and popular. At all events Logan has succumbed, for Stuart has flattered him by not merely congratulating him on his books (which is easy), but by quoting long passages from them (which is clever). Logan knew Henry James intimately, but could only guess at James's sex proclivities. He thought

Shane Leslie's disclosures in *Horizon* horrifying. James's letters were written to a young soldier in World War I and were unmistakably love letters. Shane was given 300 of them by the man's widow early this year. We talked about many things, disjointedly, leaping from one topic to another. He recounted one 'awway'* after another. Finally he expressed the hope that Stuart was not a 'marrano' – *i.e.*, a Jew in Spain who adopts Christian methods and later relapses into what he was originally.

When I told James and Stuart all Pearsall Smith had said, they laughed. They knew all the topics, all the 'awways' by heart. I was disconcerted. In fact Jamesey says he is a poor, senile old man, who repeats himself over and over again.

*Wednesday, 28th July*

I had tea with Stuart – he is no longer to be called the Sergeant and gets fretful when addressed by that term of endearment – at the Travellers. Talk was too much of personalities. His social activities arouse the worst instincts in me. While we walked afterwards across Green Park in the sun he said he had asked Lady Islington why her husband had chosen that particular title. I laughed, and remarked in a bantering way that only an American would ask that question. He was hurt. I was constantly saying such things, whereas he refrained from saying similar things to me that would be intensely wounding. Now this retort distressed me as much as my remark had distressed him. Neither of us has a grain of humour between us.

*Friday, 30th July*

I joined Jamesey at Rules restaurant. We drank quantities of Pimm's and enjoyed ourselves hugely. There is no one with whom I can be happier. We were as one tonight. Unlike Stuart he is far from being seduced by society. As we talked and laughed, two very tough-looking men at a neighbouring table were looking at us

* Expression coined by L.P.S., meaning stories that in one's dotage one tells more than once.

critically. In truth they had no right to judge us, for James is in the army, and I was.

We walked out of the restaurant into the heat, and down the Embankment. We crossed London Bridge to the south side of the river, and ambled along Cardinal's Wharf. Jamesey was extolling in the most candid manner his age (he is twenty-six), his good looks and his success, saying he did not believe he could ever die. He said, 'Our relationship is such a one that can never have existed in the past.' I said yes, I felt certain that before our time personal relations could never have been so intimate, though we could never tell what, for instance, Byron and Hobhouse talked about at nights in a tent during their travels in the Morea. I said that more people ought to keep diaries, but the trouble was that the most unscrupulous diarists were too scrupulous when it came to putting personal truths on paper. James said that Cecil [Beaton]'s diary would be the chronicle of our age, that we would only survive through it. I said Eddy Sackville-West kept one. James said, 'We could not be hoisted to posterity on two spikier spikes.' We looked at bombed churches and sat in churchyards, and drank shandies in City pubs.

*Friday, 6th August*

My birthday. I am thirty-five! The horror of it! Except for my incipient baldness, fortunately on the crown of my head and on account of my height not always noticeable, I do not think I have changed much. My figure is the same as it was fifteen years ago.

At 7 o'clock I went to Jamesey's flat. The gay little creature was splashing about in the bath. He gave me two stiff whiskies to keep up my spirits, which were actually quite high. He made me change out of my nice blue shirt and put on a white shirt of his and a blue tie with large, white round spots, which he said looked more festive. He gave me as a birthday present a little water-colour sketch of the interior of a church by Pugin. Thus fortified and encouraged I set out with him to Boulestin, where at luncheon time I had ordered a table and food for eight guests. We drank again in the bar where Harold and Stuart joined us. Then Dig and

Henry Yorke* came. I had not seen Henry since the war. He was absolutely charming and rather reserved; Dig her usual sweet self. Harold gave me a book of Freya Stark's (and later a tooth-brush!). Then Joan Moore came without Emerald, whom she had said she would bring. Emerald arrived at 8.40 just as we were about to begin dinner. Harold said in front of everybody, 'What worries me about this party is how Jim will afford to pay for it.'

I had Joan on my left and Emerald on my right. The dinner passed with perfect ease. Never was there less need for anxiety. Excellent food – fish in shells, partridge and plenty of Algerian wine; brandy afterwards. Joan was divine. I was so absorbed with her and James with Emerald that I hardly spoke to Emerald. As it happens I prefer listening to her than talking to her; just as I prefer watching a canary flit from perch to perch and scattering feathers and shrill cries, to trying to pick up its song. I enjoyed my party immensely. As we sat on, and the waiters longed for us to leave, Emerald arranged marriages for James, Stuart and myself.

When at last the party ended I walked away with Harold to stay the night at King's Bench Walk because I could not have got home so late. Harold began by saying, 'The worst of women is their selfishness. They must make slaves of men.' He extolled the advantages of homosexuality and relationships between men, who allowed individual independence. Then he praised Vita as an exceptional wife. He said that he and Vita had pledged to tell each other the moment one of them fell in love, but not to confess to casual affairs because that was rather squalid. Their marriage began badly because Vita immediately fell in love with a married woman – Violet Trefusis† I presume. He said that in his whole life he had only been in love three times, and these times were before his marriage, with two subsequent ambassadors, and a 'bedint' young man of no consequence called Eric Upton, whose only

---

* Novelist (1905–73) under pseudonym Henry Green; m. 1929 Hon. Adelaide ('Dig') Biddulph.

† Violet Keppel (1894–1972); m. 1919 Major Denys Trefusis. Her 'elopement' with Vita, and their pursuit by their husbands, is described by Vita's son Nigel Nicolson in *Portrait of a Marriage* (1973).

recommendation was extreme beauty. 'Oh, I may have fallen a fourth time, with R[aymond Mortimer].' He told Vita about this fall, and she was wonderful. But then Vita truly *is* exceptional.

*Saturday, 7th August*

I went to tea to Ivy Compton-Burnett and Margaret Jourdain. Anne Hill was there; also Dame Una and Rose Macaulay. I was the only man among blue-stockings. Rose Macaulay said the Portuguese were having bread riots. Ivy C.-B., I noticed, when she did condescend to speak, shouted everyone else down. The tea was a sit-down spread of breads of different hue, jam, potted meat, biscuits, shortbread and cake, delightful but curiously middle-class and such a contrast to Emerald's weak China and a thumb-nail of chocolate cake. Ivy, who now addresses me by my christian name, said it took Harriet Martineau* forty years to discover what it had taken her eighteen, namely that there is no God.

I joined Rick [Stewart-Jones] at 7.30 and we dined together at 97 [Cheyne Walk]. He said I was moving in a set to which I did not properly belong, that since I was far from gregarious by nature, I was behaving foolishly. I admitted that in a sense he was right, but protested that instead of acting foolishly I was acting out of curiosity, if by 'set' he was referring to those people who congregated round the Dorchester.

*Wednesday, 11th August*

Bruce Thompson is in a great state because he left behind at Temple Sowerby during our visit his file containing letters between him and me, criticising Mrs McGrigor-Philips. Some of mine were strongly worded and I remember saying she was an impossible woman to do business with. Mrs McGrigor-Philips read all the correspondence and has written to the secretary and the chairman complaining of our misconduct. She said to Bruce on the

* Writer (1802–76), originally for the Unitarian press, who had become an agnostic by 1850.

telephone, 'I thought you were both gentlemen', which upset Bruce who is 100 per cent a gentleman to my 25 per cent. I told him he ought to have retorted, 'And I thought you were a lady.' For ladies do not read other people's letters.

*Tuesday, 17th August*

It is half-past six. I have been sitting for an hour on my window seat looking at the cheerful river, with the evening sunlight dancing upon the wavelets, and at the gay motor-boats, painted black and yellow, dashing down the river and growling busily. There are water boys on them. There are old men with sticks and pipes just below my window and across the road. They are squatting on the Embankment wall, smoking and gossiping. 'Are these young men', I ask myself, 'and these old men wracked by hopeless love, a prey to their miserable natures, slaves to their emotions, and irredeemably wretched?' I think not. They may wish the war was over. They don't want to lose their lives or the lives of their sons. But this is negative wishing. On the other hand they are positively living, with a zest for being alive which they do not stop to question or understand. How sensible they are. Whereas I seldom live carelessly, with abandon. Most of the year I mope, moan, resent other people's happiness, lament my own unhappiness, and waste this precious living. And what is it all about now? Neither last night nor the night before has the voice spoken to me.* In the office today I hardly dared leave the room in case the telephone should ring. Whenever it did my heart jumped. And when the voice at the other end was not the right voice I was in despair. I became edgy, bad-tempered. I could hardly bear it when colleagues were using the line in case my voice was trying to get through to me. And what am I doing now? Waiting again for the

* In *Another Self*, J.L.-M. describes a year-long telephonic love affair with a woman he never met or even discovered the identity of (though the episode is described as if taking place in 1941). Apparently the original 1943 diary contained further references to this mysterious person, but his publishers asked him to remove them as they would have meant little to anyone unfamiliar with the other work.

telephone to ring. This is preposterous, infantile and reprehensible. I must snap out of it.

*Friday, 20th August*

James surprised me a little by repeating a conversation he had had this evening with his mother. He explained to her that the nettle-rash on his behind was diagnosed by his doctor as the effect of a nervous disorder, brought about by his being semi in love with M.A.B. and Ann Paget, yet physically desiring boys. Dame Una expressed disapproval of his going to a psychoanalyst. 'What, darling,' said James, 'would you rather that I never learnt to get an erection with women?' 'No,' said Dame Una.

*Saturday, 21st August*

Caught a morning train to High Wycombe and walked up the drive at West Wycombe just as the Eshers arrived for luncheon with Johnny and Helen. Esher was in splendid form, teasing the Dashwoods about their progeny. After luncheon we drove to the far end of the park and inspected the temples, follies and cottages on the property to be transferred; also all that distant part of the park to be held inalienably. Esher has a genius for persuading people to act sensibly against their deep-rooted inclinations by his jocular manner and sheer fun. I really believe we may acquire this beautiful house and park in the end. After tea I caught a train which was so slow and late that I missed my train from Waterloo to Woking. I did not reach Send Grove until nearly 9.

Spent the weekend at Loelia Westminster's.* Only Emerald and a dull but affable young man called Sharman staying. Send is an enchanting small Jane Austen house, symmetrical, stuccoed and washed pink. The front is covered by an enormous wisteria. It dates from the end of the eighteenth century. The prospect from the

* Hon. Loelia Ponsonby (1902–93), dau. of 1st Baron Sysonby; m. 1st 1930–47 'Bendor', 2nd Duke of Westminster (from whom she was now separated), 2nd 1969 Sir Martin Lindsay, 1st Bt.

house covers a long expanse of grass, with curving boundary to the left, and to the right, open views across a river bordered with pollarded willows in the direction of Clandon. Stuart calls this neighbourhood the New Dukeries, for in addition to Loelia, the Dukes of Sutherland, Northumberland and Alba live within a few miles.

My hostess has impeccable taste. She bought this house a year after the war began when it was not too late to buy French wallpapers. As you enter there is a charming little stairwell with a balustered staircase corkscrewing steeply upwards towards a domed ceiling. To the right and left are projecting bays forming a small dining room and library. The Duchess greeted me at the dining-room door, napkin in hand. I washed and joined the party straight away. A delicious dinner at a small round table. After dinner we talked in the library about Keats and Shelley. Emerald said Shelley had a child by Claire Clairmont* and that Mary Shelley had adopted it as her own. We then talked of eccentric people living in country houses. Emerald told us how when she was first married and lived in the English country, she went to call on the Mexboroughs.† Presently Lord Mexborough was wheeled into the room. He had a long white beard down to his knees and was wearing a top hat. As soon as he saw Emerald he let out a piercing scream, 'Take her away! Take her away!'

*Wednesday, 8th September*

At 5.20 Raymond [Mortimer] rang up Eardley [Knollys] in the office to report that Italy had surrendered unconditionally. At Brooks's it was on the tape and members were talking about it in great excitement. My first reaction was one of relief; my second of anxiety, lest worse fighting than ever against the Germans might take place in Italy. When I spoke to Harold Nicolson on the telephone he said what a relief it was that henceforth we would no

---

* Clara Mary Jane ('Claire') Clairmont (1798–1879); stepsister of Mary Shelley; her dau. Allegra (1817–22) was presumed to be by Byron, who however conceived a profound dislike of her.

† John Savile, 4th Earl of Mexborough (1810–99).

longer be under the sad necessity of destroying further Italian towns. I said I should feel no happier if the world's greatest architecture was wiped out by Germans, and not by Englishmen.

*Friday, 10th September*

Took the 9.10 from Liverpool Street to Cambridge, stopping at every station on the way. Was met at Cambridge and driven by the agent to Anglesey Abbey. On our arrival Lord Fairhaven* was strutting in front of his porch, in too-immaculate a blue suit, and watch in hand. He is a slightly absurd, vain man, egocentric, pontifical, and too much blessed with the world's goods. He is an enthusiastic amateur, yet ignorant of the arts he patronises. At luncheon I was ravenous, having breakfasted at 7.30. Even so I did not eat as much as my host, who at forty-seven has a large paunch, a heavy jowl, pugnacious chin and mottled complexion. The nice agent, a gentleman from these parts (Lord Fairhaven is not from these parts), only spoke when spoken to. After luncheon he was dismissed and we strolled down the Lode bank into the garden. This is well kept in spite of the war. It has been laid out on eighteenth-century lines. Just before the war Fairhaven planted a long, straight line of limes, chestnuts and planes in four rows with caryatid statues by Coade of Lambeth† at the far end. Unfortunately the vista does not begin from and so cannot be enjoyed from the house.

Anglesey Abbey is, like Packwood [House, Warwickshire], more a fake than not. The only genuine remains are the calefactorium, or crypt (used as a dining-room) dating from 1236, with thick, quadripartite ceiling of clunch, some medieval buttressed walls and the greatly restored 1600 south front. Lord Fairhaven put back the

---

* U. H. R. Broughton (1897–1966); cr. Baron Fairhaven, 1929 (his father, American-born oil magnate and sometime MP for Preston, for whom the peerage was originally created, having died before he could receive it); worked during the war for the Red Cross.

† Eleanor Coade (1733–1821) set up her business manufacturing artificial stone at Lambeth in 1769.

pointed gables and added the cresting to the porch. The interior is entirely his, opulent and pile-carpeted. But his new library with high coved ceiling, lined with books (first editions and un-cut), is fine. He has a desultory collection of good things that do not amount to a great collection. There is a corridor of Etty* nudes in his private bedroom wing.

Exhausted, I had a bath and changed into a dark suit. Lord Fairhaven wore a dinner jacket. We had a four-course dinner of soup, lobster, chicken and savoury, waited on by a butler. Lord Fairhaven is served first, before his guests, in the feudal manner which only the son of an oil magnate would adopt. Presumably the idea is that in the event of the food being poisoned the host will gallantly succumb, and his instant death will be a warning to the rest of the table to abstain. Port and brandy followed.

*In mid September, J.L.-M. went with his friend the artist Geoffrey Houghton Brown† to spend a week as a guest of the Duke of Argyll‡ at Inveraray Castle, his first real holiday since resuming work at the National Trust in the autumn of 1941.*

*Saturday, 18th September*

We caught the 8.45 bus [from Glasgow] to Inveraray. Loch Lomond was glassy calm and the water blue-grey like my lady's eyes of yesterday. This is my great-grandmother McFarlane's country and the beginning of the Highlands. When we reached the Pass the sun came out fitfully and spread a gold and purple patchwork on the hills. At Loch Fyne sun and sky and water were Mediterranean. As the bus turned a corner I had my first view of Inveraray, a wide bay in the loch with little boats and large ships in the harbour, and a minute classical town in the background. Then I saw the gaunt, grey block of the castle, the two classical bridges and the romantic

* William Etty (1787–1849); English painter specialising in nudes of both sexes.
† Artist, country house restorer and antique dealer (1903–93); an ardent Roman Catholic convert.
‡ Niall Dermid Campbell, 10th Duke of Argyll (1872–1949).

peaked hill with watch tower upon it. A man from the castle met us on the quay and wheeled our luggage on a trolley. We followed him through a gate and to avoid the soldiery whose huts are in the park, along the drive and among the shrubs, we took a path through the desolate garden, and crossed a bridge over the moat straight into the great saloon.

The castle is built of ugly stone, which turns grey in the sunlight and black in the rain. This is a pity, for all the old houses in the town are of a lighter, kindlier stone. The castle has been greatly spoilt by peaked dormer windows added in 1880, and unsightly chimneys stuck on turrets and steeples. Outside it is grim and forbidding like some hydropathic hotel. The bridge to the front door had a sloping shelter erected over it for the benefit of Queen Victoria. Geoffrey led me through the saloon to the library where the Duke of Argyll was writing. He was seated at a large table in the middle of the room, with a bronze replica of a Celtic cross and one lighted candle on it. He rose and was very welcoming. He is obviously fond of Geoffrey.

He is a short old man with white hair and a smooth white face, for he seldom if ever has to shave. He has handsome blue eyes. He has a woman's voice, very eunuchy. Lady Victor Paget described him to Jamesey as an elderly hermaphrodite. He was wearing an old Harris tweed, deer-red jacket with wide buttoned revers up the sleeves, an immensely old tartan kilt, old blue woollen stockings (revealing white knobbly knees), dirk, sporran, and most surprising of all, shoes *à l'espadrille.* He conducted us up a long, stone staircase with plain iron balusters curved for crinolines, and threadbare carpet. The central hall, exceedingly high, reaches to the roof of the central tower. High though it is, it always retains a smell of lodging-house cooking. Windows are never opened, and no wonder, for the castle is bitterly cold in September without fires. My small bedroom is just over the front door. It has double doors, with a moth-eaten, red rep curtain over the inner one. On the blue and white wallpaper hang a large framed photograph of the widowed Queen Victoria (looking like Robert Byron) at the time of the first Jubilee, a large oil of an eighteenth-century duke in a beautiful Rococo frame, and a foxed print of the Porteous Riots. The Victorian iron bedstead has a red plush-covered canopy. The washstand, dressing-table and clothes cupboard are solid Victorian mahogany pieces. A fire is actually burning in the grate – rather feebly. There is a lovely view from my window (which has not been cleaned for years) of the watch tower hill and a corner of the loch.

We had a delicious luncheon of mackerel and grouse, helping ourselves from the sideboard. The Duke is very voluble and he has an insatiable appetite for gossip, as well as food. Conversation revolves round people and their relationships. After luncheon he put on a Glengarry green with age, and set off to the hospital in the park with some French newspapers for wounded French Canadian troops. A soldier on guard stopped us going up the long ride. 'What's this? I can go where I like. I am the Duke,' came from a high-pitched, slightly hysterical voice. From the hospital Geoffrey and I went on to the little eighteenth-century fishing lodge by the first fall, looking for salmon. I saw one leaping, but the wrong way, not upstream but down. We continued up the burn, the Aray I presume, crossed over a bridge where I pointed to a rock in midstream, like a surrealist sculpture of a torso with one buttock incomplete, and bitten away. We tested each other on the trees we passed. I failed over a sycamore and a rowan. We found the eighteenth-century pigeon house which is at the end of the vista.

Meals here are excellent in that solid Scotch way I love – porridge, bannocks, plum cakes and game. The Duke prattles as ceaselessly as the Aray flows over the stones. Sometimes he is very entertaining; sometimes he is boring, and one does not listen. It makes no difference to him. He is a recognised authority on all church ritual, and a scholar of medieval liturgy, hagiology and Saxon coins. He is eccentric. He will rush without warning out of the room to play a bar or two of a Gregorian chant on a harmonium, or to play on a gong, or a French horn. He also has a cuckoo whistle which he likes to blow in the woods in order to bewilder the soldiers. He takes the keenest interest in the soldiers, both officers and men, learns their names and where they come from, and the names of their diocese and bishop. The great advantage of this place is that after meals the Duke disappears, and we are left to read, write, walk out of doors, or roam round the house.

After tea we looked at the rooms on the ground floor. Great bushes of laurel and ungainly spruce trees have been allowed to grow close to the house, with the result that the magnificent views from all sides are shut out. Geoffrey once suggested their being felled, but the Duke would not hear of it. It is true that today they serve as screens against the myriad Nissen huts. In the lower part of the hall are two ugly fireplaces. Over them and indeed all the way up the walls practically to the roof are ranged archaic weapons, guns, rifles, pistols, spears and daggers, in giant Catherine wheel patterns. Elks' horns are interspersed. In the blank spaces are numerous family portraits. On one chimneypiece stands a bronze equestrian effigy of Richard Coeur de Lion by Princess Louise, 'my aunt'.* The state-rooms on this floor contain some splendid eighteenth-century furniture, and on the rose damask walls of the saloon portraits by Gainsborough, Cotes and Batoni, hung higgledy-piggledy. Amongst other things is the most astonishing bric-à-brac, including a forest of framed photographs collected by 'my aunt'.

*Saturday, 9th October*

Stuart dined with me at Brooks's. It was a disastrous evening. The moral of it is that there are no limits beyond which the idiocy of adults will not go. At dinner we argued, I cannot even remember over what. I was certainly disagreeable about some friends of his. He contradicted me. I contradicted him. He said I always snubbed him, and was ruder to him than anyone he knew, and I said outrageous and insulting things to him, just for fun. I said, 'If they are funny, why don't you laugh?' He said, 'They're not funny. They make me want to cry, they're so un-funny.' 'But you never do cry,' I said, 'so they must be funny.' 'They're *not* funny,' he almost shouted. 'Remember where you are,' I said. 'We are in the coffee-room.' 'There you go again – correcting, finding fault, patronising.' There was a seething silence of several minutes' duration.

* HRH Princess Louise (1848–1939), 4th dau. of Queen Victoria; m. 1871 Marquess of Lorne (1845–1914), Governor-General of Canada, 1877–83, who s. 1900 as 9th Duke of Argyll.

He looked very put out, and ate nothing. Then he said, 'I am too tired to argue any more.' (How often have I not heard my parents say this?) And he added, 'You had better go.' '*I* had better go?' I asked. 'But it's my club we're in.' 'Oh, so it is,' he said, rising from his chair. 'No, no,' I said, 'I will go all the same.' I paid the bill and went to fetch my coat and umbrella. I said, 'I am off now, and I do not intend that we shall meet again. We have nothing in common.' He said, 'Good night!' I said, 'It's goodbye,' and left. I walked home.

*Monday, 11th October*

Q. and I sat on her sofa. She began: 'Now you are unhappy. What is it? You have quarrelled with Stuart, and it's your fault, I know.' How did she know? She has never met him. Really the intuition of women is uncanny. She gave me much advice, telling me quite severely that I must make it up with him. 'You simply can't lose a good friend for an idiotic reason', and so forth.* We found a cab and she insisted on coming with me to Cheyne Walk. In the cab she took my hands and kissed me over and over again. I lit a fire in my room. We turned the lights out, and sat on the window seat looking at the moon on the river.

*Tuesday, 12th October*

At 8.20 I telephoned Q., who I knew would still be in bed. She answered the telephone. I said, 'It's me, Q.' 'Is it you, Terry?' she said in a voice of unconcealed excitement. 'No,' I answered, and put the receiver down gently.†

*Friday, 15th October*

The wretched National Trust car would not start again. The battery was dead. So I took a train to Tunbridge Wells, and a bus to

---

* The diary shows that a reconciliation did take place within a week, the two dining (albeit somewhat uncomfortably) on Sunday 17 October.

† This is the last mention of 'Q.' in the diary.

Wadhurst. I was not feeling very grand because last night Pierre Lansel [physician] gave me my last whopping injection. Hot and cold by turns I walked, wearing my black overcoat, down the long, straggly, dull village street to The Gatehouse. For some reason I expected the owner to be a man, having addressed it as such. It was on the contrary an old woman in a mackintosh. I have never been more astonished by such squalid living. The house is a genuinely early Tudor – say, late fifteenth-century – yeoman's dwelling, typical of this region. It is of half-timber, with sloping roof, over-hanging eaves and a central brick chimney stack. There is nothing fake about it. But the condition! It has no services, no water, no drains, no light. The old creature has no domestic help, and obviously no money. For these deprivations I am indeed sorry for her. But the dust, the dirt and junk littering literally every square inch of space inside were indescribable. Filthy saucepans, opened and half-emptied tins of sardines, jam and baked beans, and worse still, piles of snotty grey handkerchiefs and other unmentionable rags littered the tables and chairs of the living-room. The garden shrubs have got so out of control that they obliterate the little light which lattice panes allow at the best of times. None of the windows open. The stench was asphyxiating. The old dame gave me a cold luncheon of salmon, lettuce and cheese, not off plates, but out of tins. I hardly dared swallow a mouthful, and when her back was turned, shoved what I could out of my tin into a handkerchief, which I stuffed into my trouser pocket. Had I seen the kitchen before luncheon I would not have eaten one mouthful. After this terrible meal she insisted upon my looking at the kingpost upstairs. Now if there is one thing which bores me it is a kingpost. However, obediently I trudged up the creaking staircase. But when I reached the top landing I dared not proceed further for fear of putting a foot through the crazy floor boards and the ceiling of the downstairs sitting-room. When I turned back she knew I hadn't seen the damned kingpost, and was very hoity-toity. She then told me that she wishes the Trust after her death to allow the Women Farmers and Gardeners Association to have the use of the house as their rest home. By which time the whole rickety old dump will have collapsed in a heap. I could not be encouraging, and I suppose I showed my boredom with her ceaseless rattle about the importance and antiquity and rarity of the house. I was not well, and I did not respond as dutifully and enthusiastically as is my wont to offers which I know from the first glance are unacceptable.

When I left her on the high road, she said, 'I don't think much of the National Trust.' 'You mean', I replied, 'that you don't think much of me, I'm afraid.' 'You have done nothing but sniff and crab the place,' she said, giving me a stiff handshake, holding her arm high up in that injured manner peculiar to the sensitive poor. I felt a little abashed, a little ashamed and sorry that I had not been more forthcoming. But I did not feel guilty of her accusation. It was just not true that I had crabbed. I may have sniffed, for I am beginning a cold. I had merely tried, possibly a little too forcefully, to check her extravagant enthusiasms with which she relentlessly bombarded me. With the exception of that odious old gentleman, Colonel Pemberton of Pyrland Hall, she is, I think, the first owner with whom I have failed to make friends.

*Saturday, 16th October*

A Georgian Group committee meeting this morning. I sat next to Dame Una and Trystan Edwards,* who fascinated me with the number of objects tied to his person by black strings: fountain pens, spectacles, magnifying glasses, etc. It was a good meeting and the Professor [Richardson] in the chair dealt well with the items. I brought up several: Claremont – the park advertised for building plots; Chiswick – Lord Burlington's little temple in poor condition; 37 Portland Place – the beautiful central façade of the last intact terrace being demolished now; Dropmore [House, Buckinghamshire] – the estate bought by speculative builders.

When I got home for tea Jamesey telephoned proposing a night of adventure. I was thrilled and for once our enthusiasm coincided. We drank first at the Ritz, then the Gargoyle, dined at the White Tower and visited disreputable pubs in that area. The only person we met was Guy Burgess,† drunk and truculent, and we soon shook

* Architect, planner and writer (1884–1973).
† Diplomatist and traitor (1911–63); friend of Harold Nicolson.

him off. We both agreed that depravity was a bore, and that on this account alone the evening would have been worth while as a gentle reminder – in the hideous sweaty faces, the human stench, the risk of beer being spilt on one's best suit, of one's pocket being picked, and ten to one the likelihood of meeting no one rewarding. We returned to the Gargoyle and joined a table of Brian Howard,* that affected, paradoxical figure of the Twenties, and two other dreary queens. As I walked home about midnight from South Kensington station I ruminated upon the loneliness of my lot.

*J.L.-M. visited Devon with Eardley Knollys.*

*Thursday, 28th October*

Woke to find the sun shining upon the sea. Salcombe is as mild as the Mediterranean. At ten we went to Lady Clementine Waring's† house, a cheerful Gothic villa in which Froude‡ wrote his history, and to which he added a wing. Lawns slope down to the sea. Lady Clementine looks at one with the intensity of a psychoanalyst. And the expression on her face says, 'I have seen the inmost recesses of your squalid little mind. You are a worm only fit to be trampled underfoot.' She is a handsome and forbidding woman, who is chairman of the small local committee which runs the Sharpitor property. This contains a perfectly hideous villa called after its donor, the late Mr Overbeck, a mysterious German quack doctor whose interests embraced stuffed birds, oriental brass, Wedgwood cameos, every conceivable form of bric-à-brac, and young boys. The garden is famed for its rare shrubs, and is as unappetising as the house. It has no layout. It is criss-crossed with serpentine paths of yellow flags and tarmac, and is adorned with

---

* Oxford aesthete (1905–58); said to be the model for Anthony Blanche in Evelyn Waugh's *Brideshead Revisited* and Ambrose Silk in *Put Out More Flags*.

† Lady Clementine Hay (b. 1879), o. dau. of 10th Marquess of Tweeddale; m. 1901 Captain Walter Waring, MP (1876–1930).

‡ James Anthony Froude (1818–94); historian (latterly Regius Professor at Oxford), influenced by Thomas Carlyle.

pergolas fashioned out of drainpipes, handrails made out of tube pipes, terracotta urns on concrete piers, and the soppiest sculpture of simpering little children. The eucalyptus trees, which really must have been attractive features, were all killed by the frosts of recent winters.

Having inspected this unprepossessing property we lunched under the eagle eye of Lady Clementine and motored to Dartmouth. After crossing the ferry we continued to Brixham. I don't like Devon in spite of the beautiful coastline and cliffs. There is a littleness about its valleys and lanes, a meanness in the cramped views, an oppression in the claustrophobic, dinky little towns. Besides it is being overbuilt, spoilt by rashes of Tudor bungalows with miniature drives of grey granite pebbles and white-washed boulders at the gates. And, oh the gates! Either made of old wagon wheels, painted orange, or the rising (or setting?) sun in cheap metalwork. Devon is too much beloved by too many of the wrong people.

Brixham is like a foreign fishing village; and is indeed filled with Flemish fisherfolk, who escaped here with their craft. We watched the fishing smacks sail in and unload, while we had tea. We reached Torquay in the dark and stayed in tremendous luxury in the most expensive hotel in England, the Imperial, decorated and furnished by Betty Joel.

*Thursday, 18th November*

I attended Kenneth Clark's lecture at Greek House, the Greek Ambassador in the chair. The subject was the influence of Greek art upon British art and architecture. K. must be the most brilliant of lecturers – superhuman learning worn with ease, diction perfect – because he makes me concentrate as though I were immersed in a book. I can say this about no other lecturer, except Harold. He sat beside me for a few moments before the lecture, talking most graciously. Gracious is the word. He makes me feel like a nurserymaid addressed by royalty. He makes me feel a snob because I record that he spoke three words to me. Is he a very great man, and am I a very small one? The answer to both questions must be Yes.

*Monday, 22nd November*

At Brooks's I talked to Simon Harcourt-Smith* about Anarchism, for he too believes it may be the only political creed that holds out a hope for peace and justice. He said that his wife, Rosamund, who is about to become a Papist, was a confirmed Anarchist. The Farm Street Jesuits told her that, far from being incompatible, Catholicism and Anarchism were reconcilable, and she could embrace both. Simon knows no Anarchist except Herbert Read,† whom he greatly admires and to whom he will introduce me. I tried to press him for light on the positive side of the creed. I admitted that I shared his dislikes, but was a bit bewildered by the negative likes, and apparent lack of constructive policy. Simon was not able to enlighten me. He said Anarchism was a state of mind, presenting a goal to be kept in the mind's eye, however distant and unattainable. When I told Carol Dugdale at luncheon that Simon was the only Anarchist I knew, she said: 'Thank you very much. I don't need to know any more to be put off Anarchism for ever.'

*Wednesday, 24th November*

This afternoon Madame de Polignac rang me up and asked me to dine tonight. At first I said 'no', because I was on fire-watching duty, then succumbed to the temptation when she said I might leave early after dinner.

I arrived at 55 Park Lane earlier than I should have done. Only Alvilde Chaplin‡ there. She told me before my hostess came in how worried she was about the Princess's health. She has angina and lately has been having as many as twenty attacks a day. Then she

---

* Writer and critic (1909–96).

† (Sir) Herbert Read (1893–1968); poet, art critic and writer, strongly marked by war experiences.

‡ J.L.-M's future wife Alvilde *née* Bridges (1909–94), then married to Hon. Anthony (later 3rd Viscount) Chaplin (1906–81), who had for some years been the Princess's devoted companion. J.L.-M. appears to have met her for the first time dining with the Princess three weeks earlier, on 3 November.

came into the room wearing a green dress and nothing on her thick grey hair. She moved slowly and sedately. Her remarkable face, like some mountainous crag, was sunset pink. I talked to her before dinner and, almost exclusively, during dinner. All the other guests were French, including her niece, Madame de Vogüé. The dinner [cooked by Alvilde] was more delicious than words can express, and ended with a succulent mince pie, followed by an egg savoury flavoured with garlic. Algerian wine to drink. She said Proust's limited knowledge of England came through Ruskin; and that one of the first things he wrote was a preface to a French translation of Ruskin. The last time she saw Proust was at a dinner party given for him in Paris. He attended pale and ill, wearing a long seal-skin dressing gown down to his ankles. The Duke of Marlborough, who was present and had no idea who Proust was, was indignant at the informality of his clothes. The Princess again told me she never liked Proust. He was always hopelessly, unrequitedly in love, and this was wearisome for his friends.

*Thursday, 25th November*

I caught the 10.15 for Stockport, where I was met and driven to Lyme Park. As we climbed the long drive there was snow lying on the ground. This vast seat is 800 feet above sea level. The park gates are at the entrance to the suburbs of Stockport. In other words, Lyme forms a bulwark against Manchester and its satellite horrors. The greater part of the 3,000-acre property stretches in the opposite direction, towards the Peak. All morning while I was in the train the sun was shining. At Lyme it was snowing from a leaden sky. A butler met me at the front door and conducted me through the central courtyard, up some stone steps and into the hall on the piano nobile. Lord Newton* lives and eats in the great library with a huge fire burning, and two equally huge dogs lying at his feet.

---

* Richard Legh (1888–1960); s. father 1942 as 3rd Baron Newton; m. 1914 Hon. Helen Meysey-Thompson (d. 1958), dau. of 1st Baron Knaresborough.

Lyme is one of England's greatest houses. The exterior is practically all Leoni's* work. The south side is a little too severe to be beautiful. Lewis Wyatt's† chunky, square tower over the pediment is ponderous, like the central imposition on Buckingham Palace. A corridor runs the whole way round the first floor (from which staterooms open), with windows looking into the courtyard (which is architecturally the most satisfying composition at Lyme). The contents of the staterooms are magnificent, notably the Chippendale chairs, the Charles II beds and the Mortlake tapestries. There is a fascinating Byronic portrait of Thomas Legh in Greek costume standing by a horse. My bedroom on the west side of the first floor has two Sargent portraits, one of Lord Newton's mother and the other of his mother-in-law.

Lord Newton is hopeless. The world is too much for him, and no wonder. He does not know what he can do, ought to do or wants to do. He just throws up his hands in despair. The only thing he is sure about is that his descendants will never want to live at Lyme, after an unbroken residence of 600 years. I am already sure that he will not see out his ownership.

There were forty evacuated children in the house, but they have now gone. The park is cut to pieces by thousands of RAF lorries, for it is at present a lorry depot.

*Friday, 26th November*

On my return I dined with Stuart at White's. I was very distressed by his greeting me with the news that the Princesse de Polignac died suddenly last night. She told me on Wednesday that she was dining with Sibyl Colefax the following night. She did so, and Jamesey talked to her after dinner. She left at 11, was unwell in the taxi, and sat with Ronald Storrs downstairs in her block of flats

---

* Giacomo Leoni (*c.* 1686–1746); Venetian Palladian architect practising in England from *c.* 1714; worked at Lyme *c.* 1725–35.

† Lewis William Wyatt (1777–1853); country house architect, of the family of builders and architects descended from Benjamin Wyatt of Staffordshire.

until she felt better, then went upstairs to bed. At 2 a.m. she died of a heart attack in the presence of poor Alvilde Chaplin and a doctor. She was a very remarkable woman indeed, and I am glad that at the end of her life I had the privilege of meeting her.

*Saturday, 27th November*

Nancy lunched with me. She was as amazed as I was at Stuart paying a call on Alvilde Chaplin yesterday morning at 10 o'clock, to find her in tears only a few hours after the Princess's death in the next room. An extraordinary thing to do, considering how little he knows either. Oh well, customs differ on opposite sides of the Atlantic!

*Wednesday, 1st December*

Harold asked me to dine tonight. To my disappointment he was not alone. There were Godfrey Nicholson, MP,* Guy Burgess and a Dr Dietmar. The last is a tall, fair young man now teaching in a secondary school in Raynes Park. Harold got him out of an internment camp a few months ago. He is immensely grateful to Harold, earnest and rather a bore. Harold gave us champagne. I ought to have been firewatching in my office, and when the siren went during dinner rose to go. Harold quite rightly was shocked, for he has never once shirked firewatching duty in the House. However, the all-clear sounded almost immediately, so I sat down again. Talk was about lying. Harold said he never lied except about sex matters. Then he and Godfrey became engrossed in political shop, which I found very tedious. I am interested in politics *per se*, but long anecdotes about how Mr Bevan† snubbed Lady Astor,‡ who got her own back by insulting

---

* Conservative MP for Farnham, Surrey, 1937–66.

† Aneurin Bevan (1897–1960); radical Labour politician.

‡ Nancy Langhorne (1879–1964); m. (2nd) 1906 Waldorf, 2nd Viscount Astor; campaigner for Christian Science and other causes, and the first woman MP to take her seat in the House of Commons.

Mr Attlee,* strike me as childish and contemptible. I also think that when MPs treat politics like a game they are behaving dishonestly towards their constituents, who have not voted them into the House of Commons for that purpose.

*Sunday, 5th December*

At Mass in Cheyne Row I felt devout again. My devoutness is more readily maintained by my having my rosary and telling beads. It is when I am distracted from my devotions – I can't honestly say, prayers – by trying to make sense of the liturgy, or indeed listening to the sermon, that everything goes wrong. The moment reason takes over, faith flies out of the door. But concentrating on my rosary to a background of symbolic acts, punctuated and not interrupted by rising for the Gospel, kneeling for the sanctus bell and elevation, and crossing myself on approaching certain well-known and loved landmarks, then I can often be devout. Then I can feel I am making contact. God preserve us from too much illumination. What I need is a twilight atmosphere relieved by myriads of twinkling candles from crystal chandeliers, a plethora of gold, jewels, rich raiment, silver vessels, clouds of incense, and the tinkling and tolling of innumerable bells. Beauty, not austerity, is what I crave in order to be religious.

*Tuesday, 7th December*

Cyril [Connolly]† has told Stuart that Cecil [Beaton]'s strongest passion is spite. So I have told Stuart to ask Cecil what Cyril's strongest passion is.

Everyone is talking of imminence of the Germans' rocket shells. The Germans themselves announced over the wireless on Saturday

* Clement Attlee (1883–1967); Leader of Labour Party, 1935–55; Deputy Prime Minister in wartime coalition, 1940–5; Prime Minister of Labour Government, 1945–51.

† Writer and journalist (1903–74); editor of *Horizon*, 1939–50.

that these shells would shortly rain upon London and totally destroy it. The War Office takes them very seriously, and soldiers are commanded to carry steel helmets again.

*Friday, 10th December*

Lying in the bath this morning, with the hot tap gently running and the water making throaty noises down the waste-pipe – a thing one is strictly enjoined not to allow in war-time – I thought how maddening it is that the worst sins are the most enjoyable. I wondered could it possibly be that these sins would recoil upon me in my old age. For at present they don't seem to do my soul much harm. And the lusts of the flesh, instead of alienating me from God, seem to draw me closer to him in a perverse way. He on the other hand may not be drawn to me. Yet I feel he ought to know how to shake me off if he wants to. Can it be that he is too polite, as I am when Clifford Smith [N.T. furniture expert] button-holes me at a party, and I am longing to escape? How oddly one's body behaves in the bath, as though it did not belong to one. Admiring my slender limbs through the clear water I thought, what a pity they aren't somebody else's.

*Thursday, 23rd December*

Today the announcement of the National Trust's acquisition of West Wycombe Park appeared in the press: at last, after protracted negotiations since 1938.

I lunched with Lord and Lady Newton at their flat in Park Street. They were pleased with the suggestion that Manchester University might rent Lyme Park from the Trust. Lady Newton must once have been handsome. She is tall, and thin like everyone else these days. But she is as languid and hopeless as her husband. Both said they would never be able to reconcile themselves to the new order after the war. They admitted that their day was done, and life as they had known it was gone for ever. How right they are, poor people.

*Saturday, 25th December*

Christmas Day. I met Stuart at the Brompton Oratory for High Mass. Children's beautiful voices singing. We walked to the Hyde Park Hotel, where we sat and talked rather sadly. I left him for Dame Una's Christmas luncheon in Ladbroke Grove. John, Jamesey and Nancy were there. We exchanged little gifts. I gave them each a piece of soap shaped like a lemon. Dame Una gave me a honeycomb, and Nancy one of her hen's eggs and an ounce of real farm butter, golden yellow. A huge turkey was carved, and we had an excellent plum pudding. We talked about Italy, the looting by British troops, and the Italians' dislike of us.

I walked with Nancy to her house in Blomfield Road. We looked at the terraces round Paddington Station and the Canal basin, and the house Browning lived in at Little Venice. It is now shabby and bombed, but so romantic. I left Nancy in the Harrow Road on her way to deliver a leather tea cosy to her charwoman who is in hospital. I went to tea with Emerald Cunard, who was alone. She gave me a book for Christmas. At first she was absent-minded. Then she warmed up and was enchanting. She talked of Chips Channon and the Stuart row. 'Do you really think, my dear, he made up to him?' She talked of the Knighthood of the Garter, mandragora, Shakespeare, Galsworthy ('who looked a gentleman and may have been one'), of a friend of hers who loved a man with £3 million, of the lack of culture among Americans and the English middle-classes. 'Do they really not care for the arts? How extraordinary of them!' I stayed until 7 o'clock.

*Friday, 31st December*

Having dined with Geoffrey [Houghton Brown] I walked home and went early to bed. I read, but the Battersea church bells started pealing across the river, contrary as I thought to the regulations. It was more than I could bear, so I went downstairs to put some cotton wool in my ears. Still I heard them. At midnight I stuffed my fingers into my ears in order not to listen to the striking of the little tortoise-shell and silver clock by my bedside. The loneliness of this moment, wholly artificial though it be, harrows me. When it had passed I went on reading. At 12.30 the telephone rang. I threw the sheets back and leapt out of bed. Book, paper and pencil clattered to the floor. It must, I thought, be the voice I longed for. It would be contrite, solicitous, loving. No such thing. It was that bore Dr Dietmar to wish me a Happy New Year, as though 1944 could augur anything but the direst misery of our lives. Only a German could be so obtuse. I was not very friendly, and pretended that he had woken me up.

# 1944

# 1944

*Saturday, 1st January*

I had tea in Jamesey Pope-Hennessy's flat. Dame Una who joined us afterwards asked me if I kept my diary for posterity. 'Perhaps,' I answered, 'but it won't be read until fifty years after my death.' 'Since *we* can't possibly die,' Jamesey said, 'that means never. Just as well.' The Dame looked wise and said nothing.

*Monday, 3rd January*

At 6 went to a meeting to wind up the Federal Union Club* at the Squires' flat. Only the Squires, Keith Miller-Jones, Sainsbury and Miss Ward present, a sad little gathering. I thought of poor Robert Byron, our President, and Derek Rawnsley, the fair, fanatical young man who was also killed. Keith and I walked to Brooks's and dined there. He recommended my reading Festing Jones's life of Samuel Butler.† When young, Keith knew Festing Jones, who told him many anecdotes of Butler. The third unpublished sonnet of Butler to Miss Savage began, 'Had I the desires of a common sailor after three weeks' abstinence', or words to that effect. Butler had a woman upon whom he vented his appetite, often, according to Festing Jones, without troubling to unbutton his trousers.

---

* Association founded September 1939 to promote a federation of the world's democracies. Robert Byron was President, and drew in socially prominent young friends – the Rosses, the Antrims, Sir Michael Duff and John Sutro. The club, which had an office near Piccadilly, held parties and organised broadcasts, but petered out after the spring of 1940: see James Knox, *Robert Byron* (2003), pp. 423–7.

† Samuel Butler (1835–1902), English writer best known for his satire *Erewhon* (1872), whose friend Henry Festing Jones published his biography in 1919.

*Tuesday, 4th January*

John Betjeman* lunched with me at Brooks's, the first time since the war. He seemed to be enjoying himself, jumping up and down in his chair and snapping his fingers in laughter. He is sweeter and funnier than anyone on earth. He never changes, is totally unselfconscious, eccentric, untidy and green-faced. He works at the Ministry of Information and simply hates it, returning every Saturday-to-Monday to Uffington. In his *Daily Herald* articles he surreptitiously damns the war and progress and the left wing. Talked about the slave state in which we are already living. Said he loved Ireland but not the Irish middle class. When the Betjemans left Ireland, De Valera sent for them. Penelope said to him, 'I hope you won't let the Irish roads deteriorate. I mean I hope you won't have them metalled and tarmacked.'

After luncheon, we walked down Jermyn Street and John pointed out two buildings by Morphew that had singular merit. Any surviving Georgian building provoked him to say, 'They ought to have that down. That's too good.' I showed him the Athenian Stuart† façade in St James's Square, which to my surprise he did not know. He is a committed High Churchman, and wishes to edit a church magazine after the war. Suffers much from guilt complexes over his youth, which must surely have been more innocent than most people's – 'but the flesh hasn't been so provoking during the past fortnight'.

As we passed the site of Pennethorne's‡ old Geological Museum he reminded me of our visits years ago during luncheon breaks. There was never a soul, either an attendant or a visitor. We used to insert into the dusty glass cases old chestnuts and pebbles which we labelled with long names in Latin, invented by us amid peals of laughter. They remained where we put them until the building was pulled down.

---

* (Sir) John Betjeman (1906–84); poet (Poet Laureate, 1972–84), critic and writer on architecture; press officer at British High Commission in Dublin, 1941–3; m. 1933 Hon. Penelope (1910–86), dau. of Field Marshal Lord Chetwode.

† James Stuart (1713–88); architect in Greek Revival style.

‡ Sir James Pennethorne (1800–71); architect.

*Monday, 10th January*

Matheson is leaving on 1st March for six months. I wrote him a note, which he showed Esher and Zetland, that I did not want to become Secretary if it meant abandoning my historic buildings work, and that I could not cope anyway with the secretarial routine. I feel very unwell nearly all the time.*

Went to Lady Crewe's party. It was hell. Not much to drink, hardly anyone I knew, and the atmosphere far from relaxed. Lady Crewe is awkward and shy. I watched Mrs Keppel† hobbling around the room and smoking from a long holder. She is rather shapeless, with hunched shoulders, and a long white powdered face. She was gazing with mournful eyes as though in search of something. Colonel Keppel, with big moustache, is very much a Brigade of Guards officer of the old school.

*Wednesday, 19th January*

This evening I dined at Claridge's with Alfred and Clementine Beit. Arrived at 8 and waited in the hall. Espied Gerry Wellington‡ likewise waiting. He said, 'Shall we have a drink?' I said, 'A good idea.' 'We will not have cocktails, they are too expensive,' he said in that well-known way. So we each paid for a small glass of sherry at 4 shillings, which was preposterous. He told me that his gross income today was £40,000. After income tax and super tax there was £4,000 left over. Out of this he has to pay Schedule A on Stratfield Saye and Apsley House, which leaves him barely enough to pay for wages and food. I asked whether he had any servants at Apsley House. He said, 'Oh yes, I have the chamberlain's wife and the house carpenter.' He did not pay death duties on either of these two houses, or the lands attached, because they don't belong to

---

* J.L.-M. nevertheless acted as Secretary of the N.T. in Matheson's absence.

† Alice Elphinstone (1869–1947); m. 1891 Hon. George Keppel (1865–1947), yr s. of 7th Earl of Albemarle; mistress of King Edward VII.

‡ Lord Gerald Wellesley (1885–1972); yr s. of 5th Duke of Wellington; diplomatist and architect; s. nephew, killed in action, September 1943, as 7th Duke; m. 1914 Dorothy ('Dot') Ashton.

him, but to Parliament. He is applying to Parliament to take back Apsley House – with the gift of the valuable contents which are his – on condition that they will make it into a museum under his guidance, and allow him to live in a corner of it. It is, he says, a perfect museum, not having been altered in any particular since the Great Duke's death in 1852.

Joan Moore joined us. At 8.30 it occurred to us that the Beits might have taken a private dining-room, which is what they had done. Joan and I talked of passionate, desperate, hopeless love. General conversation after dinner. Most enjoyable it was too. I walked in the rain to Hyde Park Corner with Gerry, who feigned to be nervous, cautious and old-mannish, as though it became his new ducal status. I think a person's age can be measured by his reaction to the blackout. Gerry was, however, charming, as he always is to me. He says that being a duke and inheriting two houses is like having a glittering present every day.

*Thursday, 20th January*

Hamish [St Clair-Erskine]* dined alone with me at Brooks's. A boozy evening. I had three whiskies and soda before dinner. We had a bottle of burgundy at dinner, and two glasses of port each after dinner. Hamish told me all about his bravery, for which he got the MC, treating it all as a great joke. His gun was shot to atoms and he received wounds all down the left side. His sergeant dragged him to safety. He denied that he was courageous. There was no alternative to what he had to do. A few times only he had a sense of personal fear when at close quarters to the enemy. The German soldiers were kind to prisoners. The Italians were only interested in their money. They have no respect for us and deadly fear of the Germans, who say, 'If you do so-and-so, we shoot', and do shoot, whereas we say the same, and don't shoot. He recounted his escape and hiding in a ditch, while hearing Germans shout, '*Fritz, wo ist er?*' I said,

* Hon. Hamish St Clair-Erskine (1909–73); yr s. of 5th Earl of Rosslyn; rakish Eton contemporary of J.L.-M. In *Ancestral Voices* J.L.-M. had reported his capture in July 1943, and his escape and return to England in December 1943.

'I suppose if they had found you, they would have bayoneted you on the spot?' He looked surprised and said, 'Not at all, they would have clapped me on the shoulder and said, "Bad luck, now we must lock you up again."' But he was anxious then. 'I had my rosary and was racing round it faster than you could have gone round the Inner Circle.' I said, 'When the Germans left and you realised you were safe, what did you say to Our Lady?' 'Whoopee, Virge!' We went back to his mews and drank beer till 2.30. He prepared a bed for me and said before he went to the bathroom, 'I hope you will be comfortable, but if you can't sleep you will have to come to mine', which was a great double bed. When he came back I said, 'You were right in saying that the sheets on my bed would only reach to my navel.' So Hamish said, 'Well, you'd better come to my bed, though I have wasted a clean pair of sheets on yours for nothing.'

*Sunday, 23rd January*

At 10.30 Stuart met me at Paddington station. While waiting for him I watched a woman passenger have a row with an officious woman ticket collector at the barrier. The first threw the other's ticket-puncher to the ground. The second threw the first's handbag to the ground, took off her own coat, and flew at her opponent. They punched and scratched and finally became interlocked, each grasping the other's hair which came away in handfuls. I felt quite sick and intervened. Then they both hit me. I roared for help, and two policemen dragged the combatants apart. The other passengers, mostly soldiers, merely looked on.

From Windsor station we made for the Park and down the Long Walk, the far end of which is felled, the elm trunks being quite rotten. Fine day with a biting wind. I had my filthy old mackintosh on which always puts me in the wrong frame of mind. It's curious how the clothes one wears dictate one's mood. Stuart kept saying, 'I do hope there is a good luncheon [at Cumberland Lodge], and lots to eat.' I had misgivings.

There were only us and the family. Lord FitzAlan is past conversing now, having become very old and deaf. Magdalen has no conversation anyway, and Alathea looked sad and cold, no wonder.

Stuart tried to be bright. I felt ill at ease, and realised I would have been able to make more effort if alone, without S. As we went into the dining-room, Magdalen said, 'I hope there is enough for you to eat. There is only soup.' It was too true. S. took some scotch broth, and Alathea said, 'I would put some potato into it if I were you.' I overheard S. exclaim, 'What! Potato in my soup? No thanks.' He soon did, however, on discovering that this really was the only dish. We got up rattling. S. was very forgiving on the way back. In Windsor we had a filthy tea at the Nell Gwynn café, to make up for the non-luncheon.

*Friday, 28th January*

Today was devoted to Sherborne Castle [Dorset]. At 10 the solicitor took me to Rawlence the agent's office, and the three of us motored to the castle grounds bordering the town. At first glance the outside of the house is disappointing. The cement rendering makes it gloomy. The plate-glass windows give it a blind, eyeless look. Yet the house reminds me of Westwood Park* in that it too has a central Elizabethan block (built as a hunting lodge by Sir Walter Raleigh) to which four arms were added in Restoration times. The dressings are of Ham stone. Fine entrance gates at the north and south sides, forming two open courts. Like Westwood the house is terribly confusing inside, for it is very tall, with many floor levels. There is little inside to take the breath away, but much that is good, notably the great marble chimneypieces of Jacobean date and, above all, the two interior porches in the downstairs dining room. At present the furniture is stored away, for American troops have requisitioned the castle.

So far the lordly owner has not appeared, and we three of low degree lunch at the hotel. Twice Rawlence is called away to be advised by the Colonel's butler at what time we are to appear for coffee, port and cigars. The Wingfield Digbys† are in Raleigh's

* Elizabethan house in Worcestershire, sold on death in 1949 of 3rd and last Baron Doverdale (who had m. an Australian chorus girl), and later turned into flats.

† Colonel F. J. W. Wingfield Digby (1885–1952); m. 1905 Gwendolen Fletcher.

lodge for 'the duration'. The Colonel is a stooping MFH with the manner of one. Very autocratic, and conscious of his not inconsiderable dignity. He addresses Rawlence as Major Rawlence, in spite of the latter's father and grandfather also having been agents to the family, and Rawlence being every inch a gent. Rawlence addresses him as Colonel, and often as Sir. An awkward interview takes place. I explain as best I can what the transaction would involve. But they are not the sort of people to welcome public access.

After the interview we sallied forth to the pleasance. The Colonel and Mrs W.D. took us over the old ruined castle and through the very beautiful wooded walks by the lake. Here we came upon Raleigh's seat, where the servant is said to have thrown the water over his master while he was smoking, and Pope's seat, where the poet wrote letters to Martha Blount. The Colonel showed little interest in these fascinating associations. 'Pope indeed,' he snorted. 'I've no idea which pope it could have been.'

The Wingfield Digbys, finding that I was to dine alone, very kindly bade me dine with them. They showed me some rare miniatures – of Arabella Stuart,* Kenelm Digby and Venetia Digby;† also a jewel given to Ambassador Digby by the Court of Spain. I liked the W.Ds, although Anne Rosse had previously warned that they might not like me. And there was one awkward moment when, à propos of nothing, the Colonel exclaimed, 'I can't stick Roman Catholics. One can smell 'em a mile off,' or words to that effect. Mrs Wingfield Digby, who, although her sentiments were clearly the same as her husband's, wished to appear open-minded, then said, 'But, Freddy, they do have a right to their own point of view,' adding after a pregnant pause, 'Of course, one can't trust them one yard.' I thought it best to remain mum.

Anne had also told me a hair-raising story of the Colonel's behaviour during a severe frost. The lake at Sherborne froze, and

* Lady Arabella Stuart (1575–1615); cousin and dynastic rival of King James I, who died in the Tower of London where he had imprisoned her.

† Sir Kenelm Digby (1603–65); courtier, swashbuckler and intellectual, founding member of Royal Society and prominent English Roman Catholic; m. 1625 Venetia Stanley who d. 1633, Van Dyck painting a famous picture of her on her deathbed.

people from near and far assembled to skate, without a 'by your leave'. So 'Cousin Freddy' climbed up to one of the Castle towers, and with a rifle peppered the ice to make it crack.

*Among those who offered their houses to the National Trust at this time was George Bernard Shaw.**

*Wednesday, 9th February*

Shaw's Corner [Ayot St Lawrence, Hertfordshire] is a very ugly, dark red-brick villa, built in 1902. I rang the bell and a small maid in uniform led me across the hall to a drawing-room, with open views on to the garden and the country beyond, for the house is at the end of the village. There was a fire burning in the pinched little grate. Walls distempered, the distemper flaking badly in patches. The quality of the contents of the room was on a par with that of the villa. Indifferent water-colours of the Roman Campagna, trout pools in cheap gilt frames. One rather good veneered Queen Anne bureau (for which G.B.S. said he had given £80) and one fake lacquer bureau. In the window a statuette of himself by Paul Trubetskoy. On the mantelpiece a late Staffordshire figure of Shakespeare (for which he paid 10 shillings), a china house, the lid of which forms a box. Only a few conventionally bound classics, plus Osbert Sitwell's latest publication prominently displayed on a table. Two stiff armchairs before the fire and brass fender. A shoddy three-ply screen attached to the fireplace to shelter from draughts anyone sitting between the fire and the doorway.

I wait five minutes and looked around, at a chronometer and the serried row of Shakespeare plays in soft leather bindings. Presently the door opened and in came the great man. I was instantly struck by the snow-white head and beard, the blue eyes and blue nose, with a small ripe spot over the left nostril. He was not so tall as I imagined, for he stoops slightly. He was dressed in a pepper-and-salt knickerbocker suit. A loose yellow tie from a pink collar over a thick woollen vest rather than shirt. Several waistcoats. Mittens

* Irish playwright, essayist and critic (1856–1950).

over blue hands. He evidently feels the cold for there were electric fires in every room and the passage. He shook hands and I forget what he first said. Nothing special anyway. Asked me to sit down, and put questions to me straight off, such as how he could make over the property now and retain a right of user. His friend, Lord Astor (*Ar*stor),* had done so. I had not expected the strong Irish brogue. This peasant origin makes him all the more impressive. It put me in mind of Thomas Carlyle, of whom, curiously enough, he spoke. I said I preferred Mrs to Mr Carlyle. He said Carlyle was out of fashion because of the prevailing anti-German prejudice; that there had been worse husbands than he. G.B.S. said he wished to impose no conditions on the hand-over, but he did not wish the house to become a dead museum. Hoped it would be a living shrine. He wanted to settle matters now, for since his wife's death he was bound to remake his will, and in three years' time he might be quite dotty, if he was alive at all. He is 88, and very agile. He showed me his statuette, which he likes, and bust (copy) by Rodin which he does not care for. Took me into his study where he works at an untidy writing table. In this room is another Queen Anne bureau. The wall facing it is covered with reference books, and all the bound proofs of his own books, corrected by him. These, I said, ought to remain here. There are no pictures or photographs of his wife to be seen. The dining-room is far from beautiful. It contains some fumed oak furniture and a portrait of him done in 1913. He ran upstairs, pointing admiringly to the enlarged bird etchings on the stair wall. He showed me his wife's room and his bedroom, and the one spare room. He has lived in this house since 1908.

When he smiles his face softens and he becomes engaging. He is not at all deaf, but comes close up to one to talk, breathing into one's face. His breath is remarkably sweet for an old man's. Having looked upstairs we descended. He tripped going down, and I was afraid he was going to fall headlong. He then said, 'We will go out to look at the cu*r*tilage' – rolling the 'r' of this unusual word. It was

* Waldorf, 2nd Viscount Astor (1879–1952) had donated Cliveden, Berkshire, to the N.T. on the understanding that he could continue to have virtually unrestricted use of it for his lifetime.

fearfully cold by now, and raining heavily. He put on a long, snow-white mackintosh and chose a stick. From the hall hat-rack, hung with a variety of curious headgear, he took an archaic rough felt hat, of a buff colour, high in crown and wide of brim. In this garb he resembled Carlyle, and was the very picture of the sage, striding forth, a little wobbly and bent perhaps, pointing out the extent of the 'curtilage' and the line of the hedge which he had de-rooted with his own hands to lengthen the garden. The boundary trees of spruce were planted by him. 'Trees grow like mushrooms in these parts,' he said. We came to a little asbestos-roofed summer-house that revolves on its own axis. Here he also writes and works. There is a little table covered with writing material, and a couch. The summer-house was padlocked. I said, 'Do you sit out here in the winter, then?' 'I have an electric stove,' and he pointed to a thick cable attached to the summer house from an iron pylon behind it. 'This will be an attraction to the *birthplace*, if it survives,' he said. We passed piles of logs, which he told me he had chopped himself. He showed me his and his wife's initials carved on the coach-house door and engraved on a glass pane of the greenhouse. Took me into the coach-house where there are three cars under dust sheets, one a Rolls-Royce. 'When I want to use this,' he said, 'I become very decrepit, and the authorities allow me coupons.' We continued down the road.

A collie puppy met us in the road and jumped up at the old man who paid it much attention. He led me to Revett's* curious church. He explained that the reigning squire began demolishing the old church because he considered it 'an aesthetic disgrace' and 'barbarous Gothic'. The Bishop stopped it entirely disappearing, but not the erection of Revett's church in 'fashionable Palladian'. G.B.S. walked up the steps and with reverence took off his hat. We walked inside. The interior is certainly cold and unspiritual. 'But it has good proportions,' Shaw allowed. The worst mistake is the ugly coloured glass in the windows. Classical churches are always spoiled with coloured glass. When we left he tapped with his stick a scrolled tombstone and

* Nicholas Revett (1721–1804); architect in Greek Revival style.

made me read the inscription. It was to some woman who had died in the 1890s, aged 76, and below was inscribed, 'Cut off ere her prime', or words to that effect. 'That', said G.B.S., 'is what persuaded me to come and live in the parish thirty-six years ago, for I assumed I stood some chance of at least reaching my ninetieth year.'

By the time we got back to the house I was wet through. Tea was brought on a tray to the drawing-room. A glass of milk only for him; tea and cakes for me. I was given a mug to drink out of. He decried the madness of the times, and the war. He said wars cease to be wars when chivalry is altogether excluded, as now, and become mass murder. Up to now conscientious objection had failed, but one day it would succeed. It would be interesting to see how it would work if ever this country declared war on Soviet Russia. The present war was due, not to man's weakness, but his ignorance. I asked, 'What would you do if you were given Winston Churchill's power and position today?' He said wisely enough, 'All action depends upon actual circumstance, but I would endeavour to bring fighting to an instant conclusion.' He condemned the folly of insisting on unconditional surrender. There can be no such thing. The Government ought to tell the Germans what conditions we would accept and terms we would impose.

We talked about Hardy's* Max Gate. 'Pull it down,' he said. He advised the National Trust to hold his house alienably, so that, supposing in twenty years we found that his name was forgotten, we could reap the benefit of selling it. He liked the idea of our holding T. E. Lawrence's† Clouds Hill [Dorset],‡ for it was good for nothing else. He talked a lot about Lawrence. Said people would not grasp that T.E.L. was physically under-developed and never grew up, scarcely shaved, and was mentally adolescent. He used to tell Lawrence that he knew no one who kept his anonymity so much

---

* See entry for 20 January 1947.

† Soldier, writer and archaeologist, 'Lawrence of Arabia' (1888–1935); author of *Seven Pillars of Wisdom*, which he endlessly rewrote (it appearing in an abridged version in 1927 and a fuller version on his death); intimate of J.L.-M's late employer Lord Lloyd.

‡ See entry for 20 September 1945.

in the limelight. He and his wife corrected the proofs of *Seven Pillars*. The published version was scarcely recognisable. The Shaws cut out much that was sheer guilt complex. Lawrence's great discovery was that the surest way of directing the affairs of any department was by enlisting at the bottom and remaining there.

At 5.15 G.B.S. jumped up, saying it was getting dark and he had kept me a quarter of an hour too long. Thanked me for coming. I said I had enjoyed the afternoon immensely. He said he had too. Before I left however he talked about his will again; said he would not leave any money to his relations because he did not wish them to grow up in idleness and luxury. He wanted to leave his money for the sole purpose of inaugurating a new alphabet of something like 140 letters instead of 26. He had calculated that the saving of expense in print and paper within one generation would be enough to finance three more world wars. And if that didn't appeal to the Government, what would? He came on to the road without hat or coat and stood until I drove off. In the mirror I watched him still standing in the road.

*Sunday, 13th February*

To tea with Emerald. How funny she was. I recall Gerald Berners'* definition of Sibyl Colefax's and Emerald's parties. The first was a party of lunatics presided over by an efficient trained hospital nurse, the second a party of lunatics presided over by a lunatic. It is impossible to recollect or record accurately Emerald's particular funninesses. She told us how Count So-and-So shocked her correct husband, Sir Bache, by bringing to Nevill Holt [Leicestershire] where they lived his Austrian mistress for a week's hunting. 'My dear, she was an Abbess' – by which she meant a *chanoinesse*, a hereditary dignity.

*The second half of February saw the worst German air raids on London since the 'Blitz' of 1940–1. (These were conventional raids, as the German*

* Gerald Tyrwhitt-Wilson, 14th Baron Berners, of Faringdon House, Oxfordshire (1883–1950); composer, writer and aesthete, friend of Harold Nicolson.

*'secret weapon' announced at the end of 1943 did not start arriving until June 1944.)*

*Friday, 18th February*

On my return [from dining with Emerald Cunard] at 12.30 Joan [Moore] telephoned, and we talked for half an hour. The instant she put down the receiver the sirens went, and the worst raid for years occurred. The noise of guns was deafening. Miss Paterson and I went downstairs and ate buns in the kitchen, trembling with fear. When the all-clear sounded, there were fires to be seen in all directions. The result is, we brought down five raiders only, and four of them over France.

*Sunday, 20th February*

By the evening I was very tired for I slept badly last night. On returning home was obliged to shelter in South Kensington tube during another severe and noisy raid. A lot more fires and a bomb dropped on the Treasury buildings. The Carmelite church in Kensington destroyed.

*Wednesday, 23rd February*

I returned to my office at 9.15 [p.m.]. Christopher Gibbs* on fire-watching duty with me. We talked until 10.30 when the sirens went. We donned our steel helmets and joined the other firewatchers from our block. We were both astonished by the unashamed way in which most of them, including the men, admitted that they were not going to take the risk of putting out incendiary bombs, or rescuing people. I said in surprise, 'But I thought that was what we were here for!' Several close crumps shook the building so that one and all ducked to the ground. Christopher and I went out several times between the bursts of gunfire to look around. A clear, starry night. It was beautiful but

* Assistant Secretary of N.T., 1935–66 (d. 1985).

shameful to enjoy the glow of fires, the red bursts of distant shells and the criss-cross of searchlights. I suppose that Nero derived a similar thrill from watching the Christians used as human torches. Then we saw the slow descent of what looked like a lump of cotton wool. Our leader lost his head, shouting, 'It's a German parachute! We must run, it's coming down here', etc. In fact it was far away. Christopher Gibbs, who had been a colonel in the last war, was furious with him. I could not help ragging him, for it seemed so funny. I am far better in raids when I have something to do, especially when others lose their heads. Fear then seems driven away by farce.

*Thursday, 24th February*

There is no doubt our nerves are beginning to be frayed. Frank telephoned this morning. I could tell by his voice he was upset. He said he was going to leave the Paddington area and thought Chelsea or Belgravia would be safer. I said I doubted whether the Germans discriminated to that extent. This evening I went to see a crater in the road, now sealed off, in front of St James's Palace. The Palace front sadly knocked about, the clock awry, the windows gaping, and shrapnel marks on the walls. A twisted car in the middle of the road. Geoffrey [Houghton Brown]'s Pall Mall flat devastated, and the Lelys from Castle Howard he had just bought presumed lost. The staircase to the flat quite gone. A colonel who lived above him has entirely disappeared, only two buttons of his tunic and part of his cap have been retrieved. In King Street Willis's Rooms finally destroyed, one half having gone in the raid of [May] 1941 when I was sheltering in the Piccadilly Hotel.* Poor Frank Partridge's shop devastated, and presumably Leonard Knight's. Drowns, the picture restorers, where I took the two Greville primitives, gone altogether. This is an ill-fated area. The London Library received a hit. Whereas fewer bombs are dropped than formerly, they must be of larger calibre, for the damage they do is greater. A huge bomb fell last night at the

* As described in *Another Self.*

World's End, killing many people. Miss P., alone in Cheyne Walk, was buffeted by the blast. Poor little Mrs Beckwith's house in Battersea bombed, and she didn't come to work today, but sent her daughter to tell us before we left for the office. This evening at 9.45 another raid of an hour. The weather is cold, the air clear, the moonless sky starry. Lovely weather for bombing. There was one ugly moment when a big bomb dropped near me. It provoked a deafening cannonade of guns in retaliation.

*Sunday, 27th February*

Read the papers in Brooks's and walked to the London Library in my corduroy trousers and an old golfing jacket. Joined the volunteers for two exhausting hours in salvaging damaged books from the new wing which sustained a direct hit on Wednesday night. They think about 20,000 books are lost. It is a tragic sight. Theology (which *one* can best do without) practically wiped out, and biography (which *one* can't) partially. The books lying torn and coverless, scattered under debris and in a pitiable state, enough to make one weep. The dust overwhelming. I looked like a snowman at the end. One had to select from the mess books that seemed usable again, rejecting others, chucking the good from hand to hand in a chain, in order to get them under cover. For one hour I was perched precariously on a projecting girder over an abyss, trying not to look downwards but to catch what my neighbour threw to me. If it rains thousands more will be destroyed, for they are exposed to the sky. It is interesting how the modern girder-constructed buildings withstand the bombs, for those parts not directly hit, but adjacent to hit parts, twist but resist the concussion to a surprising extent.

To lunch with Stuart at the Travellers where I washed and changed, although my hair remained glutinous with dirt. Hamish joined us. When the two went off to play bridge with Nancy, I returned to the London Library for another hour and a half. Again was a link in a human chain passing bucket-loads of shattered books from hand to hand. It was very exhilarating and exhausting.

*Monday, 6th March*

Went to Partridge's Bruton Street shop to look at the Blickling pictures which have suffered severely from two foot of water rushing into the strong-room at King Street during the raid. Partridge's lost a third of their own things. The Holbein of Henry VIII, Zucchero of Queen Elizabeth and Samuel Scott of the Thames, all from Blickling, very bad indeed. All the varnish off and what to my eye seemed much of the paint too, the bare canvas showing. But the restorer wiped the surface with a rag and some methylated spirit and the pictures miraculously reappeared for an instant, then faded away. If treated at once they can be saved, he maintains.

Dined at Alvilde's in the Princesse de Polignac's old flat. Exquisite dinner, a rich curry with plenty of onion, and a pudding of bananas and much beside. Eddy, his friend Mrs Richards,* and the Strathallans† there. A jolly evening discussing food ad nauseam, regurgitation and wind – favourite subjects of Eddy's.

*Friday, 17th March*

Hired a car for £1 to take me [from Shrewsbury] to Pitchford Hall [Shropshire]. A most glorious day, though keen and sharp. The black-and-white of this house is a bit too much of a good thing. The house is supposed to be late fifteenth- or early sixteenth-century, but I suspect it to be much later. The clock-tower porch is obviously Jacobean. The north wing extension of 1880 is well done, but over-contributes to the black-and-white. However today the place looked highly romantic amid the buds of spring, flowering crocuses and primroses. Met Forsyth, the architect, in the drive who told me Sir Charles Grant‡ was waiting for me. Was conducted upstairs to a small, shapeless end room in the west wing, where he sprawled, listening to the European news in the way country people

---

* Betty Fletcher Mossop (d. 1971); m. 1st 1937 Nigel Richards (killed in action, 1944), 2nd 1954 William Batten.

† John Drummond, Viscount Strathallan (1907–2002); o. s. of 16th Earl of Perth (whom he succeeded as 17th Earl, 1951); m. 1934 Nancy Seymour Fincke; in Ministry of Production.

‡ See entry for 8 July 1943.

do most of the livelong day. He is well over sixty, still handsome, and rather mischievous. Indeed a sweet man who must once have been attractive. He is an old friend of that fellow general, Lord Sackville. Eddy tells me that he remembers that, at Knole, years ago, the two men were discussing something rather excitedly. Lord Sackville said, 'What you can't understand, Charlie darl—', and stopped dead, too late: Eddy's mother, who was present, rose from her chair and stalked out of the room, head in air.

Now Sir Charles vegetates, and talks volubly and a little irrelevantly about his ancestors, his friends and acquaintances. He galloped me through the house, pointing out the contents which he thought he would give with it. But so rapid was our progress that I could not take in individual things. I don't think there is much that is very good. The rooms have a rather incongruous early Victorian air, which is sad and romantic. All the rooms are low and dark in spite of the sun shining outside, the birds singing and the water falling over the stones. He dearly loves the place. His proposals are vague however, and he does not intend to transfer any land over and above what the house stands on, even omitting the orangery and walled garden.

While he was talking to me on the lawn Lady Sibyl approached. Out of the corner of my eye I saw a fat, dumpy figure waddling and supporting herself with a tall stick. She wore a long blue coat down to her calves. One foot had on a stocking, the other was bare. On her head was an orange bonnet, draped with an orange scarf which floated down to her ankles. She had orange hair kept in place by a wide-meshed blue net. She took care to shield her extraordinary face, extraordinary because, although she is beautiful, the shape is absolutely round and the lips are the vividest orange I have ever beheld. She looks like a clairvoyante preserved in ectoplasm. As a special favour she took me to the orangery where she lives, for she hates the house, which she says is haunted. She cannot sleep on the east side for the noise of the water, or on the north because of the graveyard. She and Sir Charles send messages to each other throughout the day and night, and meet for coffee on the lawn when weather permits. She would not allow Forsyth to come near the orangery, which is her sanctum, converted by her into one large living-room with a wood fire, and one bedroom. She talked incessantly for an hour, complaining how the aeroplanes swooped so low that she lost her voice and was obliged to move into a caravan in a ploughed field to escape them. Said that her French maid 'never revealed she was mad' when she came to her, and stole all her clothes. The only way she recovered them was to send the maid to confession – the abbess made her give them all back. Her gruff laugh and low, sepulchral voice reminded me of Lady Crewe, her sister. She had sprained her ankle – hence the one bare leg – and made me pour a solution of Ponds Extract over it out of a heavy lead Marie Antoinette watering can.

Forsyth motored me to Attingham where I stayed the night. I walked into the deer park looking for Lord Berwick. Found him exercising his little dog, Muffet. He talks to me far more confidently than he used to. I think he is one of the most endearing men I have ever met – feckless, helpless and courteous. We had a good dinner of four courses, including chicken and burgundy. Lady Sibyl Grant said of him, 'Poor Tom, he should not have lived in this age. He cannot drive a car, ride a bicycle, fish or shoot. He would have stepped in and out of a sedan chair so beautifully.'

*Friday, 24th March*

Stuart told me what he considers the worst thing ever said of anyone: John Betjeman's description of Charles Fry as 'a phallus with a business sense'.

After dinner the sirens went. The guns sounded very distant, so borrowing Stuart's American steel helmet I decided to walk home from Tyburnia. While in Hyde Park and before I reached the Serpentine, the guns beside me opened up cruelly. I put on the steel helmet and cowered under a tree. As there was no building to shelter in I decided it was safer to stay under the tree branches, which might break the fall of the shrapnel raining down like hailstones. I heard it crackling through the leaves and thudding on the grass. On the road it struck sparks as it fell. There was a continuous thunder for three-quarters of an hour. Occasionally I heard German planes diving. But there were no fires, and I heard no bombs.

*Sunday, 26th March*

Breakfasted at Brooks's and rang up Clementine Beit who said, 'Yes, do bring the Sergeant', thinking I meant any old sergeant, a driver perhaps, and asked, 'Does he eat at our end of the house, or the other?' I told Stuart this, and he was not amused.

Today has been wonderful. Bright warm sun; the earth dry and brown for there has been no rain. This augurs ill for the summer, perhaps well for this horrifying impending invasion [D-Day]. I drove Stuart to Hughenden. Mrs Langley-Taylor received us in the new wing built forty years ago by Coningsby Disraeli, Dizzy's nephew and heir.* I recall being brought here in about 1930 from Oxford, and being received by Coningsby Disraeli in the library. He was wearing a dusty velvet skull cap and, if I remember right, a blue velvet jacket and string bow tie. The main part of the house is at present used by the RAF for target-spotting, and cannot be entered. Mrs Langley-Taylor told me that after the war nearly every room will be furnished for show, and that Major Abbey when he bought the property also bought the Disraeli contents. Hughenden will make a splendid and interesting National Trust property for three reasons – its historic associations, its mid Victorian architecture and furnishing, and its amenity on the outskirts of horrid High Wycombe. The park is beautiful and well maintained. Some fine trees, and the garden laid out in Victorian parterres with plenty of terracotta urns and insipid statuary of cherubs and angels, now put away, which Queen Mary called 'sugar babies' when she visited the place. I was delighted with Hughenden. It is deliciously hideous. Disraeli stripped it of its white stucco, revealed the red brick, and added the ugly window surrounds and crenellations. Mrs Langley-Taylor showed us Disraeli's bedroom, which is now her own. She says Lady Desborough remembers being patted on the head by Disraeli here, and being repelled by his greasy black curls.

---

* Major Coningsby Disraeli (1867–1936); nephew of Benjamin Disraeli (1804–81; Conservative Prime Minister 1868, 1874–80; cr. Earl of Beaconsfield, 1876). Hughenden, then owned by a trust established by the philanthropist W. H. Abbey, became a N.T. property in 1946.

After luncheon, we all lay in the sun in a field and talked. The Sergeant was a great success with the Beits.

*Thursday, 30th March*

Started off in the N.T. car at 10 o'clock for Gloucestershire and drove without a break to Nether Lypiatt Manor, near Stroud, to lunch at this wonderful little house with Mrs Gordon Woodhouse.* There were Mr Woodhouse, a little, dull old man with a flabby hand, genial Lord Barrington† with hairs growing out of his cheeks and ears, and homespun Miss Walker, daughter of Sir Emery,‡ the friend of William Morris. The house is perched high on a hill, overlooking a built-up village. It is compact and tall, with two flanking wings, one new so as to balance the other old one. It is unspoilt late seventeenth-century, and perfect in every way. In fact an ideal, if not *the* ideal small country house. It retains all its wainscoting, doors with high brass handles and locks, one lovely chimneypiece in the hall, of white stone against a ground of blue slate. The rich staircase has three twisted balusters to each tread. There is much good furniture, and several Barrington family portraits. The forecourt enclosure with stone piers and balls, the contemporary wrought-iron gates, and the Cotswold stable block complete the dependencies.

Mrs Woodhouse was wearing a kind of black satin bonnet, not becoming, and a black knitted dress. Luncheon consisted of one egg in a jacketed potato. The boiler having just burst the household was in a state of perturbation. There is one servant. It is a curious colony. After luncheon, Mrs Woodhouse and Lord Barrington took me round the house, and he took me round the

---

* Violet Gwynne (1870–1948); harpsichordist, whom J.L.-M. had heard play in London on 3 February 1944 (*Prophesying Peace*); m. 1895 Gordon Woodhouse. As revealed in a biography by her great-niece Jessica Douglas-Home (1996), she lived with four men (her husband probably being the one with whom she had the least sexual relations), as well as having lesbian associations.

† William, 10th Viscount Barrington (1873–1960); one of the men in Mrs Woodhouse's life.

‡ Fine printer (1851–1933), whose daughter Dorothy was Mrs Woodhouse's friend.

garden, which is enchanting, with modern yew walks and a flourishing young lime avenue, the trees planted closely together. There is an obelisk to the horse of the builder of the house who 'served his master good and true, and died at the age of forty-two'.

I went on to Woodchester Priory, arriving at tea time. But no tea because my host, bluff ex-naval commander Bruce Metcalfe, was conducting a small unit of American soldiers, lecturing them good-humouredly but bombastically, and boasting of English customs in a manner which I found condescending and embarrassing; but not they, it seemed. I did not take to him at first – and did later, as usual. I wondered how I was going to stick this visit until the following morning. The Commander and his wife live in this by no means small house with absolutely no servants at all. It is an H-shaped Tudor building with pointed gables, and was spoilt in the last century by insertions of plate glass, and the addition of a French-style tower. We had dinner in the kitchen. Mrs M. benignant, jolly, friendly.

I find that I take an hour or two to adjust myself to different sorts of people. Going as I do from the sophisticated to the simple, the rich to the poor, the clever to the stupid, I get bewildered. But in the end I usually manage to adapt myself. Which means of course that I am a chameleon, with little or no personality of my own. I assume the qualities of others. I am a mirror of other people's moods, opinions and prejudices. But I am pernickety, and would not doss down in anybody's bed just for a crust or a new pair of shoes.

*Wednesday, 5th April*

Walking past Buckingham Palace I looked at it critically for the first time. What a heavy, uninspired, lumpish elevation! The Corinthian pilasters are too small for the heavy entablature; the columns in the centrepiece ought to be disengaged. As for the circular basin of the Victoria Memorial, it is not too bad, and the bas-reliefs are good. But the black Michelangelesque figures are far too large and out of scale with the monument.

*Saturday, 15th April*

I caught the 1.15 to Reading where Gerry Wellington met me at the station in his small car, for he gets twenty gallons a month for being a duke. Arriving at the entrance to Stratfield Saye park we stopped at the first Duke's* great polished granite pillar, with his image by Marochetti† standing on the top. It is carefully executed, and the huge blocks of granite are finely cut. Stopped again at the 1750 church, of Greek cruciform. A Wellington monument by Flaxman,‡ and another by Boehm.§ The great galleried family pew in which the Iron Duke worshipped was swept away by an ignorant vicar just before Gerry succeeded, greatly to his annoyance, for he had been looking forward to worshipping in it.

The western view of Stratfield Saye house clearly shows it to date from Charles I's reign. The original red brick was covered with a dull compo rendering in the eighteenth century, which is a pity. Odd pilasters resting on nothing appear upon the first storey in typical Charles I non-style. The house is low-lying, unpretentious, having been built, as an early guide book puts it, 'for convenience rather than for parade', by the Rivers family. They made alterations in the 1740s and added a wing in the 1790s. Benjamin Wyatt¶ carried out work for the first Duke, and added the porch and conservatory. The east front is not so regular as the west, and the terraces are deformed by messy Edwardian flower beds. Gerry, who hates flowers, will soon have them away. The pleasure grounds contain fine specimens of every tree, hard wood and soft. Under a tree is Copenhagen's gravestone.** The heavy gilded state coach in the coach-house is in splendid condition.

---

* 'The Great Duke' (1769–1852).

† Baron Carlo Marochetti (1805–67); Italian sculptor settled in London after 1848.

‡ John Flaxman (1755–1826); sculptor.

§ Sir Joseph Boehm, Bt (1834–90); Austrian-born sculptor, best known for effigy of Queen Victoria on coinage from 1887.

¶ Benjamin Dean Wyatt (1775–1855); architect; grandson of Benjamin Wyatt of Staffordshire and son of James Wyatt (1746–1813).

** Copenhagen was the horse the Great Duke rode at Waterloo.

Having eaten little luncheon I was famished, but tea consisted of only a few of the thinnest slices of bread and butter imaginable. After tea we did a tour of the inside of the house, beginning with the hall. When my stomach started to rumble with hunger Gerry looked at it with a reproachful air, and said nothing. It went on making the most awful noise like a horse's. The hall has a gallery along the wall opposite the entrance. The open balusters were boxed in so as to prevent the servants being seen from below by the visitors. Gerry's mother used to say that nothing of them was visible except their behinds, as they crouched and bobbed across the gallery. There are some pictures so huge than they can only hang sloping. In the flagged floor are inset two large mosaic pavements from Silchester. The whole hall is painted nineteenth-century brown and the walls are hung with very faded red flock paper. Against the columns of the gallery are plinths supporting white marble busts of Pitt, the Russian Czars, Walter Scott and the Great Duke.

The Gallery is long and low – 'matey', Gerry calls it – the walls covered with prints pasted upon a ground of gold leaf. Rather attractive, but G. wishes to cover these walls with damask, without however injuring the prints but so as to allow room for family portraits, for elsewhere there is singularly little space. At either end of the Gallery are brown painted columns, forming screens. The ceilings are covered with Edwardian lodging-house lincrusta. To the north is a small room with niches. The walls are hung with a delightful, flowery, 1850 gold and cream paper. In front of the fireplace is a special device of the Great Duke, namely a curious brass rail, with rings for curtains, to keep off excessive heat. The drawing-room has a Rococo ceiling, and some Boulle cabinets and commodes by Levasseur and pictures acquired by the first Duke. The dining-room is shut up, all the Apsley House pictures being stored there for the war, and valued at a million pounds, so G. says. The library is of Lord Burlington date. In it are the Duke's library chairs as seen in the conversation piece by Thorburn of this room, hanging in the Small Cabinet Room. Beyond it a billiard table and Regency lights for colza oil, very pretty, and beyond again the Great Duke's private rooms and his original bath. These rooms G. is going to make his own. The bath is very deep and satisfactory. A curious feature of this house is the water-closets in each room, put there by the Great Duke inside great 1840-ish cupboards of maplewood.

After tea Gerry took a rod, and fished in the lake for perch with a minnow, but caught nothing. He cast with much ease and abandon. When I tried, I made rather a fool of myself. After dinner, at which there were no drinks except beer, he showed me his grandfather's collection of gems and intaglios, mounted on long, gold chains. When held against the oil lights, some of the stones were very beautiful. G. is very fussy over the key bunches, everything being carefully locked up. He has a butler, cook and two housemaids, and a secretary, Miss Jones. The last has meals with him during the week, and nearly drives him mad with her archness. 'Aren't you naughty today?' she says. She is unable to type, so when he wishes to dispatch a letter not written by himself, he types it and gives it to her to sign.

*Saturday, 22nd April*

Walked from Oxford station to the Harrods'* house in St Aldate's. Dear Billa rushed down the stairs and we embraced on the doorstep. She said I had not seen her since 1938. I can't think why not, and this visit has reminded me how very devoted to her I am. We started with a large glass of sherry. Then Roy joined us. He is quiet, and has attentive good manners. If I knew him better I might like him much. He soon left for some college function, and Billa and I dined alone, deliciously, with the candles lit, though it was full daylight and the sun shining. We gossiped in great content.

---

* (Sir) Roy Harrod (1900–78); Fellow in Economics at Christ Church, Oxford; m. 1938 Wilhelmine ('Billa') Cresswell (1911–2005), whom J.L.-M. had befriended during the 1930s, when she had been a close friend of John Betjeman and worked for the Georgian Group.

*Sunday, 23rd April*

After breakfast in bed I went to Mass next door, in Bishop King's Palace where Ronnie Knox* used to be priest. It being the first Sunday of term, the chapel was packed. After Mass we walked to Christ Church garden. The garden was a dream, and we sat on a seat like an elderly married couple, while the two Harrod children played. The elder boy is handsome, with jet black hair like Billa's, and the longest black eyelashes I have seen. The younger boy has a squint, and wears an eye-shade.† At luncheon we ate enormously, with the result that I felt languid for the remainder of the afternoon. We walked around the university, looking first at the naked Shelley memorial [University College], to which Billa is devoted. I am not sure that Shelley ought to be commemorated with a great body and that drooping penis, for one does not associate the too ethereal poet with the gross flesh. And this beautiful figure, although far from gross, is physically alluring. Then we strolled through my old college, Magdalen, where the quadrangular cloisters have been renewed, stone by stone, and did the round of Addison's Walk. The meadows were covered with fritillaries.

At 7 Roy took me to dine in Christ Church Hall, at the high table. By the time we sat down most of the undergraduates had finished their dinner and gone. Roy says that today they all eat in Hall, are all serious, and impecunious. There is none of the plutocratic gaiety of the old days. He thinks there never will be again, for the state subsidises undergraduates now. I sat next to Roy and the Dean, and opposite Dundas.‡ We had a very full and heavy dinner, with strong red wine. When it was over, the Dean rose. We all followed him, carrying our napkins according to custom, down a circular staircase, to the Common Room where the port was freely circulated round the table. I sat next to David

---

* Monsignor Ronald Knox (1888–1957); Catholic convert and theologian; Catholic Chaplain to Oxford University, 1926–39.

† Dominick Harrod (b. 1940); future Economics Editor of BBC.

‡ Robert Hamilton Dundas (1884–1960); student and tutor of Christ Church, 1910–57.

Cecil.* It is difficult to reconcile his Dresden china appearance with his ever-accelerating loquacity, twinkling of eyes, twisting of long fingers, and loose-limbed jerkiness. I felt like a slow-witted bull beside him. He talked of Hatfield and the state kept there when he was a child; also of the terrifying intellectual level of the conversation, and the devotional atmosphere. Roy talked about the declining population. Now he is talking rot, I thought to myself, though did not say so.

Billa very funny when we got back. She said that breeding was hell, and Roy must not suppose she was going to do any more. Talking of pederasty, Roy said that the late King George V, when told of Lord Beauchamp's trouble,† exclaimed, 'I thought people like that shot themselves.' 'Heavens,' said Billa, 'I hope the poor darlings won't start doing that. It would be like living through a permanent air raid.'

*Thursday, 4th May*

Martineau‡ and I lunched at the Hyde Park Hotel with Lord Braybrooke,§ who has recently succeeded two cousins (killed on active service), inheriting the title and Audley End [House, Essex]. He is a bald, common-sensical, very nice business man of 45, embarrassed by his inheritance. At his wits' end what to do with Audley End. Who wouldn't be? It was arranged that Martineau and I would visit the house with him in June. It is requisitioned by the Army and used for highly secret purposes, so that even he is not allowed into the rooms except in the company of a senior officer. Consequently he hardly knows the way round his own house. Two lots of death duties have had to be paid on the estate. When the

---

* Lord David Cecil (1902–86), yr son of 4th Marquess of Salisbury; writer and historian.

† William Lygon, 7th Earl Beauchamp (1872–1938), Liberal statesman and grandee, was obliged to resign his offices and go abroad in 1931 after accusations of homosexual practices were levelled against him by his brother-in-law 'Bendor', 2nd Duke of Westminster.

‡ Anthony Martineau, N.T. solicitor.

§ Henry Seymour Neville, 6th Baron Braybrooke (1897–1990).

present lord was only 21 he was heir presumptive. Since then however he never expected to be in the running again.

*Saturday, 6th May*

Lunched with Eddy, who was in spanking form. He spied across the room a young officer, tanned darkest brown and wearing a kilt. He was sitting opposite me. Eddy made me change places before I realised his intention. Having reseated himself he said, 'You had better put your spectacles on.' I said, 'That's a bit late in the day in view of your extraordinary behaviour.'

Geoffrey Houghton Brown called at 2.30 and we walked in Regent's Park. The walk was spoilt by the bitter cold and my new shoes, which cost me £6 10*s.* and are agony. We searched for Decimus Burton* buildings. Clarence Terrace, Cornwall Terrace and Holme Villa are his. These terraces have suffered grievously from the raids. Large pieces of plaster have flaked off and the shoddiness of Nash's methods is revealed. I said to Geoffrey I often wondered if an objective person like the Pope thought the English deserved to win this war; and I was pretty certain that, as it had dragged on so long, it would not matter in fifty years' time who had won it.

*Saturday, 13th May*

Marshall Sisson† and I reached Swanton Morley [Norfolk] a little after 2.30. Found Colonel Jack Leslie with old Mr Bullard, a brewer, the local rector and others. The purpose of this visit is very strange. Colonel Leslie had given a plot of land in the village, on which it was supposed once stood the cottage lived in by the ancestors of Abraham Lincoln, and demolished fifty years ago. With great ceremony Lord Zetland received the deeds from Ambassador Winant in February.‡ Several plans were considered for a memorial on the site, one of which was a replica of the demolished cottage. With all this

* Architect in the classical style (1800–81).

† SPAB architect, who took over W. A. Forsyth's work for the N.T.

‡ Episode described in *Prophesying Peace*, 12 February 1944.

sentiment I disagreed from the first. Sisson, who was sent on our behalf to investigate the site soon after the gift was declared inalienable, suspected that it was the wrong one. By comparing a seventeenth-century map recording Lincoln land with an up-to-date twenty-five-inch Ordnance [Survey map], his suspicions were confirmed. Finally Leslie and other local enthusiasts admitted that a mistake had in all innocence been made. It transpires that two-thirds of the old Lincoln house does indisputably exist in the present Angel Inn, belonging to Bullard. There is even a small sketch of it on the old map. Bullard is prepared to give us a strip of freehold at the back of the inn. It is important that eventually we should acquire the inn itself, which he won't surrender. Why should he? It retains a magnificent central cluster of octagonal brick chimneys and several beams with original moulds and stops. All the Lincoln fields marked on the seventeenth-century map survive today, with the same demarcations and hedge boundaries; even the lanes and the ponds are the same. The Trust is left with a useless plot of land, an old chicken run of no beauty and less historic interest which it can never get rid of except by a special Act of Parliament.

*Wednesday, 17th May*

The three Pope-Hennessys have great family pride and are very united. Dame Una said to me, 'Can't you write a book and join us?' I thought, even if I could write a book I would not be permitted to join them, however much I might want to. Speaking of Lord Hartington's marriage* they all declared it was a mistake to marry out of one's station, that people like us should not marry dukes and dukes' daughters, it was shocking. The Dame said, 'The Kennedy girl will never be able to take her place.' I could see Jamesey was amused.

---

* William Cavendish, Marquess of Hartington (1917–44); er s. and heir of 10th Duke of Devonshire; m. 6 May 1944 Kathleen ('Kick') Kennedy, daughter of former US Ambassador to London Joseph P. Kennedy (who opposed the union on account of the difference in religion); killed on active service, 10 September 1944 (his widow dying four years later in an air crash).

*Thursday, 18th May*

Took the 4 o'clock train to Lincolnshire and reached Gunby Hall in time for dinner. The old Field Marshal gave me a warm welcome. He loves to talk about Gunby, its history and problems. He and Lady Massingberd are true county squirearchy, with a high sense of public duty towards the estate and the neighbourhood. They live in easy austerity, no wine, but good solid food, and enough of it. They have a butler, his wife the cook, a pantry boy, two housemaids, a chauffeur, and lead a feudal existence on a modest scale.

*Friday, 19th May*

In the afternoon I walked around the Gunby estate with the Field Marshal. After dinner he talked about Churchill. Said that he must have learnt much from his study of Marlborough, for Marlborough also had remarkable contacts with crowned heads and leaders of countries when he dashed around Europe. The Field Marshal said that he and Weygand and Pétain were the sole survivors of the Council of the Allies held in 1918 when the fortunes of the Allies were at their lowest ebb. Churchill, then Minister of Munitions, came over to France and asked what he could most usefully do to help. The F.M. said, 'Keep an eye on Pétain. I suspect that he may let us down.'

*Wednesday, 24th May*

After a Georgian Group meeting Puss Milnes-Gaskell lunched with me. She was looking sad. She said that Fitzroy Maclean* was to have travelled in the same aeroplane as her son, Charles, which crashed, but that circumstances made him too late, and he had to take the next. I asked her whether Queen Mary would accept the

* Diplomatist, soldier, writer and politician (1911–96; cr. Bt, 1957); Conservative MP for Lancaster; recently chosen by Churchill to lead a British mission to Tito's partisans in Yugoslavia.

Presidency if asked, and she seemed to think she might, and would not be too adversely influenced by Lord Harewood.* So I have written to Lord Zetland. I would like Queen Mary to become President of the National Trust, because she is the only member of the Royal Family interested in such things. Puss told me she was in Partridge's shop with the Queen. Partridge showed them a bed cover of seventeenth-century crewel work, which Puss recognised as having come from her old home. Mr Partridge begged her to accept the bed cover as a present. Puss resolutely protested until Queen Mary turned on her, and said, 'Constance, never refuse a firm offer. I never do.' Thereupon Puss had to accept.

*Tuesday, 30th May*

Had a great shock this morning, for the Gas Company telephoned to say my cheque to them had bounced. I rang up the bank at Evesham who were sorry and said I was £200 overdrawn. I am terrified lest other cheques may be returned. I wrote to my father in desperation and shame. Now he has always implied, like George V about buggers, that men shoot themselves for such a disgrace. As for the other offence I dread to think what he supposes they should do; slowly roast themselves on a spit, I dare say. Oh Lord, he will be furious.

*June witnessed two dramas – 'D-Day', the long-awaited Allied invasion of Europe; and the launch against southern England of the 'V-1' flying bombs or 'doodlebugs', the Germans' long-heralded 'secret weapon'.*

---

* Henry Lascelles, 6th Earl of Harewood (1882–1947); m. 1922 HRH Princess Mary, only dau. of King George V and Queen Mary. The Princess had originally been invited to assume the presidency, but her husband had refused on her behalf in a blimpish letter denouncing the N.T. as sinister and socialistic (see Jennifer Jenkins and Patrick James, *From Acorn to Oak Tree* [1994], pp. 123–4).

*Thursday, 1st June*

At 6 I called for Loelia Westminster and took her to Wilton's, where we met Ann and Esmond Rothermere,* and ate dressed crab and drank sherry and white wine, as a preliminary to a charity film, *This Happy Breed* by Noël Coward, a kind of continuation of *Cavalcade*. It was in colour, and quite horribly and insidiously sentimental, so that I had constant lumps in my throat and wanted to cry, while realising all the time that my lowest emotions were being played upon. Loelia had paid I don't know how many guineas for each seat. At Ciro's afterwards they were talking of a party the other night that cost £75, and how disgraceful it was of someone or other only to have contributed £10. So I quickly thought I would not even make a gesture of contributing to this entertainment, for had I proffered £5 it would have been accepted as though it were 5*d*. None the less I felt rather uncomfortable. But they are all so vastly rich, and I am so rat-poor.

Lord Rothermere is very tall, with a mouth like a cupid's. He seems to think the Invasion will be a walk-over, 'for the Germans cannot stand much more of a licking'.

*Saturday, 3rd June*

Went to Dickie Girouard's† Nuptial Mass at Spanish Place. It was solemn and moving, and lasted one hour and a quarter. Billa Harrod was sitting in front of me. We went together to the Dorchester reception given by the bride's mother. We found Nancy there and the three of us tucked into chicken mousse and tongue, washed down with cider cup. Then chocolate, and the cocktails we had not been offered before. Billa could not restrain her greed, and ate and ate. Nancy says Peter Rodd [her husband] tells her the invading troops are penned up like prisoners in

* Esmond Harmsworth, 2nd Viscount Rothermere (1898–1978); chairman of Associated Newspapers, 1932–71; m. (2nd) 1945–52 Ann *née* Charteris, widow of 3rd Baron O'Neill.

† Richard Désiré ('Dick') Girouard (1905–89); stockbroker, member of Georgian Group; m. (2nd) 1944–5 Beatrice Grosvenor.

barbed-wire enclosures awaiting the signal; that Peter actually knows which beaches they are to land on. He keeps appearing and disappearing, stressing how frightened he is because he has already participated in two invasions, saying good-bye for ever and warning Nancy that a widow's pension is very small.

*Tuesday, 6th June*

Miss P. woke me early at 7.30 and we breakfasted soon after 8. Consequently she missed the 8 o'clock news in her bedroom to which she usually listens. I left for the 9.30 at King's Cross, bought a paper and read of the capture of Rome without destruction, which was cheering. Hubert Smith* met me at Grantham at 11.55. It was bitterly cold. He asked me if I knew anything about the Invasion. Had it begun? He said the 8 o'clock news intimated that it had. I was filled with mingled emotions, apprehension over the outcome, anxiety for my friends, regret and guilt that I was not participating, relief that I was not.

Hubert Smith drove me to Grantham House, where we were received by the two Miss Sedgwicks, old women of the churchy, godly sort. They are very north country, abrupt and spinsterish. My visit was a waste of time. Their wireless would not work, so we heard no news at 1 o'clock. Had a rhubarby luncheon, rather nasty. Miss Marion left for a funeral, and Miss Winifred took us to look at the property the other side of the river. It rained and was depressing. Never before have I been so conscious of the fatuity of my work, fiddling while Rome burns – though, thank God, the actual Rome is spared. After tea and a rock cake at 3 we left.

A long, straight drive of a mile brought us to Harlaxton Manor. The butler at the lodge said he dared not show us the house without a written letter from Mrs Van der Elst.† I hadn't got one, I explained, but the agent said I might see over. The butler accompanied us to

* Chief Agent of National Trust.

† Violet Dodge (1882–1966); m. Jean Van der Elst; eccentric rich socialist and crusader against capital punishment; purchased Harlaxton estate, where she banned blood sports and created a wildlife sanctuary, 1937.

the back premises and telephoned to London. Meanwhile Hubert and I looked over the outside. The date 1837 is carved on the parapet of the porch. The stone of which the house is built is a beautiful bronze yellow, rather like Stanway's. The design is meant to put one in mind of Burghley. The pavilions and gate piers of the forecourt are as Baroque as Vanbrugh. Mrs Van der Elst has made ghastly insipid white marble statues peer from bushes and sit on pinnacles. Mrs Van der Elst has suggested that we should sell Harlaxton for her, and with the proceeds endow Audley End, which she will rent. The butler finally reappeared, having spoken to Mrs Van der Elst. She refused categorically to let us set foot inside the premises. I was made extremely angry by this treatment.

Just before Oxford we saw about a hundred aeroplanes towing gliders, evidently returned from France. All day I have felt excited and longed to have news.

*Friday, 9th June*

This morning I trained to Leatherhead with Christopher Gibbs and his wife Peggy. They have grown to look exactly like one another – an infallible indication of a happy marriage. We lunched at Christopher's parents' house, Goddards, one of Lutyens' earliest domestic buildings, full of oak timbers and ingle nooks. Although I can see how well designed and well executed every detail is, nevertheless I do not care for a contrived 'olde worlde' flavour. We continued to Leith Hill Place where Ralph Vaughan Williams* was waiting for us. This house is fairly small, and was built about 1730 for a General Foliot. It has two flanking wings with pedimented gables, very wide and Kent-like. Inside there is not much decoration, apart from a decent feature or two. The composer showed us what had been his nursery and his bedroom when he was a boy. He wants the house to be used as an institution, which is a pity, because it is just the sort of house that would let privately. There is a large walled

* Ralph Vaughan Williams (1872–1958); composer, who had approached J.L.-M. the previous month about donating Leith Hill Place, Surrey, which he had just inherited from his brother.

garden, with trees, shrubs and an azalea walk, which is lovely. Unfortunately the property is destitute, offered without endowment.

The composer is a very sweet man, with an impressive appearance. He is big and broad and has a large head with sharply defined features, and eyes that look far into the distance. He has shaggy white hair which is not long. Slender hands and fingers with square-ended or rather bitten nails. He is very courteous and when it began to rain in the garden, offered to return to the house to fetch my Burberry. I had some difficulty preventing him. He is longing to disembarrass himself of responsibility for the estate. When asked by Christopher to resolve some estate matter, he replied, 'We will let things continue as before, for the present.' He told me that when young musicians came to him for advice he always discouraged them, for those who seriously intended to make music their career would always do so willy-nilly. He has a quiet, dry humour which expresses itself in very few words. He laughs in a low key.

*Friday, 16th June*

I lunched with Philip Frere,* who is working in the Ministry of Aircraft Production. He told me that last night 140 pilotless planes came over. They are guided by radio and when they land, their bomb of 2,000 lb explodes. This is like an H. G. Wells story. It is almost inconceivable. Some of these things have landed in Surrey, some around and in London, doing great mischief.

*Saturday, 17th June*

Worked in Brooks's library this afternoon. I am always happy in this stuffy, dingy Victorian library, in which the silence is accentuated by the relentless ticking of the old, stuffy clock. I love the old stuffy books on the stuffy brown shelves, books which nobody reads except Eddie Marsh, and he falls fast asleep over them. The very atmosphere is calculated to send one asleep, but into the gentlest, most happy, nostalgic dreams of nineteenth-century stability, self-satisfaction and

* Aesthete and peacetime solicitor, with a passion for genealogy (1897–1981).

promise of an eternity of heavenly stuffiness, world without end. How much I adore this library, and club, nobody knows. May it survive Hitler, Stalin and all the beastliness which besets us.

I had to return to prepare tea for Nancy in Cheyne Walk. When we had begun Stuart walked in. Talk was of little else but the pilotless planes. They came over again all evening. We kept rushing to the window to look for them, but were always disappointed. I have only seen plumes of smoke across the river where they have landed. I believe they are hardly ever shot on the wing either by our fighters or our anti-aircraft guns. Nancy cracked very bad-taste jokes about them, implying that she welcomed them as a hilarious diversion during these dull days.

Nancy agreed to dine with James and me. When she and I were outside Bridget [Parsons]'s flat in Mount Street, suddenly Michael Rosse in battledress and wearing a beret approached us round a corner. He had unexpectedly come up from Wanstead with his brigadier for an hour and a half. The whole Guards Division is there, and have not yet gone to France. They wait, like caged swans, for the north wind to drop before they can sail. We accompanied him to Bridget's flat. I talked to him while he had a bath. He said that in a few days' time a huge offensive would be launched, but that unless things went very wrong, his company would not be in it. He wants Bridget to tell Anne this, for he dares not do so on the telephone, and letters are censored.

We met Jamesey outside Rules, which was shut. So we dined at Simpson's, Nancy dashing to the window whenever we heard a rocket. She made us laugh a lot. Told a story about a tart in Curzon Street who, when asked how the war was treating her, replied that for a reserved occupation, £700 a week tax free, plus emoluments from the Government for reporting the indiscretions of her soldier clients, was so satisfactory that she only wished she could open a second front.

*Sunday, 18th June*

At Mass at 11 there was a great noise of gunfire and a rocket. In the afternoon Stuart walked in and said that a rocket had landed on the Guards' Chapel during service this morning, totally demolishing it and killing enormous numbers of Guards officers and men. Now this did shake me. After dining at the Churchill Club we walked through Queen Anne's Gate, where a lot of windows with the old crinkly blown glass panes have been broken. In St James's Park crowds of people were looking at the Guards' Chapel across Birdcage Walk, now roped off. I could see nothing but gaunt walls standing, and gaping windows. No roof at all. While I watched four stretcher-bearers carried a body under a blanket, a siren went, and everyone scattered. I felt suddenly sick. Then a rage of fury against the war welled inside me. For sheer damnable devilry what could be worse than this terrible instrument?

I left Stuart in St James's Park underground, and walked to Victoria. On getting out of the bus in Beaufort Street I saw and heard my first rocket. It was rushing overhead at great speed northwards. Half an hour ago, while writing this, I heard another, and saw one out of my west window, like a dagger with a flaming beacon at its tail. Then the engine cut off, and I watched it dive over the World's End. In a second the windows rattled, and a thin plume of smoke rose to the sky. There was a faint, distant sound of wailing. Dame Una tells me that today they have destroyed Tyburn Convent [Bayswater] and the Charing Cross Bridge.

*Tuesday, 20th June*

Another fearful night. Nothing dropped in Chelsea that I know of, but before midnight one just across the river made a hideous clatter, and the house shook like a jelly. The guns have ceased firing now because they merely bring the rockets down – when they hit them – to explode in the streets, just as they do if they fall of their own accord, which is sometimes in open counry. Whereas previously I cursed the guns for the noise they made throughout the night, now without them I find I am more frightened. Instead I lie awake for hours, my ears waiting for the sound of rocket planes. Here in Cheyne Walk we have distant trams, trains, motor vehicles and river traffic which one mistakes at first for a plane.

*Monday, 26th June*

At midnight the siren went, and I put on my boots and watched the flying bombs from the Embankment. Because of clouds the beacons from their tails lit up the sky in a weird, uncanny manner. A number came over. I went to bed soon after 1 a.m., and fell asleep. At 2.30 I was woken abruptly by the most terrific concussion, sat up in bed, and heard a cascade of glass, plaster and broken woodwork. But the house stood up. I was intensely alarmed, and went down to Miss P., now sleeping in the disused dining-room. I did not know whether I should find her alive or dead, since not a sound came from her direction. She had been awake, heard the plane approaching and covered her head with a pillow, which with the rest of the bed was strewn with fragments of broken glass. A tiny muffled voice came from under the bedclothes. I said, 'Don't move an inch until I can see what's happened.' My feet were crunching glass on the floor. I found the torch. Her bed looked as if buried under a snow drift. I removed the glass as carefully as I could and disinterred her. She was not even scratched. Neither of us was hurt a bit. The bomb had fallen in the river opposite Turner's house, which had already been blitzed, 100 yards from us. We walked into the kitchen, and even in the dim light could see the air filled with clouds of dust. A cupboard had burst open and disclosed a chimney belching a heap of soot. The only window in the house not broken was my bedroom one. My big room was inundated with glass fragments, which had shot across the room through the blinds and curtains, which were cut to ribbons. None of the furniture or objects was broken. All rugs inundated with soot and muck. The back door was blown across the passage. Window casements and wooden surrounds torn out, and the poor little house terribly shaken. Oddly enough this bomb killed no one.

*Saturday, 1st July*

All afternoon, planes came over. For the first time I am feeling a bit despondent and dispirited. Miss P., having tidied the house up a bit, left for the country. The workmen are still in the house, and the head workman was almost as drunk as I was last night.

At six I met James at King's Bench Walk, and we tubed to Aldgate East. We walked down the Commercial Road to the river. God, the squalor, the desolation and the dreariness of the East End! Poor inhabitants. We passed one beautiful church, burnt out, which I thought must be by Vanbrugh. J. identified it from his pocket guide-book as St George's-in-the-East, by Hawksmoor. We were smartly dressed underneath, but wore over our suits dirty old Burberries buttoned up to the chin. Went into a pub for a drink, and a robot came over, nearer and nearer, exploding a few yards away. The pub keeper turned us out and shut the door, saying he had had enough for one day. We wandered through Wapping, to Wapping Old Stairs where Judge Jeffreys was captured trying to escape to France dressed as a sailor. Then to the Prospect of Whitby on the water, with its rickety galleries built over the river on piles. Found Philip Toynbee* there with a pretty little girl, a Communist. We sat together on the gallery drinking beer and eating sandwiches, watching large boats struggle up the river, pirouette in front of us, and retreat into the docks. From here Jamesey saw his first robot. It scurried through the clouds at a great rate, and seemed to be circling and not going straight. By 9.30 the inn was full, and a piano and clarinet were playing hot music. Women sang into a harsh microphone, sailors stamped, and peroxide blondes and the worst characters in London danced like dervishes, sang and swilled gallons of beer. It was a strange, gay, operatic scene. J., who was looking forward to meeting his romance of two nights ago, was bitterly put out when the romance turned his back on him and was frankly rude. Philip said he did not know life yet, for the masses were incorrigibly fickle and perfidious.

---

* Writer and journalist of Communist sympathies (1916–81); m. 1939–50 Anne Powell.

*Sunday, 9th July*

I arrived at B. House at 1.30 in time for luncheon. When I told Stuart where I was going, he laughed and said, 'Lord — has the worst reputation in the world. His taste is Lascars.' Well, I thought, then I am all right. He is a natty, foxy little man with blue eyes and a boyish figure and boyish hair cut, though well over 60. A young American with a baby face was staying. He disappeared after luncheon. Lord — took me round the grounds and then round the house which has thirty-six bedrooms. In one we came upon Baby Face fast asleep in an enormous bed, just a turned-up nose projecting over the top sheet. In every room a delicious smell of rose water, or furniture polish, I was not sure which, mixed with that sweet mustiness of calf-bound books. Lord — inherited B. from his mother who lived here until her death. She had no commerce with her children, and would not see a soul. She never left the house. She slept all day, and prowled around the house by night. I was bound to tell my host that I much doubted the Trust being able to help him. He was very nice about it. I left before tea.*

*Saturday, 15th July*

At 9.30 Stuart walked in [to the dining-room at Brooks's]. He said, 'Well, I go tomorrow. I have come to say good-bye. It was in this room that we met in 1938.' There was little to say, and what I did

* The anonymous peer sounds very like the millionaire Labour politician and notorious homosexual rake Gavin Henderson, 2nd Baron Faringdon (1902–77). He owned Buscot Park in Oxfordshire, which he donated to the N.T. in 1949; his mother, Lady Violet Henderson, owned Barnsley Park in Gloucestershire. However, Faringdon was only in his early forties at this time, his mother was still alive, and she eventually left her house to her younger son. Possibly J.L.-M. altered details in order to preserve the anonymity of Faringdon, who died the year this entry was published. On 20 December 1946, J.L.-M. visited Buscot and met Faringdon, who had 'a youngish, ogling, rather raddled American staying, or perhaps living with him' (*Caves of Ice*). Meeting him again years later, on 6 January 1974, after he had been rendered 'harmless' by a stroke, J.L.-M. recalled his 'lithe, panther movements', 'cat-like eyes', and 'dangerous, evil and malevolent' personality (*Ancient as the Hills*).

say was fatuous. 'Yes, I was sitting in that chair by the door.' 'No,' he said, 'you were standing against the fireplace.'

*Sunday, 16th July*

Nancy told me that her upbringing had taught her never to show what she felt. I thought how lamentably my upbringing had failed in this respect, and how too perfectly in her case, for there is a vein of callousness in her which almost amounts to cruelty. All Mitfords seem to have it, even Tom,* who has never directed it at me, though I have seen him turn it upon others, and have blanched at the spectacle.

*Tuesday, 18th July*

On walking past the Ritz I heard Nancy give a cry, and there she was with Tom, back from the Mediterranean after two-and-a-half years' absence. He almost embraced me in the street, saying, 'My dear old friend, my very dearest and oldest friend', which was most affecting. He looks younger than his age, is rather thin, and still extremely handsome. We went up to his suite in the Ritz – how civilised and pretty after the modern jazz of the Dorchester. There he telephoned Harold Acton† and Bridget [Parsons], bidding them to dine this evening, rather cross with me because I simply would not cut the Girouards' dinner party.

*Wednesday, 16th August*

Near Devizes, we [J.L.-M. and Eardley Knollys] were slowed up by a troop of German prisoners. We felt ghoulish staring at them. They stared at us just as hard, but with impassive, expressionless faces. They showed no sign of either chagrin or relief, poor brutes. First

---

* Hon. Thomas Mitford (1909–45); only brother of Mitford sisters, whom J.L.-M. had loved at Eton.

† Writer and aesthete (1904–94), who had been an older boy in J.L.-M's house at Eton.

came the officers, then the men, all hatless. They were a fine looking lot, bronzed and with only a day's growth of beard, and had presumably been captured some twenty-four hours before. Among them were a few very young boys, and some quite old men. They marched well and made an impressive spectacle. A few feeble-looking American soldiers, physically infinitely their inferiors, were in charge of them, holding rifles with their fingers on the trigger.

*Sunday, 27th August*

Tom and I dined at Brooks's. I asked him point-blank if he still sympathised with the Nazis. He emphatically said Yes. That all the best Germans were Nazis. That if he were a German he would be one. That he was an imperialist. He considered that life without power and without might with which to strike fear into every other nation would not be worth living for an Englishman. I absolutely contradicted him. Told him I was an unrepentant pacifist, and would prefer to live in a country of tenth-rate power, provided there were peace and freedom of action and speech. The sweet side of Tom is that he never minds how much an old friend disagrees with him. But woe betide an acquaintance.

*Tuesday, 12th September*

At about 6 a.m., I with thousands of others in London was woken up by an explosion like an earthquake, followed by a prolonged rumble, which I at first mistook for thunder. The explosion was followed by a second. Both, I learned later, were caused by V-2 rockets which other people have heard before. I am told that quite thirty have so far been dropped on different parts of the country. This morning's are said to have fallen on Chiswick. They have greater penetrative but less lateral destructive power than the V-1s. They are very exciting and not frightening at all, for when you hear them you know you are all right.

*In September, J.L.-M. completed six months as Acting Secretary of the National Trust during Matheson's absence. He had applied to go to France as an ambulance driver at the end of this period, but was rejected on medical grounds (probably owing to the influence of Esher, who did not want to lose him). Feeling exhausted and far from well, he spent a month's leave visiting friends and relations in various parts of the country, returning to London on 16 October.*

*Tuesday, 17th October*

Today we had our monthly [committee] meeting and also the annual meeting. Lord Zetland announced the gift of two Queen Anne's Gate houses, which we may make into our offices. As regards situation they would be very suitable.

During my long absence from London nothing has been done to my house. But today, twelve hours after my return, an army of builders have begun putting glass to the windows, mending frames, the bedroom ceiling, door-locks, etc. Thank goodness, but the mess is once again appalling.

To my intense surprise and delight, the Committee have given me a bonus of £200 for my work during Matheson's absence.

*Saturday, 21st October*

Looked over 17 Alexander Place [South Kensington], which Geoffrey Houghton Brown has just bought with a view to my fitting myself into it too. A nice little house, but I don't see how it can easily be divided up.

Caught a train to Bradford-on-Avon and stayed the night with Mrs Moulton at the Dower House. Had a long talk after dinner, when his mother had gone to bed, with Alex Moulton* about the future, which promises to be less black for his generation – he is about 24 – than for mine. In actual fact I don't think this applies to me particularly because I have never known riches or pre-war luxury, unlike most of my Eton contemporaries. I am not gloomy

---

* Engineer (b. 1920), who later invented the Moulton bicycle and motor-car suspension.

about the future for myself. He is a rather appealing young man in that he is very earnest, intelligent and already successful, with a fine grasp of business. The youngest of three children, he is the one who loves The Hall, and is about to return to work in his family business, Spencer-Moulton, at the bottom of The Hall garden. The works are screened by trees. He is determined to and undoubtedly will make money. He will be a conscientious manager, for he has enlightened views about the condition of the workers, who number 700 Bradfordians. He is very proud of the proximity of the factory to The Hall, and rejoices in it. He is also determined to do his duty by The Hall. He is going to live in the stables, which he is about to convert into bachelor lodgings, and eventually move into The Hall when he has made enough money. We went all round the house, which was heavily restored by his great-grandfather in the 1840s. The furniture which I saw the last time I was here has been sold since. The house has distinct academic interest.

On Sunday afternoon I drove over to Westwood Manor and stayed the night with Ted Lister. I enjoyed it but Ted will not go to bed until the early hours and thinks one offensive if one slips away before 3 a.m. John Leslie* and Sir Orme Sargent† dined. The latter is a tall man with a sloping forehead, nose and chin: all slopes. An agreeable evening with much Edwardian gossip and laughter. These three elderly gentlemen are given to story-telling. Have you heard this one? The hotel commissionaire saying confusedly to the lift-boy, 'Take this lady up to P. I mean to letter P. I mean to letter P. on the door' – and others of this calibre.

*Wednesday, 25th October*

I lunched with Lord Carlisle‡ in the House of Lords. Found him in the library, which was as dark as pitch. Several other peers emerged from the half light. I thought what a seedy, drab bunch of

---

* Aesthete, normally resident in Italy, then living at Little Westwood Manor.

† Foreign Office mandarin (1884–1962).

‡ George Howard, 11th Earl of Carlisle (1895–1963).

old crocks, and above all how out of date. Lord C. on the contrary is very spry. He has spent three years in Turkey; his wife is an ATS General in India; his son is fighting in Italy. He may be sent on a mission to Yugoslavia in a few weeks' time. He talked of Naworth [Cumberland], which is, he believes, the king of all castles. His son loves it too. He may never live in it again, and wants the N.T. to have it. He suggests a school renting it. Asked me to come and stay there in a fortnight's time, which I shall enjoy doing.* After luncheon the House sat, and I stood behind the bar for a few minutes in the Chamber, which is now the Robing Room, smaller, cosier and more intimate than the old Chamber. There were the Lord Chancellor in his wig, the bishops in their lawn sleeves, and the stately attendants in boiled shirt-fronts and tail-coats, with medals hanging round their necks on chains, which clattered against the starch. The peers, mostly decrepit, looked gaga in the dim yellow light, and remarkably nineteenth-century. This is the best place in which to recapture nineteenth-century atmosphere. I love it, and would not have it any different.

*Monday, 6th November*

I dined at the Travellers with Harold Nicolson to meet a young poet and playwright, by name Michael Clayton-Hutton, aged 23.† I took an instant dislike to him, for he is rather off-hand and hideously pleased with himself. Shaftesbury Avenue looks, moreover. Harold talked politics over port wine. He said Hitler told a friend of his, the Swiss Governor of Danzig,‡ that Hitler lamented there was no prominent English statesman to whom he could speak freely in his or our tongue. The Danzig Governor asked what he would say to the Englishman. Hitler replied: 'Supposing it were

* J.L.-M. did indeed enjoy the visit; though he was doubtful about the castle, which was huge and ugly, having been rebuilt after a fire in the 19th century, and offered without endowment.

† He later committed suicide.

‡ Carl J. Burckhardt (1891–1974); League of Nations High Commissioner for Danzig, 1937–9.

Lord Halifax, I would say – I offer your country the ports of Antwerp, Dunkirk, Le Havre, etc., absolutely, on the understanding that I take Poland and the Balkans without interference.' Harold said that when the Germans walked into Czechoslovakia, he was with Winston Churchill and Lord Cecil.* After serious discussion Lord Cecil said, 'Well, Winston, things are desperate. I feel twenty years older.' Churchill replied equally seriously, 'Yes, Bob, things are desperate. I feel twenty years younger' – and these words convinced Harold that Churchill was a great man. They convince me that Churchill enjoys war.

*Sunday, 12th November*

Had a glass of sherry at Brooks's with Tom, who walked in. He tells me he is soon off to Burma at his own request, for he does not wish to go to Germany killing German civilians, whom he likes. He prefers to kill Japanese whom he does not like. Tom makes me sad because he looks so sad, and I am so deeply devoted to him.

*Friday, 24th November*

Had a postcard this morning from Father Francis Moncrieff, written from Hambleton [Hall, Rutlandshire], saying that old Mrs Astley Cooper† died last Sunday after three weeks' illness. Mrs Cooper was very good to me when I was in disgrace with my family ten years ago,‡ and gave me my missal. She was a remarkable old woman with a first-class brain, a man's attitude to life and its problems. She hated pettinesses, and had no patience with small irritations or small points of view. Accordingly, few women liked her. She had a sad life, in losing her favourite children and

* Lord Robert Cecil, 1st Viscount Cecil of Chelwood (1864–1958); yr s. of 3rd Marquess of Salisbury; architect and leading figure of League of Nations, awarded Nobel Peace Prize in 1937.

† Evangeline Marshall (1854–1944); heiress to shipping fortune; m. 1877 Major Clement Astley Cooper.

‡ After J.L.-M's conversion to Roman Catholicism in 1934.

quarrelling violently with the others and her relations. But she had a magnificently embracing sense of humour, was a realist and a cynic, and could never be taken in or deceived. She discovered Noël Coward* as a boy, was an intimate friend of Malcolm Sargent† and Scott Moncrieff,‡ whom she helped translate Proust's novels at Hambleton and who dedicated the series to her in the moving poem published in *Swann's Way*. She was a convert, who loved and revered the Church, respecting it for its intellectual, rational and ruthless approach to life. Although she frequently rebelled, she always returned to it. People were frightened by her direct manner, her immediate circumvention of all conventional and social façades. I have had many a meal with her, she sitting, groaning and shaking with mirth at some foolish person's expense, a massive, shapeless lump of a woman, over the most delicious English food. Fred, the tall, stately, respectful P. G. Wodehouse butler, was always in the background. Rarely can two people have had a more profound affection and admiration for one another. Unfortunately Mrs Cooper became more and more self-adulatory in a sly way, and her constant, roundabout fishing for praise exasperated me. I had not seen her for three or four years. I shall always respect and love her, for she contributed a lot to my life. There was absolutely no nonsense about her. Her trouble was that she was a woman with a brain, born into English upper-class county circles.

James telephoned just before midnight that tomorrow evening he is at last to sleep with his first woman. Everything has been arranged. He dreads it and is terrified, and will telephone first thing on Sunday morning to let me know how it proceeded. Asked me to think of him and pray for him.

---

* Actor, singer, songwriter, playwright, and possessor of other talents to amuse (1899–1973).

† Conductor (1895–1967; KB 1947).

‡ C. K. M. Scott Moncrieff (1889–1930); poet and writer, best known for his translation of Proust.

*Saturday, 25th November*

Went to tea with Logan [Pearsall Smith] who told the same stories over again, but one new saga about the wickedness of Lady Ottoline Morrell,* who succeeded in breaking up happy relationships, and tried to separate Ethel Sands and Nan Hudson. Lady O. was constantly throwing herself upon men. Logan asked me if I liked foul-mouthed men who otherwise led blameless lives. I said, No, I preferred clean-mouthed people who gave physical expression to their lusts. He seemed shocked. For two hours he criticised everyone, asking me if I did not agree. Since half the people criticised were unknown to me, I was unable to agree.

At the Ritz bar Guy Burgess called to me. I dined with him and Charles Fletcher-Cooke† at the Gargoyle. Drank too much beer and gin mixed, and talked a great deal about politics and sex, disagreeing with Guy over both. He does and says the most dangerous things. However, we laughed a lot. Mary Churchill‡ who was there joined us. She is prettier than her sister Diana§ and looks like her mother. She talked all the time about her father, whom she adores unreservedly.

*Sunday, 26th November*

James telephoned this morning, and said tersely, 'I am still alive. It was quite easy, but not riotous.'

I fear that in this diary I disclose the nastier, the more frivolous side of myself. I sincerely believe and fervently hope that I am not as nasty as I may appear. It is difficult to be entirely honest about

---

* Lady Ottoline Cavendish-Bentinck (1873–1938); m. 1902 Philip Morrell, MP; châtelaine of Garsington Hall, Oxfordshire; lover of Bertrand Russell and friend of members of Bloomsbury Group.

† Subsequently Sir Charles Fletcher-Cooke, QC, MP (1914–2001); obliged to resign as a Home Office minister in the 1950s owing to a brush with homosexual scandal.

‡ Yst dau. (b. 1922) of Winston Churchill; m. 1947 Christopher Soames (later Baron; d. 1987).

§ Diana Churchill (1909–63); m. 1st 1932–5 Sir John Bailey, 2nd 1935–60 Duncan Sandys, MP.

oneself because one does not necessarily know oneself. One thinks one knows. The consequence of being as honest as I try to be must surely be that readers of these lines would pronounce me worse than many of my contemporaries who do not keep frank records of themselves. Frank? Not entirely, because I withhold things.

*Friday, 8th December*

I walked to Albany [Piccadilly] to meet Lord Wilton* at Johnny Philipps's.† He is about 23, tall, fair, handsome, and very shy. He is passionately interested in architecture and wants to buy a large country house, but cannot find one large enough. I intend to find one for him.

*Wednesday, 13th December*

I took Tom Mitford to tea with Logan. I think Tom, whose manners can be abrupt, was bored, and certainly Logan was rather boring, for he would read from his own books and from the *Dictionary of National Biography* about all the Mitfords that had ever been. But he is a dear old man, and when he got up, all bent, and fumbled in the shelves I rather loved him. When Tom and I left it was pitch dark, the fog having thickened. It was almost impossible to see a thing. By tapping with my stick against the kerb, he clinging to my left arm, we reached the King's Road. After a fond farewell, and Tom's farewells are so fond they always touch me, we separated. Slowly and cautiously I followed in the wake of motor lights and walkers' torches, presuming that I was on my way to the Chelsea Hospital Road. After half an hour, not knowing where I was, and almost desperate, I bumped violently into someone. I apologised. The victim apologised. It was Tom. Peals of laughter. We clove to one another, and agreed not to separate again. We staggered to his flat, and abandoned our different projects for the

---

* John Egerton, 7th Earl of Wilton (1921–99).

† Sir John Philipps, 3rd Bt (1915–48); of Picton Castle, Pembrokeshire.

evening. Instead we ate scrambled eggs and drank red wine. Once I am indoors I love pea-soupers, the cosiness, the isolation, the calm broken by distant squeals of taxis and thuds of wary footfalls, the tapping of sticks against area railings, and the blessed expansion of confidence between two friends.

*Friday, 22nd December*

I drove to Hampstead, to Fenton House, which belongs to Lady Binning,* an elderly, delicate hot-housey lady. Fenton House was built in 1693 of beautiful red brick and has wrought-iron gates of the period. It is large for London, and has a large walled garden. Much of the pine wainscoting has been stripped by Lady Binning. She intends to leave her excellent furniture, and wishes the house to be a museum, but I feel it ought to be put to some use. Her porcelain collection is first-rate and at present bequeathed to the V&A, but she is prepared to alter her will. She gave me tea, and we liked each other, I fancy. At the end of tea she disclosed that she was anti-democratic and very pro-Nazi. She denied that the Germans had committed atrocities, and declared that the Jews were the root of all evil. Oh dear! She ought to meet Tom.

*Wednesday, 27th December*

All this Christmastide my father has been perfectly charming, and companionable. I believe that by taking the initiative and showing sympathy for his not inconsiderable difficulties, which I ought to have done years ago, I may at last have broken down his suspicion and reserve. At least I hope so.

An extremely frosty morning, the air glacial, and all living things arrested. The sun came out once and made the trees, swathed in hoar frost, glitter like fairy godmothers in the pantomime. I left Wickhamford after breakfast and reached Swinbrook at 10.30.

* Katherine Salting (d. 1952); m. Major-General Lord Binning, e.s. of 11th Earl of Haddington (killed in action, 1917, their son succeeding as 12th Earl).

Lady Redesdale gave me sherry and cake. Bobo[*] made Tom laugh a great deal. He is perfectly sweet and patient with her. Indeed with those of whom he is fond his manner is irresistible. He said good-bye to his mother, who was brave about his departure, which he told me might be for three years. He is my oldest friend, whom I first met in 1919, and have loved from that moment onwards.

*Sunday, 31st December*

Dined at the [Anthony] Chaplins'. Lady Kenmare,[†] James and Derek Hill[‡] there. Anthony talked marvellous uproarious nonsense for two hours about a bogus Constable he had bought. James and I left at 11.20. We walked in the moonlight. At Hyde Park Corner we heard a crash, followed by the roar of a rocket that made our hearts beat. Then we laughed. Just before midnight I left him at Sloane Square station and continued homewards. Crowds were singing in the square like zanies. There were sounds of merriment from lighted windows. They seemed forced to me. There were no church bells, and for the first time I did not feel left out, nostalgic or particularly sad, merely indifferent to it all.

[*] Unity Valkyrie Mitford (1914–48); the third-youngest Mitford sister, who became enamoured of Hitler and attempted to commit suicide in Munich in September 1939, returning to England mentally as well as physically damaged.

[†] Enid Lindemann of Sydney NSW (d. 1973); m. 1st 1913 Roderick Cameron of New York (d. 1914), 2nd Gen. Hon. Frederick Cavendish (d. 1931), 3rd 1933 (as his 3rd wife) 1st Viscount Furness (d. 1940), 4th 1943 (as his 2nd wife) 6th Earl of Kenmare (who d. same year).

[‡] Portrait and landscape artist (1916–2000), whom J.L.-M. had met through the Mitford sisters.

# 1945

# 1945

*As 1945 began J.L.-M., apart from his normal work for the National Trust, was engaged in two literary projects for the publishers Batsford – the editing of a volume of essays (one by himself on the history of the English country house) to celebrate the Trust's fiftieth anniversary, and a book on the architect Robert Adam (1728–92).*

*Friday, 5th January*

The year has opened in a melancholy way. Tom has gone to Burma and James to Washington. The V-2 rockets have begun again to some tune. One fell on Tuesday morning with a terrific explosion and roar on the eastern wing of Wren's Chelsea Hospital, completely wrecking it and breaking windows for miles around. In the afternoon I walked down St Leonard's Terrace and asked after Logan. He was in bed, but he and the servants were unhurt. All the windows on both sides of his house were smashed, doors wrenched off, both outer and inner; and partitions and ceilings down. Much of his furniture was destroyed. Yesterday rockets fell like autumn leaves, and between dinner and midnight there were six near our house. Miss P. and I were terrified. I put every china ornament away in cupboards. The V-2 has become more alarming than the V-1, quite contrary to what I thought at first, because it gives no warning sound. One finds oneself waiting for it, and jumps out of one's skin at the slightest bang or unexpected noise, like a car backfire or even a door-slam.

Jamesey sailed. On Wednesday we drank whisky at the Allies Club, and with much affection pledged a renewal of friendship and confidences. We agreed that during the last year there has been a coolness.

Last Saturday Major Benton Fletcher* died suddenly at no. 3 Cheyne Walk. He was found fully clothed on his bed on Sunday morning. I was called. He was evidently in the process of cooking something on an electric ring. The saucepan had burnt into an unrecognisable tangle of metal, but did not set the room on fire. Benton Fletcher was lying hunched up, as if frozen stiff. Indeed I believe he may have died of the cold, for he would not spend a penny on heating. The neighbour said to me it would only be decent for us to lay him flat. We tried. It was impossible to bend the limbs and straighten him. All the while there were those glazed and staring eyes. I felt sick, and said to myself, 'Give me V-2s every minute rather than a repetition of this experience.'

As there was absolutely nobody to take matters in hand I had to arrange the post mortem, the funeral, and caretaking of the house. I went through all his papers. He had hardly any personal belongings and only very few clothes. He lived entirely alone, with no one even to clean for him, in great dirt and squalor. This sort of death is a bourgeois business. I only hope to die in splendour. I want my body to be burned immediately on a pyre, not at Golders Green, preferably at Wickhamford, close to the church, and my ashes scattered there. Then an enormous marble monument, two, three storeys in height, to be erected in the nave above our pew, with a lengthy epitaph in complicated Latin, so that the stranger reading it will not make head or tail of whom it commemorates, or what it means. It *must* be beautiful.

*Sunday, 7th January*

I picked up John Wilton and drove him to Audley End. I like his quiet intelligence and his taste in things and people, which concurs with mine. Lord Braybrooke met us in Audley End which was perishingly cold. We had a sandwich luncheon in the lodge over a fire which was not hot enough. The troops are out of the house which

---

* Donor to N.T. of Old Devonshire House, WC1, and a historic collection of keyboard instruments. The house was destroyed in the war, the instruments later finding a home at Fenton House, Hampstead.

has barely suffered from them, and is quite clean. John liked it very much, but in Lord B's presence was shy and never once spoke what was in his mind. However, on the way home J.W. opened up and suggested buying the house, endowing it and living in it. It would be too wonderful to be true. He stayed to dinner and talked till 11 when I went firewatching.

*Tuesday, 9th January*

At 11.30 Matheson and I drove to Brompton Cemetery to pay our last respects to Major Benton Fletcher's remains. Deep snow lying, and intense cold. I wore a thick pair of snow boots over my shoes, but this made my feet so unnaturally gigantic that I kept tripping over my toes, once dangerously near the grave's edge. At the chapel no one but ourselves, a nephew by marriage, and Roger Quilter* the composer, his only friend, who appeared grief-stricken. We watched the old man, who had had so many acquaintances, lowered lonely into his grave. We promptly turned and left him to his own devices. Oh, the cruelty of it all. The nephew told me that before 1914 Benton Fletcher's name was to be seen at the end of every list of those attending dinner parties and balls in *The Times*. He quarrelled with nearly everyone but me, and died unloved, neglected, and mourned by Mr Quilter.

*Thursday, 11th January*

The cold persists. It is appalling, and I have run out of anthracite. Had tea at Emerald's, after the office shut. Mr Partridge was brought in. E. tried, I like to think, to put him at his ease, but her thin manner overlaid an inclination to show him the social differences. She introduced him to us all in turn: 'Princess Kallimachi, who lives at the Ritz; Lady Kemsley,† whose husband owns all the newspapers;

* English composer (1877–1953); yr s. of Sir Cuthbert Quilter, 1st Bt.

† Edith Dresselhuys; m. 1931 (as his 2nd wife) Sir James Berry, Bt, Chairman of Kemsley Newspapers Ltd, cr. Baron, 1936 and Viscount Kemsley, 1945.

Mr Peter Hesketh,* who owns a whole town; and Mr L.-M., head of the National Trust, who looks after all the public houses.'

*Saturday, 13th January*

Yesterday I resolved not to be disagreeable and cross, or rude, or to show envy, pique or malice. The day went fairly well, for I was at home most of it, though I was not too pleasant to poor Miss P., who has a cold, and *will* sniff. But this morning in the office I was distinctly unpleasant to Matheson in complaining that the agents never came into the office on Saturdays.

John Wilton dined at Brooks's. He is complaisant and will agree to eat what one suggests, drink what one suggests, and do what one suggests. Yet I feel there is a will of iron underneath, which if one struck it would send out sparks and dent the offending instrument. His is one of the most curious minds I have come across. It resembles the Princesse de Poliganc's – questioning, cautious, non-committal, tentative, then – crash! Out comes a devastating bomb, but muffled, for he seldom raises his voice. Nothing escapes him, and his memory is alarming. He is acutely observant, like Cecil Beaton. Every blemish of others is recorded on that photographic retina. If he could write he would be a great novelist in the George Sand manner. Or is he just a Disraelian young duke, Byronically moody and damned? He seems determined to take Audley End, and has steeped himself in the history of the Nevilles. We drank at Brooks's until midnight, then went to Cheyne Walk in spite of my warnings that there was no fire. At 2 there was a siren and four flying bombs shook my windows. At 3 John Wilton left in a hired car.

*Saturday, 20th January*

It is so appallingly cold – snowing again and freezing – that I cannot, without anthracite, face my room in Cheyne Walk.

---

* Peter Fleetwood-Hesketh (1905–85), architect and illustrator; his family owned much of Southport, Lancashire (where his brother Roger was later Mayor).

Went to Brooks's and there worked by the fire, interrupted at times by Sir Warren Fisher's* chat about the superiority of Brooks's to all other clubs. At 3.45 I set out to walk in the snow to Westminster Abbey. I found Robert Adam's grave slab in the south transept, simple and worn by the feet which have trampled over it these 150 years. There is no other memorial or monument to him, whereas there are tablets to Wyatt and Taylor, who are less distinguished architects. I look at many monuments. How dirty they are. How wonderful though. The Abbey enshrines England's history. It is a volume of a thousand pages, England's most precious sanctum.

I had a drink with John Philipps. He showed me Beatrix Potter's† drawing of 'Johnnie the town mouse' and said, 'That's me to the life. I am just like that. I saw a woman in the street the other day, just like that too. So I went up to her and said, "You are a mouse. You should have married me."' Whenever I see one of these delicious drawings, I find it hard to reconcile the Mrs Heelis I met with the Beatrix Potter who conceived and produced them. For Mrs Heelis was an unbending, masculine, stalwart woman, with an acute business sense. She was rather tart with her dim husband and adored her sheep, not for sentimental Beatrix Potter reasons but for hard-cash Heelis ones. She drove bargains with farmers at sales and the National Trust over her benefactions.

*Wednesday, 24th January*

A terrible day. Arctic cold. I caught the 9.40 from King's Cross, reaching Darlington at 4. Changed for Scorton, arriving at 4.45. Already getting dark, and a leaden, snow-filled sky of the most ominous description, the silence promising the blackest frost.

---

* Civil servant (1879–1948); Permanent Secretary to the Treasury, 1919–39.

† Children's writer and illustrator (1866–1943); m. 1913 William Heelis, solicitor; bequeathed 4,000 acres in the Lake District to the National Trust, one of whose founders, Canon Rawnsley, had been a friend of her parents.

There was no car to meet me at the station. Consequently I walked two miles from the station to the village, carrying my bags. My hands were numb with cold. On reaching a garage and thawing them before a fire, I feared they were frostbitten, so badly did they hurt. A taxi drove me to Kiplin Hall, put me down and drove away. There was no Miss Talbot who had asked me to stay. I trudged round the empty house, in which not a glimmer of light was to be seen, and could not get inside. What I did see in the twilight was enough to convince me that this house was not acceptable. The centre part, the brickwork and the eccentric towers, almost French Renaissance in plan, were interesting; but there were too many nineteenth-century alterations and additions.

I chased round the village enquiring for Miss Talbot. Finally a friend of hers told me she had telegraphed that she was not coming down from London after all. I was furious, and returned to Darlington, catching the 7.50 p.m. back to London. In the train there was no heating, and I reached King's Cross at 3.35 a.m. frozen to the very marrow. There were no taxis at that hour, and there was no alternative to walking with my bags to the far end of Cheyne Walk. Got home in my wet and clammy clothes at 5.30. As I tried to force a comb through my hair, which was stiff with hoar frost, I cursed that wretched Miss Talbot.

*Saturday, 27th January*

Walked to the Adelphi [by Charing Cross] to see what, if anything, remained of Adam's work there. Nothing to speak of. Just the butt-ends of some buildings with the familiar wide pilaster bands of terracotta, disporting huge honeysuckle emblems. What a monstrous abomination of a building the new Adelphi block is. Utterly and absolutely without merit. While I was at Charing Cross there was a terrific V-2 explosion. Dined at the Etoile. Cyril Connolly at the next table said he had come back from Paris two hours ago; that in Paris you felt the French were living, whereas in London you knew the English were dead.

*Wednesday, 31st January*

Dr Wittkower* of the Warburg Institute lunched at Brooks's. He is so hesitant, and so burbling in that irritating German accent, that I can barely listen to what he says. Yet he is a great scholar. Within that huge head one senses, almost sees, cavern after cavern crammed with documents in German, French and English, and rolled parchments covered in the dust and must of ages. He offers any amount of help [with J.L.-M's Adam researches], and will put numerous books of reference at my disposal at Denham, where the Institute staff is living during the war. A kind and generous man, ready to impart information from his great store, which is by no means always the case with scholars.

At 2.30 to Batsford's where, with Mr Harry Batsford† and Charles Fry, I made a final selection of illustrations [for the National Trust book]. Mr B. is the dirtiest, yet the sweetest old person I ever saw. He smokes, and coughs, and shakes incessantly, while the cigarette ash spills down the front, saliva also. His eccentricities are Dickensian. He adores cats, and fills his coat pockets with the heads, tails and entrails of fish. As he stumbles down the pavements he distributes these remnants to the congregating cats. The scene is like the Pied Piper of Hamelin, and the smell of his clothes is overpowering.

*Saturday, 3rd February*

This morning in the office I typed out a memorandum I composed in the train yesterday with much care and thought, suggesting that the museum aspect – for lack of a better phrase – of the Trust's work should be recognised to be as important as the agents', solicitors' and accountants' departments now are; suggesting that, instead of Country Houses Secretary, a foolish title,

* Rudolf Wittkower (1901–71); German-born art historian, holder later of chairs at London and Columbia universities.

† Publisher, bookseller and architectural historian (author with Charles Fry of *The Cathedrals of England* [1935]), whose family firm had celebrated its centenary in 1943.

there should be a chief curator or some such officer, responsible to a new Committee of Taste. I feel very strongly on the subject, and pretty confident that Esher, who is my consistent ally, will agree.*

*Sunday, 11th February*

I was taken last night to a *louche* club. What we saw going on was disturbing in general and disgusting in particular. There is something horribly genteel about brothels and their equivalents. Male and female harlots talk politely about the weather, and their talk, for they have no conversation, is laced with prurient innuendoes and punctuated with adolescent giggles. Why the hell don't they get down to business straight away, and hold out their hands for the notes? Instead they perch like suburban housewives on the edge of their stools, prolonging the ghastly farce as though to make believe they are respectable dowagers on gilt chairs in a Mayfair ballroom. I walked home alone, sickened and unsatisfied.

*Wednesday, 14th February*

At 7 p.m. the doorbell rang, and there was my father who had called unannounced in a taxi. We welcomed him and Miss P. gave us dinner in the kitchen. He told me how my grandfather,† on inheriting Crompton Hall, sent every single piece of eighteenth-century furniture to Druce's to be refashioned, as well as the priceless oak beds. All of them were ruined. The oak four-posters, which had been in the Crompton family for generations untouched, were

* This marked the beginning of a twenty-year struggle in the N.T. between those who dealt with artistic and with financial matters – the 'aesthetes' and the 'agents'. As J.L.-M. surmised, Esher took his side on this, overruling Matheson (see entry for 12 March 1945); but the situation was reversed during the 1960s, when the 'agents' came to predominate.

† Through his mother, J.L.-M's grandfather James Henry Lees-Milne (1849–1908) inherited one of Lancashire's leading cotton mills, along with much property in and around Oldham. He retired to Ribbesford Hall, Worcestershire a few years before his death.

made into buffets, pedestals for aspidistras and ferns, and overmantels for Ribbesford [Hall]. My grandfather 'improved' Crompton itself in the most ghastly way. My father was delightful, because totally relaxed. When it was time for him to go no taxi was obtainable. I walked with him to the bus stop, for I don't think he has ever been in a bus in his life. Immediately the bus drew up there was a flash, and the terrific explosion of a rocket.

*Saturday, 17th February*

After lunching I went to Lansdowne House.* I need make no comment on the mess made of the exterior. The interior is worse. Of poor Adam's work, what has been allowed to remain is now a travesty. The façade has been pushed back one room's width, so that the glorious entrance hall and ante-room no longer exist. The bow room is left, but the niches have been ruthlessly cut into disproportionate openings. The room-for-company-before-dinner seems to survive, although I suspect that the apsidal end of the ante-room has been stuck haphazard on to the east end of this room. The two rotundas at the end of Smirke's† gallery have been hacked about, and galleries introduced. The whole maelstrom is a deplorable instance of Thirtyish decadence – total lack of respect for the great architecture of the past, and total lack of confidence in that of the present. The result a shamefully hideous mess and muddle.

*Sunday, 18th February*

After tea, I called by pre-arrangement upon Aunt Katie, my grandfather's sister, the sole survivor of that large family. My grandfather, born in 1847, was a second son, so Aunt Katie must be about ninety. She is very blind and quiet, but distinguished and sedate.

---

* The house, built in the 1760s, was formerly the London residence of the Marquess of Lansdowne, who sold it in 1929. The grounds and the original façade were sacrificed to property development and road-widening schemes, the remnant being remodelled as the Lansdowne Club, which opened in 1935.

† Sir Robert Smirke (1781–1867); favoured architect of the Tory establishment.

She hardly uttered, and derived no pleasure from my visit. She was somewhat out of humour and growled at her companion for knocking against her chair. 'For the last time I must ask you not to do that,' she barked. She did however tell me she was brought up at Clarksfield Lees,* and the view across the valley, though magnificent in her day, looked upon distant factory chimneys.

*Wednesday, 21st February*

George Dix† took me into 9 Clifford Street. It was once a great town house, called Clarendon House. It is now divided into tailors' shops. An extraordinary discovery, a huge staircase hall of late seventeenth-century date, a double flight staircase with Ionic columns and thick balusters of acanthus leaves. A ribbed plaster ceiling over all, and pedimented doorcases, like Coleshill in miniature.

I took the train to Richmond and walked to Ham House. Sir Lyonel is now aged 91; young Lyonel is 60. The old man is courteous and charming, rather deaf, but very sprightly and straight. He wears an old-fashioned black cravat. Lady Tollemache looks younger, but they were married in 1881. This time conversation took a more positive turn. As at Osterley [Park, Middlesex], so here we must ask the Government or the London County Council for help. Ham is superb, but far more impracticable than most great houses. Quite impossible for a private residence these days, and not suited to any institutional use. The first floor is all state-rooms; the second all intercommunicating rooms. The attic floor not fit for animals, far less modern servants, when obtainable. The basement vast, dark and rambling. All the best pictures and furniture are away in the country. I had tea with the family and then walked round the garden with young Lyonel. Rather touching, but oh what an unhappy man. All of them seem hopelessly defeatist, anti-Government, anti-people and anti-world. More so than me really. Of course their difficulties are formidable, but unlike the French

* Country estate near Oldham, owned by the Lees family since the reign of James I.
† Lieutenant in the US Navy, whom J.L.-M. had first mentioned in his diary on 6 January 1945.

aristocracy the English usually manage to adapt themselves to current trends, if only to survive.

*Saturday, 10th March*

A sunny, balmy day. I walked without an overcoat to lunch with Alice Harding at the Basque Restaurant. The Sachie Sitwells, their son Reresby* and George Dix there. Sachie has old-fashioned good manners. Anecdotes fly from his lips like little birds from an open cage.

Dined with Rory [Cameron]† and Lady Kenmare. A large party. When the women left the dining room Beverley Baxter‡ and Lord Margesson§ started talking about the recent debate on Yalta. They said it was perhaps a pity that the Prime Minister claimed the Polish settlement, which they agreed was the only possible solution, to be a wise and beneficent one. Quite suddenly I became furious and, red in the face, exclaimed, 'Beneficent, my foot! Expedient doubtless. It is a disgrace and an indictment of Parliament that only twenty-one members had the courage of their convictions to vote against you. The Poles have every reason to feel betrayed by our country.' I was somewhat surprised at myself. Lord M. became indignant, and said, 'What would you have the Government do?' I said rather truculently, 'What the Government ought to do is something honourable. It is not for me to dictate, I'm not a professional politician,' which was a bit lame. He said that politicians were just as other men. I checked myself from saying what I thought of him and most of them. In the course of the argument

---

* Sacheverell Sitwell, writer and poet (1897–1988); m. 1925 Georgia Doble; s. brother Osbert as 6th Bt, 1969, and was succeeded as 7th Bt by his son Reresby (1927–2009).

† Anglo-American horticulturist and society figure (1914–85); son of Enid Kenmare by her first marriage; friend of Alvilde Chaplin.

‡ (Sir) Beverley Baxter (1891–1964); Canadian protégé of 1st Baron Beaverbrook; editor, *Daily Express*, 1929–33; Conservative MP, 1935–64.

§ Captain David Margesson (1890–1965); Conservative MP for Rugby, 1924–42; Chief Whip of National Government, 1931–40; Secretary of State for War, 1940–2; cr. Viscount, 1942.

I said that the Russians were less to be trusted than the Germans, and were far more dangerous. We had got our enemies wrong. And I defended the Pope against the charge of condoning Fascism, for the Pope had to put ideals before countries. Lord M. and the other men present were, I could see, shocked and annoyed. Not an enjoyable evening.

*Monday, 12th March*

In between the two [committee] meetings today I lunched with Esher, who was very outspoken in his objection to the agents' encroachment upon the aesthetes' work. He laughed mischievously and said, 'After all, they are only plumbers.' At this morning's meeting it was decided to extend the functions of the Country Houses Committee, henceforth to be called the Historic Buildings Committee.

*Friday, 16th March*

Dined at the Argentine Embassy. Jacqueline Killearn,* whom I haven't seen since I was 18, told me that her father, Senator Aldo Castellani, is incarcerated in the Quirinal with the Prince of Piedmont, and that all parties have treated him abominably. He is not the least interested in politics, only in medicine and his friends. She has not seen him for six years. Lord Margesson was polite to me in spite of our differences the other evening. There was one row at dinner, when Chips foolishly belittled the K[enneth] C[lark]s, saying they were bourgeois and not in society. At this I spoke up, saying that I hardly knew the Cs, but he was undoubtedly one of the most brilliant and distinguished men of his generation. Emerald said to Chips, 'You are as much an upstart as K.C., and so am I. We are both from across the Atlantic. As for you,' she continued, turning to Lord Margesson, 'you know nothing about the arts or

---

* Jacqueline Aldine Leslie, dau. of Senator Count Aldo Castellani; m. 1934 (as his 2nd wife) Sir Miles Lampson (1880–1964), British Ambassador to Egypt, 1934–46, cr. Baron Killearn, 1943.

the intellect, and are only fit for politics and love.' Chips then said that Mrs Corrigan* was in the best society, and that anyone in Paris who was not received by her was 'beneath consideration'. Jacqueline and I agreed that talk about 'society' was unintelligible, and parvenu.

*Thursday, 22nd March*

G. M. Trevelyan† came to the office with the proofs of the National Trust book I have edited. He showed me the first half of his Introduction, and asked what he should say in the last half. I said, 'Please stress the Trust's opposition to museumisation, and its wish to preserve the face of England as it was under private ownership.'

*Saturday, 24th March*

I called for Mrs Fellowes‡ at the Dorchester. We got to Compton Beauchamp [Berkshire] at 5.30, exactly the same moment as Chips Channon and Terence Rattigan.§ For so sophisticated a woman, Daisy – this is what Mrs Fellowes tells me to call her – has simple country tastes. Yet I cannot help seeing her as Reynolds's Mrs Graham, the society lady masquerading as a housemaid with a broom. She keeps a cow which she likes to milk herself, and asked someone the other day if the cow would mind her going to Paris for a long weekend without being milked in her absence.

---

* Wife of American steel magnate who established herself as a London hostess, known for her lavish hospitality and malapropisms (d. 1948); in France during the Second World War, she devoted herself to good works and was decorated by Marshal Pétain before returning to England in 1942.

† Historian (1876–1962); Master of Trinity College, Cambridge, 1940–51; Chairman of N.T. Estates Committee; brother of Sir Charles Trevelyan, donor of Wallington to N.T.

‡ Marguerite (1890–1962), dau. of 4th duc Decazes by his American wife Isabelle Singer; Anglo-French society figure; m. 1st Prince Jean de Broglie (d. 1918), 2nd Hon. Reginald Fellowes; niece of Winaretta de Polignac.

§ Playwright (1911–77); loved by Channon.

Compton Beauchamp combines so many qualities that are desirable in a country house. It is completely surrounded by a moat, for romance. It has a pleasant, square courtyard, for shelter. The approach is by a symmetrical forecourt with two detached flanking stable wings, retaining wall, stone piers and magnificent iron gates, for grandeur. The principal façade is classical Queen Anne of rustic simplicity, for cosiness and dignity. The other façades are mediaeval and Jacobean, for historic continuity. There is an extremely pretty garden at the back with contemporary raised terraces. A box garden behind that; another magnificent iron gate between piers, cut and set askew to the wall. It is a small paradise in the fold of the downs, with tinkling fountains in the forecourt and courtyard. A dream country house in which I could gladly be incarcerated for the rest of my life.

*Tuesday, 27th March*

To St Leonard's-on-Sea to inspect some furniture which a Mrs Tate wants to leave to the Trust. While I was under a table running my fingers in a professional manner up and down the legs, like a horse-coper examining fetlocks at a sale, I realised how ignorant I was, with no pretensions to judge what is genuine and fake in furniture. I rely upon instinct, sharpened by years of experience, rather than upon imbibed knowledge from books.

*Wednesday, 4th April*

My anticipated-with-apprehension but pleasurable dinner with Daisy Fellowes. There she was, splendid in black lace and a black mantilla over her hair, with violets in it for my benefit, so she said. A limousine took us to the Basque Restaurant in Dover Street. There was no wine, so we had to be contented with two glasses of sherry each. The bill came to £4 10*s.* with tip, which was monstrous. There was no actual breakdown of conversation, yet there were awkward pauses. I felt mesmerised like a rabbit by a stoat, and frightened to death until, come the pudding, I pulled myself together with 'Fool!' and pinched myself with 'To hell!' and proceeded to enjoy the rest of the evening mightily. Anyway, I am to go to the theatre with her next week.

When I got home I read in the evening paper that poor Ava [Lord Dufferin] had been killed. Ava was with Tom the friend I most admired at my private school and at Eton, where the three of us edited magazines together. I saw little of him at Oxford, and rarely met him afterwards. He had the best brain of my generation, and was at school a brilliant scholar, winning prizes after doing the minimum of work, always at the last moment. As a boy he was eccentric in that, during intense concentration, he would literally eat his handkerchief or suck ink from the end of a pen without realising what he was doing. I think he was ruined for life by the late Lord Birkenhead, who at Oxford taught him and others of his group to drink. Consequently he became a sad physical wreck before he was thirty.

*Sunday, 8th April*

And now what I so long foreboded and dreaded has happened. At 6.30, when just about to leave for Bridget [Parsons]'s and take her out for dinner, Nancy rang me up to say Tom had been killed in Burma. They heard yesterday. He was wounded in the stomach, and died on Good Friday. Whether he was with Ava they don't know. I could barely finish speaking to Nancy, who was very composed. She says her parents are shattered. Beloved, handsome Tom, who should have been married and had hosts of beautiful children; Tom, caviare to the general possibly, but to me the most loyal and affectionate of friends. It is hell. Bridget was wonderful, calm and sympathetic, and wretched too. I loved her for it.

*Thursday, 26th April*

*Angst* is the strangest, most unpredictable enemy. It assails one for no apparent reason in the most unlikely places. Today in Manchester walking from the station to the Midland Hotel I was so overwhelmed with a sense of my own futility that I was terrified lest someone might speak to me. It was most unlikely that someone would, for I know nobody and nobody knows me down here. But I skulked close to the wall on the side of the street away from the sun so as to be as inconspicuous as possible. I have noticed that April is always the worst month for this kind of nonsense.

*Friday, 27th April*

A bitter east wind, in fact the Protestant wind, so named by James II when he feared the beastly Orange's armada. I called myself at 7 and caught a train for Mow Cop [Cheshire]. Yesterday (apart from the skulking episode) and today have been blissful because I have been totally alone. From Mow Cop station I climbed the steep hill to the ridiculous castle folly which belongs to the N. Trust. It blew so hard at the top that I could scarcely breathe. Having inspected this monument associated with the Primitive Methodists, I descended across the fields to Little Moreton Hall. A truly picturesque scene, with the cows lying – it is going to rain – before the moat. The house looked more grotesque than ever; the gallery is so uneven and undulating that it must topple over into the moat. The chapel end subsides in an acute angle. And yet it stands like the Tower of Pisa. How, I wonder? I love the old-fashioned farmyard atmosphere, the heavy, polished Victorian furniture in the great hall, the brown teapot, the scones and marmalade and eggs for luncheon. Charming farmeresses waiting on me, and gossiping with each other, and for ever polishing.

*Tuesday, 1st May*

I worked and dined alone at Brooks's. At 10.30 a member rushed into the morning room announcing that Hitler's death had just come through on the tape. We all ran to read about it. Somehow, I fancy, none of us was very excited. We have waited and suffered too long. Three years ago we would have been out of our minds with jubilation – and with prognostications of a happy issue out of all our afflictions.

*Tuesday, 8th May*

This is V-day at last. I got home at 9.30,* had a bath and changed. At midday went to Bridget's flat, and with her and Anne to lunch with John Sutro† at Driver's. We were joined by Oliver Messel and a quiet, mystery man of about 50. We ate oysters and lobsters and drank sweet champagne. Then returned to hear Churchill's speech at 3 o'clock. It was merely a short announcement that peace had been declared. We were all rather disappointed, and wondered what the necessity was for telling us what we already knew.

I went to John Sutro's house and found Bridget there. Had it not been for the mystery man arriving uninvited at 8 o'clock, the evening would have been unalloyed fun. The three of us being such old friends were perfectly contented by our own company. Bridget was more beautiful and alluring than ever I remember her. We drank muscat wine, and listened to the King's speech at 9. It was perfect, well-phrased, well-delivered in his rich, resonant voice, expressed with true feeling and tinged with an appropriate emotion for the occasion. Bridget and I cooked the dinner, she scrambling eggs, I frying the bacon in great quantity. This was all we had, but it was delicious. We drank a bottle of excellent white wine and some very old brandy, sitting till 11.45 at the table. All the while the sad mystery man sat speechless. John played Chopin on the piano. At midnight I insisted on our joining the revels. It was a very warm night. Thousands of searchlights swept the sky. Otherwise there were no illuminations and no street lights at all. Claridge's and the Ritz were lit up. We walked down Bond Street passing small groups singing, not boisterously. Piccadilly was however full of swarming people and littered with paper.

We walked arm in arm into the middle of Piccadilly Circus which was brilliantly illuminated with arc lamps. Here the crowds were yelling, singing and laughing. They were orderly and good-humoured. All the English virtues were on the surface. We watched

* The previous day's entry had ended with J.L.-M. 'jubilating' in Piccadilly with the garden designer Lanning Roper.

† Film producer and *bon vivant* (1904–85).

individuals climb the lamp posts, and plant flags on the top amidst tumultuous applause from bystanders. We walked down Piccadilly towards the Ritz. In the Green Park there was a huge bonfire under the trees, and too near one poor tree which caught fire. Bridget made us push through the crowd collected on the pavement to a ring of people round the bonfire. Six or seven people were struggling under barricades of wood including whole doorways from air raid shelters which they dragged on to the fire. The fire's reflection upon thousands of faces, packed on the pavement, squatting on the grass and cramming the windows of the Piccadilly houses reminded me for some reason of a Harrison Ainsworth illustration of the crowds witnessing Charles I's execution. One extraordinary figure, a bearded, naval titan, organised an absurd nonsense game, by calling out the Navy and making them tear round the bonfire carrying the Union Jack; then the RAF; then the Army; then the Land Army, represented by three girls only; then the Americans; then the civilians. If we had been a little drunker we would have joined in. As it was Bridget took a flying leap over the pyre in sheer exuberance of spirits. The scene was more Elizabethan than neo-Georgian, a spontaneous peasant game, a dance round the maypole, almost Breughelian, infinitely bucolic. No one was bullied into joining who didn't want to, and the spectators enjoyed it as much as the participants. I thought, if we could have a V-night once a month, and invite the Poles, Germans, even Russians to do what we were doing now, there might never be another war.

We left Bridget at Mount Street. John and I went to his house where I slept the night. This was about 3 a.m.

*During June 1945 J.L.-M. was in the throes of two moves. Having to leave 104 Cheyne Walk, he accepted Geoffrey Houghton Brown's offer of accommodation at 17 Alexander Place, South Kensington; but this was in a state of disrepair, and it was not easy to find labour and materials to make it habitable. The same was true of 42 Queen Anne's Gate, a fine house recently donated to the National Trust, to which the Trust now moved from its pre-war offices at 7 Buckingham Palace Gardens, the imminent departure of Matheson, its long-standing Secretary, adding to the turmoil.*

*Friday, 1st June*

The lengths to which I have gone, the depths which I have plumbed, the concessions which I have (once most reluctantly) granted to acquire properties for the National Trust, will not all be known by that ungrateful body. It might be shocked by the extreme zeal of its servant, if it did. Yet I like to think that the interest of the property, or building, rather than the Trust has been my objective. I have to guard against the collector's acquisitiveness. It isn't always to the advantage of a property to be swallowed by our capacious if benevolent maw. These pious reflections came to me in the bath this morning.

*Wednesday, 13th June*

Brian Fairfax-Lucy* lunched with me at Brooks's and I found myself speaking too frankly about his odious father. When I excused myself, he agreed with what I had said, and elaborated to some tune. He said that all Sir Henry's children were terrified of him, and the lives of all of them had been ruined by him. After luncheon, Professor Richardson introduced me to Lord Crawford,† who was absolutely charming. One must beware of charmers.

*Saturday, 16th June*

This morning the telephone man came to Alexander Place to say he would install my telephone on Monday. My bureau is to arrive that day. My bookshelves and curtain rods are to be put up next week. So things are moving. The bath however is still unattached to the pipes. The house painter and I picnic together. I leave the house each morning at 7.30 to bathe, shave and breakfast at Brooks's, where I virtually live.

---

* Yr son (1898–1974) of Sir Henry Cameron-Ramsay-Fairfax-Lucy, 3rd Bt, who had died in 1944, leaving the decade-long negotiations over Charlecote unresolved; s. brother as 5th Bt, 1965; m. 1933 Hon. Alice Buchan (1908–93), dau. of 1st Viscount Tweedsmuir (the novelist John Buchan).

† David Lindsay, 24th Earl of Crawford (1900–75); Chairman of N.T., 1945–65.

In Heywood's shop I met Diana Mosley* and Evelyn Waugh with Nancy. I kissed Diana who said the last time we met was when I stayed the night in Wootton Lodge [Staffordshire], and we both wept when Edward VIII made his abdication broadcast. I remember it well, and Diana speaking in eggy-peggy† to Tom Mosley over the telephone so as not to be overheard. Diana looks radiant as ever. She was the most divine adolescent I ever beheld. Divine is the word, for she was a goddess, more immaculate, more perfect, more celestial than Botticelli's seaborne Venus. We all lunched at Gunter's and Harold Acton joined us, the first occasion he and Evelyn had seen Diana since her marriage to Tom. Her two Guinness boys from Eton also joined us: Jonathan,‡ a little cross and supercilious, Desmond§ good-looking like his father. He, aged 13, said to me, 'I wish Bryan would not go on having more children, for the money won't go round at this rate.' Diana said she had ordered a taxi-cab; she supposed it would come. 'The driver, I think and hope, is a fifth-columnist.' She *is* funny. Evelyn said his book [*Brideshead Revisited*] is already sold out – 14,000 copies.

Kathleen Kennet, who took me to the theatre, said Peter Scott's new book on battle boats has 24,000 copies printed. The play, *The Skin of our Teeth* [by Thornton Wilder], was hell. We could not be bothered to understand what it was all about. I had tea with the Kennets at Leinster Corner. K. and I are the best of friends again. Indeed I love her dearly.

I dined with Simon Harcourt-Smith, who said that in my Adam book I ought to discuss Adam's relationship with Chippendale,¶ his

---

* Hon. Diana Mitford (1910–2003); m. 1st 1929 Hon. Bryan Guinness (who s. 1941 as 2nd Baron Moyne), 2nd 1936 Sir Oswald ('Tom') Mosley, 6th Bt.

† Children's private language that involves adding 'egg' after the first letter of every syllable, invented to confuse and annoy grown-ups

‡ Elder son (b. 1930) of Diana Mosley by 1st husband, whom he succeeded, 1992, as 3rd Baron Moyne; writer and politician.

§ Hon. Desmond Guinness (b. 1931); founder-president of Irish Georgian Society, 1958–91.

¶ Thomas Chippendale (1718–79); furniture maker.

importance compared to Gabriel* and contemporary foreign architects, and the Roman–Greek controversy. At 10 I left Brooks's for home and ran into a friend in Piccadilly. 'Where are you hurrying?' I asked. 'To the Music Box,' he said. 'Come too.' There Sandy Baird,† whom I have not spoken to since Eton days, introduced himself to me, and me to a *louche* little sailor. The sailor called me Jimmie, and while Sandy was getting us drinks, said, 'Give me your address.' 'Ask Sandy for it,' I replied. He hissed in a whisper, 'God, no, I can't ask him.' So much for fidelity, I thought. He also said to me, 'I don't want your money, only friendship.' I was flattered, but would not accompany them to another club. I hate these places. They disinter one's dead adolescence and point to the pathetic loneliness of old age.

*On 23 June, with both his new rooms in Kensington and new office at Queen Anne's Gate in a chaos of building works, J.L.-M. escaped for a fortnight's holiday to Blickling Hall in Norfolk, where he hoped to make progress with his book on Adam.*

*Sunday, 24th June*

I am blissfully happy this afternoon. I write this at my table on the raised platform at the south-east end of the Gallery, as I had for so long pictured myself doing, surrounded by 12,000 calf-bound books, looking on to the beautiful but unkempt, unmown garden, and Ivory's temple at the far end of the vista. Here I intend to work for a fortnight, and pray to God no distractions will prevent me. But my character is weak, and I bow before temptation. I sleep and breakfast in Miss O'Sullivan's flat in the wing; I take all my other meals at the inn, where the landlady Mrs O'Donoghue is my friend. It is a warm sunny day. The air smells of roses and pinks. The tranquillity accentuates the extreme remoteness of Blickling, this beautiful house which I love.

---

* Court architect to Louis XV.

† A.W. B. G. Baird (b. 1908); nephew of 1st Viscount Stonehaven.

*Monday, 25th June*

And here is temptation literally at the door. At midday Wyndham Ketton-Cremer* called on me as I was working in the library. He plans to come over next Tuesday week (another temptation) and take me to Wolterton. After he had left I was told that Lord Wilton was on the line. He seemed anxious to see me, so I suggested his coming for the weekend, and he accepted. Temptation wins every encounter.

*Monday, 2nd July*

Worked all day till dinner, John [Wilton] sitting around the state rooms reading and apparently content. Stuart [Preston] telephoned this evening from London. He is back from the Continent. I can see further temptation looming.

*Tuesday, 3rd July*

Wyndham Ketton-Cremer spent the morning with me in the library, which, he says, contains the finest collection of seventeenth-century tracts he has ever come across. We lunched at the inn, and he agreed to take John on our tour. We called at Heydon first. The large house is let by the Bulwers to Lady Playfair, an old woman. It is a pretty house, centre part 1580, with Reptonish additions in the same style. Mrs Bulwer is a widow, charming, living in the dower house. She showed us her collection of teapots, hundreds of them, all English, mostly porcelain, some pottery, and a few very eccentric. Her house is overcrowded with treasures. There is a Queen Anne dolls' house, inherited by her husband from a direct ancestor. The outside is dull, but the contents are fascinating, particularly a chandelier enclosed in a glass bubble for protection, ivory forks and knives in a shagreen case, the servants and the owner and his wife with their names inscribed.

* R. W. Ketton-Cremer (1906–69); bachelor squire of Felbrigg Hall, Norfolk (which he bequeathed to the N.T.), and man of letters.

Among other extra dolls' house treasures were a pair of velvet shoes which belonged to Charles I.

Then to Wolterton. Lady Walpole* showed us round and gave us a good nursery tea. The house of beautiful, coursed brickwork. A heraldic achievement in the pediment finely carved. One wing has been added, which is a pity. The porch on the north front is unfortunate, and should go. The *piano nobile* is raised high, and the rooms on the ground, or basement, floor are quite habitable and cosy for the cold winters they get in Norfolk. The state rooms are splendid, though at present in a mess, for until lately Lady Walpole had officers billeted on her throughout the war, Lord Walpole still being in the Army. Ripley† may have been a second-rate architect, but the quality of his craftsmanship is far from shoddy. The carving of the doors is on the other hand coarse. Chimneypieces of a variety of marbles. Wolterton could be made a wonderful place in spite of the flat terrain. The troops are still in Nissen huts along the drive under the trees. John and I walked back to Blickling from the house.

*Thursday, 5th July*

Polling day,‡ but not for me. I simply cannot make up my mind how to vote. My dislike of Socialism is almost equalled by my dislike of what Mr Churchill stands for. What has the end of the war in Europe brought us? Perhaps the answer is that it has brought us nothing positively good, but has saved us from something infinitely bad. But it has brought us something else infinitely bad, if not worse, namely Russian occupation of Eastern Europe. Moreover, this damnable occupation of Christian countries which form part of our civilisation will spread like a disease, and we, being too tired and feeble to resist, will complacently defer, in our phlegmatic

* Nancy Harding Jones; m. 1937 Robert, 9th Baron Walpole (1913–89).

† Thomas Ripley (*c.* 1683–1758); protégé of Sir Robert Walpole, for whom he built Wolterton.

‡ To general surprise, the election, the results of which were only announced on 26 July, resulted in a massive defeat for Winston Churchill and the Conservative Party, a Labour Government coming to power with a majority of almost 150.

British way, resisting this disease until it is too late. No, politically speaking, I am miserable. Nevertheless, my joy at the ghastly fighting having stopped is great. This relief makes me so complacent that, if asked tomorrow whether I would be prepared to resume fighting Communists instead of Nazis, I would hesitate – I hope not for long.

*Friday, 6th July*

A glorious day of full sun. I worked and walked in my shirt sleeves. The RAF were bathing in the lake and lying in the sun. After dinner I bicycled to Erpingham where the N.T. owns a small detached parcel of the Blickling estate. I looked through the windows of Ingworth church, shut at this hour, and noticed a rood screen that seemed to be Jacobean. On the way back a delicious evening smell of amber hay. Bats flitting across the pale lemon sky.

Last night I had a dream about Tom [Mitford]. He was reading and sucking his pipe in the morning-room at Brooks's. I rushed up to him and he threw his arms around me. I said, 'Tom, they told me you were dead, and here I see and know that you are alive.' He laughed and said most convincingly, 'Yes, it was all a mistake.' Then I woke up.

*Saturday, 7th July*

Train punctual, and there on the platform was Stuart, smiling with pleasure. He was in his sergeant's uniform, unchanged in face and figure, though a little red like a porcupine without quills – the suns of Normandy. We went straight to the inn where he had an enormous meal at 3.30 of eggs and tea. It was as though there had been no break in our relations. Indeed there had been none. We went to the house and looked at the state rooms, then walked round the lake, and reclined under the trees in an Elizabethan fashion, chins hand-cupped. He had a bath in the bathroom next to the Chinese bedroom before we dined. The Sissons, having arrived to stay at the inn, ate with us. I don't think either party liked the other much. Incompatibility of interests; lack of common acquaintances; and instantaneous, suspicious antipathy of strangers. I am always naively surprised when my friends do not immediately click. After dinner Stuart and I left the Sissons and strolled round the lake, pausing at the remote end to take in the view of the house. Across the placid water it looked like a palace in a dream. Returned to the inn where we smoked and talked. It was past midnight when I left. The front door being barred and bolted, and no key anywhere visible, I let myself out of a window into a bed of nasturtiums and ran home. Luckily Miss O'Sullivan does not lock her front door.

*Sunday, 8th July*

We left Blickling after luncheon for London. In Alexander Place the bath is installed, but no hot water connected. The house still occupied by the painter, and in a filthy mess.

*Thursday, 19th July*

After cursing the caretaker at Polesden for neglecting his duties, and taking away two silver teapots bequeathed to Sir John Bailey, I arrived at Petworth at 3.30. I stopped at the street entrance, walked through a long, gloomy passage, crossed a drive, passed under a *porte-cochère* into a hall, and was ushered into Lord Leconfield's* presence. He gave me a hurried handshake without a smile, and told the housekeeper to show me round inside. This she did, bewailing the damage caused to ceilings and walls by Saturday's storm. She and one housemaid look after this vast palace. All the state rooms being shut up and the furniture under dustsheets, I had difficulty, with most of the shutters fastened, in seeing. I liked the housekeeper. She keeps the house spotless and polished. Then I was handed back to Lord Leconfield.

My first impression was of a pompous old ass, with a blue face and fish eyes. He seemed deliberately to misunderstand what the National Trust was all about. He was highly suspicious. He looked

* Charles Wyndham, 3rd Baron Leconfield (1872–1952).

up and said, 'Understand, this visit commits me to nothing. I much doubt whether the National Trust can help me.' He complained, understandably enough, of surtax, and would not grasp that the Trust was exempt from taxation. He implied that we would turn him out of the house the moment we took over. He walked me very slowly round the park. He said that the Victorian architect Salvin,* when summoned by his father, stood on a mound in the park, and pointing to the house, said, 'My Lord, there is only one thing to be done. Pull the whole house down and rebuild it.' His father replied, 'You had better see the inside first.'

At 5.45 Lord Leconfield, tired out, led me to the street door where he dismissed me. Pointing to a tea house with an enormous notice CLOSED hanging in the window, he said, 'You will get a very good tea in there. Put it down to me. Goodbye.'

*Tuesday, 31st July*

Matheson left the office today, and we are in chaos. I had luncheon with Eddy, who goes this week to live with Eardley and Desmond [Shawe-Taylor]† at Long Crichel in Dorset.

*Wednesday, 8th August*

John Wilton telephoned that his trustees refuse categorically to sanction his buying Audley End. I am very disappointed but not the least surprised.

All day I have been made to feel despairing, careless and numb by the atom bomb. Nothing has any purpose any more, with these awful clouds of desolation hanging over us. I am shocked, shocked, shocked by our use of this appalling bomb, a tiny instrument of the size of a golf ball, dropped on the Japanese and devastating four square miles. It is horrifying, and utterly damnable.

---

* Anthony Salvin (1799–1881).

† Music critic (1907–95); friend of Eddy Sackville-West and Eardley Knollys. Their household at Long Crichel was to become a haven of civilised hospitality for their friends, including J.L.-M.

*Friday, 10th August*

Oh the onslaught of age! I met Lord Redesdale* in Heywood's shop. Nancy said, 'You know Farve,' and there, leaning on a stick, was a bent figure with a shrunken, twisted face, wearing round, thick spectacles, looking like a piano tuner. Last time I saw him he was upstanding and one of the best-looking men of his generation. I suppose Tom's death has hastened this terrible declension. I melted with compassion.

I had to lunch Charles Fry my publisher at the Park Lane Hotel. He was late, having just got up after some orgy *à trois* with whips, etc. He is terribly depraved and related every detail, not questioning whether I wished to listen. In the middle of the narration I simply said, 'Stop! Stop!' At the same table an officer was eating, and imbibing every word. I thought he gave me a crooked look for having spoilt his fun.

My delight in Churchill's defeat, disapproval of the Socialists' victory, detestation of the atom bomb and disgust with the Allies' treatment of Germany are about equal.

*Wednesday, 15th August*

Miss Ballachey telephoned at 9 to say the war was over, and today and tomorrow were public holidays. I am strangely unmoved by this announcement. The world is left a victim of chaos, great uncertainty and heinous turpitude. This morning no buses are running, and everything is very tiresome, including the drizzle. Nevertheless I went to the office and drafted letters. Worked all afternoon.

I dined at Sibyl's Ordinary† and didn't enjoy it one bit, although several friends were present, including the Nicolson boys.‡ Nigel was looking wonderfully healthy and handsome. He

* David Mitford, 2nd Baron Redesdale (1878–1958); father of the Mitford sisters; portrayed as 'Uncle Matthew' in Nancy Mitford's novels.

† Luncheon and dinner parties towards which the guests were expected to contribute financially according to their means.

‡ Benedict Nicolson (1914–78), art historian, Deputy Surveyor of the King's Picture, 1939–47; Nigel Nicolson (1917–2004), soldier, writer, publisher and politician; sons of Harold Nicolson and Vita Sackville-West.

astonished me and embarrassed Ben by saying loudly, 'I do wish men would make up their faces.' I can think of several who might improve themselves in this way, although Nigel has no need to do it. He made wry references to James [Pope-Hennessy]'s behaviour as though he were surprised and pained by it.* I left with Desmond Shawe-Taylor, and we walked against a stream of people coming away from Buckingham Palace. We stood for three-quarters of an hour on the Victoria Monument gazing expectantly at the crimson and gold hangings over the balcony. Floodlit the façade looked splendid, but the minute Royal Standard was out of scale. Desmond could not bear waiting, being an impatient man, but I was determined to wait. Besides I easily get myself into a sort of cabbage condition and can't be bothered to uproot myself. The crowd showed some excitement, calling 'We want the King', 'We want the Queen', but not uproariously. At last, just after midnight, the French window opened a crack, then wider, and out came the King and Queen. They were tiny. I could barely distinguish her little figure swathed in a fur, and something sparkling in her hair. The gold buttons of his Admiral's uniform glistened. Both waved in a slightly self-conscious fashion and stood for three minutes. Then they retreated. The crowd waved with great applause, and all walked quietly home.

*Monday, 20th August*

Charles Fry wants the National Trust to apply for more paper for Batsford to print another 10,000 copies of my N.T. book, which is selling beyond their expectations. The 7,500 copies they printed have gone in under a week.†

*J.L.-M. travelled to Ireland with Michael Rosse to stay at the Rosses' seat in County Offaly, Birr Castle, his first trip outside Great Britain since 1940.*

---

* Nigel had been infatuated with James Pope-Hennessy at Oxford in the 1930s, and shocked to discover that James was one of his father's lovers.

† On 2 August J.L.-M. had reported that the book was out, but looked 'rather thin and cheap'.

*Saturday, 25th August*

I woke at 5.45 and at 6.45 the car ordered by Michael Rosse called for me. It picked him up in Mount Street and drove us to Euston for the 8.15 to Holyhead. Travelled in comfort and ease. I read several books during the journey, Michael much amused because I read standing in queues on the boat. I always do this, for what is the point of letting the minutes roll by in vacancy?

At Holyhead Anne's two Armstrong-Jones children* joined us. After a smooth crossing we reached Kingstown at 7.30. I was at once struck by the old-fashioned air of everything: horse-cabs on the quay, cobbled streets with delicious horse-droppings on them. Met by a taxi-cab come all the way from Birr, for £8. Letter of greeting from Anne to Michael. Vodka for Michael and me in the car. We drove straight to Birr. Even through the closed windows of the car I caught the sweet smell of peat in the air. Curious scenes, ragged children on horses drawing old carts along country lanes. Our driver sounded his horn loudly through Birr, that pretty, piercing foreign horn. The gates of the castle shot open as if by magic. A group of people were clustered outside the gate. We swept up the drive. All the castle windows were alight, and there on the sweep was a large crowd of employees and tenants gathered to welcome Michael home from the war. Anne, the two Parsons boys,† and Mr Garvie the agent on the steps. Behind them Leavy the butler, the footman, housekeeper, and six or seven maids. A fire blazing in the library and everywhere immense vases of flowers. We heard Michael make a short speech from the steps, followed by cheers and 'For he's a jolly good fellow', a song which always makes me go hot and cold, mostly hot. The crowd then trooped off to a beano and drinks, while we sat down to a huge champagne supper at 11 o'clock.

---

* Antony Armstrong-Jones (b. 1930; m. 1960 HRH Princess Margaret; cr. Earl of Snowdon, 1961); Susan Armstrong-Jones (d. 1986; m. 1950 John Eustace Vesey, 6th Viscount de Vesci [1919–83]).

† Hon. William Brendan Parsons (b. 1936; s. father as 7th Earl, 1979); Hon. Martin Parsons (b. 1938).

*Sunday, 26th August*

I rose late this morning, just in time for Mass in the town 'with the natives'. The church very full and crowded, and somehow horribly sectarian and un-Roman; but clean and polished. Indeed there is an air of well-being and contentment in Ireland, and almost of prosperity after England. The house-fronts in the town are painted and the inhabitants well clothed, whereas before the war I remember them as squalid and poverty-stricken. This shows how English standards and conditions must have deteriorated during the war years. The streets in Birr are swept. There is as little traffic as before the war. The smell of horse-dung everywhere is very refreshing after the petrol fumes.

*Tuesday, 28th August*

Bridget came from Abbey Leix* yesterday, and today Lord X. He is an agreeable, plump, intelligent Irishman, a Catholic from Galway.† He says the priests are so bigoted and politically minded that he fears there will be a strong reaction against Catholicism in Ireland within the next generation. Most of the priests are peasants' sons, with no true vocation. They become priests because it gives them social status. He blames Maynooth College.‡ A generation ago the neophytes went to Rome. Now they are totally nationalistic and provincial in outlook. The Cardinal is positively chauvinistic. Lord X. blames the Vatican for not taking the Irish hierarchy in hand. The people are kept in great ignorance, as in Spain.

We went for a walk this afternoon with the children, in the bog, leaping from tuft to tuft. The wide, flat expanse of bog with purple heather growing on it, and the purple hills, always just in sight, very nostalgic. I find the climate extremely relaxing. I eat a lot, am

---

* Seat of Viscount de Vesci in Queen's County, built by James Wyatt; the current châtelaine (Lois Lister-Kaye [1882–1984]; m. 1st 1905 5th Earl of Rosse, 2nd 1920 5th Viscount de Vesci) was Michael Rosse's mother.

† Probably Michael Morris, 3rd Baron Killanin (1914–99), journalist and author.

‡ Catholic seminary in Co. Kildare, established in 1795 with assistance from Ireland's Protestant Government.

sleepy, and wake up feeling doped. The food is rich after England, and the cooking full of cream and butter.

*Thursday, 30th August*

We motored up the mountain, got out and walked over the heather in the sun. The heather smells acrid. It is curious how quite high up you come upon soggy patches of bog where the turf has been sliced away. Oh yes, the climate of Ireland is far too relaxing. There is something dead about the country and the people. It is like living on a luxuriant moon. I dislike the way individuals remain for hours on end standing and staring into space. We passed this morning one woman sitting on a stile, with the face of a zany, staring, not at the view, but at her toes. When we returned this evening, she was still there in the same idiotic posture. This gives me the creeps.

*Friday, 31st August*

Michael and I motored thirty miles to Abbey Leix to fetch his mother, Lady de Vesci. I was last here at Easter 1936 staying with Desmond Parsons.* I had forgotten the extraordinary beauty of the park and trees. The vivid fresh green of Ireland in August after the aridity of England is startling. The house was built about 1780 and is Adam-like. A beautiful hall with columned screen, delicate frieze, and the whitest statuary marble chimneypiece. Two drawing-rooms with thin decorated ceilings, one with deep sky-blue Morris wallpaper which, though wrong, is very attractive with the gold mirrors and frames. The library has pink scagliola columns, green walls, mud-coloured bookcases and Siena doorways, all dating from about 1850 and very charming: facing full south. The exterior has been too Victorianised, balustrades added, window-surrounds altered, and some plate glass inserted.

* Hon. Desmond Parsons (1910–37), Michael Rosse's younger brother, whom J.L.-M. loved at Eton.

At Roscrea, on our return to Birr, a large brown dog walked under the car which drove right over its body. Lady de Vesci made the driver pull up, get out and apologise. I saw the poor dog kicking in the road, but by the time the driver reached it, it was dead and being dragged to the verge. I felt rather sick. This is the first time such a thing has happened to me, though I expected this driver would kill a dog sooner or later. In Ireland dogs are not well trained to avoid motor-cars, as they seem to be in England. Michael and his mother were quite unmoved, and so it seemed were the owners of the dog. What a contrast to my mother's behaviour. If she had been present she would have created the most embarrassing scene, tearing out the driver's hair in rage, hugging the corpse and emptying her purse into the lap of the owner.

*Saturday, 1st September*

Before leaving Birr for Dublin I spent the afternoon with Anne alone, the others having gone for a walk in the woods. She conducted me round the castle, showing me all the portraits and little things belonging to Parsons ancestors that mean so much to her. She is a proud châtelaine and looks after her possessions with tender care. I have the greatest admiration for her efficiency, her vitality, her keen wit and good nature. She always has the ready answer.

The train to Dublin was packed with folk going up to the Games. There is only one train each weekday, and none on Sundays. At Dublin I spent three-quarters of an hour in an appalling jam trying to extricate my bag, which unfortunately the chauffeur had put in the [guard's] van because he thought I should not get a seat and would have no room for it in the corridor. A typical Irish scene of muddle and confusion. Before we got to the van it left the platform, to our dismay. Eventually it returned, whereupon porters and passengers screamed and scrambled over each other, the passengers complaining vociferously at the inadequacy of the system which, they maintained, could only be experienced in Ireland. Had a foreigner agreed with them, they would doubtless have set upon him. In Dublin I was pushed into a four-wheeler with two other passengers, and we bowled over the cobbles to the Hibernian

Hotel. Here I found Geoffrey Houghton Brown and we dined after 10. No difficulty getting a meal at this hour, and plenty of waiters.

*Sunday, 2nd September*

Walked this morning to the Municipal Museum. Quite a good collection of modern pictures: Lavery,* Jack Yeats,† and the Hugh Lane‡ collection (corresponding to our Tate Gallery). All the churches so crowded that we could hardly enter one. The devotion of the men and women is not so much exemplary as alarming, for the Irish are not a spiritual people.

You see no platinum blondes, no tarts in Dublin streets. There is absolutely no evidence of vice on the surface. Yet the squalor of the slums is formidable. We walked into several doorways in Henrietta Street. Splendid mid Georgian grand houses, now tenements in neglect, dirt and disrepair. But what a wonderful town. Streets of flat-façaded houses, dull maybe, but of long unbroken elevation and layout. The atmosphere created by the four-wheelers, the side-cars, the smell of ammonia from horses and the stale straw from mews is of the 1890s. The bouquets of ferns and geraniums tied round lamp-posts conjure up 'Art Nouveau' poster designs. We looked at the Customs House, the Four Courts, the Castle, Trinity College and several churches. We bought sweets§ and ate them in the streets. The view across the river, which reminded me of the Arno, of the magnificent elevation of the Four Courts is spoilt by mean little trees.

*J.L.-M. returned to London.*

---

* Sir John Lavery (1856–1941); Irish artist.

† Jack B. Yeats (1871–1957); Irish artist, brother of the poet William B. Yeats.

‡ Sir Hugh Lane (1875–1915); Irish-born London art dealer, who established Dublin's Municipal Gallery of Modern Art in 1908.

§ Strictly rationed in Great Britain.

*Tuesday, 4th September*

At 4 Anthony Martineau and I had a painful meeting about Ham House in Richmond Town Hall with the town councillors and the Tollemache family: old Sir Lyonel and his son. The town clerk and councillors were gushing and deferential: the Tollemaches proud and patronising. When the Tollemaches left we stayed behind and the town councillors became outspoken in their derision and dislike. I was horribly and uncomfortably aware of the hostility between the two classes.

*Saturday, 15th September*

Arrived [in Edinburgh] 8.30. Breakfasted and established myself at the Railway Hotel. Had a full and successful day. First I visited Adam's Register House and was shown round by a dour Scot, the curator of public records. Was rather disappointed with this building. Then to the National Library and looked at two manuscript letters of R. Adam. Then to St Giles's Cathedral, which did not please me greatly. Adam's University however I thought very fine indeed, in particular the street elevation and Playfair's inner court. After luncheon I climbed Calton Hill, which is Edinburgh's Acropolis, with its temple of Lysicrates, etc., and crossing the road looked at Adam's tomb for David Hume. The city is splendid from this site. A strong, warm wind was chopping the distant sea below the Forth Bridge. Arthur's Seat a prominent feature from here. In the afternoon I walked an unconscionable amount, admiring the architecture of the New Town, George Street, Adam's Charlotte Square. Was duly edified by Steel's memorial to the Prince Consort, with sentimental groups at the corners of aristocrats, bureaucrats, peasants and artisans, paying ridiculous homage to him. The iron railings and lamp standards in this square survive intact. There are some truly majestic Squares and Crescents with palatial houses, like those in Moray Place, on a grander scale than Dublin's, Bath's or Brighton's. Edinburgh is a very black city due, I suppose, to the railway line, which really should not be allowed to run in the great valley. After looking at numerous Adam houses I caught an evening train to Berwick.

From Berwick I was driven to Beale foreshore, where I changed into a ramshackle, rusty old car which drove me in the dark across the sands to Holy Island,* quite three miles away. Although the tide was out we splashed through water on parts of the causeway, for the sands are never thoroughly dry. Sometimes a horse and cart have to be used, and when the tide is up, a motor-boat. There are two lines of posts to guide vehicles, for off the track the sands are treacherous. A weird, open, grey expanse of mudflat with millions of worm-casts, flights of duck over one's head, and pencilled hills in the distance. The car mounts the bank of the island shore, and bumbles along a tolerable road through the little village of Lindisfarne. Beyond the village is Lindisfarne Castle, perched high up on an abrupt rock. The car bumps over the grass and stops. Mr de Stein† and a friend were there to greet me. We walked up a cobbled path to the portcullis, and then further steps. A family of islanders looks after the Castle, and serves de Stein whenever he comes here.

De Stein is a peppery, fussy, schoolmasterish man, with whom I should hate to have a row. He has not got a good manner. After dinner we had a talk about mysticism. He recommended a book by William James‡ on the subject. The friend staying is about my age, fair-haired, stocky, an expert botanist who has worked in East Africa, attached in some way to Kew Gardens, and now in the Army. Rather nice. I can't quite make de Stein out. He is prudish and disapproving, yet he puts his arm round one's waist and makes rapid, sly remarks which I think it best to leave unheeded.

---

* Site of Anglo-Hibernian monastery of Lindisfarne, founded by St Aiden and the Irish monks of Iona in 634; subsequently the seat of St Cuthbert (d. 687), in whose memory the celebrated volume known as the Lindisfarne Gospels was produced (now in British Library).

† City financier who had bought Lindisfarne Castle from the Hudson family (who had commissioned Lutyens to redesign it in 1902), and presented it with its contents to the N.T. in 1944.

‡ American philosopher and founder of the science of psychology (1842–1910); brother of the novelist Henry James.

*Thursday, 20th September*

Clouds Hill, T. E. Lawrence's cottage, is in the middle of Bovington Heath [Dorset], which is a blasted waste of desolation, churned feet-deep in mud by a thousand Army tanks. The cottage is embowered in rhododendrons. It is a pathetic shoddy little place. The visitors have stolen all they could lay their hands on, including the screw of the porthole window in Lawrence's bedroom, and the clasps of the other windows. The bunk gives an idea of his asceticism. Pat Knowles, his batman, is back from abroad. He and his wife, a pretty, gazelle-like woman, live in another cottage across the way where Lawrence fed with them. They conduct visitors over Clouds Hill, and dare not let them out of their sight for a minute. Knowles is a high-minded, cultivated proletarian, a youngish 45 with vestiges of gold hair. Bespectacled face now a bit puffy, but must once have been handsome.

*Saturday, 22nd September*

Lord and Lady Bradford* conducted me round Castle Bromwich Hall.† It is a fine red-brick house of Elizabethan date with several late seventeenth-century ceilings of the compartmented, bay-wreath type. Much early and much William and Mary panelling. The painted ceiling over the staircase by Laguerre.‡ The house is empty, having been vacated by the troops, and in consequence is a filthy mess. Every window broken by bombs dropped in the garden, all the heraldic glass destroyed in this way. Yet in other respects suprisingly little structural damage incurred. The most alarming threat to the building is the dry-rot which is rampant. The garden, now very neglected, is contained within a brick wall. It has

* Orlando Bridgeman, 5th Earl of Bradford (1873–1957); m. 1904 Hon. Margaret Bruce, er dau. of 2nd Baron Aberdare.

† The Hall eventually became the headquarters of a property company, while the gardens were preserved by a trust.

‡ Louis Laguerre (1663–1721); French artist who worked on decorative schemes at English country houses.

descending terraces, a contemporary maze and holly hedges in the formal style. I would say it is an important and complete garden of *circa* 1700.

Lord Bradford is a very courteous man, the epitome of good breeding. Lady B., whom I like, kept snubbing him. She told him he ought to give the place to the Trust without further thought. What was the good, she said, of letting it to unsatisfactory business firms who had no idea how to look after it? The family would never want to live in it again. This I think is incontrovertible. She pointed out that he had let the stable block to some depot for £100 p.a., out of which he receives, after tax, £2 10*s*. I suggested that perhaps Birmingham might have some use for this marvellous old house, still so tranquil, so well sited on its hill and yet now so close to the city.

*Saturday, 29th September*

Went to tea at Emerald's. Violet Trefusis was there – a large, clumsy, plain woman wearing a top-heavy hat, and sitting in such a way that one could see a naked expanse of thigh. Young Giles Romilly* also there. He is distant and distraught. He told me he had not yet recovered from being a prisoner of war; that being out of prison has no savour – it is like wanting to smoke after a cold. He is a Communist, which I don't find endearing, but an interesting young man. Although he can't be more than 25, he has grey streaks in his black hair. He said he hated society women, the sort that were know-alls, in the know, in the swim, had to be 'in with' everything, and were merely pretentious pseudo-intellectuals. I asked him why he mixed with them. He said he only did so to glean material for the novels he hoped to write. I said I too detested the sort of women he described, but all rich and grand women were not like that, nodding at Emerald, whom I never think of as a 'society woman', that hateful term.

---

* Journalist (1916–67); correspondent during Spanish Civil War; captured in Norway and imprisoned in Colditz (owing to his being Mrs Churchill's nephew), later writing a book about his escape; his brother Esmond (killed in action, 1941) m. Hon. Jessica ('Decca') Mitford.

When the guests left I started talking to Emerald about the world's great novels, about the discontent of the rich and the still greater discontent of the poor. 'It's less sad to be rich,' Emerald concluded. When Emerald gets talking about literature and music, about which she knows so much and loves so passionately, I realise that, for all her faults, she is a woman out of the common run. She is almost a phenomenon, and a rare and inspired talker. When she is with company her nonsense can be funnier than any nonsense I have ever enjoyed.

Esher was for once wrong when he criticised her yesterday. She shocked him by telling him how she took off her shoes to show her beautiful feet to a young man. 'Just fancy an old woman of eighty-two doing a thing like that,' he said. I said I thought it was enchanting of Emerald, for her feet are still beautiful, and her spontaneity is beautiful. Lady E. on this occasion asked if she might call me James, since everyone else seems to do so. I said I was delighted, for James was well on the way to Jim, which my friends called me. Lord E. chuckled, for out of policy he steadfastly calls me Mr L.-M. 'If we were on Christian name terms,' he said, 'it would be awkward if I had to sack you.'

*Monday, 1st October*

This morning I went – oh never mind where. It is not interesting. Besides, my old typewriter has broken down, and I have cut the index finger of my right hand. Besides too, this diary ought to have an end. Its background was the war. Its only point was the war. And the war is now over – to all intents and purposes – isn't it?

# 1946

# 1946

*For reasons explained in his entry for 6 January, J.L.-M. resumed his diary in 1946. These postwar journals have a different flavour from the wartime ones. Life in battered Britain was grim, with Socialist 'austerity', continued rationing and shortages, and a succession of freezing winters; and J.L.-M's mood of weary discontent reflected that of the nation as a whole. He was also busier than ever, for the National Trust was overwhelmed with offers of country houses whose overtaxed owners saw no possibility of continuing to live in them independently, as well as having to prepare properties for opening to the public and negotiate with the Labour Government for financial and legislative support. Such social life as J.L.-M. had time for lacked the excitement of the war, when one lived for the moment.*

*As 1946 began, J.L.-M. was still living at 17 Alexander Place – though within a few months he followed his landlord Geoffrey Houghton Brown, a restless buyer and seller of houses, across the street to 20 Thurloe Square (which was to remain his London base for fifteen years). He was putting the finishing touches to his first work of architectural history,* The Age of Adam.

*Tuesday, 1st January*

No one asked me to a party last night, so I dined at home and went to bed early. At midnight heard the sirens and distant cheering. The idiocy of it. Buried my head in the pillow and turned over.

Went to the dentist who said it is trench mouth I am suffering from. It sounds too disgusting, and I haven't been near a trench. I am destined to suffer from sins uncommitted. Had tea with dear Lady Throckmorton whose nephew Nicholas Throckmorton,*

* Nicholas Throckmorton was born in 1913 but predeceased his cousin Sir Robert (who d. 1989).

Robert's heir, called. Consequently I couldn't talk to her as intimately about Coughton as I would have liked.

*Wednesday, 2nd January*

One of the coldest of days. Midi lunched, or rather didn't lunch with me. We could not get a table anywhere so finally went to her club where she gave me a scratch meal at 1.45. Drank sherry with old Logan, aged eighty, lying on a bed in his cosy room. He calls it a deathbed cocktail party. He told me a long story of an American cousin of Henry James who stayed with James in Paris. The cousin was known to all as the Sir Galahad of the New World. He invited the novelist to sleep with him. I longed to hear the sequel but Logan was overcome with a fit of coughing.

*Sunday, 6th January*

Why do I resume this diary which three months ago I brought to an end? There is no explanation. I merely missed it like an old friend. It has never intentionally been a confessor. And being a bad Catholic I used, when I went to Confession, to skate lightly over sins I had a mind to while emphasising those I was less inclined to, and fancied I might with an effort abandon altogether. So too, being cowardly, I treated and shall continue treating my diary like an intimate friend who mustn't know everything. If a man has no constant lover who shares his soul as well as his body he must have a diary – a poor substitute, but better than nothing.

*Wednesday, 9th January*

A meeting of the Historic Buildings Committee this morning. The Committee turned down Hever Castle as a gross fake. I lunched with Lord Esher and he agreed to support me in appointing Robin Fedden* curator of Polesden Lacey; also agreed that I should write the guide book to the place. Esher spoke most eloquently about

* Writer and mountaineer (1909–77); J.L.-M's successor (1951–68) as Historic Buildings Secretary of the N.T.

the civil service mind as we crossed St James's Park – the footbridge is closed for they are digging a bomb from beneath it. Began by saying that he never believed in hari-kiri [*sic*]. Many people after 1911* thought the House of Lords was doomed and gave up the struggle, whereas it still survives, and fulfils another and no less necessary function. The same could be said of the Monarchy, now that it is constitutional. This is why he believes the National Trust will survive, and profoundly disagrees with George Mallaby's,† the new Secretary's, defeatism in assuming that the Government are bound eventually to take over the Trust's activities. He, Esher, said this attitude was typical of the civil service mind, which is perfectionist. He said the aristocratic mind was quite different: it was pragmatical, and made the best out of indifferent materials.

*Friday, 11th January*

Jamesey dined at Brooks's. He was his enchanting old self, indiscreet and communicative. He is madly in love with a Communist Pole who won't allow J. to go in a taxi because it is patrician. J. being a masochist enjoys this sort of treatment. In his book on Lord Houghton he intends to have a showdown of the upper classes for their cruelty. The Pole's influence, of course. J. says he has no manners at all. When bored in other people's houses he takes up a paper and reads. Sounds hell to me.

*Saturday, 12th January*

Motored in the office Morris to Uppark in Sussex. Lady Meade-Fetherstonhaugh‡ kindly gave me coffee – stone cold – from a pot she held over a log fire. She was welcoming and friendly and most

---

* Year of the Parliament Act, which deprived the Lords of their legislative veto.

† (Sir) George Mallaby (1902–78); served in military secretariat of War Cabinet, 1942–5; succeeded Matheson as Secretary of N.T., 1945–6; later Civil Service Commissioner.

‡ Margaret Glyn; m. 1911 Admiral Hon. Sir Herbert Meade (1875–1964), yr s. of Admiral of the Fleet 4th Earl Clanwilliam, who added the name Fetherstonhaugh on inheriting Uppark, 1932.

anxious that our scheme should succeed. The country round here is heavenly, rolling downs under a pellucid sea-light. Backed by a belt of trees the house commands a panoramic view of sheep-cropped sward and the sea. A romantic house, yet it disappoints me a little. Perhaps because it is so tumbledown, and the slate roof is shiny purple and the elliptical dormers are too spotty. Lady M.-F. showed me all round. She has done wonders repairing the curtains and stuffs and bringing back their old colours by dye from her herb garden. Saponaria is her great secret.* She is a first-rate needlewoman and, before the war interrupted her work, spent years labouring away. During the war she had to do her own housework and so the fabric repairs were neglected. She showed me one curtain which was a heap of dull silk tatters, and another, which she has retrieved from a like state. It is a deep, live mulberry colour, minutely hemmed and stitched. The contents of the house are marvellous. She told me that Eddie Winterton† was ruled out of inheritance by old Miss Fetherstonhaugh before she died in 1895. He was brought there as a child by his mother and was rather rude; asked his mother why Miss F. dropped her h's, and if he was to own the place one day. The Lady Leconfield of the day was ruled out too. Miss F. asked her what she would do with the silver, if the place was left to her. 'Take it to Petworth of course,' she said. There are no servants in the house now at all. Lady M.-F. and the Admiral gave us luncheon and tea in the basement. Their lives are completely and utterly sacrificed to the house, and they and their son love it. Mr Cook's agent, Hill, is determined they shall part with all the contents for the inclusive offer of £50,000, with which sum they have to endow the house. So they, poor things, will get nothing in cash out of the transaction.

*Monday, 14th January*

Went to Cecil Beaton's birthday cocktail party. Talked to Daisy Fellowes who had been to Strawberry Hill, and Loelia Westminster

---

* Not in fact a dye, but a herbal cleanser.

† Edward Turnour, 6th Earl Winterton (1883–1962); Irish peer who served as a Conservative MP for forty-seven years; Chancellor of the Duchy of Lancaster, 1938–9.

who introduced me to her beau, Whitney Straight.* Talked to a charming young Norwegian over here with his delegation to UNO. Said I would be surprised if I knew how stupid most of the delegates were, especially Mr Spaak.† I left with Jamesey who was in tears because his Pole has been recalled to Warsaw. J. now hates Stalinism because he says the individual is sacrificed to the Party. I could have told him that before.

*Tuesday, 15th January*

Made a regrettable and most extraordinary discovery this morning. *Pediculus pubis*‡ Dr Black's dictionary calls it, in its genteel phraseology. Now this honestly is not through physical contacts for I have had *none*. I can suggest only the proverbial lavatory seat, perhaps the one in the train last Friday. Public places and conveyances these days are absolutely filthy. I know curates invariably give these reasons and excuses. But I am not a curate with a necessity to lie. Anyway it is a sad record, trench mouth and creepy-crawlies within a fortnight.

*Wednesday, 16th January*

Mallaby and I had an interview in the morning with Sir Somebody Robinson, who is permanent head of the Ministry of Works. Briefly, he postulated that the Government were just as fit persons to hold country houses as the National Trust, if it was a case of their having to provide funds. Mallaby, being a civil servant, was about to agree, but I gave him no chance to do so, interjecting, 'By heaven, you're not!' rather rudely, then explained why. Michael Rosse, Bridget [Parsons] and Clarissa [Churchill] dined with me at

* American-born racing driver (1912–79); fought with RAF in Second World War and twice captured; later Chairman of BOAC.

† Paul-Henri Spaak (1899–1972); Belgian Foreign Minister, who chaired inaugural meeting of UN General Assembly in London that month.

‡ Lice in the pubic hair, otherwise known as 'crabs'.

a new restaurant, the Lyric, in Dean Street. No one spoke much. I was longing to go to bed. Before this lamentable meal I went to Uncle Ian Hamilton's ninety-third birthday party at 1 Hyde Park Gardens. When I went to say goodbye he did not recognise me. Watched him sitting among the boys of the Gordon Highlanders, as obsessed with the conjurer as they. Poor Blight, the parlourmaid, in her pale blue uniform, now crippled with arthritis. The ghost of darling Aunt Jean still hovers in that house of Roger Fry's* pitch black and green.

*Friday, 18th January*

A Rolls-Royce is the only car that has aesthetic merits. It has solidity, dignity and beauty even when fifteen years old. It purrs and it glides.†

*Saturday, 19th January*

Bitter cold and frozen snow in patches along the street. Got through very little of my [Adam] book this weekend. Very dissatisfied with what I have so far written. That intolerably stilted, cumbersome style of mine when I try too hard.

*Tuesday, 22nd January*

Lunched with John Wilton at Wilton's. He took me in his luxurious black Rolls to my office, we sitting in the back under rugs, driven by the chauffeur. Surprisingly sybaritic young man. Dined at Sibyl Colefax's Ordinary and sat next to Lady Esher and Daisy. Lady E. said, 'You are sitting next to the siren. I shan't be allowed to talk to you.' Only too true. John Russell's new wife,‡ a plain dark

---

* Bloomsbury artist and critic (1866–1934).

† J.L.-M. had bought the car on 5 January from an 'odious Mr Marcus' for £600.

‡ Alexandrine Apponyi; m. 1945 (as 1st of his three wives) John Russell (who launched his literary career that year with *British Portrait Painters*).

girl, there, and John fatter, more prosperous than of yore, the ethereal Shelleyan looks gone already.

*Wednesday, 23rd January*

Picked up Robin Fedden and Ben Nicolson and motored them down to Polesden. I think Fedden, who is serious in his wish to be curator, will do very well. We picnicked in the little room next to the library. I left them there and went to Worplesdon to collect some books and letters and a lacquer work-box, Goethe's present to the Carlyles for their wedding. On my return the telephone rang. It was Rick Stewart-Jones, back from Palestine. So I put off my homework, and gave him dinner and Australian burgundy at Brooks's. Came back here and talked till 12.30.

*Friday, 25th January*

Set off on tour of the Eastern counties – not perhaps the time of year most people would choose. I don't choose. Got to Anglesey Abbey for tea. Wonderfully appointed house, soft-treading carpets; full of semi-works of art, over-heated, over-flowered, and I do not covet it or anything in it. We had a frugal tea but sumptuous dinner prefaced by whisky and epilogued by port. Lord Fairhaven is precise, complacent and dogmatic. Hospitable and kind, though aloof and pleased with his noble position. Who is he, anyway? The son of an American oil magnate. We talked till midnight and groaned delightedly about the way the nation is going to the dogs.

*Saturday, 26th January*

Woke with slight hangover from whisky and port, and my over-heated bedroom. The chauffeur who has two Rolls-Royces here discovered my clutch was slipping and put it right for me.

I reached Huntingdon and Hinchingbrooke at 1 o'clock. What a contrast to the Hollywood Anglesey Abbey. No answer from the front door bell, so I drove round to the back. Walked in and found my way through a labyrinth of passages, finally emerging into the square oak room at the corner where Hinch* was squatting over an inadequate fire. He greeted me with, 'My dear Jimmie, has no one helped you find the way in?' He and Rosemary most welcoming. Gave me sherry and a rabbit pie cooked by Rosemary, for the staff consists of army batmen and wives, and no cook. The Hinchingbrookes are picnicking in the house, still full of hospital beds and furniture. The hospital has only just vacated. Hinch took me round the outside and inside of the house. The gatehouse and nunnery, with gables, and the large 1692 bay window are the best features. Hinch has contracted for £400 to have the 1880 wing of red brick pulled down, also the ugly pepper-box tower of that date. This will make the house far more manageable and improve its appearance. It will also reveal the nunnery from the gardens, all sloping gently down to a lake with fine elm trees close to the house. The raised terrace overlooking the road is a Jacobean conceit. There is absolutely nothing to see inside the house, apart from the Charles II dado of the staircase.

At 3.30 I found Rosemary on her knees scrubbing the kitchen floor, and I helped her to swab it over. The kind Hinchingbrookes made me stay the night in the house, so I cancelled my room at the inn. Very cold and most primitive bathroom with no mat, no soap, etc. Rosemary a true bohemian, untidy and slapdash, and for this reason admirable, and tough. She is like a very jolly able-bodied seaman. Has four children and intends to have lots more. After dinner she showed me the contents of the crops of pigeons shot that afternoon. Gave a precise anatomical lecture as she tore open their guts, squeezing out undigested acorns and berries. Then started on the gizzards and stomachs, by which time I felt rather sick and turned away. She has studied medicine and wanted to become a qualified doctor, but Hinch put a stop to that.

* Victor Montagu, Viscount Hinchingbrooke (1906–95); MP for South Dorset, 1941–62; s. 1962 as 10th Earl of Sandwich but disclaimed peerages, 1964; m. 1st 1934–62 Rosemary Peto, artist (1916–98).

*Sunday, 27th January*

Today brilliantly sunny, crisp and cold. At midday arrived at Woolsthorpe Manor, now empty but very clean. The spirit of Isaac Newton still hovers shadowy against the panelled walls waiting for that apple to drop. Met Mr Smith, a retired electrician who wishes to rent the house. Got to Gunby by tea time. The dear old Field Marshal seems older, slower and more ponderous. By midnight I was worn out by ceaseless talk about Gunby affairs. They have no indoor servants apart from the wonderful Whartons, and old Lady Massingberd, seventy-five, polishes the stairs on her hands and knees every morning. Still, we had an excellent dinner, waited on by Wharton in tail coat and white tie, I of course in dinner jacket.

*For most of February, J.L.-M. was ill with mumps.*

*Wednesday, 20th February*

Considering myself free of infection today, I lunched at Sibyl Colefax's house. Violet Trefusis looks like a basilisk, upright in carriage, and very ugly. On my right Mrs Hudson.* Remembering how Jamesey shocked her lately, I said I was not a Conservative, nor a Liberal, nor a Socialist, but an anarchist. I was certainly a papist and would like to be ruled by the Pope. I heard her asking Raimund von Hofmannsthal† afterwards who I was and whether I was a lunatic.

Dined with Charles Fry, back from the States. He drank seven whiskies and soda while I was with him. He is violently pro-American and anti-English. He said he had been away eleven and a half weeks and slept with forty people during that time. Said the Americans are to a man anti-English (I can't believe Charles is their

---

* Hannah Randolph of Philadelphia; m. 1918 Robert Hudson (1886–1957), MP for Southport, 1931–52, cr. Viscount Hudson, 1952.

† Son (1906–74) of Hugo von Hofmannsthal, Austrian playwright; m. (2nd) 1939 Lady Elizabeth Paget (b. 1916), dau. of 6th Marquess of Anglesey.

single exception); that life there is life, and England so dead that people living here have no idea just how dead. In America you can get up at 3 p.m. if you wish, and lunch at 4.30 a.m. I am glad I am English and live in England.

*Friday, 1st March*

I reached Upton [House, Warwickshire] at 6.30 to stay with the Bearsteds.* He and Lady B. both charming, with the unassuming manners of the well-bred. At midnight Lord B. took me round the house. Inside there is nothing of consequence architecturally save a few early eighteenth-century chimneypieces and a beautiful Coleshill-style staircase, rearranged by Lord B. and extended. Morley Horder, the architect, built on to the house in the 1920s. But heavens, the contents! There is a lot of Chippendale-style furniture and some marvellous Chelsea china of the very best quality. The picture collection superb, as fine as any private collection in England. Many of the pictures are not yet back from the Welsh caves where they were stored with the National Gallery pictures.

*Thursday, 7th March*

Nancy lunched with me at Wilton's. She is radiant because she has already made £2,000 out of her novel *The Pursuit of Love* and has high hopes of it being filmed in America. She told me that Tom died intestate and so his estate, quite considerable, was divided between his six sisters. When that fiend Decca† was notified she cabled from America, 'Give my share to the Communist Party.'

This evening went to see Doreen [Colston-Baynes],‡ one of my dearest friends. After a couple of glasses of South African sherry

* Walter Samuel, MC, 2nd Viscount Bearsted (1882–1948); Chairman of Trustees of National Gallery, 1942–3; m. 1908 Dorothea Montefiore.

† Hon. Jessica Mitford (1917–96); m. 1st Esmond Romilly (1918–41), 2nd Robert Treuhaft (1912–2001); emigrated to USA, 1939; the 'Communist' Mitford sister.

‡ Writer of popular historical works under the name of Dormer Creston (1881–1973); friend of J.L.-M. in the 1930s, when she had advised him on his writing; she had spent the war in Scotland.

she, and consequently I, become acclimatised, and indulge in confidences. She told me she had never been interested in sex, either subjectively or objectively. For example, she cannot bring herself to deal in her book with 'the highly sexed woman' which, she is told, Queen Victoria was. The idea bores as well as repels her.

*Friday, 8th March*

Had a shock this evening to receive a letter from Stuart referring to Logan Pearsall Smith's death. He died after a quick heart attack, his last words being, 'I must go and telephone to the Pope-Hennessys'. He has made John Russell his literary executor, which will infuriate many older friends.

*Sunday, 10th March*

James telephoned to explain why he had not been in touch lately. For the past seven weeks he has been madly in love with a French 'cellist. His life has been a turmoil. I drove to lunch with Joan and Garrett Moore and there found both James and the 'cellist. Both looked very alike, two little black-headed objects, dissipated, green and shagged. James had scratches over his face.

*Thursday, 14th March*

Went to Sibyl's Ordinary. My respect for her kindness and gallantry has developed into true fondness. She is old now and the worldly are always pathetic. Sat next to Joan Oglander* who told me that Desmond MacCarthy† was trying to persuade John Russell to surrender Logan's literary executorship. Stephen Spender said that Julia Strachey‡ attended the reading of the will and protested aloud at the fortune having been left to J.R. Spender said it was a real

* Joan Oglander of Nunwell Park, Isle of Wight; m. 1927 (as his 2nd wife) Brig.-Gen. Cecil Aspinall (1878–1959), he adding 'Oglander' to his surname.

† (Sir) Desmond MacCarthy (1877–1952); critic.

‡ Novelist and journalist (1901–78); niece of Lytton Strachey.

Henry James sequel to Logan's life. Rose Macaulay, with whom I sat after dinner, said she saw J.R. in the London Library looking sheepish and embarrassed. I feel sorry for him, it was not his fault that Logan took a fancy to him.

*Sunday, 17th March*

Horrible rainy day. Sung Mass in Bath not very inspiring, but the church full. On to Corsham Court [Wiltshire] with the Methuens* in the Nash library. They believe they have let the Victorian centre part of the house to an art teaching establishment, the state rooms to be used by them only occasionally and shown to the public regularly. Paul and Norah are to live in the north wing which has ten bedrooms. At present the hospital is still in the house. After luncheon talked to Paul until 5 o'clock tea-time about Corsham and the N.T., and gave him data for his speech to *La Demeure Historique* in Paris in May.

After tea I left Corsham at 6 o'clock. About a mile from the village on the Bath road I saw a small car facing me, up the grass bank as though run into a wall, on its wrong side. I pulled up and was met by a man frantically waving, and holding a handkerchief up to his head which was covered with blood. I asked him if he had had an accident. He said he had been assaulted and robbed by two sailors to whom he had given a lift from Bath. I stopped an approaching car and asked for help. They seemed bewildered and did not wish to be involved. So I pushed the man into my car, turned round and drove hell for leather to Corsham again, holding the man's shoulder with my left hand and talking to him without cease. Drove straight to a Maternity Home, which I remembered passing in the morning, rang the bell and handed the man to two nurses, then ran down the street for a doctor. The doctor was off duty and at first reluctant to come. But I made him, while I telephoned the police. They came and took all particulars. The man was badly knocked about, but not unconscious. He had

* Paul, 4th Baron Methuen (1886–1974); artist; member of Historic Buildings Committee of N.T.; m. 1915 Eleanor Hennessy.

complained about the terrible pain all the way in the car and I was afraid he might be going to die. The moral is not to give lifts to more than one person at a time, and then not to let one sit behind you. For it transpired that the sailor in the back seat had biffed the man over the head while the sailor in the passenger seat opened the driver's door and pitched him out, after rifling his pocket of ten shillings!

*Wednesday, 20th March*

Eardley and I motored to Melbury [House, Dorset] where we had a quick luncheon with Lord Ilchester, Lady I. being ill in bed. He conducted us round the house, which is huge and in a state of desolation. Lord I. said that unless he could get some more servants he would have to leave the place. Although seven-eighths of the house is unused, little attempt has been made at dust-sheeting. The rooms and furniture are consequently untidy and dreadfully dusty. I understand that Lord Stavordale* will pull down the Victorian wing. We did not go inside it. Lord Ilchester's father built it in the 1880s in imitation perpendicular, well designed, well built and not at all to be despised. The library by Salvin, built in the 1870s, is very fine: simple and effective roof, book shelves of pine. Salvin impresses me more and more favourably. The 1690 wing is very beautiful. The material yellow Ham stone, glowing like honey, the columns and dressings of silvery Portland stone, as are the cornices, for they are still sharp. One contemporary long room has survived, but most of the ceilings are modern and indifferent. One 1690 ceiling, painted with gaily plumed birds, is unusual. Good and indifferent furniture. Interesting collection of family portraits.

*Saturday, 23rd March*

Bridget dined with me at the Ritz, I having ordered dinner for 9 o'clock. Found oysters waiting for us on our plates and had a

---

* Edward Fox-Strangways, Viscount Stavordale (1905–58); e.s. and heir of 6th Earl of Ilchester; killed on active service in Cyprus.

delicious meal. Took her back to her flat and walked home in the middle of the night.

*Thursday, 28th March*

Went to Logan Pearsall Smith's memorial service at St Margaret's, Westminster. The Pope-Hennessy family in the front row. The Dame said to me reproachfully, 'I have been in my new flat six months and you have not yet visited me.' The lesson from Ecclesiastes, beginning 'cast thy bread upon the waters'. And what did the bread bring back to Logan? Three volumes of *Trivia*, a reputation as a grammarian, and a sad, lonely, unfulfilled old age. Was struck by one passage in Jeremy Taylor's prayers, 'Accept the stupid and the fools to mercy'. How many did Logan accept? John Russell and wife sat in front of me, he with golden hair like spun treacle.

*Friday, 5th April*

Had to give evidence today in the robbery and assault case at Chippenham. Kind John Wilton called for me at 7.45 in his beautiful Rolls-Royce and motored me down. Weather broke and it rained incessantly. The Chippenham Police Court was Dickensian; a bare Georgian room up a steep staircase. The benches inches thick in dust. First we listened to a bigamy case. The magistrate, an old fool, might have been John Sutro mimicking. Then our case came on. The two sailors stood handcuffed in the dock. One aged twenty-one, a terrible rough type; the ringleader, aged twenty-two, very small like an eel, very pretty but very wicked, by name Tulip, who in the dock kept winking and giggling with the other, unchecked, which surprised us a lot. We were kept until 3 o'clock without being allowed so much as a cup of tea, as though we were the criminals. I was bound over – or whatever it's called – to attend the Salisbury Assizes when the case is referred to them in three weeks. The whole business is a damned nuisance and waste of time.

John dined at Brooks's. Told me he pays his chauffeur £8 a week.

*Wednesday, 10th April*

At the end of each day I think of what I have accomplished. Today I had tea with Lady Binning in Hampstead. She loves me with the passion of friendship and would lavish costly presents upon me, were I to allow it.

*Thursday, 11th April*

Today I went with one of our new agents to St John's Institute in Hackney, the first time I have ever visited this property. And what a wretched one! It is no more important than hundreds of other Georgian houses left in slum areas. Very derelict after the bombing all around it. Tenanted by a number of charitable bodies. It does have one downstair room of linenfold panelling. I found it terribly depressing and longed to hurry away.

At an SPAB meeting we discussed Chelsea Old Church. As before I was alone in voting against it being rebuilt on the grounds that there is too little of it left. I was in a minority of one – decision taken to rebuild over what rubble remains and to retain absolutely those surviving fragments, but not to reproduce an exact fake. But an exact fake is what they will have to produce, can only produce.

*Friday, 12th April*

Dined with Charles Fry at Rules after trying some six restaurants in Soho and not getting a table. Charles less drunken tonight, but more sinister. He said I was in bad form, whereas I thought I was in better form than for some days. He took me to task for not being on good terms with Jamesey. Jamesey told him last night that he was very fond of me except when I was 'diabolically malicious'. Now that is the very expression which he and I have consistently used in describing Charles. This has given me something to ponder over. Charles also told me in a flat sort of voice that I was a great snob. Now if that is not diabolical malice I don't know what is. Of course I am a snob, not a social snob but an intellectual one. I like the company of my intellectual superiors.

*Saturday, 13th April*

This afternoon finished off additions to my book and went to tea with Margaret Jourdain and Ivy. Did not enjoy it at all. How these women eat! And how horrible their food is! And talking of social snobs, that is what they are. Their conversation is all about the most worthless society people they have recently met and admired at tea parties. Dined excellently at the Ritz with John Philipps who leaves tomorrow by air for a hospital in Switzerland. His blood pressure is too low. Didn't enjoy this either.

*Good Friday, 19th April*

Before I left [for Wickhamford], Geoffrey [Houghton Brown] took me round his Thurloe Square house which is in process of redecoration by that horrible H.* and his pals. G. wants to move himself and me there in the autumn. The prospect of moving again appals me. To him it is the breath of life.

At Wickhamford they were in the throes of preparation for a cocktail party this evening which they held in the garden. I hardly knew a soul. A few recognisable wizened faces of pre-war good-timers. Nothing but pleasure-seeking and inanities. They have nothing, *nothing* to communicate. The only possibly interesting person present was Pug Ismay,† who as Military Adviser to the PM during the war must at least be intelligent. He was being jolly and gay, living down I suspected. He spoke to me most warmly of George Mallaby, towards whom I feel cool.

*Saturday, 20th April*

I motored to Birtsmorton Court – most luscious, low-lying Worcestershire country, my very favourite – under the lee of the Malvern hills, so long-backed, naked, nobbly and impressive. The

* Probably Geoffrey's friend Felix Harbord, artist and decorator.

† General Sir Hastings Ismay (1887–1965); military adviser to premier, 1940–6; cr. Baron, 1947.

dreadful Mr Bradley-Birt* received me. House surrounded by a moat and very romantic, were it more genuine. The remains of the gate-house are thirteenth-century, the house fifteenth- and sixteenth-century, I judge, rather like Baddesley Clinton, which is of course the genuine article. But the old boy built just before the last war a wing to the east on the foundations of a wing destroyed by fire a hundred years previously. He did it well outside in half-timber and rosy-red brick. Swans swim in the moat and peacocks preen on the walls. The moated grange (not quite) all right. Two or three rooms of interest, Elizabethan panelled parlour with early Renaissance frieze, plain plaster ceiling. Mullions have been inserted where sash windows were shown in the old *Country Life* article. I could see no contents of quality save a shove-halfpenny table. Most of the furniture heavy black-stained Victorian reproductions of lodging-house baseness. Brass pots and pans in plenty, table-cloths of plush, and doilies. Everlasting flowers in vases of plate. Pretty little church in the garden with monuments by White of Worcester.† The house is so cluttered with dusty, frowsty things that it appears a mess in spite of four servants, perhaps because all male. Mr Bradley-Birt spoke almost exclusively of his friendship with Prince Ruprecht of Bavaria and the Kaiser, of whom he has an enormous photograph on the piano.

*Monday, 22nd April*

Called on poor old Canon Allsebrook‡ in the Evesham hospital. He is a wraith of what he used to be; sitting up beside his bed, looking extremely handsome, but so ill and resigned. He spoke

---

* Francis Bradley-Birt (1874–1963); m. 1920 Lady Norah Spencer-Churchill (1875–1946), dau. of 8th Duke of Marlborough (though she resumed her maiden name the following year).

† Thomas White (*c.* 1674–1758) – though Pevsner seems disinclined to allow him the credit for this monument (which is to Admiral William Caldwell, 1718).

‡ William Carmont Allsebrook (d. 1947); Chaplain, Christ Church, Oxford, 1897–1903; Vicar of Badsey and Wickhamford (livings in the patronage of Christ Church), 1903–46; Rural Dean of Evesham, 1921–45; Hon. Canon of Worcester Cathedral, 1930–46.

slowly about the Sandys tombs in the church. How often have I listened to this conversation over the years, almost since he christened me? He is an educated but not wise old man. Devoted to the classics, and taught me Latin. Treated abominably by the family who would hide when he called uninvited at the manor, because he, who knew nothing of hunting and shooting, bored them. I can see him retreating shamefacedly and disappointed from the front door down the drive. But I always loved him.

*Saturday, 27th April*

This afternoon I trained to Eastbourne where Paul Latham met me at the station. Just the same in appearance, like a bounding retriever puppy, hatless, his hair still yellow, clustering and curly. Complexion slightly sunburned. I had not seen him since my disastrous visit in the summer of 1943. He was giggly and rather endearing. We dined with his old mother who is staying in Eastbourne to be near him. She is a dear, ordinary old woman of seventy-nine, adoring her son. Paul is angelic to her. She, he told me, befriended him while he was in prison, never missed writing, never reproached him, and never has done since. Paul is living in a different house in Herstmonceux, on the road: not very comfortable, and ceilings very low. He is greatly improved. Far less hysterical and more reconciled. Less sex mad. I sat on his bed until 3 a.m. out of affection and a desire to console. He talked non-stop.

*Tuesday, 30th April*

This evening went to 41 Yeoman's Row [Knightsbridge] where Geoffrey Lemprière, my Australian friend, is staying. I have not seen him for seven or eight years, perhaps nine. He is exactly the same, like a startled kangaroo, and his age is only betrayed by the tight fold behind the ear. He is no more a ball of fire than he used to be, but thoroughly, intrinsically decent. He told me he loved me very much when we first met in Corsica [1933]. He was in a Japanese prisoner-of-war camp for three years and seven months and spoke of his sufferings quite cheerfully. They were starved and beaten all the time. The Japanese have no redeeming qualities – not even good looks – and are treacherous, insinuating and cruel. He says he will take me as his guest to Sweden the first week of June by air. This will be a treat.

*Wednesday, 1st May*

Bridget dined with me here. Anne's son Tony [Armstrong-Jones] is very ill with meningitis, supposed to be of a fatal kind. At 10.30 Bridget made me accompany her to Emerald Cunard's. Neither of us had changed. We found a dinner party still at the table, all in evening dress: Lord Bruntisfield, Lady Milbanke,* Mary Lady Howe,† the French Ambassadress‡ and the King of Greece.§ Ambassadress thanked me for the synopsis of British architecture and furniture I sent her. Was presented to the King as the man who looks after all the public houses of England – Emerald always does this – and shook hands, while bowing slightly. Should one shake first, or bow first? Or simultaneous? Then B. and I were left talking to each other, and left as soon as we could.

*Friday, 3rd May*

Dined with Malcolm Bullock¶ at the Turf. What is the matter with me that I find a staleness and futility in those of my friends whose tacit superiority is that they are sophisticated and in the swim? Lord Ilchester joined us for dinner, telling us how corrupt the police are.

---

* Sheila Chisholm of Sydney, NSW (d. 1969); m. 1st Lord Loughborough, s. of 5th Earl of Rosslyn, 2nd 1928 Sir John Milbanke, 11th Bt (1902–47), 3rd Prince Dmitri of Russia.

† Mary Curzon (1887–1962); m. 1907 (diss. 1937) her cousin 5th Earl Howe.

‡ Odette Boissier; m. 1932 René Massigli, French Ambassador to London, 1944–55.

§ King George II of Greece (1890–1947); then awaiting a plebiscite on his future (which took place in December 1946 and resulted in his resuming the throne for the last seven months of his life).

¶ Conservative MP and closet homosexual (1890–1966; cr. Bt, 1954); m. 1919 Lady Victoria Primrose (d. 1927), dau. of 17th Earl of Derby; friend of Harold Nicolson.

It goes against the grain for me to criticise the police, naively believing all policemen to be like our dear old Sergeant Haines at Wickhamford and Badsey who spanked the boys for stealing apples and succoured old women and lame cats; and, after the Vicar, was the pillar of village society.

*Saturday, 4th May*

Took Alvilde to the White Tower and gave her a delicious dinner; then to a news reel. I almost loved her this evening, and kissed her affectionately on leaving her at her hotel.

*Thursday, 9th May*

Harold [Nicolson] said he would not consider the National Trust secretaryship because he was intent on returning to politics. He told me he scarcely required sex any more these days, and that having two sons living in his small house anyway precluded it. I too find sex without savour or even degrading unless with someone who attracts me mightily, and with whom I believe myself to be in love – or is it in lust? I feel I may be on the verge of a breakdown, my melancholy is so consuming.

*Sunday, 12th May*

At tea Miss Sibyl Paley Ashmore came to talk about the Baileys, but was a little disappointing. She is aged sixty-nine and my second cousin. It is curious suddenly to meet someone who remembers my grandfather who died in 1889, and my grandmother in 1896.* I had a photograph of the latter on my mantelpiece, and she said 'There's Christina!' Said she had a beautiful, low Scotch voice; that all the family loved her. That our great-grandfather amassed the

* J.L.-M's maternal grandfather Henry Bailey (1822–89); yst son of iron and railways tycoon Sir Joseph Bailey, 1st Bt (1783–1858); m. (2nd) Christina Thomson (1849–96).

family fortune and between his two marriages led a gay life and begat many illegitimate children. He was perfectly hideous, so there's hope for us all.

*Thursday, 16th May*

Trained this morning to Aylesbury and was motored by Mrs James de Rothschild's* agent to Waddesdon Manor. What a house! An 1880 pastiche of a François Premier château. Yet it is impressive because it is on a grand scale. There is symmetry, and craftsmanship and finish. I suppose most people today would pronounce it hideous. I find it compelling. A nursery school, which was here throughout the war, has just left. It is being scrubbed and cleaned. The Rothschilds are moving back into the whole of it, which is huge. They have been living in the wing. Most of the rooms are panelled with gilded Louis XV *boiserie*. One drawing-room is lined with marble. Furniture French of the highest quality. One room stacked with pictures, taken out of their frames. Could not see them. A hundred acres of grounds offered too. Beautiful trees. In all a better Cliveden. I have written a report, which is by no means contemptuous, upon it.

*Wednesday, 22nd May*

Motored to Salisbury to the Assizes. Was not called upon to give evidence for the two sailors pleaded guilty and were given only eighteen months on account of their youth, service and previous good record. The judge was young, about my age, and looked resplendent in his red robes. There was a subsequent case of a man who had raped his daughter, aged fourteen, which I could not wait for and was sorry to miss.

---

* Dorothy Pinto (d. 1988); m. James de Rothschild (d. 1957), who inherited Waddesdon from his cousin Baron Ferdinand de Rothschild (d. 1922), its creator in the 1870s.

*Friday, 31st May*

A really terrible day spent at Charlecote.* It rained cats and dogs and was bitterly cold. The Lucys all rather overwrought. The guide books have not come and, worst of all, the British Legion attendants never turned up. They were expected today in order to learn the history of the house and be told what to do at the opening tomorrow. Not a sign of them. Returned to Wickhamford almost ill with nerves and anxiety.

*During the summer of 1946 J.L.-M., who had not been abroad since 1939, enjoyed holidays in two countries which had remained neutral during the war, as the guest of friends not seen since the 1930s – in Sweden with the Australian Geoffrey Lemprière, and in Switzerland with Georges Cattaui, formerly a Jewish attaché at the Egyptian Legation in London, now a Catholic theologian in Fribourg. His descriptions tell the reader as much about the deprivations experienced in England as about the countries he was visiting.*

*Sunday, 2nd June*

Woke at seven, finished packing, breakfasted at eight and called at 41 Yeoman's Row. Went with Geoffrey Lemprière to the Imperial Airways House where we were weighed in. Drove in a bus to Northolt Aerodrome, where we drank coffee and ate a roll. Everything is efficiently done and the attendants polite. At 10.30 we got into the aeroplane. This was my first flight since I was sick looping the loop in Captain Butler's Moth over Broadway Hill in 1925. While the machine was revving up Geoffrey said I looked scared and started to read to me. This I resented, but I *was* scared,

* Charlecote had finally been accepted by the N.T. from the Fairfax-Lucys, despite lack of endowment, and was due to be opened to the public the following day – 'about the first country house of which I supervised the showing after the war', wrote J.L.-M. in *People & Places*. Despite his apprehensions, all was well on the day, with the missing elements turning up at the last moment, and ringing speeches from the Shakespearean director Sir Barry Jackson and the historian G. M. Trevelyan, the latter launching an appeal for funds with a donation of £5,000.

and would not look out of the window for quite a time. Then I took courage and first noticed what I think was Boreham Hall with its canal in Essex. England looks small, compact and very beautiful from the air. Most striking features are the fields and hedgerows, chequer-board fashion, and the number of country houses and demesnes. It was not a very clear day and at times we were flying blind. I had taken a pill and a Luminol and did not feel ill at all. Only over Denmark was it bumpy. I do not like it when the machine drops like a stone. Jutland is flat and neat. It has straight canals and roads with regimented trees. The number of old farmhouses, all in square formation round a courtyard, uniform. Few villages, but the area thickly populated by those scattered homesteads. Reached Copenhagen at 2.15 and bussed to the centre of town. Walked in the Tivoli Gardens where we had tea. All gay and bright. The sun shining. It is far warmer than in England. It took us precisely a quarter of an hour to fly on to Malmö, which is ugly from the air.

Were met by Geoff's firm's agent who walked us round the town. I was particularly struck by the modern theatre, of simplest lines, severe and unadorned, faced with grey-white marble. The shop windows are replete with everything one could possibly want to buy. The air of well-being and luxury at the Hotel Kremer where we are staying is wonderful and exhilarating. The beauty of the boys and girls. Everyone is young. The cream complexion of the men, their blond thick hair. Women with pale blue eyes and bare arms. The standard of good looks immensely high.

We dined in the smart restaurant in the Kungspark, the waiters in trim uniforms, clean as clean can be. Speciality here the hors d'oeuvres which go on and on, accompanied by schnapps.

*Monday, 3rd June*

I wandered round the town this morning while Geoff and the agent had business appointments. In the afternoon we were taken by Allström the agent, a nice little man who has lately lost his wife, to the outskirts of Malmö and shown some of the recent suburban development. Extremely impressed by the wholeness, convenience and neatness. Everything is neat here. A garden city of two-storey buildings in rows, each alternate house facing the opposite way to ensure privacy. Air of gaiety and happiness. We went into Allström's house, a little, low, long villa, quite prettily furnished with modern birch-wood furniture in traditional eighteenth-century style, but not absurd. A lot to be said for middle-class taste and existence. Complacency breeds content.

Allström took us to dine with a rich merchant's family, by name Mueller. They live well and modishly. Meal began with cocktails, then red wine, port and brandy. You must not start drinking until your host or hostess says 'skoll'. Then you 'skoll' the other members of the family before drinking yourself. You may never 'skoll' your hostess. Whole paraphernalia a terrible bore. We dined at six, the normal time here, and caught at 9 o'clock train to Göteborg. You must make a speech before rising from the table, and on leaving the dining room the host and hostess shake hands with every guest.

*Tuesday, 4th June*

Göteborg a charming town of intersecting canals. In the morning I was free to roam around. Examined the Dom, the Museum and all the eighteenth-century houses along the canals, including the Town Hall by Tessin.* Bought a few ties and handkerchiefs. We caught 2.30 train to Stockholm. For six hours the country never varied: fairly flat, heathy, birch wood with green glades of poor grassland, and many lakes. On arrival we drove to the Stockholm City Hotel, on the sixth floor of a huge, grim, gaunt building. We had eaten a delicious dinner of grilled salmon on the train. Walked round the town till midnight, wondering open-eyed at the combination of ancient buildings, grand shop windows and brilliant lights.

* Nicodemus Tessin the Younger (d. 1728).

*Wednesday, 5th June*

In the afternoon Allström conducted us round Skansen in the boiling sun. Looked at primitive Swedish wooden houses, brought from the north and re-assembled here, complete with furniture, utensils, etc. No protection to prevent the public from stealing. They just don't steal in this country, and the stacks of chopped wood for winter fuel lining the side streets are never looted. We drank lemonade to a band. This evening Jane Denham, the Naval Attaché's daughter, dined with us; also Allström's young lady whom we pronounced bossy. We ate at the most expensive restaurant, and afterwards went to the Tivoli. Went on roundabouts and swings, and I felt and was sick. The lights and merriment are something I never remember in England before the war.

*Sunday, 9th June*

There seems little point in enumerating my doings in Stockholm. Since Geoff left on Thursday I have literally not spoken a sentence to a soul. I have visited the Town Hall, the modern Hagersten Church, the new hospital, the state apartments of the Royal Palace (disappointing), the Palace of Drottningholm (enchanting French formal garden and unique 1760 theatre, complete with contemporary stage equipment), the Hagaslott Pavilion (by far the best rooms I have seen; a veritable Petit Trianon), the National Museum and Northern Museum (the one pictures, the other period furnishings). I have also been to the Ballet Joos and two cinemas, one showing the film of *Henry V*. I have eaten in the best restaurants and the cheapest, and have bought quantities of clothes, though not as many as I would like to for fear of paying duties. Only occasionally in the evening have I felt lonely. Only once I bought some pleasure. Flat, stale and unprofitable it was too. Experienced little elation and no disgust. On the other hand, the sun has shone and I feel well.

*During June and July 1946 J.L.-M. and his colleague Eardley Knollys, 'the dearest and best companion', were busy preparing Montacute, Somerset, for opening to the public. This house had been bought for the National Trust by the philanthropist Ernest Cook in 1931, but was devoid of contents, making it necessary to find furniture and pictures from other sources with which to fill it.*

*Friday, 14th June*

Meetings today. Our new Secretary, Admiral Bevir,* in attendance, although George Mallaby was in the office for the last time. Admiral seems jolly, if too inclined to be facetious. Of course he has been warned by the Chairman that we are not a bureaucratic team of experts, but a dedicated group of happy-go-lucky enthusiasts, who ought not to be bossed about. Lord Crawford pressed me to stay at Haigh Hall next weekend, to see his pictures in case a few would do for Montacute. He is packing up and leaving the place for good. I said how sad it must be for him. He looked desperately unhappy for a moment and replied, 'Really, it is just terrible how much I mind.'

*Saturday, 15th June*

At six went to Doreen [Colston-Baynes]. She said that when she got going on her writing she became an instrument, a gigantic machine or fountain pen through which outside thoughts and ideas poured, sometimes to the extent of thoroughly alarming her, the *she* remaining such a passive, uncontrolling feature of the process.

*Monday, 17th June*

With Hubert Smith to Darlington. After a late supper we went for a walk to Ecclestone Priory, belonging to the Ministry of Works. Did not like the heavy black pointing of the stonework which they have done there. The situation is very romantic. I disliked the ugly little wooden hut which they have erected just in front of the ruins.

* Vice-Admiral Oliver Bevir (1891–1967); Secretary of N.T., 1946–9.

The Ministry lacks taste and sensitivity in spite of its academic superiority. Listened to the curlews. Hubert told me that corn-crakes are practically extinct in the south.

*Saturday, 22nd June*

Took midday train to Wigan and was met by Lord Crawford, hatless, grey and charming. What a nice man he is; what John Wilton calls 'grand', and comparatively young still. He is cultivated, civilised, urbane, polite, industrious on behalf of the arts, dutiful, a patron – in other words, an anachronism in this detestable age, fighting a losing battle with no rancour, good-humouredly, agony gnawing at his heart.

The drive to Haigh Hall is entered directly from Wigan. It twirls, twists uphill through massed hedges of rhododendron and laurel. The house lies on a plateau overlooking the chimneys of Wigan, pit-heads and hills beyond. It is the house of Mr Gradgrind, but a well built classical house of 1830, actually designed by Lord C's great-great-grandfather, a very pleasing house of white stone, machine cut. The lines are concise and clean, compact and symmetrical. Lady Crawford was away, for which he apologised, but his white-haired mother there and a genteel secretary. Hardly any servants. We waited on each other. House in a state of utter muddle for all the pictures and furniture are stacked, and in process of removal. Claret for dinner. He and I talked of all sorts of things, including the N.T., until midnight over a very rare rum, which is 200 years old. Very strong and we drank it as a liqueur.

*Sunday, 23rd June*

Lord Crawford took me round the house to look at the stacked pictures of which there are hundreds. I made a list of twenty-five that might be suitable for Montacute. They included several Teniers, a Ruysdael, Ostades, van der Neer, a Pintoricchio, Reynolds of Lady Eglington at the harp, Opie of Dr Johnson, Romney of the young Pitt, and so forth. Superb collection of pictures, and the Duccio one of the finest pictures in existence. Much of the library has already gone to Balcarres, but he showed me a First Folio Shakespeare rebound, and a Second Folio in original boards. Interior of the house is good of its date. No furniture of much consequence.

*Tuesday, 25th June*

Today we had a Reports Committee at which the bewildered Admiral was present. He does not know much about the National Trust and is, besides, not an intelligent man. He pierces one with a cold blue eye like a schoolmaster trying desperately to assess a new boy; only he is the new boy. Clarissa [Churchill] dined at the White Tower. I tried a technique of rapid talk, which answered well for one hour. After that for lack of collaboration I subsided into an exhausted heap.

*Friday, 28th June*

We [J.L.-M. and Eardley] finished our work at Montacute and had tea with Mrs Knollys in Bath. Then called on Mr [Ernest] Cook the mysterious benefactor's house in Syon Place to see two Raeburns he offers the Trust for Montacute. Before my finger was off the bell he opened the front door himself. Was not the shy, shifty little eccentric I imagined, but a tall, self-possessed man rather like Bogey Harris. Not prepossessing; cunning I should say. His house is decorator's Georgian; his pictures likewise decorator's, mostly English school and indifferent specimens at that. He showed us with justifiable pride the façade of the beautiful early Georgian house from Chippenham which he bought when Woolworth's pulled it down. He has re-erected it not too badly. Eardley dropped me at Westwood [Manor]. Alex Moulton dined and on leaving embraced Ted good-night on the drive, very charmingly, unostentatiously. I was surprised. So too was Ted, but he was delighted.

*Friday, 5th July*

With Geoff Lemprière to the American Ballet. Also present a young sub-lieutenant in the Navy, stupid and dull. *Would* call me

Jim; but I knew neither his Christian name nor surname. Dined well at Prunier's, with champagne and green chartreuse. Geoff's farewell party for he flies to America tomorrow. Went back to Yeoman's Row for a short time. Oh God, these blatant queens! An ugly Greek prince with a soldier from the Horse Guards. And the conversation. Feel awfully out of sympathy with these people who must rub one's nose in it. I am most grateful to Geoff for his great kindness to me for he would receive no payment for my Swedish trip. Yet I feel guilty for receiving so much and returning nothing. Do tarts who fail to requite the attentions of rich business men ever harbour these guilt feelings?

*Sunday, 7th July*

A heavenly day [at Wickhamford], hot and mid-summery. Hay smelling. Evening primroses, Canterbury bells, mock orange wafting. Lay about the garden all day with Mama in deck-chairs. The parson's daughters are a help in spite of Mama calling them useless, unable to cook, slow and stupid – sometimes to their faces, I fear.

*Friday, 12th July*

At 6 I left in the car for Montacute where I arrived at 10 o'clock, having dined in Basingstoke. I drove with both windows down, and the smell of new-mown hay and hedgerows, of eglantine and elder, was intoxicating. How I love these long, gentle, Shakespearean summer evenings.

*Saturday, 13th July*

Busy day spent entirely at Montacute. I selected wall space for every single picture and for Lord Rochdale's tapestries. Made progress but there is much to be done by [the opening to the public] today next week, when I shall be travelling across France. I found the arrangement of this house so agreeable that I did not want to go abroad, even for a fortnight, while there was still so much to be done.

*Saturday, 20th July*

Up early, having packed last night and fetched some sandwiches from Brooks's which I had the foresight to order during dinner there. At 9.30 my train left London. I had an early luncheon on the Channel boat, my last proper meal until the next morning. Reserved a second-class seat in the French train, but the seats are narrow. I was very uncomfortable in consequence. Calais is extremely bombed. In fact there are hardly more than a dozen houses standing. At Lille I had some coffee (acorn juice) at the station, but nothing to eat. Indeed there must be very little food in France. The people look shabby, but not so hang-dog, discontented and truculent as the English. I was prepared to sit up all night, but the resolution waned as I got sleepy. By bribing the nice conductor I got a sleeper, which I shared with a pretty, English Mrs Miniver.*

*Sunday, 21st July*

Arrived one and a half hours late. The Basel customs authorities easy enough. At the station I had a good breakfast, with boiled egg. At 2.30 reached Fribourg. Was greeted by Georges Cattaui who came running up the stairs of the station platform. He is little changed, perhaps greyer, balder, now nearing fifty. He leads an ascetic, holy life, having done his seven-year stint of theology at the University here. He at once took me to the new University buildings. The rooms have many points to recommend them, ingenious mechanisms, a variety of beautiful woods. But there is much that is ugly. I felt very tired at the end of this inspection.

Tonight we dined at the hotel with the University architect, who is called Denis Honegger, and Monsieur Barraud, who is considered Switzerland's leading artist, a handsome, bluff, pleasant man who smokes a pipe. He speaks no English.

The smell of the lime trees is all pervasive.

---

* Character invented during 1930s by the writer Jan Struther (Joyce Anstruther [1901–53]; m. 1931 Andrew Maxtone Graham), the 'ideal' English wife and mother, with sharp observations and great zest for life. She had been made much use of by Allied propaganda in wartime books and films.

*Monday, 22nd July*

I sleep profoundly and late. Georges goes to bed at 8 o'clock every evening and, rising at 6, attends Mass. These hours would not suit me. Today the sun shone. Greedily I inhaled the strong, dry, torrid southern heat, which I have not experienced for seven years.

*Tuesday, 23rd July*

Hotter than yesterday, and cloudless, but by no means too hot. Georges and I went to look at St Michael's church which is Rococo, and the Priests' College attached, founded by St Canisius. Georges fusses about his health more than anyone I have ever met. Must not get too hot, too cold, wears a muffler and coat, which he puts on and takes off, and talks of his ill health ceaselessly. He also asks after everyone I have ever heard of and never heard of, which is extremely irritating. While we were sitting on a bench, he lamenting his ailments, along came a good-looking, sprightly Englishman called Bennet, whom Georges greeted and with whom I shook hands. This man could not linger to gossip because he was in a hurry. He is Professor of English Literature here and aged eighty-five. Georges explained that he had been a pupil of Gerard Manley Hopkins* at a Jesuit school. Hopkins used to read fairy stories to him and his other pupils when they tired of their lessons. I think he is the only person I have met who knew Hopkins personally.

Georges left for Berne to lunch at the French Embassy. I, pleased to be left alone, visited the three churches in the middle of the town, looking at the sixteenth-century fountain heads, and walked across the river over the 1840 suspension bridge, which is of wood. The cables seem most insecure, and when a lorry passed over it full of people the bridge swayed like a ship in a rough sea.

Georges is a cultivated, educated man, but withal a terrible bore. He jumps from one subject to another so that conversation never sustains a level. He never allows me to speak. He is disturbed by

* Poet and Jesuit (1844–89), of whom J.L.-M. had attempted to write a biography in the 1930s.

what he calls my Fascist sympathies and remarked tellingly that I was a Catholic rather from political than religious motives. That later I am almost bound to turn to God. So be it.

This afternoon we went to tea at a château just outside Fribourg called La Poya, belonging to the Comte and Comtesse de Grafenried Villars. It was built in 1701 by an ancestor, and is thoroughly Palladian, and no larger than a villino. The present owner added two 'tourelles' at either end in good taste. In the centre is a high square hall with Rococo plaster ceiling and Baroque figures in stucco over the doorways. The enrichments are picked out in gold. There are Empire rooms with pink damask walls upstairs, very pretty. Some of the eighteenth-century furniture is French, and all exquisite. Oh, the impeccable taste. The Countess was gracious, and gave us tea. There were present the Count, who only talked of *la chasse*, an Italian marquis who is a Fascist, and a daughter and son-in-law, Baron Rambaud, who did the honours and showed me round the house. Balustraded terraces descend in front of the house which has a splendid view over the town and the snow-capped mountains beyond. The trees in the park are ancient and deciduous, and the lawns green and luscious. But on close inspection the grass is very poor, full of dandelions and weeds.

*After an unsettled few days, during which he suffered from a stomach upset and had some trouble obtaining Swiss currency, J.L.-M. moved to a hotel in Lugano.*

*Sunday, 28th July*

The situation of Lugano is very beautiful, surrounded by close, high mountains. The lake is in a hole. Today the sky is thundery and there is no breath of wind. Wandered in the public gardens along the lake under tall beech and chestnut trees.

*Monday, 29th July*

Today feel very unwell, I think due to slight sunstroke. I overlooked the fact that I am getting bald on top of my head, damn it. Have a feverish feeling about the eyes. There is not a soul in this hotel to speak to. All dagos when not English, and when English, dentists. Have finished *The Last Chronicle of Barset.*

*Wednesday, 31st July*

Took photographs of the Renaissance façade of San Lorenzo early this morning, then did some shopping. Shops not as good as in Sweden, nor is the food. This afternoon crossed the lake to Campione and photographed the Baroque front of the little Madonna dei Ghirli, which has flights of steps descending into the water. Campione is by some curious chance an island of Italy in Switzerland. At the south extremity is a rather noble Mussolini arch of grey and white striped granite. Some of the Fascist architecture is good, though abused by all left-wingers. The sun in the full glare of day was almost too much for me. Happily found a train back to Lugano in time for a delicious tea. Am reading Shakespeare's sonnets with care. Poetry and architecture are my two great loves. I judge the latter more academically and less subjectively than the former. One should fight with poetry, hammering it, thrashing it with the mind if one is to appreciate it properly.

*Thursday, 1st August*

Although I have passed my time this week as I had intended and hoped, yet I shall be glad to leave on Sunday. Ten days of complete solitude are enough. Besides, I am anxious about that accumulating pile of work at home.

Today there is some sort of *festa* and all the shops are shut. I went to church next door (Sant' Angioli) at 9.45. I stayed till the end of Mass and studied very closely the Bernardo Luini *Passion*, a splendid thing, in excellent preservation. Visited the Museum in the Villa Cacci, a good late classical building of *c.*1840, but internal decoration poor, Museum itself neglected and absolutely lifeless. After luncheon took the steamer to Morcote. Extremely hot and muggy, the sun sheltering behind high clouds. Climbed the steep eighteenth-century stairs to the S. Sassa church, with splendid square Romanesque campanile, which I photographed.

*Friday, 2nd August*

Today's jaunt was to walk along a path cut out of the rock, under the roadway, along the northern arm of the lake as far as Gandia. This is an old medieval village, the houses tumbling over each other and intersected by labyrinthine passages in the rock. In the evening I bathed in the Lido. I do not stay in the water long, nor do I much care to exhibit my nude body to the public. The corporate diversion of bathing does not appeal. And if I see a beautiful body it merely disturbs me.

*Saturday, 3rd August*

My last day. Paid my bill at the hotel which amounted to just under 300 francs. I was so horrified that I did not buy the little gold toothpick I had coveted in a jeweller's window all the week. Today I took the funicular up San Salvatore. Less than twenty minutes to climb 3,000 feet. The incline to the summit 6/10, rather frightening. A little too much haze, but the view of the lake in its entirety very lovely.

Two things never cease to astonish me. That despite the hysterical devotion Latin men and women lavish upon male babies, they grow up to be normal extroverts, which is not what one would expect. And that the English race manages to keep its end up in the world, considering how, when confronted with Europeans, of no matter what class, Englishmen never fail to appear intellectually inferior.

I rather dread my journey home of two days and one night without a sleeper and without food on the French train, in this torrid heat.

*Saturday, 10th August*

All this week has been very dull. No visits because my car is not yet ready. Very busy indexing the list of properties for the annual report.

Spent three evenings at the Soane Museum looking through Robert Adam drawings. The versatility of the man.

*Tuesday, 13th August*

Had a session at Batsford's with Charles Fry and Mr Batsford. It was settled that I should add an appendix to the third edition of *The National Trust*, inclusive of new properties acquired since the first edition was published a year ago; that I should write a guide book of all N.T. buildings to be sold at six shillings, this to come out next year; and that I should write a book on the dawn of English classicism from Henry VIII's reign down to and including Inigo Jones.* We furthermore made some progress with illustrations for *Adam*, and settled that Batsford's would have photographs taken of a selection of the drawings in the Soane Museum.

At dinner tonight at Brooks's I sat with Eddie Marsh who is selling many of his books, amongst them twenty presentation copies to him from Mrs Belloc Lowndes. He complained that he had to tear out all the fly-leaf inscriptions. 'Why tear out?' I asked. 'The books will fetch more if you leave them in.' Eddie frowned, thinking my remark in bad taste. Then he told me how Sir James Barrie† once sold a number of his books. One day a friend informed him that the shop which had purchased them was displaying them in their window and asking a high price for each copy that contained a dedication to him. Poor Barrie was obliged to buy back all these books at a higher cost than he had received for them. Silly ass.

*Wednesday, 21st August*

Woke up from another vivid dream about Tom Mitford who was dressing to go to a luncheon party. He was in his trousers and shirt sleeves and slung round his waist the gold key-chain he always

* Published in 1951 as *Tudor Renaissance*.

† Sir James Barrie (1860–1937); Scottish playwright and novelist, creator of Peter Pan.

wore, and patted his thighs in self-satisfaction. He was cracking jokes and laughing at himself in his most engaging manner.

Today I motored George Dix on a small N.T. tour. We first went to West Wycombe, Helen [Dashwood] accompanying us. After lunching at the Apple Orchard, where I bought for £35 a chest of drawers, we went to the house. Prepared to be angry, I was angry with the guides for not being at their places. House looking bare but clean and very beautiful. At Cliveden [Berkshire] we walked round the grounds before going on to Hatchlands [Surrey], which George liked best of the three houses. We dined late at the Allies Club and there was Malcolm Bullock. Apparently he had invited me to dine and received no reply. He sat with us while we ate and came on to Brooks's where we met Randolph [Churchill] and had drinks. Randolph has a huge belly and is very grey. George could not believe him to be thirty-three and younger than us. Randolph boisterous and argumentative. Talked of Chartwell, wanting to know if there was some snag in the arrangements with the National Trust. He abused Mrs Greville roundly. Then we all remembered the unwritten law never to discuss women at a club, and laughed.

*Monday, 2nd September*

Tonight dined at Lady d'Avigdor-Goldsmid's* house, 47 Hans Place. She looks just the same, improved if anything in looks, and obviously enjoys her London widowhood. Always hated the country. Harry† joined us at eight, without his wife. He won the MC and DSO in the war and was apparently seriously wounded in the face. But he has been well mended and I saw no sign of wounds. He is still bombastic, rude and snubbing to his mother, but there is great kindliness underneath. He is very happily married and loves his two daughters. He is probably going to give up bullion broking, for by not earning income he will be better off, he

---

* Alice Landau; m. 1907 Osmond d'Avigdor-Goldsmid (1877–1940; cr. Bt, 1934).

† Major Sir Henry d'Avigdor-Goldsmid, 2nd Bt (1909–76); Oxford friend of J.L.-M., who had often stayed at Somerhill, his house in Kent; Conservative MP, 1955–74; m. 1940 Rosemary Nicholl.

maintains. I don't understand it. I only know that if I gave up work I would starve.

*Wednesday, 4th September*

My watch stopped again. I was so angry that I hit it against the table and the winding handle fell out and disappeared. I doubt it will ever go again. Rather perturbed this morning to receive a letter from Lord Esher enclosing a letter to him from Christopher Hussey,* complaining about the Trust not giving *Country Life* the National Trust Guidebook to publish – complaining, in fact, about me. But damn it, it is *my* book. To the Treasury where talked to Sir Alan Barlow† about Audley End and Ham House.

Saw Osbert Lancaster this evening. Rather grey and pustular. Full of gossip about our surviving mutual friends. Says it is all a piece of Nancy's nonsense claiming that she is loved by Palewski‡ who, he maintains, is uninterested (which is absolutely untrue); that Patrick [Kinross] has gone quite queer again;§ that Joan is divorcing and living with a man, and so on.

*Sunday, 8th September*

I read that Peter Acton¶ and his wife had been killed in an air liner. Peter was my neighbour and close friend at Magdalen, Oxford. He was so neurasthenic that for weeks he would not leave his rooms or speak to a soul. When he did his low, drawly, exaggerated voice was so like the Fleetwood-Hesketh** that for long I imagined they

---

* Architectural historian (1899–1970); architectural adviser, *Country Life*, 1930–64 (editor, 1933–40); m. 1936 Elizabeth ('Betty') Kerr-Smiley.

† Sir Alan Barlow, 2nd Bt (1881–1968); senior Treasury official.

‡ Colonel Gaston Palewski (1901–84); principal wartime aide of General de Gaulle, with whom Nancy Mitford was in love, he holding her in affection while tired by her attentions.

§ Following his divorce in 1942.

¶ Hon. Peter Lyon-Dalberg-Acton (1909–46); bro. of 3rd Baron Acton.

** Roger Fleetwood-Hesketh (1902–88) and his brother Peter (1905–85); Lancashire landowners and architectural conservationists.

were Catholics, like him. He was tormented by religious inhibitions, and never wholly natural.

*Wednesday, 11th September*

Lunched with Ian McCallum* at Kettner's. Not quite enough to assuage the pangs of hunger. At 6.30 to Sheila de Rutzen's.† [Her brother] Johnnie Philipps there with a new Bentley which goes a million miles an hour. Michael [Rosse] says he [Philipps] disgraced himself at Brighton by sliding down the banisters of a rather stuffy hotel at 8.30 a.m., stark naked, just as the bishops and schoolmaster guests with their wives were descending to breakfast.

*Saturday, 14th September*

Spent day at Blickling. There are eight gardeners now and the grounds are greatly tidied up. Miss O'Sullivan is slow and tired and looks ill. Went on to Felbrigg for dinner. Wyndham Ketton-Cremer's mother staying, a sweet, white-haired old lady. Although physically flaccid he is mentally stimulating. Plenty of serious talk. House huge, but Wyndham is well looked after by his couple, and lives comfortably. No electric light, and I had to walk miles with a candle from my bedroom to the w.c. at the far end of the Stuart wing.

*Sunday, 15th September*

Lord and Lady Templewood‡ (Sir Samuel and Lady Maud Hoare that were) came to luncheon [at Felbrigg], which we have in the

---

* Architectural historian (1919–87); conscientious objector during Second World War; later Curator of American Museum at Claverton near Bath.

† Sheila, dau. of Sir Henry Philipps, 2nd Bt; m. 1st Major John Foley, Baron de Rutzen (killed in action), 2nd 1947 (as his 2nd wife) Hon. Randal Plunkett (1906–99), who s. 1957 as 19th Baron Dunsany.

‡ Sir Samuel Hoare, 2nd Bt (1880–1957); Conservative statesman, related to the Hoares of Stourhead; Ambassador to Madrid on Special Mission, 1940–4; cr. Viscount Templewood, 1944; m. 1909 Lady Maud Lygon, sister of 7th Earl Beauchamp.

Paine* Rococo dining room. She is a big, gauche woman, but easy enough to talk to, and a devoted wife. He is a small, dapper man, every inch a politician, or rather now a statesman, wearing smartly cut blue serge suit and brown suede shoes; silvery hair, youthful. Spoke of the Government with utmost contempt, particularly of Bevan. Said his book on his Embassy in Spain had proved an unqualified success and even the left-wing papers praised it. They are close friends and neighbours of Wyndham, whom they call Bunny. Wyndham and I went for a long walk in the woods after tea; a gorgeous evening.

*Thursday, 19th September*

This evening I spent packing up, and moving china and breakable objects to 20 Thurloe Square, preparatory to the proper move tomorrow. My rooms there are not yet finished which is unsettling and annoying.

*Sunday, 29th September*

Today I practically finished my new flat, having worked hard at it all the weekend. Last night was my first at 20 Thurloe Square.

Jamesey dined at Brooks's. Without any reference being made to our recent estrangement, a *rapprochement* was, I suppose, effected. Our confidences seemed as sincere and easy as of yore. There are certainly enchanting sides to his volatile little character.

*Thursday, 3rd October*

Eddy Sackville-West lunched at Brooks's. His appearances in London get rarer. He seemed fairly satisfied with the efforts I am now making at Knole. He asked me for a weekend, which surprised me. Then I found it was because he had somebody staying whom no other friend could be persuaded to meet.

---

* James Paine (1717–89); worked at Felbrigg 1751–6.

Had our Annual General Meeting at the Mansion House. Lord Mountbatten* was the chief speaker. He was in admiral's uniform and is, I think, the handsomest man I have ever seen. At 20 Thurloe Square improvements gradually happen.

*Thursday, 10th October*

Tony Gandarillas dined.† Very sweet and eccentric. I asked him how he, aged sixty-two, managed to keep his youthful figure and complexion. He said it was the 'green pipe', explaining that he smoked opium every day of his life.

*Wednesday, 23rd October*

Today Professor Richardson lunched with me. We left Brooks's arm in arm, he in a long, thick topcoat, limping now since he broke his ankle and carrying a stout, unfurled umbrella. Slowly we walked up St James's Street. I imagined the scene to be like William IV and a cabinet minister, as might be depicted by Creevey.‡ The Hanoverian Professor took me to his new offices, above Lenygon's shop in Old Burlington Street. The building is, appropriately, by Kent and his room furnished with incomparable old furniture and a deep Savonnerie carpet. He pointed out with pride and merriment his chair of Queen Anne date, with original covering, and then his gold-headed cane in the corner. 'I like a touch of gold in a room,' he said. He is a darling old man. 'The devil is a real person. You meet him everywhere, James,' he said seriously, shaking his head.

*Monday, 28th October*

Tonight went to Tony Gandarillas's house at 7.30 to find him and Daisy Fellowes drinking champagne downstairs. Daisy looking

* He had just stood down as Supreme Allied Commander, South-East Asia, and been cr. Viscount.

† Rich bisexual Chilean diplomatist and patron of artists (d. 1970).

‡ Thomas Creevey, MP (1768–1838); author of gossipy *Creevey Papers*.

younger, thinner and seductive. Her gaiety is infectious. We went to dine at the Savoy in her large Rolls-Royce. It has a glass roof which can be revealed by pushing aside the inner covering; also the glass partition between the back and the driver's seat gently opens or closes by a handle operated by Daisy. I sat next to Carmen, Tony's sad daughter, and to Georgia [Sitwell], whose appearance was lovely – she was wearing little velvet bows in her hair and a heavy gold wrist chain with enormous seals. Sachie and Peter Quennell too; also Daisy's married French daughter Jacqueline, who has just left a French prison for having betrayed her girlfriend to the Gestapo during the war. This party such a contrast to my six o'clock talk with darling Doreen, with whom I can communicate for hours on all subjects. This time we discussed the mystery of the 'gentleman'. She said the 'lady' was no mystery. The quality of the first was indefinable, a gift of God; that of the second mundane, merely a social acquisition.

*Tuesday, 29th October*

The Eshers motored me down to Polesden. They went round the museum and were delighted with it. Lord E. has approved Michael [Rosse]'s memorandum on the proposal that we should have area 'representatives' as well as 'agents'. Lord E. wants to call them area 'artists', but Lady E. and I think that a bad name, which will cause resentment in those who are not artists. I have engineered this little scheme.*

*Saturday, 2nd November*

After luncheon motored to Watlington to stay with the Eshers, arriving tea time. No one in the world is more delicious company than Lord E. After dinner, and indeed before and during, he talked incessantly. He is amazing for a man of his age. He honestly

* The system of 'representatives' survived until the early twenty-first century (by which time they had long been professionals, whereas originally the posts were mostly honorary and unpaid).

thinks the world pleasanter and more interesting than ever before, and that the post-war life is the most interesting adventure. He sees a resurgence of interest in the arts on a wide basis, and praises the Government for being more progressive in patronising the arts than any in history. He says he has had a wonderful and enjoyable life, and even sees a great future for the British aristocracy. He possibly overlooks the fact that his life has been a peculiarly easy one.

*Tuesday, 5th November*

Staying with the Bearsteds. More of his pictures are back from war storage, including the Italian primitives. The whole make a superb private collection. An undergraduate from Oxford, David Carritt,* came to look at the pictures. Lord B. warned me beforehand to be kind to him for he would probably be shy. He was by no means shy. A perky youth of eighteen dashed into the room with abounding self-confidence. Within minutes he was disputing the entries in Lord B's catalogue. I must say his knowledge of pictures and of everything else touched upon was astounding. I was amazed. Though polite he is a little too sure of himself.

*Friday, 8th November*

Saw Sibyl [Colefax] in hospital. I hate going there and then feel ashamed of myself for so nearly not going. I overheard her telephoning to a friend about Lady Anglesey's† death. 'No, no, my dear, it was the left lung; you're quite wrong. She spoke to me herself only four days before she died. The children rang me up at nine in the morning, three hours after she died.' Sibyl must 'be in at' every death, even that of her greatest friend.

---

* Art expert (1927–82); later to be renowned for his 'discovery' of lost or unrecognised masterpieces; lover of Harold Nicolson's son Ben.

† Lady Marjorie Manners (1883–1946), dau. of 8th Duke of Rutland; m. 1912 6th Marquess of Anglesey (1885–1947).

*Monday, 11th November*

Dined with Rory [Cameron] at Claridge's: Alvilde, Tony, Emerald and a beautiful French woman, *circa* fifty, called Norah Auric, wife of composer.* She rolls her lovely eyes and shows the whites, like first-quarter moons. After sitting in the lounge (what hell restaurants are), Alvilde and Tony and I went to Angus Menzies's† house, where Barbara Ward,‡ Jimmie Smith,§ Lennox Berkeley¶ and Angus M. were playing and singing. Barbara Ward *would* sing in a very missish voice which no one applauded. Angus's voice is deep and mellifluous. What a seductive creature he is. Just slightly affected. He has glossy black hair and a Michelangelo mouth and eyes.

*Saturday, 16th November*

Trained to Neath in Glamorganshire. There are restaurant cars again on the trains, though the food is poor. Was met by an old chauffeur in an old car and motored to Derwydd in Carmarthenshire, inhabited by Miss Stepney-Gulston. The outside is just like a modern villa, stuccoed over. An ugly house which in England would be of no account, but here is held in some esteem. It does contain several chimneypieces and ceilings of rather remarkable post-Restoration work in crude, provincial Inigo Jones style. Sheila de Rutzen came for tea and motored me to Picton [Castle, Pembrokeshire]. Just she and [her brother] Johnnie [Philipps]. Good dinner at which we drank hock and a bottle of port. Johnnie is totally irresponsible and what the older generation would call a rotter. But he can be very funny.

*Thursday, 28th November*

Ate at Brooks's with Ben Nicolson, who told me how deeply he regretted not having been more dissolute in his youth.

---

* Georges Auric (1899–1983); French composer, member of 'Les Six'.

† Decorator (1910–73); bachelor cousin of Alvilde Chaplin.

‡ Writer and broadcaster (1914–81); m. 1950 Commander Robert Jackson.

§ Hon. James Smith (1906–80); unm. yr s. of 3rd Viscount Hambleden; director of W. H. Smith, and musical personality, later Chairman of Sadlers Wells Foundation.

¶ (Sir) Lennox Berkeley (1903–89); composer; m. 1946 Freda Bernstein (b. 1923).

*Saturday, 7th December*

Very showering but beautiful day. After breakfast motored across the Tamar into Cornwall, up and down narrow lanes and up steep hills until I reached Cotehele, which faces east over Calstock and the river. Were it moved just a little further southward the house would be better situated. Then it would overlook the lovely ribbon loop of the river. As it is, the situation is romantic, wild and wooded. The caretaker was away with the key, but the farmer's wife most kindly motored to fetch the daily help from Calstock who had another key. This kind and intelligent woman showed me round the house which is fully furnished. Meanwhile the old coachman, seeing my motor, came and talked. Told me that until 1939 he drove a 1911 Rolls for Lord Mount Edgcumbe.* He expressed himself very concerned about my 'points'. He left and presently returned, wearing a topcoat with velvet collar and old-fashioned billycock, to present me with the distributor points of his old Rolls. I was charmed by him. Didn't know what to do with object presented.

Cotehele House is not striking from the outside, being squat and spread. It is actually far larger than one is led to suppose from the front, for it has two courtyards. It is uniformly old, late medieval with pointed windows, all of granite. The great hall is as fine as any I have seen, with curved windbraces in the roof and plastered white-washed walls, hung with armour. In the oldest wing all the rooms are panelled, walls plastered and the Stuart furniture upholstered in needlework, none later than the eighteenth century. The contents are untouched, superb. Indeed it is a superb house.

Lunched at Tavistock and motored to Pixton [Park, near Dulverton], arriving for tea. Mary Herbert,† my hostess, came

---

* Kenelm Edgcumbe, 6th Earl of Mount Edgcumbe (1873–65); m. 1906 Lilian Arkwright.

† Hon. Mary Vesey (1889–1970), dau. of 4th Viscount de Vesci; m. 1910 Hon. Aubrey Herbert (1880–1923), 2nd son of 4th Earl of Carnarvon, politician, diplomatist, traveller and secret agent; J.L.-M. had been her frequent guest at Pixton before the war.

just before dinner. Only Eddie Grant* and an Austrian countess† staying.

*Sunday, 8th December*

Pixton is a little more orderly than usual. The evacuee children have all gone of course, but the house is left rather knocked about. Mary is as majestic as ever, tall, robust, windswept, exceedingly untidy. Her tweed coat and skirt are stained and torn, and the pockets have holes in them. Her breeding and dignity are impeccable; her views are uncompromising, proud and right. Her humour is unimpaired. She is a splendid creature with a massive soul. Today it poured in cascades from morn till eve, the north wind driving blankets across the valley. So I sat indoors all day, talking to Mary and that kindly, silly Eddie Grant.

*Thursday, 12th December*

Dined at Lennox Gardens at Mrs Carnegie's.‡ This interested me historically for here was a pre-Great War upper middle-class regime in full fig. Large, ugly, late-Victorian house. We assembled in the capacious drawing-room on first floor. Lots of silver in evidence, silver photograph frames, silver boxes and bric-à-brac displayed on dainty tables. Dining-room table with white brocade cloth and silver candlesticks, spoons and forks shining very bright. Butler and footman both in white ties. Circular metal suspended centre-light with Edwardian electric fitting, called, I think, an electrolier. Sixteen candles burning. Present the Petos§ and Mrs Carnegie,

---

* Captain Eddie Grant (1894–1947); racing personality; m. 1934 Bridget Herbert (1914–2005), 2nd of Mary's three daughters (J.L.-M. once having been in love with the eldest, Gabriel).

† Gretel Coudenhove-Kalergi, who had been marooned there since the outbreak of war in 1939.

‡ Mary Endicott of Massachusetts; m. 1st 1888 (as his 3rd wife) Joseph Chamberlain, Unionist statesman (1836–1914), 2nd Canon W. H. Carnegie (1860–1936), Sub-Dean of Westminster.

§ Lt-Col Sir Michael Peto, 2nd Bt (1894–1971); of Iford Manor, Wiltshire; m. 1920 Frances Carnegie.

whose last husband was Frances Peto's father Canon Carnegie, and her first Joe Chamberlain, whom she referred to as 'Mr Chamberlain'. Mrs C., grey, wispy-haired, tall, upright like a ramrod, dressed in black tulle, thin Edwardian waist, low V front, and long grey kid gloves. Opposite me at dinner hung a splendid portrait of her as a young woman by Millais. In the drawing-room is another of her in her early thirties by Sargent, this one full-length depicting a feather plume in her hair. Very pretty she must have been. Now be-pince-nezed, severe, correct, but oh such a delightful woman. There is a third portrait of her as a child by William Hunt.* There is one of Joe Chamberlain by Sargent in the dining-room. After dinner she and I talked of Millais, whom she much liked – 'he was so jolly' – and of 'Mr Sargent', whom she liked too. I wondered how this impeccable, immaculate lady could have allowed herself to have two husbands, even though she was a widow when she married the second, the first being satisfactorily in heaven. Which would she belong to when *she* reached heaven?

Such a flavour of Edwardian London this evening conveyed to me, of hansom cabs and artificial flowers in a long, frilly vase, for a dense yellow fog enveloped us, percolating through the closed windows for a time, and the street outside chill and muffled. Mrs C. is still young in spirit and quick in uptake, with her perfect old-fashioned manners. Speaks with a low, slightly husky Bostonian voice, very beguiling intonation.

*Sunday, 15th December*

M. Jourdain and I. Compton-Burnett came to tea at 5 o'clock, which we had before the fire. I must tell Emily† not to put paper mats under the cakes. Bought cakes today are detestable enough, without mats. James and Maurice [the French 'cellist] came in later. They were longing for the ladies to go, and made it plain. But the ladies made it plain that they were not going to leave just to please

* William Holman Hunt (1827–1910); inaugurated with Rossetti the Pre-Raphaelite Brotherhood.

† The housekeeper at 20 Thurloe Square, Miss Emily Bradford.

these two young men and stayed and stayed until 6.45. Then James and Maurice both leapt to their feet, saying goodbye. So the ladies had to leave while the boys stayed behind. Maurice spoke not a word until they left, and then asked in French English, 'Who are those impossible governesses?' J. explained that one of them was the foremost novelist of our time.

*Thursday, 19th December*

It was snowing when I left for the office. Was invited to three cocktail parties, and went to one, John Murray's, at delightful No. 50 Albemarle Street, surrounded by Byron relics. The party was given for Freya Stark. Why, when dozens of other guests were just as distinguished? I was much moved by Byron's glove in a case, and the shirt worn at his wedding which had been George II's (shirt, not wedding).

*Friday, 27th December*

Papa and I drove to Brockhampton near Bromyard [Herefordshire] in the morning where we met Admiral and Mrs Bevir, Ruby and Christopher Holland-Martin,* and Colin Jones. Lunched in the cold, cold hall and walked round the house where Colonel Lutley's personal belongings are left lying about since the day he died.† Something poignant in a house which has suddenly ceased to exist with the last owner. Life arrested in old tobacco jars with the lids off, smelly old pipes, books turned face downwards on tables, the well-worn favourite chair with deep imprint of the late 'behind' and threadbare arms, and the mournful, reproachful gaze of dozens

* Edward 'Ruby' Holland-Martin (1900–81), of Overbury Court, Worcestershire, Director of Bank of England and Hon. Treasurer of N.T.; his yr bro. Christopher (1910–60), Director of Martin's Bank, Eton contemporary of J.L.-M., MP for Ludlow 1951–60. (Both were bachelors at this time but subsequently married.)

† Following a visit from J.L.-M. in 1938, and having no direct heirs, Colonel Lutley had bequeathed his entire property to the N.T., the bequest taking effect on his death in 1946.

of forgotten ancestors on the walls. Estate, house and contents all left to the National Trust. The house, which has a situation of unparalleled Midlands beauty overlooking valley and woods, could be made decent by the removal of Victorian trimmings round the windows, and the installation of sash-bars. No furniture of museum quality but very nice plain utility Georgian, as genuine as the old squires who for centuries loved it. Two good Georgian bookcases. The Admiral being incredibly muddleheaded and Ruby as friendly as I am sure a swordfish can be. Christopher shocked me by warning me that G.,* whom I had proposed for election to Brooks's, would be black-balled. What possible reason could there be other than personal spite? No one is less offensive or more amiable to all and sundry. Ruby who drove over in a luxurious Bentley produced a luncheon basket with fittings like a bar, complete with gin and whisky and coffee. Papa and I rather humbly drank our milk. The dear old butler with his sweet, sad smile is stone deaf and speaks in a whisper. The housekeeper, dignified and courteous like the one at Chesney Wold,† speaks like a BBC announcer. Papa and I drove down to Lower Brockhampton and examined this little black-and-white manor and gatehouse with enthusiasm. It is just the sort of house my father cares for.

---

* Identified in original typescript as George 'Grandy' Child-Villiers, 9th Earl of Jersey (1910–98), of whom J.L.-M. had seen much during the previous three years to discuss his donation of Osterley Park, Middlesex, to N.T.

† Lincolnshire seat of Sir Leicester Dedlock, Bt in Dickens's *Bleak House*.

# 1947

# 1947

*Wednesday, 1st January*

Doreen [Colston-Baynes] telephoned and I went to her at six o'clock. She told me she has a medium who regularly visits her; that she sees visions of the departed, unfortunately too often of the people she most disliked when they were alive; that, notwithstanding, she is eagerly looking forward to death, which her medium tells her takes the form of life being gently drawn through the fingers. She is not the least melancholy and enjoys *her* life, which is not life as enjoyed by most people. From true life she is too divorced to care whether she exists any longer in this alien world. We all feel like this, but most of us cannot withdraw from it in the way she manages to do, shut up in her bedroom and adjoining sitting room, with curtains tightly drawn, for days on end.

*Friday, 3rd January*

Took the manuscript of my National Trust *Guide* to Batsford's. Met Mr Harry who with no explanations put me in a taxi and drove to Marylebone station. There we met Sachie [Sitwell]. Mr Harry produced packets of minute negatives from his capacious pockets. They smelled very strongly of the fish which he keeps in the same pockets for his cats. He spread the negatives on the platform, produced a huge magnifying glass and, while spluttering and coughing, examined them on the ground with Sachie. The two made an odd group among the hurrying passengers, Mr B. wearing a green hat with a huge feather in it.

*Sunday, 5th January*

Cold, leaden skies. It must snow soon. Left Wickhamford for Mass in Evesham in that hideous church. On to Charlecote. Alianore Lucy* there, and Wicker the caretaker. All is serene. Then to Packwood and lunched with Baron [Ash].† We had sherry and *pâté de foie gras*, as good as it used to be; omelette with quince jam and rum blazing; port wine. Baron conducted me over the house which is now in pristine condition. He showed me a Victorian lithograph of the house looking much as it does today. Saw the servants' wing adapted for the caretaker, and discussed this. B. wants a disabled ex-officer, not an artistic person. We don't see eye-to-eye over this.

*Monday, 6th January*

Deep snow this morning. At two Emily Empey's‡ funeral took place in Wickhamford churchyard. The short service with 'Abide with Me' and the Nunc Dimittis sung in a very high key to the squeaky harmonium moved me deeply. Papa, Mama and I sat in our pew, and nostalgic memories were revived. The beauty and poignancy of this little church amount to the most exquisite thing in the whole world, a sort of sacred island always at the back of my mind which I can retreat to in my thoughts wherever I may be. Em was I suppose one of the unrecognised saints of this world.

*Tuesday, 7th January*

To see Sibyl [Colefax], now in her own house, but seated in a chair. I believe she hardly walks at all. The Ambassador of Spain there, very annoyed with our Government for having broken off relations, entirely owing to pressure by Russia, he says. And Mrs Oglander,

---

* Unmarried daughter of the late Sir Henry Fairfax-Lucy, who looked after the gardens at Charlecote.

† Graham Baron Ash (1889–1980); Midlands industrialist; donated Packwood House, Warwickshire to N.T., 1941, continuing to live there until 1947.

‡ J.L.-M's mother's beloved governess, whom she had brought to live in the village.

wearing a ridiculous, over-smart Parisian hat with vast ostrich feather curling under the chin. She is not young or handsome enough for this extravagant bedizenment. Jamesey present, telling me later how much he disliked her; also Harold, to whom she abused the *New Statesman* and 'Kingsley Wood' – meaning Kingsley Martin,* foolish female.

*Saturday, 18th January*

I stayed the weekend at Long Crichel, Paul Hyslop† the other guest. Eardley, Desmond and Eddy live a highly civilised existence here. Comfortable house, pretty things, good food. All the pictures are Eardley's, and a fine collection of modern art too. After dinner Desmond read John Betjeman's poems aloud, and we all agreed they would live.

*Monday, 20th January*

In the morning Eardley and I went over Max Gate which was built by Thomas Hardy and his brother in 1885. It is perfectly hideous and shapeless. Of scarlet brick, with two ugly square angle towers. All Hardy's things were long ago removed to Dorchester Museum, so there is little connected with him of interest. Besides the house was shoddily built, with lean-to odds and ends added by him. It will be a constant expense. I shall advise the Committee to sell it – it is held alienably – and keep the money for buying his birthplace one of these days.‡

*Thursday, 23rd January*

Dined with Malcolm Bullock at the Turf off grouse and champagne. The Duke of Devonshire§ joined us as we were finishing

---

* Sir Kingsley Wood (1891–1943), Conservative Chancellor of the Exchequer, 1940–3; Kingsley Martin (1897–1969), socialist editor of *New Statesman*, 1930–60.

† Architect in the classical tradition (1900–88); friend of Raymond Mortimer.

‡ See entry for 27 January 1948.

§ Edward William Spencer Cavendish, 10th Duke of Devonshire (1895–1950).

and talked for an hour. He was what is called 'lit up'. Rather curiously we spoke of old Mr Holmes's association with the National Trust. The Duke said he is known as the chief bugger of the Peak. Next morning a telegram came to the office announcing that Mr Holmes had died at precisely the moment we were talking about him. I have before been told a story of the Duke killing a man at a public meeting merely by speaking *at* him.

The Duke becoming rather a bore I started fidgeting to induce Malcolm to leave the dining-room and shake him off. The D. said that Princess Elizabeth had been staying with him. She is just like the young Queen Victoria with the old Queen's sagacity. She makes it very plain to the Queen that whereas she, the Queen, is a commoner, she, Princess Elizabeth, is of royal blood. After church in Eastbourne she said to the Vicar, aged seventy-five, 'Your sermon was excellent.' He bridled with pleasure. 'But', she added, 'you spoilt it in the last ten minutes.' The Duke said that royalty are always happy if you organise their visits and make them play games, but you must never leave it to them to make suggestions. He is devoted to Mrs Corrigan, that ridiculous woman, famous for her malapropisms. 'My doctor said to me, if you want to avoid indigestion, you must masturbate, masturbate.'

*Saturday, 25th January*

Yesterday it began snowing and doing worse things. It is so extremely cold that even with two fires and a rug over me I was cold sitting at home. Dined with the Glenconners* in Regent's Park, driving there in the snow. He has a beaming, smiling face, yet is inscrutable. Lady G. is pretty, sympathetic and intellectual. Dinner was to celebrate the return from the States of Cyril Connolly. Cyril had for him a good colour and behaved less like an inspired oracle, though the star of the evening. He told funny stories of his adventures in America, notably flying experiences and

* Christopher Tennant, 2nd Baron Glenconner (1899–1983); m. (2nd) 1935 Elizabeth Powell.

encounters with anti-British feeling. Cyril says our Palestine policy has alienated the American Jews, whose power is out of all proportion to their percentage of the population. Alfred Beit came in after dinner. He said that Clementine is very happy in South Africa and they are to live out there permanently.* That is our loss.

*Wednesday, 29th January*

Today the cold has been unbelievable. The papers say it is the coldest day for fifty years. Wearning my snow boots and fur-lined coat I was not once warm. All my pipes, including w.c. pipes, are frozen, so a bath or wash is out of the question. Throughout the country electricity has been cut off and the gas pressure is so low that it is not worth turning the fire on. Even the basic elements of civilisation are denied us. Dined with that horror Charles Fry, drunken, dissolute and destructive.

*Monday, 3rd February*

Caught the 11.18 to Pulborough where I was met and driven through slush and snow to Petworth. Lord Leconfield, now indeed slow, old and blue-faced, waddled to meet me, clad in yellow gaiters and followed by a black retriever who seems to be his only friend. He is a pathetic old man. Today he was very friendly and not at all pompous or absurd. Wished me to see all the furniture, and hoped I would be pleased with its condition. Said in fact he was convinced he was wise in handing over to the N.T. We lunched together, I not sent to the servants' hall. Promptly at 1.30 he summoned the nice old housekeeper to take me round the house. Furniture in splendid condition, smelling of mansion polish and camphor. Lord Leconfield joined us upstairs and waddled around. He is sweet with the servants, they curiously subservient and sycophantic. He made me walk in the cold, steely hail outside. I don't

* They returned in 1952 owing to their disapproval of *apartheid*, and went to live in Ireland.

believe he was aware of it. The back of the house, with its buttresses, is really very ugly. I left by bus for Pulborough at four, Lord L. accompanying me to bus stop.

*Friday, 7th February*

John Wilton took me in his big, blue Ford car to Knole, in the snow. Bitter cold. I piloted him round the house, like a refrigerator, and the garden where no man had hitherto trod. In our snow boots we crunched over a foot of snow.

*Saturday, 8th February*

The jolly news is that all fuel is to be cut off. The cold is appalling.

*Thursday, 13th February*

This week is being a veritable nightmare. On Sunday afternoon it started to thaw and the snow mostly went. On Monday it froze again very hard, so that the slush is like slippery brick. Since Monday we have had no heating in the office apart from one electric fire. And now this is turned off from 9 to 12 and again from 2 till 4 each day. Wrapped in my fur coat with three pullovers underneath, my snowboots kept on, I am still too perished to work properly. People are unanimous in blaming the Government for a hideous muddle, yet Mr Shinwell* remains Minister of Fuel. I seldom sit in the office now but walk about and dictate letters. Have twice been to the National Gallery, which is heated, to look at the Spanish Exhibition of Velázquez, Goya and El Greco. A number of poor old people sit on the benches for hours at a time, their feet wrapped in brown paper, striving to keep warm. At an Historic Buildings Committee yesterday all sat in fur coats, moaning in misery, for no one could concentrate on the agenda.

---

* Emanuel Shinwell (1884–1986); Glaswegian Labour politician; Minister of Fuel and Power, 1945–7; Secretary of State for War, 1947–51; cr. life peer, 1970.

Lord Esher however was as cheerful as ever. He told a member of the Cabinet, 'You Labour people never let us have a dull moment.' Bridget [Parsons] says that if this Government goes an extreme left one will take its place, and that she is quite ready to go to the barricades and shoot. I asked, whom? Well, almost anyone, she replied. Most of the large shops are closed; those that are open have no electricity, and no light except from the odd candle. The streets are blacked out, as in war time, and millions are unemployed for industries have come to a standstill. Food is becoming very short and the situation is as critical as ever it was during the war.

*Wednesday, 19th February*

Eardley met me at Salisbury station and motored me to Long Crichel. Eddy and Desmond there. The house very adequately heated and comfortable. Brilliant fireworks from Desmond who is the gayest, sweetest-tempered, most informative person in the wide world. After dinner, a curious discussion about homosexuality. Eddy maintained that born homosexuals could never become heterosexuals, whereas I maintained, with no intent to annoy, that this was not the case. People were not necessarily born one way or the other; heterosexuals could become homosexuals, and vice versa; and there were people capable of falling in love equally deeply with men and women. Eddy stoutly denied the possiblity of persons being ambisexual, and with vehemence quoted himself as the overriding disproof of this notion, assuming that his case was a precedent all the world over. He adopted a highly self-pitying attitude, became furious with Desmond, and after much querulous, high-pitched shouting, left the room. Afterwards Eardley and Desmond admitted it was impossible to carry on discussions with Eddy. In spite of this I have a great affection for him. He told me the next day that he knew he ought to be contented with his lot, but his chronic ill-health and difficult temperament prevented him acknowledging his good fortune. Every day, he said, he was pursued by angst. I understand this because in lesser measure I am too – but not, perhaps, every day.

*Thursday, 27th February*

This morning went to a very enjoyable performance – the centenary service for Ellen Terry in St Paul's, Covent Garden. It was cheerful, and inspiring. Very cold, yellow day, in which no woman looked her best. I arrived at 11.30 and was put in the nave. The Sadlers Wells choir sang anthems; Edith Evans,* Sybil Thorndike† and Peggy Ashcroft‡ read three Shakespeare sonnets; the lessons were read by Ralph Richardson,§ Léon Quartermaine¶ and Harcourt Williams.** With the exception of the last, who is a handsome elderly man, all the others looked remarkably plain – Richardson a flunkey, Quartermaine a Glasgow thug masquerading as an undertaker, E. Evans a painted clown (male), and Thorndike a downtrodden school-teacher. Miss Edith Craig was present and Christopher St John, wearing a fawn teddy-bear coat, man's porkpie hat, and waving a gigantic bunch of golden daffodils at her friends behind her. The Bishop of London, a mealy-mouthed creature, gave the address.

*Saturday, 1st March*

I have never been colder. Huddled over a coal fire that gives out an imperceptible flutter of heat I managed to write with great speed an account of Petworth for my National Trust *Guide*.

*Wednesday, 5th March*

All day long it continued to snow [at Wickhamford]. This is the worst storm in these parts ever recorded. A blizzard rages and the snow is piling up. Papa, Mama and I began after luncheon to walk to the Table Land. Bitter wind and twice my hat blew away.

---

* Actress (1888–1976; DBE 1946).

† Actress (1882–1976; DBE 1931).

‡ Actress (1907–91; DBE 1956), once married to J.L.-M's Eton friend Rupert Hart-Davis.

§ Actor (1902–83; ktd 1947).

¶ Actor (1876–1967); m. the actress Fay Compton.

** Actor and producer (1880–1957).

Outside the Idions' house and along the Badsey road were drifts six feet deep. We sent Mama home. The two of us walked on to Badsey, to Cull the baker's to fetch some bread, which, with the milk, had not been delivered today. On the edge of the village we saw Cull's van about to leave for Wickhamford, so we returned. At the top of the hill over Bully Brook, where a snow drift was rapidly building up, we stopped, and talked to two men. Sure enough the van came and was stuck in the drift. By dint of much pushing the four of us succeeded in extricating it.

*Thursday, 6th March*

Brilliant sunny day but the snow lying in huge drifts. Haines [the chauffeur] says no one remembers anything like it before. There are icicles over three foot long hanging from the thatch of the cottages. I spent the morning on the roof of the pantry at the Manor shovelling the snow off. It has even blown through the roof of the motor-house loft and is lying in piles on the trunks. My hunting boots were completely buried. In the middle of the squash court was a heap of snow, two foot deep. After luncheon I walked with the Cooks to fetch some milk from the farm at Bower's Hill. There we saw an amusing sight – about twenty men attaching an old cart to a tractor, they following behind and holding the shafts and supporting the milk churns. This curious procession, like a funeral, advanced to Badsey and Wickhamford over snow drifts. I wished I had a camera. There is something harsh, metallic and savage about the Vale yokels, something extremely primitive, yet unpeasantlike, very material and earthy. Their voices are grating and discordant. When Dick and I were children we spoke broad Worcestershire perfectly. This afternoon they were very good-humoured and, though professing to dislike the snow, were enjoying it.

*Sunday, 9th March*

J[ohn] F[owler] dined with me and we discussed sex problems and how to overcome them by the most practical, mechanical and cynical means.

*Tuesday, 11th March*

Lunched with Ann Rothermere at Warwick House overlooking Green Park. Very pre-war, butler and footmen, wines and desserts. A heterogenous party consisting of Ann (hostess), Bob Boothby,* Lady Crewe, James P.-H., Sibyl Colefax, the editor of the *Evening News* and me. Lady Crewe makes no attempt to be friendly or interesting and must be a disagreeable woman. Occasionally she melts into a bland, cow-like smile, which has the effect of putting her neighbour ill at ease. We talked politics, and Lady Crewe began by hoping the Liberals would never unite with the Conservatives. Sibyl and James both agreed in deploring the present Government, but both voted it into power. Warwick House has little architectural character, but its site, with terrace over park and proximity to St James's Palace, is enchanting.

*Friday, 14th March*

At the Finance Committee this morning the staff were dismissed and salaries discussed. Mine was raised to £1,000. Harold [Nicolson] said to me in the afternoon, 'You should have heard the nice things I said about you. They would have made you regret the unkind things you said to me', referring to my reproofs over his joining the Labour Party.†

This evening I had Nancy, Bridget and Tony Gandarillas to dine [at Thurloe Square]. At least the food tasted, as Bridget said. They all complimented me over my room. Somehow I did not find the party wholly enjoyable, for Nancy, though I love her, is not always congenial, and her unkind witticisms are often less funny at first hand than when repeated.

---

* Robert Boothby (1900–86; cr. life peer, 1958); Conservative politician, friend of Harold Nicolson and the Kray Brothers.

† He had made this transition in February – to the astonishment of his friends, and the embarrassment of his son Nigel who was endeavouring to become a Conservative parliamentary candidate.

*Sunday, 16th March*

Mama telephoned me last night not to motor to Worcester today on account of the bad floods. She said that their cottage was under water and in Oxford the swans were swimming into people's bedrooms. However, I set off. Nothing very bad until the Cotswolds where single traffic because of the heaps of snow still on the verges. At Moreton-in-the-Marsh water was cascading through someone's house into the street. Then it started to rain again and a great gale arose so that I feared elm trees would fall across the car.

I am now staying in Worcester at The Crown. There is a musty smell in my tiny bedroom under the eaves. It is so dirty that I do not like to put any of my things in the wardrobe or on the table. Sluts instead of servants who chatter and giggle behind the screens of the dining-room, and the proprietress in grubby black satin has a cigarette hanging out of her mouth when she speaks. God, I wish these English hotel proprietors could be forced to see what Swiss hotels are like! Food here practically uneatable.

In Worcester I saw the water in the bedrooms of all the cottages along the river. There has been nothing like these floods since 1770.

*Saturday, 22nd March*

I showed Professor Richardson Sir Donald Somervell's* letter [about the blackball of J.L.-M's candidate at Brooks's]. He [Richardson] said he knew the reason was that G. was considered by staider members of the election committee to be a 'pleasurer', and that they wouldn't have him on account of his treatment of his second wife. He added that twenty years ago such a consideration would not have been taken into account, but today the aristocracy were tightening themselves up. He advised me to withdraw the name without ado, and not to resign myself. I know that disapproving old prude Lord Ilchester is at the back of the blackball affair. The Prof. said that after forty no man cherished illusions; and that after fifty all he cherished was personal comfort and freedom from agitation.

---

* QC and MP; Attorney-General, 1936–45 (1889–1960).

*Thursday, 27th March*

Went to Victoria & Albert at Leigh Ashton's* invitation to a buffet luncheon to see the French tapestries. Met Clarissa Churchill and we ate together. I only saw the Louis XIV and eighteenth-century tapestries, but shall go again tomorrow. The twentieth-century tapestries are hideous beyond belief. As Sir Eric Maclagan† said to me, even if one had one of the least offensive, what would one do with it? Bertie Abdy‡ told me at Emerald Cunard's this evening that the rise and fall of tapestry weaving coincided with the fluctuations of the economy. In what he esteemed the greatest periods, namely the seventeenth and eighteenth centuries, there were 600 different colours available. Today there are less than sixty. Lady Diana Cooper came into Emerald's for tea. I don't care for the insolent way she looks through me.

*Sunday, 30th March*

I have been to the tapestry exhibition again. I know nothing more symbolical of pure poetry than the lady outside her tent, '*en toi mon seul désir*'. It transcends anything I have ever seen, and makes me want to cry.

Have been thinking over what Professor Richardson said to me. Every man is damned by his own sins in this life at any rate, if not the next. I am certainly damned here by my defeatism and chronic despair. The outward form my despair takes is persistent ill-humour and an abandon to selfishness and hardness of heart, which bespeak a shrivelled soul. I realise that in this life one should love all humanity and care for it. I do not, and so am a dissident. My ill-humour is all-besetting.

Since Friday I have felt very unwell, pains in my stomach and nausea. I hope it may be merely a form of internal chill; but at

* Sir Leigh Ashton (1897–1983); Director of Victoria & Albert Museum, 1945–55.

† Art historian and museum curator (1879–1951).

‡ Sir Robert Abdy, 5th Bt (1896–1976); m. (2nd) 1930 Lady Diana Bridgeman, dau. of 5th Earl of Bradford.

nights I imagine it to be cancer. I have for weeks past also experienced a curious burning in the legs; this I attribute to phlebitis. And a pounding of the heart, which I suppose to be angina pectoris. In short, something is the matter.

*Wednesday, 2nd April*

Had a good-humoured reply from G. agreeing to withdraw his candidature for Brooks's, but expressing surprise and regret. I shall never feel the same towards Brooks's for this behaviour; shall never forget or forgive.

All Easter it was perishingly cold, with relentless rain. Harry Ashwin* motored me to Charlecote, where I stayed the night with the Lucys. The bedrooms at Charlecote are cosy and Victorian: flowered wallpapers, washstand with pretty flowered china, maplewood furniture, four-poster bed with old chintz hangings, a fire in the grate. Bath with polished wooden rim, brass taps and brass spray on end of a long pipe; deep red, thick, comfortable bath mat.

*Thursday, 10th April*

Dined with the Johnnie Churchills. It is odd seeing Johnnie so conventionally established in a tidy and well-appointed house. This entirely his wife's, Mary's, beneficent doing. Sarah Churchill was there and I sat next to her. She is beautiful and attractive; physically unlike her father, Winston, and prettier than her sister Diana Sandys. Johnnie described to me his father's† death and the keen interest which his uncle Winston took in his brother's illness. He kept telephoning and giving elaborate directions to doctors and nurses as though commanding a battle, using Churchillian phrases like, 'Backs to the Wall!' and 'Certainly Jack must fight to the finish.' On Jack's death he worked himself up to a tremendous

---

* Childhood friend and Eton contemporary of J.L.-M. (d. 1983); neighbour of the Lees-Milnes at Bretforton Manor, Worcestershire.

† Major John Strange Spencer Churchill (1880–1946).

emotional pitch and literally, as Johnnie described it, rained tears around the room. He gave elaborate instructions as to the hymns to be sung at the funeral, quoting dozens of them by heart. Then, Johnnie said, on the very night of his brother's death he read to Johnnie sixty pages of his first book on the South African War, as though to console him, ending with the words, 'I wish I had the power of writing as well as that today.'

*Friday, 11th April*

A most beautiful day, sunny, clear and balmy. I walked from Queen Anne's Gate to Paddington after six o'clock and all Londoners were singing or whistling with joy over escape from an appalling winter. Spent quarter of an hour with dear Kathleen Kennet, who is much iller. She looks very tired, her face is softer and her voice perceptibly slower. I was mightily depressed by her appearance and languor. As I left I thought the rarity of this woman lies in the fact that I can talk to her as to myself. I asked myself as I walked, was my distress selfish? Was it my loss I was lamenting?

*Sunday, 20th April*

After tea went to Melbury where I stayed the next two nights with the Ilchesters. Lady Ilchester is adorable; about seventy, with a blue face and few teeth. Extremely welcoming, she at once puts you at ease. Makes one feel one is a great success. Also very funny and full of gossip. Drink flowed.

Lady I. told me that her mother Lady Londonderry was a bosom friend of Lady Blanche Hozier, mother of Mrs Winston Churchill. Lady Blanche confided in Lady Londonderry at Aix just before Mrs Winston was born that the child's father was Lord Redesdale, her brother-in-law and my Tom's grandfather.* This makes Tom and Randolph first cousins as well as second.

---

* Lady Blanche (1852–1932; m. 1873 Colonel Sir Henry Hozier) and Lady Clementine (1854–1932; m. 1874 1st Baron Redesdale); daughters of David Ogilvy, 5th Earl of Airlie (1826–81).

I returned to London on Tuesday very late, for I was invited by Sibyl Colefax to her box at the opera. I hastily changed and dashed off to Covent Garden in the car. With my bows right across Piccadilly Circus, the car stopped dead, having run out of petrol. It was a bad dream come true. Traffic piled up, hooting behind me. I got out, walked up to three policemen on the pavement and begged for help. They pushed and shunted the car to the kerb. Then I walked to three garages before one would sell me petrol in a tin. I missed the first act of *Rosenkavalier*, an all-English production, libretto translation by Alan Pryce-Jones, scenery and décor by Robert Ironside – conventional Rococo drawing-room style.

*Friday, 25th April*

Charles Fry dined. He promised that Batsford's would pay for my holiday in Rome this autumn, and gave me a fine book of coloured reproductions of the USA National Gallery pictures, which was kind. But he made me drink contrary to my determination to do nothing of the sort, and boasted of his sexual prowess in a way that sickened me. Terrible man, the worst and most depraved I know.

*Monday, 28th April*

Went to see Kathleen Kennet in the Paddington Hospital; and took her Ciano's *Diary* which she was delighted to have. She looks terribly tired and definitely older. Complains of fainting and then falling into deep sleeps. There is no sign of improvement. She said she hoped to pass out quietly in her sleep, if she cannot recover, and is going to ask Bill [her husband] and her doctor to arrange it, if they are convinced there can be no recovery. 'What is the point of life the moment one cannot live it in a full-blooded manner?' I left and walked home across the Park sick at heart and impressed by the realisation that this woman is dear to me because with her I need never dissemble – which is a very rare thing – in mind or spirit; with her there is no call for flattery or insincerity, no barriers of any kind. Yet I can't determine precisely wherein the intimacy between us lies. This evening, having given me a selection of photographs of Peter [Scott]'s portrait drawings to look through, she remarked: 'You are of course only interested in those of the male. The young women bore you.' 'Oh,' I said, 'but so do the young men very often.'

*Wednesday, 7th May*

The office puts me in constant rages. The Admiral's incompetence is really reprehensible. How a man like this could be given responsibility for the welfare of a fleet I do not understand. At midday I left for Cornwall. The luxurious train journey dispersed my choler. I reached Gunnislake at 7.30 and Cotehele at 8 for dinner. Lord Mount Edgcumbe is in bed with a temperature, but his Countess, a little, gentle, sweet and pathetic old lady, was about. Their story is a tragic one. They inherited during the war, and their only son was killed at Dunkirk. They are now packing up to leave Cotehele which since the thirteenth century has been in their family. I am given a bedroom at the top of the entrance gate-tower, approached by a twisting stone staircase, and in isolation.

*Thursday, 8th May*

Slept ill: lightning during the night which flashed through my casements and lit up the great tower and courtyard. I worked all day in the state-rooms, listing those contents which the N.T. would like and a few things to be got rid of. Most of the contents are very good indeed, if only they were not so sadly perished. These state rooms are of the class of the Knole ones and this house is a miniature Knole of the West. It is so remote that I do not suppose great numbers will visit it. I hope not. There are two rather bedint, virginal sisters staying to help the Mount Edgcumbes pack. At first their vapid giggling annoyed me, but now I quite like them. Lady Mount E's cairn puppy has eaten a chunk out of the Turkey-work Queen Anne settee, and she thinks it rather naughty, that's all. There are a butler and some charming servants, all of the old school. The splendid Mt Es, having lost their son and heir, are taking to live with them their unknown heir and his wife, who are New Zealanders.

*Friday, 16th May*

Before the Executive Committee Lord Crawford hinted that he might take his pictures away from Montacute for the Travellers Club. I implored him not to, and made a sudden, earnest appeal, telling him how they made Montacute what it now is. 'There you are,' he said to Harold Nicolson, 'that is precisely how he wheedles things out of the old ladies.'

*Wednesday, 21st May*

Motored Eardley to Somerset. We reached Stourhead* at 3 o'clock. By that time the sun had penetrated the mist, and was gauzy and humid. The air about the lake and grounds of a conservatory consistency. Never do I remember such Claude-like, idyllic beauty here. See Stourhead and die. Rhododendrons and azaleas full out. No ponticums, but pink and deep red rhododendrons – not so good – and, loveliest of all, the virginal snow white ones, almost too good to be true. Azaleas mostly orange and brimstone. These clothe the banks of the lake. The beech are at their best. We walked leisurely round the lake and amused ourselves in the grot trying to remember Pope's four lines correctly by heart, and forgetting, and running back to memorise. The temples are not in bad order, the Temple of Flora and the Pantheon being particularly well kept. We had tea at the inn at Stourton; then walked rapidly round the first floor of the house. We were staggered by the amount of first-rate furniture and pictures. There is more than enough upstairs to fill the whole *piano nobile.*

*Friday, 23rd May*

An unforeseen experience tonight. Put on my velvet coat and dined with V.P. When the other guests left at 11.30 I stayed on talking to V. on the sofa. She told me how tired she was of looking after selfish bachelors and wanted to be looked after herself for

---

* The N.T. had taken possession following the deaths of Sir Henry and Lady Hoare in March.

a change. Then vouchsafed that on Wednesday next she was dining with someone rich, presentable and suitable who would propose to her. What should she do? In a flash I found myself taking her in my arms and sympathising too much. I knew I was getting myself up to the neck, yet could not extricate myself, and also did not particularly want to. The situation was intriguing. I was asked if I would not marry her. I parried this gently without committing myself. And left at 1.30. This puts me furiously to think.

*Thursday, 29th May*

Went to Styal village [Lancashire] today. It is interesting as an example of an early cotton industrial community, with eighteenth-century mill, master's house, manager's house, apprentices' house and artisans' red brick cottages. Then lunched at Little Moreton Hall which is greatly improved; then visited Mow Cop and Maggoty's Wood. Very hot and thundery day. Called on the Archdeacon at Astbury and saw round his beautiful Georgian house which he is converting into two and ruining in the process by ripping out all the Georgian fireplaces. It is the most extraordinary thing how holiness and hideousness are compatible.

*Saturday, 31st May*

Sat in the garden at Wickhamford correcting proofs. So hot that I had to be in the shade. Papa went dog-racing at Gloucester, an extraordinary diversion. Mama spent the day watching birds fly in and out of the house, she telling me which each one was, and its habits. When tired of this she looked at caterpillars climbing threads to the tops of trees and wondering how and why they did it. One of her most endearing qualities is adoration of nature and creatures.

*Monday, 16th June*

Motored to Brockhampton, arriving in the cool of the evening. How beautiful this place is. I walked down to Lower Brockhampton just before dark, the trees dead quiet, not even whispering, and the undergrowth steaming. Two enormous black and white bulls gave me a fright by noiselessly poking their great faces over a gate and peering at me in a meditative manner. This evening the whole tragedy of England impressed itself upon me. This small, not very important seat, in the heart of our secluded country, is now deprived of its last squire. A whole social system has broken down. What will replace it beyond government by the masses, uncultivated, rancorous, savage, philistine, the enemies of all things beautiful? How I detest democracy. More and more I believe in benevolent autocracy.

*Thursday, 19th June*

I would definitely put Holkham [Hall, Norfolk] among the first twenty great houses of England. With its collections it forms one very great work of art indeed. Lord Leicester* is a charming and cultivated man. There were, besides Michael [Rosse] and me, [Lady] Sylvia [Combe],† Lord L. and his son, Tommy Coke,‡ a nice, weak person, and my contemporary. Delicious dinner of cold venison eaten in a low-ceilinged, long room on the ground floor between the family and the strangers' wings. I sat next to Lord Leicester who said how disappointed he was that the family entail prevented him handing over Holkham. His last words to me were: 'If you can find any means whereby the Trust can take over this house and its contents, I shall be prepared to leave it, should my not staying on make the transfer easier.' After dinner we walked round the house. The high quality of the architecture and contents takes the breath away. The planning too is astonishingly convenient. There are four complete wings detached from the centre block. Yet when inside the house you get the impression that there are no breaks and the five entities makes one house, huge though it be. You get vistas from one wing through the centre block into another wing, conveying a surprising effect of grandeur. The other

* Thomas Coke, 4th Earl of Leicester (1880–1949); m. 1905 Marion Trefusis.

† Lady Sylvia Coke, dau. of 4th Earl of Leicester; m. 1932 Simon Combe (J.L.-M's company commander in Irish Guards, 1940).

‡ Thomas, Viscount Coke (1908–76); s. father 1949 as 5th Earl.

impression made upon me was the marmoreal, classical simplicity of unadorned wall spaces contrasting with the rich ornamentation of ceilings and doorways and fireplaces. The sculpture gallery in particular struck me in this way – so pure, correct and serene. We spent some little time at the end of the tour in the library where I was chiefly interested in the detailed account book kept by the first Lord Leicester who amassed his collections before the age of twenty-five. Lady Leicester is away, staying in Sylvia's house, with a nervous breakdown brought on by the anxiety and worry of keeping up Holkham with practically no servants. What these wretched landowners have to go through! Yet Holkham is superbly kept up, all the steel grates, for instance, shining brightly, the work of one devoted daily.

*Tuesday, 1st July*

Took a morning train to Appledore in Sussex and walked to the village in warm, drizzling rain which made the hedgerows and hay smell like amber. Perhaps my renunciation of cigarettes has restored my sense of smell, or made it acuter. Miss Johnston's furniture was of no account. A wasted visit, except that I read and slept in the train. The rhythm of the carriage wheels over the track induces delicious fantasies sacred and profane. Sometimes I am in the arms of God, sometimes of Satan, as a priest once remarked when I confessed to one of the loveliest lovers I ever enjoyed. There is romance in the queer, flat marshland of these parts, where the sea has receded within history and left low, flat pasture and elevated straight roads.

*Thursday, 3rd July*

I motored to Great Hampden, arriving 11.30. Was met by Lord Buckinghamshire,* aged about forty-one, whom I now remember at Eton as Hobart. He is single, reserved, and rather charming, ugly, with a turned-up nose and moustache. He seems very much older

* John Hampden Mercer-Henderson, 8th Earl of Buckinghamshire (1906–63).

than me, I am pleased to say. I liked him for his forthrightness and excellent manners. He offers Hampden House and about 100 acres to the Trust. The house is let to a girls' school who pay a rent of £800 a year. It is not really first-rate. The property was granted to the Hampdens by Edward the Confessor. The house dates from every period, from King John even, having two arches of his reign. The great hall with roof was brought from an old barn on the estate, the late seventeenth-century balustrade being original to the gallery. A suite of rooms in the south wing decorated *c.* 1740 in Palladian style is handsome, but spoilt by use as classrooms. The staircase is Jacobean and painted with arcaded panels on the dado to give a perspective effect. The south façade is symmetrical with escutcheons in stone on the roof. The windows tame Vanbrughian. The demesne now much gone to seed. I think it is a borderline case. John Hampden* of course lived and died here.

Lunched most excellently at The Hampden Arms, a tiny pub. Under the inn's name is inscribed on a board, 'The Earl of Buckinghamshire licensed to sell beer and tobacco.'

*Monday, 7th July*

To the theatre – *Annie Get Your Gun* – with Bridget and Lady de Vesci, other guests being Countess Borromeo and her son Carlo. She is Lady de V's first cousin, their mothers being daughters of the Duke of Newcastle. Bridget and I called for the Borromeos and motored them to the theatre. After the first interval Lady de V., accompanied by Mark Ogilvie-Grant,† swept in, embraced Countess Borromeo on both cheeks and took her front seat, all in one regal gesture like the Empress Eugénie. We dined at the Savoy – Alsatian wine – and I motored them home. Then took Mark to Kew. We walked in his garden, smelling the strong lilies and sipping brandy. How cosy, easy and sympathetic he is, like all my friends of that generation.

---

* Parliamentarian (1594–1643); one of the five MPs whose attempted seizure by Charles I in 1642 precipitated the Civil War.

† Old Etonian bachelor (1905–69); friend of Nancy Mitford; former prisoner-of-war in Germany.

*Tuesday, 8th July*

Had my hair cut and look shorn and ugly. However I feel in good form and none the worse for last night's lateness and drink. I feel unaccountably social and gay – so unlike me. I am in a 'swimgloat'* and don't want to be out of it so long as the season lasts. There is still a flavour of The Season in London, even now, with all the exhibitions and theatres in full swing. I called for Sibyl and motored her to Wyndham's Theatre where she was given two stalls by Binkie Beaumont† for *Deep are the Roots*. Sibyl climbs nimbly into my car which at least has leg room (although she hardly has any legs to speak of), and then scurries through the crowds, head down. I follow behind keeping a protective finger on her rounded back, rather like bowling a hoop. Our seats were behind the Eshers. It was a most enjoyable play, beautifully acted. Deals with the Negro problem in the Southern States. Sibyl took me to Binkie B's party in Lord North Street afterwards. All the cast came in. I talked to the Negro and his mother who were sweet and as earnest off the stage as on. Both looked darker and more natural than on stage where, I suppose, they were lightened so as to engage our sympathies. The Carisbrookes‡ were there and I was caught by him in a corner where he talked for hours about Mrs Greville. He said she never minded about people's morals or what they did. That was their concern. He said he was cross with someone or other because that person had expressed disapproval of Ivor Novello's 'nancy manner'. Oh gosh! Lady Carisbrooke is thin and pretty; also rather tired and embittered. They both pressed me to luncheon at Kew next Sunday, or rather he pressed and she

* A word from the private language of 'the Souls', taught J.L.-M. by Logan Pearsall Smith.

† Hugh 'Binkie' Beaumont (1908–73); theatrical impresario.

‡ Alexander 'Drino' Mountbatten, 1st and last Marquess of Carisbrooke (1886–1960); o.s. of Prince Henry of Battenberg and HRH Princess Beatrice (1857–1944), yst dau. of Queen Victoria (whose favourite grandchild 'Drino' claimed to be); assumed Mountbatten surname and reluctantly exchanged German titles for English peerage, 1917; m. 1917 Lady Irene 'Iris' Denison (1890–1956), dau. of 2nd Earl of Londesbrough.

acquiesced. Then I went up to Noël Coward and said to him, 'You and I have two great friends, both dead, in common – George Lloyd and Mrs Cooper, Aunt Eva.' He recalled who I was and made me promise I would ring him up when he returned from the States and we would dine and have a long talk about both of them. His white teeth flash when he smiles, but his smile is unconvincing. He is a very ugly man with rather bloated, sagging red cheeks and hollow eyes. He has moreover a thin, flat behind which implies shallowness of character.

*Sunday, 13th July*

Lunched with the Carisbrookes. Drove to Mark [Ogilvie-Grant]'s house and walked across Kew Green to the King's Cottage where they live. It is a shapeless house with little character. Just the Carisbrookes, Mark and a fat, middle-aged woman in gloves, a sort of fortune teller. Lord C. dispensed very strong martinis before luncheon (which was excellent), running around, helping us to potatoes like any little waiter. He was immaculately dressed in a well-pressed check suit, padded shoulders, and jangling with gold bracelets and rings. He reminded me of an old, spruce hen, cackling and scratching the dust in a chicken run – really, a typical old queen. He jabbers away, yet is not altogether stupid; has good taste, and is sophisticated. Lady Carisbrooke is very sweet and has a languorous charm. We talked about brain. She said it was possible for a man to lose a third of his physical brain and yet for his mind to be unimpaired. We conjectured from this that the mind was not a physical attribute nor even dependent on physical structure for its being. It might in consequence well be immortal. After luncheon Lord C. took me all round the house, even into the cellars and attics, complaining how inadequate was the house, which the King has given him. He showed me portraits of his mother, Princess Beatrice, and his sister, Queen Ena of Spain.* No talk however of

* Princess Victoria Eugénie of Battenberg (1887–1969); m. 1906 King Alfonso XIII of Spain (1886–1941).

the present Royal family or the young betrothed couple,* for which good marks. He said that Queen Alexandra was the most beautiful woman he had ever seen. All her limbs were of a like excellence to her face. However, he did vouchsafe that Queen Mary hates wearing black. He likes bringing the topic of conversation to venereal disease and unnatural vice; and he chases one into a corner and talks so close that one expects him to pounce at any moment. 'And if one resisted,' Mark said, 'would it be *lèse-majesté*?'

*Thursday, 17th July*

Mama has stayed with me this week. I was delighted to have her and meant to be nice but was constantly irritated by her ceaseless jaggering. Oh and she used to be hilariously funny. Poor darling. When she is with intelligent people she is hopeless, for she either airs her views which are totally ignorant or criticises what she knows nothing about. It saddens me more than I can say that she and I can no longer be the companions and confidants we once were, because there is no understanding between us. God, what a cad I am! I am sadly aware of Eddy's statement that one is irritated most by those people who share one's own faults to an enhanced degree. Now Miss Paterson and Mrs Dance, both of whom met her, think her wonderful. Mrs Dance told Miss P. that she could not take her eyes off her, she was so beautiful and both were amused without end by her sallies.

*Tuesday, 22nd July*

Mrs Hugh Dalton† called for me at the office punctually at 11.30 in a large Daimler limousine, driven by the Chancellor's faithful and respectful chauffeur. With her a French boy, Marc Viénot. We drove to Queen's Gate and picked up the Iraqi Ambassadress,

* It had been announced on 8 July that Princess Elizabeth was to marry Prince Philip of Greece on 20 November.

† Ruth Fox; m. 1914 Hugh Dalton (1894–1962), Old Etonian Labour politician, Chancellor of the Exchequer, 1945–7.

Princess Zeid,* whose husband is uncle of the present King, and her daughter.† The Princess is middle-aged, rather big with handsome, beaming lacquer face and two pairs of eyebrows: her natural brows still visible and the pair pencilled over them forming Moorish arches. She has dark, frizzy hair in curls kept together under a web of hairpins. Fat, friendly and an artist. The daughter, who is on holiday from a college in the States where she has led an independent sort of existence, has ugly oriental lips, like Georges Cattaui, and spots. But she is an exceedingly well educated girl. We motored to Sevenoaks where we lunched. At luncheon the girl tells me that when she returns to Iraq she will have to retire into purdah, and this prospect appals her. No wonder.

At The Royal Oak I forestalled criticism by offering Mrs Dalton some bread, already placed on the table, by saying, 'Come along. We are breaking the law but next year we won't have this golden opportunity.' She made a wry face, and took a piece. The two Iraqis made intellectual observations throughout the visit and, I think, enjoyed themselves hugely. The Princess pointed out that the carnation and tulip emblem on the Elizabethan chairs at Knole was of Arabian origin; likewise the Jacobean strapwork ceilings. The early rugs impressed her favourably. On the way home the daughter sang songs from *Annie Get Your Gun*. She is what you might call a forward miss for she takes on whatever subject is broached; and the arts and English literature are her passion. She is going to have a rude shock when she gets back to the harem.‡

Today I understood the qualities of Mrs Dalton without liking her. She is very intelligent indeed. She has a clear, practical mind. Her interest in culture is sincere. Her sense of historic tradition is genuine and I believe that she does not mean to break with it. Yet one cannot forget the diabolical venom poured out by the husband whom she undoubtedly loves and reveres. How this man can care for tradition, as he protests, is beyond my comprehension.

* Princess Fahrelnissa; great-niece of Ottoman Grand Vizier Shakir Pasha; abstract artist; m. Prince Zeid, yst bro. of King Feisal I of Iraq, Iraqi Ambassador to London.

† Her daughter by an earlier marriage, Shirin Devrim.

‡ In the event, she made an independent life in the USA as an actress.

Mrs Dalton has, needless to say, no charm whatever, and she petrifies.

*Wednesday, 23rd July*

Lady Crewe came up to me at the Allies Club and asked me to speak on her behalf to the Ministry of Planning. She says she opened the local newspaper last week to read that West Horsley [near Leatherhead, Surrey] was to be made a satellite town and a main road was to be driven through her garden. But her house would be saved by serving as the centrepiece of a round-about.

*Friday, 25th July*

At breakfast I opened a letter from Wayland Hilton Young* saying his mother's state had rapidly worsened in the last few days. I was miserable of course but not surprised. Remorseful too because I was thinking last night that I must ring her up and go to see her again. I telephoned Keith [Miller-Jones] who had been trying to get me at the office. He said that Kathleen died early this morning.

I motored to Cranbury Park, the other side of Winchester, by appointment. A glorious day and very hot. I was alone with my thoughts. I wept as I drove along. Not since Tom's death do I remember weeping for the loss of a friend.

I don't know at what hour K. died this morning, but I suddenly woke up at about 4.45 and remained awake for three-quarters of an hour. It is most unusual for me to do this once I have fallen asleep. I experienced a strange heaviness and depression.

*Saturday, 26th July*

Grief is an odd emotion. How much of it is self-indulgence? Today I have been very cheerful. Yesterday I was genuinely sad and yet

* Wayland Hilton Young (1923–2009); s. father 1960 as 2nd Baron Kennet.

never felt more tormented by sex. Perhaps the two conflicts have some association.

*Monday, 28th July*

I drove to Wickhamford, had a quick luncheon and fetched my Vi-spring mattress from the manor, which was sold last week.* I did not want to go into the house again yet could not avoid doing so because my father came with me to help carry the mattress. Luckily the new owners were out. I tried not to look but could not help noticing how beautiful the garden was in spite of the fearful desolation. A horrible land-girl, cigarette dangling from lower lip, showed us where the mattress was in the hall. I hurried away to Brockhampton for the night.

*Wednesday, 30th July*

Lunched today at Sibyl Colefax's. Other guests were the Eshers, the Chancellor of the Exchequer and Mrs Dalton, Malcolm Sargent, Barbara Ward, Binkie Beaumont and the Chancellor's PPS, a smug young MP, by name Christopher Mayhew.† I being the least important guest sat between Binkie Beaumont, to whom I have little to say, and the young MP, whom I cordially disliked. Mr Dalton fulfilled all my preconceived ideas of him. He is affable, bombastic and diabolically clever. I am sure he is also dishonest and evil. He is a big, tall man, bald with a pointed skull – Mephistophelean. He has an insinuating, ingratiating manner. He flattered himself that he had spent money on patronage of the arts and amenities and said he was surprised that, when his proposed gift of lands to the National Trust was made at the Annual Meeting of the Trust last year through Lord

---

* Being short of money and staff, J.L.-M's parents had sold Wickhamford Manor and its garden, but they continued to own much of Wickhamford village, and moved into a neo-Jacobean villa there known as Hody's Place which George Lees-Milne had erected in the 1920s.

† Politician (1915–97); Labour MP, 1945–74; Minister for the Navy, 1964–6; joined Liberal Party, 1974; cr. life peer, 1981.

Esher, it was greeted by the members in stony silence. Had Lord Esher announced that some millionaire had made a fraction of such an offer, it would have evoked loud applause. So I piped up, 'Why should the announcement be greeted with applause when the members learnt that *you* were prepared to make the National Trust a present of their own money and lands?' At this Mr D. rubbed his hands and guffawed with hideous laughter. Malcolm Sargent and Binkie Beaumont then complained to the Chancellor that Board of Trade regulations prevented foreign artists being employed here, with the consequence that the standard of opera and theatre must remain low. Dalton very obligingly asked us all to brief him with our complaints. After the meal he came up and thanked me for acting cicerone to his beastly wife. My neighbour Mayhew, the young MP, infuriated me by his condescending manner. He asked me if I was 'one of us'. I replied, 'By this I infer that you ask, am I a Socialist. Look again.' Then he said, 'You are a Tory?' 'No', I replied, 'I am far too right wing.' 'Just a reactionary, then?' 'Yes, against your Government.'

*In August 1947 J.L.-M. enjoyed a ten-day architectural motoring tour with Harold Nicolson and Vita Sackville-West, Vita driving.*

*Tuesday, 5th August*

I got to West Wycombe after one just before Harold and Vita arrived. We lunched at the Apple Orchard and walked round the village; drove up to the church on the hill and looked at the Mausoleum. Then to the house, where Helen Dashwood welcomed us. We left at four, drove through the Hambleden Valley. The Nicolsons have a habit I like of driving up to houses. This we did at Fawley Court. The house has been refaced with very ugly scarlet brick. We had tea at the Red Lion, Henley. Then on to Newbury. I pointed out the gates of Shaw House, so up the drive we went. Walked round the house which we greatly admired. Then to Sandham Memorial Chapel, which they did not much like and thought should not have been accepted. Stayed at the Chequers Hotel, Newbury. We pool our money and I am made treasurer and pay the bills. Vita went early to bed and H. sat up reading a book on

Lenin for a review. At dinner we guessed what fearful impositions Attlee would announce tomorrow. Harold admits that he foresees no solution to the predicament we are in, and his reason for becoming a Socialist is that socialism is inevitable. By joining he feels he may help by tempering it. He says the sad thing is that no one dislikes the lower orders more than he. Vita keeps saying how hungry she is. It is true that in hotels one does not get enough to eat.

*Wednesday, 6th August*

At 8.30 I met Vita who said she had just sent a telegram to Ben whose birthday it is. I said, 'Oh, and not to me? for it is mine too.' So she bought me some lavender-water as a present. A very full day. We drove to Avebury and diverged to see the isolated gate-piers in the field at Hampstead Marshall, for they move me strangely. Then to see Inkpen Rectory. The gardener let us in for the owner was away. H. and V. delighted with the little formal Le Nôtre layout and H. made drawings of it in his pocket-book. We drove up to Littlecote and the gardener said Sir E. Wills was away, so we walked round this house. Large; I did not like the orangery additions to the main front. The place was purring with gardeners, but very much a rich man's garden, tastelessly laid out. Emboldened by our adventures we overreached ourselves and met our Waterloo at Ramsbury Manor. Vita drove straight up the drive and stopped at the front door. We admired the house when lo! the owner, Sir Francis Burdett,* wearing yachting jacket, with bulbous face and waving a newspaper, descended the steps. Vita said, 'Shall we drive off?' but it was too late. Colonel Blimp angrily asked us what we wanted. Vita said we had made a mistake and turned to me. I said, 'Littlecote'. Harold squared his shoulders and sat dumb and miserable, trying not to be seen.† At Avebury we looked at the stones and went into the museum, very well arranged, and saw the manor and church from

* Sir Francis Burdett, 6th Bt (1869–1951); Boer War veteran.

† In his own diary, Harold Nicolson wrote that the episode 'combined four things that I most dislike: intruding on the privacy of others; telling lies; being scolded; being made to look foolish.'

the outside. Lunched at Marlborough and drove through Amesbury to Dinton. Were shown over Little Clarendon by Miss Engleheart and pursued by the old mother,* aged ninety-two and without memory. We walked round Hyde's House and the chauffeur told us about Mr Philipps's† will faked by a strange valet in the hotel at Mentone where he died. Went to Dinton House and were given tea by the YWCA lady warden. The Nicolsons did not care for this house, or Hyde's, preferring Little Clarendon of the three.

We finally drove to Wilton to have a drink with David Herbert in his strange little garden temple, the front decorated with lavish stone carving. Here we were told that Attlee's news was not at all drastic. From there to Long Crichel, arriving at 7.30. Eddy greeted us, Eardley and Desmond being abroad. After dinner, Harold again talked of his belief that only the Labour Party can save us from the terrible situation we are in. He says all the factories are controlled by Communist shop stewards.

*Thursday, 7th August*

Extremely tired today. At twelve we left with Eddy for Amesbury where V. and H. parted from us to lunch with Stephen Tennant.‡ E. and I walked into Amesbury Park which is still full of soldiers who have destroyed the entrance gates and one of John Webb's gate-piers. Park overgrown and desolate. House Victorian; the portico impressive. On the Nicolsons returning we drove to Stourhead. While the others walked round the lake I went to the house and talked to Rennie Hoare.§ He doesn't know what he

* The eccentric mother had donated the house in 1940, on condition that the N.T. never instal electric light, radiators or telephone (*Ancestral Voices*, 27 November 1942).

† Bertram Erasmus Philipps, er bro. of 1st Baron Milford, had donated Dinton House (subsequently known as Philipps House) to the N.T. in 1943. The main house was let to the YWCA at this time; Hyde's House was a lesser property on the estate.

‡ Aesthete and idler (1906–87); yst s. of 2nd Baron Glenconner; lived at Wilsford Manor, Wiltshire.

§ Henry Peregrine Rennie Hoare (1901–81), to whom Sir Henry Hoare, his distant cousin, bequeathed that part of the Stourhead estate not donated to the N.T., along with the right to live in the house.

wants and is already shifting our things about. When they met him V. and H. thought him sinister. They did not like the house.

*Friday, 8th August*

Harold worked until eleven when we left. We agreed that Eddy had been the perfect host. Drove to Ven [House, Somerset] and straight up the drive to the house in Vita's usual abrupt fashion that upsets Harold and now alarms me. There was a woman at the door whom I asked if we might see the garden by ourselves. She readily consented and showed us inside the house as well. Then we drove to Montacute where we lunched and walked round the garden, V. and H. telling me what flowers to plant in the forecourt borders. They were not as enthusiastic over the interior as I had hoped. Harold had to write his *Spectator* article so V. and I left him alone in one of the empty rooms. We drove to Ilchester where I bought a Lowestoft jug from an antique dealer. Had tea at an inn; and on to North Cadbury Court. I prevented Vita driving up to the front door. She does this thing not as a tripper but as an eighteenth-century aristocrat who has a right. We went to the church, and she walked straight from the churchyard into the garden. I rang the bell and Sir Somebody, the owner, a nice old buffer, appeared, munching his tea. He let us in. The entrance front is grey-cold stone, Elizabethan; the garden front Regency with central semi-circular bay and iron balcony, a surprising contrast. Drove past Mapperton which turned out not to be the house we expected, and quite dull. Vita drove straight through the gate and round the sweep in her inimitable manner. Then back to Montacute, where I am staying in the bedroom Eardley arranged for the public. The Nicolsons stay in Yeovil.

*Saturday, 9th August*

This morning brought the first signs of autumn. Montacute was silvery with faint dew in the early light. H. and V. called at 9.45 and walked round the outside, much moved by the silent beauty of the house. We drove straight to Stoke-sub-Ham and looked at the Little Priory. To my surprise they thought this might prove a worthwhile property. The little 'great hall' can undoubtedly be made very attractive. At one o'clock we reached Knightstones, one mile south of Ottery St Mary, belonging to Colonel Reggie Cooper,* a funny old thing who was at school with Harold, is round as a humpty-dumpty, and wears an eye-glass. He bought this house just before the war. It is a plain, granity, Cornish-looking house with carved 'Jacobean' barge-boards, *c.* 1820. He has made a pretty little garden with fountains, and has sumptuous farm buildings for his Guernsey cows. There is a large great hall with open roof and wide frieze with dolphins. He gave us a superlative luncheon of chicken Maryland with fried bananas, mangoes, junket and Devonshire cream. Cocktails and white wine. Then on to Killerton where we had tea with Sir Richard and Lady Acland.† We all disliked this property, the garden, the ugly shrubs, the house, the ménage, the dogmatic owners, the two plain little boys. In the house is established the Workers' Transport Company, people smelling of disinfectant. We saw no point in this property, which is no more beautiful than the surrounding country.

We stayed at the Royal Clarence Hotel, Exeter, and walked through the Cathedral. Fine roof. I liked a tablet in the north aisle to a young organist, dated 1586, the carved marble organ-case of remarkably modern design.

*Sunday, 10th August*

We had an extra hour's sleep and I went to Mass at eight behind the Cathedral. Then to Bradley Manor which the Ns thought shockingly neglected: the entrance unkempt, fields a forest of thistles and the paths choked with weeds. We continued to Saltash Ferry, having driven miles out of the way because Harold ventured upon map-reading. He has no geography sense whatever. We crossed the Tamar in the ferry and drove round Saltash to Trematon

* Lt-Col R. A. Cooper (1885–1965); Wellington schoolfriend and sometime diplomatic colleague of H.N.; garden designer and restorer of country houses.

† Sir Richard Acland, 15th Bt (1906–92); eccentric landowner of radical political views, shortly to be elected as Labour MP for Gravesend; m. Anne Alford.

Castle. Lunched there with the Claud Russells.* All of us disappointed with this plain Regency house within the curtilage of an old castle, where the Black Prince is said to have lodged. The view towards Devonport impressive. Sir Claud a bit of a stick, distinguished and aloof like all Russells, says Harold. He enunciates his vowels like Mr Gladstone masticating. Thence to Cotehele where the Mount Edgcumbes were assembled to greet us and give us tea. The Ns slightly disappointed with this house too, V. finding it inferior to Knole, but agreed the Mount Es were charming, with the most unaffected good manners.

Today gloriously sunny and hot. The Nicolsons do not really care for classical buildings, only liking the Gothic and Elizabethan. Harold is wonderfully untidy, dust and ash over his hat and clothes. Vita wears one terracotta dress, very shiny and long in the skirt, and brown espadrilles, yet is always distinguished and 'grande dame'.

*Wednesday, 3rd September*

Found at the office a parcel from darling Vita, containing present of a silver pencil with engraved inscription, 'J. from V., August 5–15 1947', a souvenir of our tour. Nothing could have given me more delight.

*Friday, 5th September*

At 11.30 I went to see Lady Astor in Hill Street at her request. Although over sixty she is a great beauty. White hair, healthy complexion and vital movements. She has dignity and deportment, in spite of her vulgarisms. She wanted to impress upon me the necessity of keeping Miss O'Sullivan at Blickling. As she advanced into the room she said, 'Why are you a convert to that awful Catholicism? Do you not bitterly regret it?' I replied, 'Not in the very least.' She said, 'My greatest fear and horror is Communism. Roman Catholicism breeds it.' I replied, 'Roman Catholicism is the only hope left in the world of combating Communism which

* Sir Claud Russell (1871–1959); diplomatist; m. 1920 Athenais Atchley.

I too abominate.' She said, 'It is only Catholic countries that go Communist because of the poverty and discontent fostered by the priests. No Protestant countries become dictatorships.' I protested vigorously and she hissed, 'How dare you say so? You wicked child. Philip Lothian left them. He saw how evil they were.' All this was delivered with vehemence and good humour. Then she said, 'You are in earnest and you feel passionately, and I like that.' As I said goodbye I replied, 'And you care passionately, and that is why I have always admired you.'

*In late September J.L.-M. set out for a month's holiday in Italy, where he had not been for nine years. The journey there was adventurous.*

*Thursday, 25th September*

At 4.40 Emily calls to say my bath is ready. It is pitch dark but a hired Rolls comes punctually. My aeroplane does not leave airport till eight. A sunny morning. From the air one sees that London is sprinkled with reservoirs, as though the metropolis were in flood. The fields and hills of Kent are wreathed in mist like dirty snow, but I watch the sun literally scoop the mist away. Over Deal we run into a dark storm and there are splashes of rain against the glass windows. I think how lumbering and slow aeroplanes are, like old buses. In an hour and a quarter we circle over Brussels and land. There is no time for breakfast. We immediately change into another Sabena, and are off. I am writing this in the air over France, at a great altitude, rising over dense forests. It is getting cold. I wish they would bring me something to eat.

We find ourselves over the Rhône because they say the weather is too bad to risk the Alps. Passing Marseilles and over the sea it becomes stormy. Angry purple clouds gather. It is becoming bumpy. Many passengers are sick. Then we turn back and there is some difficulty landing at Marseilles at 2.45. We stay at the airport until 6.30. Every kind of inanity takes place. All our luggage from the aeroplane is taken to the *douane* and the French go through our bags, which are then returned to the plane. At last rooms are found for us at Cassis, fifty kilometres away. The bus driver loses the way, and we do not arrive until nine. We dine and are then sent to a tiny lodgement to sleep. A terrible storm gets up in the night and at 6 a.m. we are woken up with a bowl of nasty acorn coffee and hard black pellets of bread.

*Friday, 26th September*

All the telephone wires are on the ground and the battery of the bus has been allowed to run down. We cannot therefore go to Marseilles to catch a train, and the weather is too bad to fly, so we may have to stay here another night. At seven I walk into town. All the fishermen's boats in the quay are smashed by the storm. It is a nice little old town, endurable no doubt in sunny weather, but with no buildings of any distinction. There is hopelessness, inefficiency and depravity in the faces and mien of the French here. Many of my fellow travellers say they will never again travel by air.

This unexpected visit to Cassis is like a story by Rose Macaulay. We are cooped up in a horrid hotel, cut off from the world. Inevitably the party separates into little groups of companionable malcontents. My group consists of an American of Italian extraction who speaks indifferent English, is President of some international company, cashes cheques and drinks steadily; an English-born Mrs Gregory, married to an American pilot; and a Russian lady, age about fifty, who lives in Milan. We become intimate friends and are quickly on Christian name terms. With one it looks as though I shall become still more intimate before another twelve hours have elapsed.

In the afternoon we hire a taxi to Marseilles and discover that our aeroplane has been damaged on the ground during the storm last night and cannot leave until tomorrow. We despatch cables and telegrams and drink Dubonnet and eat good cakes at a café, watching the crowds of ugly, shoddy, sullen, hard-faced, hostile French men and women. On our return to the hotel at Cassis there is a fearful row with the taxi driver who, supported by the proprietor and his wife, certainly would cheat us, did we not prevail. The consequence is that the hotel staff is uniformly unpleasant for the rest of our stay. During dinner my group becomes still more intimate: the Russian confesses that she has loved her husband consistently for thirty years; the American that he has loved his wife for six months and now has mistresses whenever they are available; Mrs Gregory that she has had two husbands, plans to have a third, and, looking me straight between the eyes, indicates that she intends to have me tonight as a sort of supplementary. I have nothing to confess, at least in this company.

*Saturday, 27th September*

To my horror, we are called this morning at 4.45, in fact just after I have got back to my own bedroom, like a thief in the night. Consequently I am dog-tired all day. We are given a horrid breakfast at the big hotel. Poor Mrs G., having as I alone know had no more sleep than I, is in despair how to feed her baby of under two. We drive in the charabanc to Marseilles airport and leave at nine. We fly over huge, ugly Marseilles, and over that sink of iniquity Cassis, and Toulon where the sunk battleships in the harbour are clearly visible. There are still clouds and lightning storms, and over Lombardy there are low, fleecy white clouds, pierced by shafts of sun like sharp lances. The fields are inundated by the torrential rain of the past days. We make for Bergamo but turn back because they tell us we may land at Milan after all. We are the first plane to do so for three days. Here we wait four hours. I decide not to stay in Milan since there is a spare seat on the plane to Rome. With the kind assistance of officials and a friendly Italian traveller, I book this seat, for which I am to pay at the other end. There are only coffee and biscuits here, but both taste delicious, and the Italians are politer, just as they are cleaner than the Frogs.

At 2.30 Mrs G., her child and I get into an LAI* plane and fly for Rome. The weather over the plain of Lombardy is clear. The country looks incredibly neat, smiling and gracious. The Po is yellow as ochre. Stepping out in Rome one is struck as by the air of a conservatory. An American friend greets Mrs G. and by some extraordinary act of generosity which I do not understand settles my extra

* The Italian national airline (later Alitalia).

fare, plus 700 lire for extra luggage, as though I had been a guardian angel and not a wicked seducer. Yet I cannot like this tall, middle-aged, slouching, oh-yahing, utterly philistine American friend. Nor do I care for the husband, when we meet him. They are all very kind to me however, and even send me in their car after profuse goodbyes (Mrs G's slightly guarded perhaps) to the Hôtel de Ville where I am staying. Here I wash and try to undeafen myself before calling on the Moores at the Hassler next door. Joan welcomes me with an embrace and Garrett orders himself a drink which he has in his dressing-gown on the terrace of their room overlooking the Spanish Steps. I dine alone in my hotel for 1170 lire, a fearful price.

*Monday, 29th September*

I looked at the Pantheon, the prototype of so much I love and endeavour to preserve. Lunched alone at a *trattoria* and after a siesta met Garrett and Sarah Churchill. She, an intelligent girl, has lived in Rome six months and yet has never been to the Pantheon, or St Peter's. Her skin is translucent like alabaster.

*Wednesday, 1st October*

Walked to the Palazzo Doria, stopping at the Trevi Fountain, that Rococo delight, on the way. At ten o'clock Prince Doria* greeted me. He is so exceedingly polite and smiling that I deduce he shuns intimacies. He is rather bent from the waist like an old apple tree. He has had tuberculosis of the spine, poor man, and was tortured by Mussolini, I believe. His Princess, with broad Scotch accent, like a comfortable nanny, is an angel. To my surprise we were joined by Garrett and Barbara Rothschild,† brought by the friendly Italian father of Yvonne Hamilton,‡ whom they call Papageno. For two

* Prince Filippo Doria-Pamphili-Landi di Melfi (1886–1958); m. 1921 Gesine Mary Dykes.

† Barbara Hutchinson (d. 1989); m. (1st) 1933–46 3rd Baron Rothschild.

‡ Countess Yvonne Pallavicino (d. 1993); m. 1940 (as his 2nd wife) Hamish 'Jamie' Hamilton, publisher (d. 1988).

hours we were shown round the *piano nobile* of this gigantic and gloomy palace. Pictures v. important. Memling and Lippi and to crown all the Velasquez of Pope Innocent X. Beautiful rich Genoese velvet stuffs, curtains and chair covers. Some curtains of Neapolitan yellow ground. Some terracotta wall hangings, others crimson and brown. The grisaille ceilings in arabesques poor. In one room stands the Pope's velvet-covered throne turned to the wall, a customary protest among the Roman nobility against the Pope's incarceration within the Vatican City in 1870. A few princes only have the right to invite the Pope to their palaces. Another princely privilege among the Black Nobility is the Baldacchino* (the Doria one sheltering the portrait of Innocent X) on either side of which repose the velvet cushion and umbrella carried in the Prince's carriage in case he meets the Pope's equipage in the street. In which event he is obliged to descend and kneel, if needs be, in the rain and mud. Nearly all the gilded furniture in the Palace is swathed in thick leather case-covers. Prince Doria says that only the Palazzo Colonna is still inhabited as a private dwelling by the family, in addition to his own.

At 12.15 we parted and I looked at the Palazzo Linotte and Palazzo Lante. Then went to the flat the Moores have been lent for two days in the via Margutta. Sir D'Arcy Osborne and Barbara Rothschild there. After luncheon we questioned Sir D'Arcy about the Vatican. He said he had the highest opinion of Vatican diplomacy although they were not as well informed on foreign affairs as might be expected. The Pope [Pius XII] was a saint, and had the charm of our Queen Elizabeth. He was now launching into unequivocal condemnation of Communism. He had hated the war and went to every endeavour to end it. But so rigidly did he maintain his neutrality that he pleased no one. Far from being Machiavellian the Cardinals were the kindest of men. Sir D'Arcy ought to know, having spent the whole war shut up in the Vatican, and being an unprejudiced Protestant to boot.

---

* Canopy covering throne or altar of the Pope and other senior ecclesiastics (the most famous being Bernini's immense ornate architectural canopy over the papal altar at St Peter's), to a version of which senior Roman nobles are also entitled.

This evening I walked miles, past the Quirinale and Colosseum to the Tiber, finding myself beside the temples of Fortuna Virile and Vesta, two of the best preserved in Rome. I walk everywhere, intending to know every street and square inch of the city before I leave. Dining with the Moores, Barbara Rothschild said that Garrett and I made the oddest spectacle walking the streets on Sunday, two of the tallest, slimmest and seemingly most disdainful men who could not be anything but English.

*Sunday, 5th October*

Sarah [Churchill] dined with me at a *trattoria*. Her beauty is of a very frail sort, her hair Botticelli gold. She is of a romantic disposition. There is something guileless about her, like Johnnie, and she will be the victim of disillusions. She says that Randolph, to whom she is devoted, is most unhappy. But then it is his own fault for being so objectionable to everyone he meets.

*Wednesday, 8th October*

After a cocktail at the hotel we [J.L.-M. and Sarah Churchill] dined at Nino's. How good it all was. She has a way with her which melts the susceptible hearts of Italians. We ordered prosciutto and salami, and her favourite dish of grilled turkey wrapped in bacon with cheese over it. We drank much red wine. It was a successful evening. She is bright, independent, bohemian, yet elegant, which is a welcome contradiction. She has a sense of humour and poise (awful word, but what other is there?). She is quite uneducated, which is strange considering who she is. She is dedicated to her own art [of acting] however. She explained to me why she loved Rome. She does no sight-seeing and has no understanding of architecture. She says it is the movements of the statues, the fountains, the bridges, the curves of façades of churches, the actions of the Romans in the streets, even the mud-guards of the *carozze*. I really am intrigued by her. I walked her home and was amused by the impression this blonde beauty, apparently unnoticing, makes upon the staring, lascivious Italians.

*Sunday, 12th October [Florence]*

A lovely, clear autumnal day, in so far as there is any sense of the seasons here. Drove to San Miniato, listened to a Mass and sat for an hour ensconced in one of the deep walnut choir-stalls. Seldom have I seen a more exquisite church, eleventh-century; Byzantine mosaics in the apse; tabernacle by Michelozzo, soffit of glazed terra cotta, sea-blue ground with white rosettes by Della Robbia. Marble pulpit Romanesque.

At 12.40 the Berenson* car called to take me to I Tatti to lunch with this grand old man, of whom I am mortally frightened. I found Raymond Mortimer there, very friendly. Signorina Mariano† lives here as hostess. Sweet woman who relieves tension and makes one happy. She said she had received six letters from Sibyl [Colefax] about me. Then in came the great man, who is tiny, white-bearded and eighty. Looks frail and tired, and is neat. When he speaks it is to the point. No irrelevancies, no pleasantries. I felt very shy and tongue-tied. He saw at once that I had nothing to communicate to him. But I was fascinated by his talk to others. My fellow guest was Mrs Bliss, a grand Henry Jamesian lady, old, and described as a wise goose. Berenson is tiresome in that he is very conscious of being the famous art-dictator and sage, surrounded by applauding disciples. This expectancy of deference does not make for ease. And no small talk is allowed, a modicum of which does, after all, oil the wheels. In stony silence he dismisses a conversational advance as a triviality, which it doubtless is. When he talks he demands attention, and is not the least averse to obsequious confirmation of his utterances. He speaks scoffingly of religion and observers of the Christian principles, like T. S. Eliot.

* Bernard Berenson (1865–1959); American art historian living in Florence; expert on Renaissance painting, who became prosperous by (sometimes dubiously) authenticating masterpieces for the art dealer Duveen.

† Berenson's devoted secretary-housekeeper.

In the late afternoon while the others were having siestas I wandered into the library. I have never seen a larger private library. Every art book published must be here. And portfolios of every work of art recorded. I took out a book about the Villa Madama, Rome, and read it on the terrace. Probably this was against the rules. Before tea Raymond and I strolled up the hill, he expatiating upon the beauty of the grey-green landscape. I thought the little brown farmhouses, villas and villinos dotted upon the hills were what constituted the Italian landscape, which is essentially suburban, the very quality which in England we consider an affront to the landscape.

During tea in the loggia Berenson sat in the full sun, talking of London. I asked him if he had not thought London beautiful before 1914. He said No, the mews were filthy slums, the fogs were stifling, and the number of drunk women and their smell overpowering. Talked about the Italian temperament. When Italians complained to him that the Americans were plutocrats, he told them they were heliocrats. He is a little deaf. He conveyed to me the impression of a great man striving to be something which he isn't. Perhaps he wishes he were an aristocratic connoisseur, and not a self-made professional expert.

*Thursday, 16th October*

The Pitti Palace is full of middle-aged spinsters making miniature copies of the Raphael Madonnas and, if one so much as looks over their shoulders, trying to sell them to one. Like Hampton Court there are too many state rooms in a line, broken by no passages. Found Peter Rodd and Adelaide Lubbock* still in the hotel; we lunched at our cheap and good *trattoria* where the charming waiter looks like Oliver Messel and runs up to our table with a skip and a jump, showing very white teeth. I saw them off in their car and went and read in the Cascine, very uncomfortably, for in Italy there

* Hon. Adelaide Stanley (1906–81), e. dau. of 5th Baron Stanley of Alderley; m. 1926 Hon. Maurice Lubbock (1900–57), yst s. of 1st Baron Avebury; their o.s. is the Liberal politician Eric Lubbock, 4th Baron Avebury (b. 1928).

seem to be no benches with backs to them, and only cold marble slabs at the best.

Harold [Acton] gave me dinner tonight. He walked all the way from his parents' villa, carrying a large stick with a knob in case of trouble late at night. An excellent dinner; felt rather sick through over-eating. We walked down the Via Tornabuoni, along the Arno, and after admiring the Palazzo Pandolfini, parted there.

Observations on Florence. (1) One should walk at night, when the main streets are empty and quiet. The narrow, tortuous streets are mysterious and forbidding by lamp- and particularly by moon-light. Then you can appreciate the vast, rugged, abstract beauty of the palaces in the sharp shadows of semi-darkness. Things not noticeable by day loom into sight – here a window pediment, there an armorial escutcheon suspended over a doorway. (2) Although mercifully the chief monuments have escaped the fighting, the spirit of Florence has been very seriously impaired by the destruction of the bridges and houses along the Arno. (3) The Florentines are not quite so beautiful, nor so lively, as the Romans. (4) A Vespa (motor scooter) would be an ideal vehicle in London, nipping in and out of the lumbering traffic and the queues. (5) Berenson is a vain, blaspheming, tricky Jew. (6) Italians don't like sitting down, nor do they mind about comfort.

On my return by foot along the Arno I met the handsome young Italian who had been in the hotel with a party of tiresome English young people last night. He was sitting on the embankment wall tapping the stone with his heels. Very sweet he was. He took me in a taxi to the Porta Latina where we got out and walked arm-in-arm towards the pitch darkness of the Boboli Gardens, which were shut now. 'But I know a way in,' he said, 'and we shall have it entirely to ourselves.' We did. I followed him blindly through a hole in the hedge which meant crawling on all fours. We reached a bench below a statue of Clio. Because of the distant roar of the traffic the solitude and quiet of the gardens were somehow intensified. Mysterious lights of cars and bicycles from the surrounding roads flashed momentarily across our tense bodies. His fine classical features were illuminated as in a succession of celestial visions. It was as though the whole history of Tuscany was bared to me in that strange, silent conjunction of understanding and love. When we parted I walked home under the stars. I salute his evanescent youth and beauty.

*Saturday, 18th October*

Reached Venice at 8.10. Already dark. To my great relief was met by the Chavchavadzes'* gondolier at the station, who said, '*La Principessa ha detto che Lei era grand' uomo.*' What a lovely gondola! Jet black and sumptuously upholstered with brass figureheads at either side, brightly polished, crests and a coronet and black silk ropes and tassels. There is etiquette about gondolas too. The gondolier sees to it that you sit in the proper seat. When you accompany the Princess, her seat is on the right, yours on the left; and you, the man, must get out first. The first gondolier, wearing livery with wide sailor's collar, brass buttons, striped waistcoat, knee breeches, a biretta with a big, black pom, takes the prow. Behind him stands Mario, the second gondolier. There can be few things more romantic, more transposing from this dismal modern age, than to find yourself, at dead of night, under the stars and dim spangled lamps, skimming down the small canals, the gondoliers shouting, '*Hoih! Hoih!*' as you approach a corner. Rhythmically, swiftly you glide, your wake gently lapping the palaces, faster seemingly down the narrow canals, slower into the Grand Canal, where indeed the romance is not lessened, if anything intensified at this hour by the noisy *vaporetti*, whose rough wake rocks the gondola and rudely smacks against the prow. Never once do the *gondolieri* pause.

We reached the Palazzo Polignac, very sombre in the darkness, its great striped *pali* rising from the water at the steps. This is a fine Lombardi palace and the Chavchavadzes rent the second and top floors, which are splendid and high. There are many servants, all male, silent and respectful. We dined at 9, the Cs' usual

* Prince George Chavchavadze; bisexual Russian concert pianist with whom J.L.-M. had had an affair in the 1930s; m. Elizabeth de Breteuil (*née* Ridgeway), American heiress, who died with him in a car crash in 1962.

hour. George delighted to see me and as charming as ever. Elizabeth, bigger than before. Hamish [St Clair-Erskine] and a young 'cellist staying. A brigadier and wife, a daughter of Bourne & Hollingsworth [department store], dreary folk, came to dinner. When they left we talked till two.

*Sunday, 19th October*

I woke at 9.30 and rang for coffee and fruit. My room is large, with a floor of scagliola, a large bed with white and gold posts, raised on a dais, the windows looking up the Grand Canal through the high-arched Accademia bridge to the Palazzo Fornari, and down the Canal towards the Salute. Elizabeth says Venice is so fragile that each time she returns, it is with relief that she finds it still there, and not dissolved. How long can it survive, its huge palaces supported on wooden piles? She and I went to the steps of the Piazzetta in the gondola, and walked to High Mass in St Mark's, standing tightly wedged, for Mass was said by the Patriarch himself on account of the 700th anniversary of the visit of St Somebody from Hungary. He was behind us in a glass case, embalmed and wearing red gloves and slippers. I did not feel in the least devout. There is a cold wind blowing through the *calle*. But we were sheltered and warm, drinking coffee in the Piazza.

*Monday, 20th October*

It is distinctly cold. In the Palazzo large wood fires are lit, and the stoves are being cleaned out. Walking in Venice today I caught, mingling with the smell of fruit and the moist, excretal smell of the lesser canals which I love, a scent of firewood that is faintly English and preposterous. I am not taking my sight-seeing very seriously here. I did too much of it in Rome and Florence. Furthermore I am luxuriating in the superb meals of the Palazzo, the flow of wine and the late hours. The first night at dinner here there were, after martinis with fresh lemon peel in them, white and red wine and two sorts of champagne. After soup there is invariably a fish or some such course before the meat. After tea I sit upstairs in

George's attic while he practises the piano. Then at eight have a bath. This afternoon Hamish and the 'cellist, Dimitri Marcovitch, who is twenty-five and of some renown, went by gondola to look for Tiepolos in the Madonna del Orto and San Giovanni in Bragora. Hamish says that Mario, who stands at the helm of the gondola, looks as proud and beautiful as Michelangelo's Adam.

*J.L.-M. returned to England.*

*Thursday, 30th October*

An American girl in the train between Dover and Victoria, her first sight of England, said to me, 'My, what a number of chimneys! In our country we have one chimney to each house; here it must be one chimney to each room.' That is one manifestation of England's cosiness before the war when every chimney would be smoking. Now the grates are empty, or nearly so.

*Sunday, 2nd November*

Everyone I meet complains of distended stomach and attributes it to the starchy food. The food in England is worse than during the war, dry and tasteless, even at Brooks's.

*Monday, 3rd November*

Motored to Brockhampton. In the afternoon members of the Barneby family arrived and by a sort of muddled arrangement we distributed to them certain things they wanted, for which they paid probate figures. The Admiral, who was present, behaved very well, and saw the point of the Trust behaving like gents and not bureaucrats. Now the Ministry of Works would never have allowed these poor people to have a few family trinkets, which have little monetary value and mean all the world to them.

*Friday, 14th November*

Immensely surprised to read in the paper at breakfast that Dr Dalton had resigned on account of having given away to the press the headings of his Budget speech before delivery. There was much speculation in my office this morning whether Mrs Dalton would come to the Executive Committee. She did come, not early as she normally does to discuss with the staff before the meeting points of interest to her, but, wisely, just after the meeting had begun so as to avoid general conversation. She was rather more truculent and talkative than usual, doubtless trying to maintain her sang-froid, yet I have seldom seen any woman so betray her true feelings by her looks. Her face when in repose was drawn, mauve and sagging. She was far from tearful, or abashed, just downright broken. I felt sorry for her. It shows how ambitious she is, how much she relished her horrible husband's position. It is interesting that humans, when deeply moved, cannot disguise their expressions, however successful they may be in disguising their manner of speaking and their gestures.

*Wednesday, 26th November*

Today went to Harewood [House, Yorkshire]. Took the train to Leeds and arrived at one o'clock. Was met by a nice, old-fashioned chauffeur, not in livery, and a brand new small Daimler limousine with a large silver owl on the bonnet, and driven to Harewood village. Immediately on leaving Leeds one enters the Harewood estate, on either side of the road. God, what England owes to the landed gentry for the trim appearance of their estates. Harewood village is a fine specimen of a planned eighteenth-century community. The little houses are uniform, for they were all built of a piece by John Carr. I lunched with Mr FitzRoy, the Agent. He told me the estate was faced with 75 per cent death duties, but the family were resolved to remain at Harewood notwithstanding. I suggested that the family might approach the Treasury and ask for the house, some 4,000 acres of land around it, and also the chief objects of art to be taken in lieu of death duties and handed over to the Trust. Mr F. was interested. Then he took me in his car down the Leeds road, and through the lodge gates to look at the house across the valley towards the Wharfedale and high ridge of hills beyond it. At once saw how important it was that a large area should pass with the house which is visible from such long distances.

We drove back through the main entrance, past the stable block by Chambers,* to the house. Were shown into the old library to the left of the hall, and stood before a fire. While I was debating to myself how I ought to make my first obeisance, suddenly HRH† ran swiftly into the room and shook me by the hand without saying a word. When I realised who she was I just had time to incline my head. My first impression was how good-looking she is, far more so than photographs suggest. She has a beautiful complexion, neat greyish hair, cropped but wavy at the back. She wore a grey tweed skirt, thick mesh wool stockings, dark leather indoor shoes, a grey jumper and one string of pearls. The effect not dowdy, but simple country dress. She is extremely shy, but dignified; sensible and natural in manner. Rather abrupt and has little small talk. When interested in a subject she becomes vivacious and communicative. It was now 3.30 and already getting dark. She took us round the state rooms until 5 o'clock. The hospital which occupied them has recently gone, and the rooms are being cleaned and put back. There were men working on the floor boards with a machine like a tennis court marker, sandpapering them. The Princess picked her way through, opening shutters, removing dust-sheets and talking affably to the workmen. In the centre library one workman was re-laying boards by the glass door, wearing his hat and smoking. When he spoke to the Princess he neither removed his hat nor his cigarette. When we left him HRH was very worried lest he set fire to the house. I thought his behaviour abominable.

Tea was in the breakfast-room, as were all meals. I always sat on the Princess's right. She kept jumping up to fill the teapot from an electric kettle. She has a smooth-haired dachshund called Bruna, to which she is devoted and with whom she keeps up a flow of banter. It sleeps in a basket in her bedroom. The other day she upset milk on the silver tray and let the dog lick it up,

* Sir William Chambers (1723–96).

† HRH Princess Mary, Princess Royal (1897–1965); only dau. of King George V and Queen Mary; m. 1922 Henry, Viscount Lascelles (1882–1947), who s. 1929 as 6th Earl of Harewood, and d. 23 May 1947, leaving the Harewood estate heavily encumbered with death duties.

then, for fear of what the butler might think, washed the tray herself. Miss Lloyd and Mrs Balfour, ladies-in-waiting, were in attendance. The younger son, Gerald,* came in from shooting. He is stocky, with large chin, slightly oafish, and mixture of David Lloyd and Auberon Herbert in appearance only. Has drooping, sensual mouth. He is very jolly with his mother, whom he teases.

The Princess has a remarkably beautiful deep voice, and rolls her 'r's' slightly. She has fine white teeth and a curious mark on the upper lip, as of a scald.

After tea she took FitzRoy and me to her private sitting-room where some of the best Chippendale satinwood tables and commodes are; also a pair of Sèvres inlaid cabinets. I then explained my ideas about the Treasury scheme and she asked many questions quietly and intelligently about domestic arrangements under the National Trust. Asked if she might have a small strip of terrace to herself and dog on opening days, and proposed providing tea for the public in the stable block. 'One can get used to anything,' she observed rather pathetically. We talked until 7.40 when the Agent left us together.

My bedroom was in the semi-basement. It had a coal fire. There was no time for a bath. In fear of being late I changed quickly and dashed up to the old library just as it struck eight. At dinner there was no waiting, the Princess going first to the sideboard, helping herself, the rest following. There was plenty of banter during dinner. The P. having rung the bell for coffee said, 'Now what is the betting that they won't answer it,' and two minutes later, 'I thought so.' The son then said, 'I will try, Mummie,' and his peals brought a response. The P. had changed with inordinate speed into a black dress, very plain, with black shiny belt and velveteen coatee, for she is still in mourning. After dinner, sitting till nearly twelve in the old library, stifling yawns, was a bit of a trial. Talk was about the crowds in buses and tubes during rush hour, the smell of human beings on a muggy, rainy day (things she can never have experi-

* Hon. Gerald Lascelles (1924–98).

enced), and then politics, and keen, anxious speculation over the Gravesend election. She says a little naively that, whatever happens, we mustn't emigrate or desert this country, however much we are tempted. I thought to myself, Royalty never emigrates. It either stays put or is pushed out.

*Thursday, 27th November*

Breakfast at nine. I was up at 8.50 in case the Princess should arrive first. The ladies assembled in the breakfast-room. HRH then came in. The two ladies curtseyed and I bowed. This was all the ceremony. Every sentence has a Ma'am in it, a slightly denaturalising suffix. And reference to her presence or absence is to 'Her Royal Highness'. I like this. After breakfast I was allowed to walk outside on the terrace and round the house by myself. Was specially commanded to examine the small group of playing children in a painting by Baurscheit, dated 1725. I could not admire these insipidly mischievous children as much as the urns the Princess has bought at the Clumber sale and put in the Barry parterre garden. At 10.30 the Princess reappeared and until 12.20 conducted me round the house again. She takes great pride in and has considerable knowledge of the contents. Her taste too struck me as very good. Indeed the rooms are superb and the long gallery one of the noblest apartments I have seen in an English house. It is amazing how convincing the wooden curtain boxes are, carved to resemble drapery. The quality of the French-style Chippendale furniture the finest possible. Together we pulled off covers, compared the suites of furniture, examined ceilings, pier-glasses, door-locks and handles, chimneypieces, carpets and pictures, about which she knows a great deal. We went into every bedroom and bathroom, deploring the effects of last winter's damp on many ceilings. Went into HRH's bedroom, with large, brown, mahogany double-bed, dog's basket and dozens of photographs of Queen Mary, the late King, present monarch and family. Rather wistfully she kept saying, 'I do hope I shall not have to sell this, or that.' We even descended into the cellar to examine the china. At the end I was asked if I was tired. Valiantly I denied it, although nearly dropping, and expressed the same anxiety about her. She said she was never tired showing the house to people who appreciated it.

*Saturday, 29th November*

Lunched with Patrick Kinross at the St James's Club. He is finally back from Egypt after seven years and is to retire to Devon where he intends writing a novel about his past and all his friends.* God help us all. This will be no contribution to literature. I was delighted to see dear old Patrick who has grown enormous in length and breadth. He sprawls over chairs and tables and puffs a great deal. He is not notably chic or clean, but otherwise unchanged. The same good-humoured, quizzical, gently cynical, kindly individual.

*Tuesday, 9th December*

Eardley and I motored to Stourhead where, from 12 till dark, now 4.30, we worked in the house. This we continued the following day, and Thursday, I staying at Long Crichel. Stourhead in turmoil. We had to start from scratch, sorting, rejecting, with the minimum of help, carrying heavy furniture and busts together, back-breaking yet giggling work. We sold a collection of sheer junk for £75 to the local antique dealer in Mere, for which I hope the Trust will be pleased. We tried to trace all the younger Chippendale's pieces of furniture scattered about the house to put them in those show rooms to which they rightly belong. It was the greatest fun, and oh, how I enjoy Eardley's companionship. We make a splendid team, because we never spare criticism, neither taking offence; on the contrary each relishing outright condemnation of the other's efforts. I know we shall eventually succeed in making this house look splendid, having picked the brains of all the experts, sifted, endorsed or rejected their advice. The late Alda, Lady Hoare has

---

* *The Ruthless Innocent* (Hamish Hamilton, 1949), dealing mostly with his brief marriage to the siren and notorious 'bolter', Angela Culme-Seymour.

become a mythical figure at Long Crichel. Eddy deplores our eradication of her appalling bad taste, and is going to write a novel about her. Desmond calls us the despoilers.

*Friday, 12th December*

Eddie Marsh at luncheon at Brooks's told me three stories in his clipped, Edwardian manner. Someone congratulated Lady Tree on the colour of her hair which he supposed she had recently dyed. 'How sweet of you', she replied, 'to say, *my* hair.' Winston Churchill, when told that Mr Attlee had decided not to visit Australia, remarked, 'he feared that when the mouse was away the cats would play,' and described Socialism as 'Government of the duds, by the duds, for the duds.'

*Thursday, 18th December*

A harrowing visit this afternoon to see an old woman, Mrs Walter Tibbitts, in a private residential hotel in Inverness Terrace, Bayswater. She had offered her 'collections' to the Trust. From her descriptions of the Benares ware, Poona brass, marquetry furniture, and from the photograph she produced of a Hindu carved screen, it sounded appalling and unsuitable. Yet she had not a flicker of doubt that it was important and insisted that the collection be kept together. She is seventy-eight and must find a home for it before she dies. I left her feeling more depressed than words can describe. When the old have to live in soulless drabness, which this hotel is, alone, ridiculous and unwanted, they are pitiable. When they are slightly truculent, to keep their end up, it moves me beyond compassion to a sadness which haunts me for days. The agony of it.

*Friday, 19th December*

This afternoon, after the dentist, I called at Batsford's and collected five advance copies of *The Age of Adam*, of which the jacket is the prettiest I have ever seen. Met Mr Harry in the shop. He made me talk with him upstairs, and promise, rather against my will, that

I would help in the editing of some guide books. I could not quite understand, because of the coughing and spluttering, whether or not it was the same old Methuen guide books on which he is so keen. 'Now then, Jim darling,' he went on and subsided into catarrhal chuckles. The house telephone rang. 'God damn the bloody swine,' he shouted. 'Is that you, Sam darling?' without a break between the two ejaculations.

*Saturday, 20th December*

Bridget [Parsons] took me to Covent Garden. Three ballets, *Les Patineurs, The Three-Cornered Hat* and the new Lecoque one, very gay with Derain scenery. On the way to the Ivy – the best food I have had since my return from Italy – a man accosted me and I, so Bridget said, was very snubbing. Indeed I did not recognise him until we had passed on. Then I suddenly remembered the sad, second-rate, hopelessly unpractical member of the ARP who was in my platoon at the beginning of the war. The last person in the world I would wish to be unkind to. I left B. and tore after him. Alas, he had gone. Now for ever he will remember me as a cad, a man too proud, while with a beautiful woman, to acknowledge him. He looked so thin, yellow and *dégringolé,* which makes my behaviour worse. Perhaps he is starving and would have welcomed five shillings. Instead B. and I continued to her flat in Mount Street where we drank whisky, were warm and happy.

*Wednesday, 24th December*

I have given thirty-seven Christmas presents and, so far, received one, a wireless set from my parents. Financially, I am utterly broke. Most of my presents go to servants, and friends like old Mrs Strong, the caretaker of Carlyle's House. I suppose it is always the way.

*Friday, 26th December*

The family went to Wolverhampton Races in the extreme cold wind. Papa's horse was third and Mama says it is a dud. All morning

I read Virginia Woolf's latest essays. I really believe she is the best prose writer of this century. In the afternoon went to see Maggie, my old nursery maid. Her little boy, aged five, has fair hair and the most beautiful and patrician face, yet he hardly speaks. His eyes are melancholy, and beseeching. Maggie says she is forty-nine but looks as pretty and young as when I first knew her. They have thirty acres of fruit trees.

*Wednesday, 31st December*

Dined at Brooks's with Dick Girouard whom I met there. Walked home to bed at 10.30 and read *Dombey and Son* contentedly. Party-lust seldom irks me nowadays. That is one consolation. Heard the distant cacophony and catcall of sirens, and the cretinous shouting at midnight.

I read Virginia Woolf's latest essays. I really believe she is the best prose writer of this century. In the afternoon went to see Maggie, my old nursery maid. Her little boy, aged five, has fair hair and the most beautiful and patrician face. Yet he hardly speaks. His eyes are melancholy, and beseeching. Maggie says she is forty-nine but looks as pretty and young as when I first knew her. They have thirty acres of fruit trees.

*Wednesday, 31st December*

Dined at Brooks's with Dick Girouard whom I met there. Walked home to bed at 10.30 and read Dorothy Osborne contentedly. Party-lust seldom irks me nowadays. That is one consolation. Heard the distant cacophony and catcall of sirens, and the cretinous shouting at midnight.

# 1948

# 1948

*The year began with J.L.-M. busy preparing Stourhead for opening to the public. His book on Adam had just been published.*

*Saturday, 3rd January*

Paul Hyslop lunched. He explained to me that the word 'rag' was coined by Eddy to mean a cagey queer, the opposite of a 'tearing' queer, the term 'rag' applying to pages of children's books made of that material. A 'billiard ball' is the smart, dandified, smooth, City type of queer, who tries to appear otherwise. Well, one lives and learns.

*Monday, 5th January*

Drove down to Long Crichel. Lunched excellently at my favourite eating place, the Wheatsheaf Inn, and stopped at Winchester. In the Cathedral choir were one old man reading the New Testament to himself, very loudly in an affected voice, and two ladies discussing hats, each party oblivious of the other. The three had evidently sought refuge in the warmth rather than spiritual consolation. At the bookshop I was lucky to buy the architectural book I saw there last July and always meant to go back for – *Some Designs of Mr Inigo Jones and Mr William Kent*, by John Vardy, 1744.

*Tuesday, 6th – Friday, 9th January*

Each day Eardley and I went to Stourhead, arriving at 10 every morning. We worked like blacks. There is hardly one piece of furniture in the state rooms that we have not shifted ourselves. At last we broke the back of our difficulties and assembled all the furniture in the rooms allotted to them. It is astonishing the amount of stuff left over which we cannot place. Nearly every day it rained and the rooms are pitch dark. But we have enjoyed ourselves.

Raymond Mortimer is staying at Long Crichel. A wise man. He warned Eardley and me against looking up all the words we did not know in the dictionary when reading French books, advising us to look up only a word that recurs frequently. Talking about some silly-billy, he observed that most of us have our own censor that prevents our uttering all the foolish thoughts that tumble into our minds. I returned to London on Friday afternoon. All the inmates at Long Crichel, Eddy, Raymond, Desmond and Eardley, are angelic to me, and this house has become a sort of second home.

On my return I dined at B.S's. There was present another man, Archie Colquhoun,* whom I met years back. B.S. terribly tied up and adolescent. At 10.15 Harold Nicolson arrived and ate a sandwich supper. He had come from Croydon where he was adopted as the Labour candidate. He was rather silly and bumble-beeish. Memo: not to be bumble-beeish with younger persons in twenty-five years' time.

*Monday, 12th January*

At 6 went to Doreen [Colston-Baynes] in Ovington Square. She was very kind about my book, but has not read it. Says her brother has taken and is reading it. I told her of Sachie Sitwell's charming letter of congratulation I received this morning. It was unsolicited for I had not sent him a copy. Evenings at Doreen's are a bit of a strain at times for she can be goosey, dear thing that she is. She has been introduced to Chips Channon by Peter Coats† and is thrilled to the marrow. Theirs is no more her *monde* than the Crazy Gang would be Queen Mary's. Doreen confessed to me this evening that she preferred the company of stupid, well-bred people to that of

---

* War hero and translator, best known for his 1960 translation of Lampedusa's *The Leopard*.

† Distant kinsman of J.L.-M. (1910–90); close friend of Chips Channon; ADC to Lord Wavell as Viceroy of India; later a garden writer; known as 'Petticoats'.

intelligent, common people. I think I do too, on the whole. She complained how dirty were the hands of bus conductors, so that she tries to avoid their touching her gloved hand when they give her change, and in consequence is apt to drop her coins on the floor of the bus. I said it would be surprising if at the end of a long day their hands were clean, poor things.

*Tuesday, 13th January*

Went to see Sibyl Colefax in bed today and brought her my book as a present. Anything to give the kind old woman slight pleasure; this sounds horribly condescending. Lady Anderson came in before I left in such a cloud of scent that I smelt it on me all the way back in the tube to South Kensington. Bowler-hatted commuters sniffed me suspiciously.

*Friday, 16th January*

I have seen a good deal of Michael [Rosse] these few days, he being very important and taking the chair at numerous meetings. A trifle too gracious. I was pleased to be able to reprove him for ordering Anthony Martineau to get in touch with the Princess Royal's solicitor without her authority. 'How could *you* do such a thing? Such an unwonted lapse by you of all correct people.' M. was for the first time in his life abashed, and actually blushed.

*Tuesday, 20th January*

I arrived after tea at Gunby. Lady Massingberd, only recently widowed after fifty years' bliss, was extremely cheerful and just like her old self. I do admire her. No complaints and she is making the best of her situation. She says that so long as the Whartons stay, she can remain at Gunby. The Field Marshal's pension of £1,700 a year is now gone. He died quietly, having had his first seizure nine months before. A tired heart finished him off. Wharton gave me some more particulars with the relish servants always indulge in. He confirmed that the F.M. suffered no pain, just declined, adding that 'not a drop came out of his body anywhere, after his death'. The Whartons were much moved and are erecting an iron gate, chosen by Lady M., with the inscription 'To the memory of our beloved Field Marshal'.

*Tuesday, 27th January*

In pouring rain E. and I in my car motored to Higher Bockhampton [Dorset]. Looked at Hardy's birthplace. The little house and surroundings are just as Hardy must have known them, the rising heath behind the property surely unchanged. The cottage of brick and thatch is of the simplest. The two nice elderly lady tenants are very anxious to stay on and show visitors round. Educated women, yet content to live without a bath and with oil lamps. We stayed with Patrick Kinross at Easton Court Hotel, Chagford. Charming and friendly; greatly improved in health and looks since I saw him on his return from Egypt. We were shown photographs of all of us, Patrick, Christopher Hobhouse,* Alan Pryce-Jones and me – all quite nice-looking too – when we were here in 1932.

*Friday, 30th January*

E. is patient and sweet, and helps dispel my ill humours. There is no one in the world with whom I have shared more cherished moments of giggling, *vide* yesterday carrying the grandfather clock down the stairs at Cotehele, clankings coming from the mechanism. I thought I would have a stroke we laughed so much, yet could not put it down. This morning we looked at the Old Post Office, Tintagel, a dreadful Hans Andersen gingerbread witch's house. It was streaming with damp. I hated it. Such a sweet old caretaker showed us round, a toothless hag with a beautiful voice and the manners of Lady Desborough.

---

* Writer and barrister, killed in action (1910–40); intimate of Harold Nicolson; author of a book on Charles James Fox.

*Saturday, 31st January*

On my return B.S. telephoned and dined with me at Brooks's. He is a strange, unbalanced youth, with whom the world should be careful for he is sensitive and neurotic, torn between religious mysticism and the usual lusts of the flesh which he sublimates to his own unhappiness. Since he is handsome and engaging and intelligent I am tempted to advise him to make discreet hay while the sun of youth still smiles upon him, yet I don't want to influence him. He left at midnight, then early Sunday morning dropped a note through the letter-box at breakfast time. Note conveyed that he did not wish to 'hurt' me, who am anyway unhurtable nowadays. I gathered from the strange effusion that he meant he could not fall in love with me, who have not the slightest inclination to fall in love with him.

*Sunday, 1st February*

B.S. called to explain away his note, poor youth. So I tackled his problem at once and counselled him thus – remain celibate provided you lead a truly saintly life and can maintain it; otherwise, live life to the full without restraint. The first path is undoubtedly preferable if you mean to enter the priesthood. And please let me hear no more about it.

Had a dinner party of Viva King,* Janet Leeper† and Burnet Pavitt.‡ Janet is in a wild sort of way intelligent and earnest; Viva more intelligent, not at all earnest, on the contrary wicked and amusing. I thought they would never go. They left at 11.40 but Burnet stayed on for half an hour. He confided that he could have done without either lady, I having invited them for his benefit. Burnet a very sympathetic man, extremely musical. Tells me he plays duets with Joan Moore who is a great friend.

* Neighbour of J.L.-M. in Thurloe Square.
† Author of *English Ballet* (1944), and other works on theatrical subjects.
‡ Businessman with musical interests (1908–2002).

*Tuesday, 3rd February*

I dine in and work, but at 11 p.m. go to a party given by Hamish Erskine and Jennifer Heber-Percy in the next street to mine. In spite of the number of 'old friends', I hate it. I believe my generation to be, for the most part, 'unreal'; cliquey, dated, prejudiced, out of touch with the new world and preposterously exclusive – arrogant, arrogant, with few redeeming qualities of any kind. They have nothing original to impart. I do have one conversation with Roy Harrod and Sachie Sitwell about Roy's biography of Keynes;* Roy has been through Lytton Strachey's correspondence with his brother James† before 1914, a lot of which is purely (I don't know why I write 'purely') about human organs. I return home, not depressed, for Burnet rings me up and we have a jolly chat, but intensely irritated by pretence. I don't truly care if I never see these people again. They are only tolerable singly or in very small groups. In a mass they are detestable and contemptible. Am I one of them?

*Wednesday, 4th February*

This evening took John Fowler‡ to a box lent to Grace Davenport at Covent Garden for *Die Meistersinger*. English performance. What a cock-teasing opera. Thence we took Grace D. and Mrs de Freville to the Savoy. John was angelic and lent me money. The whole evening cost us about £4 10*s*. each. Agreed later, as we sat here after midnight, what *hell* affected, rich, smart, spoilt society women could be. He is a kind, cosy, good-natured man to have put up with the evening I landed him in.

---

* John Maynard Keynes (1883–1946; cr. Baron, 1942); economist and member of the Bloomsbury Group, whose biography by Roy Harrod appeared in 1951.

† Lytton Strachey (1880–1932), man of letters; his brother James (1887–1967), friend of Rupert Brooke and editor of the works of Sigmund Freud.

‡ Decorator, former partner of Sibyl Colefax, who was to do much work in N.T. houses (1906–77).

*Thursday, 5th February*

Received from poor B.S. a long letter of a very compromising nature about himself, bemoaning his hopeless effeminacy, and confessing that he wanted love to be made to him the other night; that his Sunday letter was all nonsense – which I suspected. There is nothing I can do to help him for he is ineducable.

*Friday, 6th February*

Tonight I dined at Mrs Carnegie's in Lennox Gardens. She has been ill but is now recovered, and as upright and sprightly as ever. The party was to meet the American Ambassadress, a good-looking, charming woman. There were three old butlers waiting in the hall in evening dress. At dinner I sat next to Frances Peto's sister, Cathleen, and Diane Maxwell, Austen Chamberlain's* daughter, not handsome but very agreeable. The large dining-room table covered with a huge snow-white cloth and sprinkled with silver candlesticks, cups and bric-à-brac. Dinner meagre compared with the old days; a little fish, a little hot ham (deemed a luxury and American no doubt), a tiny savoury, and dessert of one tangerine; a little red wine and a little port. Yet I had no appetite and ate sparingly of this sparse fare. During port I talked to Lord Courtauld-Thomson† who expressed a wish to read my book. I said there was nothing to prevent him. After dinner I talked to an American woman accompanying the Ambassadress. She spoke in that low Boston voice which I find the loveliest of the English-speaking voices. She said thousands of Americans will visit England this summer and she hoped they would not stay in the smart hotels but the lesser ones, in order to see how little the English still have to eat today.

---

* Conservative statesman (1863–1937; KG 1925); e.s. of Joseph Chamberlain.

† Colonel Sir Courtauld Courtauld-Thomson (1865–1954; cr. Baron, 1944); wealthy industrialist, of whom J.L.-M. had seen much during the war in connection with his desire to leave Dorneywood, his house in Buckinghamshire, to the N.T., to be used as a residence for Government ministers (a gift which took effect in 1947).

*Sunday, 8th February*

Sarah Churchill to whom I spoke yesterday on the telephone attracts me much. The sound of her voice again, mocking, independent and gay, quite made my heart jump to hear. I have only one trouble just now – money, or the lack of it. Bills fly in and I have nothing with which to meet them. I suppose I am extravagant, yet consider I live very simply, and have little to show for it. And I work very hard. I just don't earn enough. It is all very sad.

*Thursday, 12th February*

Had a hangover this morning. Burnet feels just as I do about parties. We telephone nearly every day.

*Friday, 13th February*

Sarah dined with me alone and brought me one of Mr Churchill's Havana cigars as a present. Alas, I do not smoke cigars. We talked and talked. She told me that to leave Vic Oliver she had to adopt a sudden cruel course, and just bolt. There was no other way. She is curiously ignorant of books and painting and music. Just not interested. Only knows about the stage. This is odd for she is bright, quick with an answer, and naturally intelligent. I like her much.

*Saturday, 21st February*

I went out this morning; otherwise stayed at home, huddled by the fireside, perished. The grip of winter has descended and the snow is thick outside. My pipes are frozen and I cannot have a bath. Heywood Hill told me my book is now his best seller.

*Tuesday, 24th February*

Called on Bill Astor* at 12. He is always very friendly. I persuaded him to write and ask his father to agree to Cliveden house being

* Hon. William Astor (1907–66); Conservative politician; s. father 1952 as 3rd Viscount Astor.

opened at least one afternoon this season. I stressed that the public could not be expected to understand how Lord Astor found this impossible. Then I lunched with Lord Braybrooke who thanked me for what the National Trust had done in persuading the Government to buy Audley End from him. I am sorry that the N.T. has not got it all the same, because I am convinced that they can present houses better than the tasteless Ministry of Works.

Dined tonight at Dick Girouard's. The Eshers were there. We talked about the seven deadly sins which Lord Esher thinks are mostly misnamed. Gluttony and sloth he called 'perfectly divine sins'. He said that class feeling today is infinitely less strong than during the Eighties. He remembered how as a child he, and the grown-ups, were in living terror of the East End marching to the West End. His mother could not drive to Buckingham Palace with the windows of her carriage open for fear of the 'mob' spitting into it. He said the poverty and rags were deplorable and terrifying. 'Things get better every day,' he finally said – and meant it, too.

*Thursday, 26th February*

Oh, the dreariness of Society with a large 'S'. Went to a cocktail party given by Diane [Abdy] in her 'twee' little flat, as Anne [Rosse] would call it. He! he! he! and giggles and pretentiousness. Would I sign my book and would I put 'from the author', for how could posterity know who 'Jim' was? How indeed? But I would not, and that was the end of it. I hadn't *given* it.

*Friday, 27th February*

Went to the Chagall* exhibition at the Tate which I was prepared to hate. On the contrary found the surrealist pictures gay, inspiring and dreamlike. Jamesey dined with me here. He says that when he finds himself in bed with someone incompatible he prays all the time to St Teresa, who sympathises. Told me that Harold is very

* Marc Chagall (1887–1985); Russian-born French painter and designer.

shocking about his by-election. In the coldest weather he fears to wear his fur-lined coat. He dissuades Ben from visiting the constituency because his voice sounds too patrician; expresses the hope that the Communists, not De Gaulle, will get to power in France. James had a row with him and told him he was unprincipled and defeatist.

*Saturday, 28th February*

Worked in the British Museum Reading Room morning and afternoon. This vast domed room with galleries of bookshelves ought to be a national monument, if it isn't already. In the evening I had B.S. to dine and insisted on going to a film, *Cry Havoc*. Very bad film but I could not face an evening alone with this young man who bores me, with his unhealthy odour of sanctity and bottled-up lechery. I am trying to get him a job with *Country Life*.

*Monday, 1st March*

Lunched at the Dorchester with Sibyl Colefax in a very overheated little room on the top floor overlooking the park, the sun shining directly upon us. A curious party – the Hartingtons,* T. S. Eliot,† Ava Anderson,‡ Georgia Sitwell, Peter Quennell, Alan Pryce-Jones. I sat between Alan and Lady Anderson. T. S. Eliot dark, swarthy, professorial, retiring, quizzical, diffident – a medical practitioner or undertaker's clerk. Alas, I had no chance of talking with him. Lady Anderson, rather blowsy, resembled the Hayter§ portrait

* Lord Andrew Cavendish (1920–2004); s. father 1950 as 11th Duke of Devonshire (having been known as Marquess of Hartington since his er brother's death in 1944); m. 1941 Hon. Deborah ('Debo') Mitford (b. 1920), youngest of the Mitford sisters, who had known J.L.-M. since her earliest childhood.

† Poet (1888–1965).

‡ Ava Bodley; m. 1st Ralph Wigram, 2nd 1941 (as his 2nd wife) Sir John Anderson, member of War Cabinet (cr. Viscount Waverley, 1952).

§ Sir George Hayter (1792–1871), English historical and portrait painter; 'Principal Painter in Ordinary to The Queen' from 1841.

of Queen Caroline at Battersea House. I was very pleased to see Debo [Hartington] again. She said she would ask me to stay at Chatsworth in June. Wants to take me round the big house, now empty. She was pale, with no make-up; beautiful and melancholy-merry.

*Tuesday, 16th March*

Went this afternoon with the Admiral and Lord Esher to the Treasury for a meeting with the permanent official, Sir Bernard Gilbert, and the Ministry of Works official, Sir Eric de Normann, two smug, obstinate, unimaginative civil servants. The meeting was about Harewood House. In spite of Esher's ably presented case, these men implied that they might advise the Chancellor to let the Government hold the house and estate, if they were asked to take them in part payment of death duties, and not hand them on to the N.T. A dangerous precedent indeed. Nothing we could say would convince them that we were the qualified body to hold and run country houses inhabited by their previous owners. Esher and I were distinctly depressed by the interview. The two brushed aside our argument that, in a disintegrating world, country house owners disliked the N.T. far less than the Government.

*Monday, 22nd March*

Went to a lecture at the SPAB this evening by Sir Sydney Cockerell* on William Morris, whose secretary he was and whom he knew intimately. To listen to him talking of him, Ruskin, Burne-Jones, Philip Webb as his close companions conjured up the past vividly. Morris had fits of violent rage, once tearing his own clothes to ribbons; then immediately subsided and was penitent like a spoiled child.

* Director of Fitzwilliam Museum, Cambridge, 1907–38 (1867–1962); friend of the famous, having been literary executor of William Morris, Wilfrid Scawen Blunt and Thomas Hardy.

*Wednesday, 24th March*

Lunched at Harewood with the agent, Mr FitzRoy, then went to the big house. HRH was opening something, but young Lord Harewood* received us, and we talked for an hour in the library. He is shy and bashful. Has a head shaped like his father's, but a large Hanoverian mouth, and the same resonant, deep voice as his mother. Is hopelessly defeatist about the future of Harewood. Nevertheless is definitely opposed to the Government holding it and practically insisted that it must be held by the N.T. and no other body. Being semi-royal must be tormenting, for one is neither fish, flesh nor good red herring, and to have one's mother in the house, with two ladies-in-waiting at every meal, curtseying and Ma'am-ing, yet oneself to be an ordinary human being subject to the kicks and pricks of this mortal life, most unsatisfactory.

*Bridget Parsons took J.L.-M. to spend Easter at Monk Hopton House, Shropshire, the house of her mother and stepfather, Lord and Lady de Vesci.*

*Monday, 29th March*

I left Monk Hopton after luncheon today, Bridget staying on for a week. As usual I was glad to leave, although I have enjoyed myself and am grateful for the kindness received. I suffer from *gêne* in other people's houses and from guilt in that I do not pull my weight, i.e. don't garden, which is always a welcome assistance from guests these days. The other three gardened all the time. Not once did I offer to do so. Stooping makes me giddy. Yet the delicious food, deep sleep and long lies in the morning did me good. In spite of the nearly complete relaxation was obliged to take one Epanutin pill per day. Back in London shall be obliged to take three a day. One admitted drawback here is the dreadful, inescapable proximity

* George Lascelles, 7th Earl of Harewood (1923–2011); after being a prisoner-of-war in Germany, he became both a Cambridge undergraduate and a member of the Council of State which was periodically convened to sign official documents during the ill health of his uncle, King George VI.

of Lord de Vesci,* with whom I repeatedly found myself alone, being the only other male. He is an arch-bore, who never stops talking and grumbling about the decline of the country, the incompetence of the Government, and the menace of Communism – what I am fairly apt to do myself. In another it is intolerable. He is the most reactionary man, bar none, I have ever met. On the other hand there is something rather likeable about him – that truculent bewilderment as of a spavined horse. And it cannot be agreeable to be despised by both your wife and stepdaughter.

*Thursday, 1st April*

At the Connaught Hotel this evening met Archie Gordon† and Blewitt of the television BBC who are organising a broadcast, if that is what it is termed, about the National Trust. They invited me to cooperate in finding suitable performers and to attend the performance. I declined to play a part on the screen because I cannot talk impromptu.

*Friday, 2nd April*

This week has been very bad. Terrible depression. Pierre Lansel says I am to go away and stop my pills and take others in their place. Michael and Anne [Rosse] have pressed me to go to Birr, which is noble and sweet of them.

*Friday, 9th April*

Arrived at St Paul's Waldenbury [Hertfordshire] at 7.30 to stay with Burnet whose fortieth birthday it is. He has taken a little red brick farmhouse called Bury Farm, and just moved in. It is not yet furnished, only the small dining-room in commission. We lived in

* Yvo Richard Vesey, 5th Viscount de Vesci (1881–1958); a Representative Peer for Ireland.

† Lord Archibald Gordon (1913–84); formerly on staff of CPRE, now Director of Talks, BBC Radio; s. 1974 as 5th Marquess of Aberdeen.

the kitchen, cooked our own dinner, or rather heated what had been prepared for us by the daily charwoman. Bedrooms with no carpets down, etc. B. is rather depressed by the whole business, the loneliness, the expense of the move, but he will make it pretty and comfortable. He is not really a countryman. The house is on a corner of one of the finest landscape gardens of England. On Sunday we whitewashed the ceiling of the servants' hall and distempered the walls, as we thought, beautifully, but the following day revealed a very indifferent performance.

*Monday, 12th April*

Picked up Mrs Esdaile* and drove her to Stourhead. Never have I been in close contact with a more unkempt female; yet she is an old pet. Her stockings hang in folds, covered with stains; her face and fingers are yellow from cigarettes which she inhales. Her clothes are a nightmare of cobwebs and must. She is rather vague now and walks with difficulty. Yet at Stourhead she gallantly plodded round the house and told us what she knew about each piece of sculpture, which was everything. I took notes as we went around. Eardley there for the day, and Bob Gathorne-Hardy† came for tea to start cataloguing the books in the library. Mrs Esdaile kept prattling about a monument she wished to see in a church three miles from Stourton, at Silton. 'A stunner,' she called it. It was by Van Nost, she assured me, of a Windham. We took a look at it. I admit it was a splendid affair, dated 1684, full-blooded Charles II Baroque, standing in face of the open door.

*Monday, 19th April*

After luncheon went to my first meeting as a member of the National Buildings Record, of which Sir Eric Maclagan is chairman. Not very

---

* Katharine Esdaile (1881–1950); authority on post-Reformation English sculpture.

† Hon. Robert Gathorne-Hardy (1902–73); 3rd s. of 3rd Earl of Cranbrook (and brother of Lady Anne Hill to whom J.L.-M. had been engaged in 1935); bibliophile; sometime private secretary to Logan Pearsall Smith.

interesting perhaps, but I am proud to be on the Council for I approve of what it is doing and make much use of its photographs.

*Tuesday, 20th April*

At the airport I met Alan Lennox-Boyd,* also going to Dublin to a Guinness Brewery ball tonight. We took off at 11.15 but when in sight of the Irish Sea turned back because we were told that we could not land in Dublin owing to ground mist. Went back to London again, and at the Service's expense ate an excellent cold luncheon. I was glad to be with Alan whom I like. We set off again at 3.30 and landed safely at Dublin, seeing little *en route* because of the clouds. It was too late to catch the last train to Roscrea, so I went with Alan to Farmleigh and stayed the night with the Iveaghs, his in-laws. Patsy and the three children were there, and Chips Channon's son Paul,† a curiously sophisticated, plump little boy, perhaps cunning. There was a ball in the house and, had I not had a lot to drink, I should have been most unhappy. Farmleigh is a large Georgian house, ugly and Edwardianised inside, but luxurious. Lord and Lady Iveagh paid little attention, but seemed not the least surprised to see me. Late at night Alan said what a tiresome necessity of life dissimulation was, for he has for four years been in love with a young man. He kept saying, 'Isn't Patsy a wonderful wife?' I could not deny it. He says she was jealous of the young man to start with, but is resigned to him now. Lady Iveagh once complained to Alan, 'Can't you change your friends a little more often?'

*Wednesday, 21st April*

Left Farmleigh at 8 with Alan. From Kingsbridge station to Roscrea the journey quiet and uneventful, through low-lying fields

* The 'X.-B.' who had been infatuated with Stuart Preston (see notes to 22 March 1943).

† Future Conservative cabinet minister (b. 1935); son of 'Chips' Channon and nephew of Lady Patricia Lennox-Boyd; cr. life peer 1997 as Baron Kelvedon.

without a labourer in sight and stations with no one on the platform. A dead landscape, all the trees looking as though they were part of the earth and a thousand years old in spite of the green buds. The faces of the inhabitants express no surprise and, as they stare, are utterly vacant. When they are animated they are the faces of demons. Arrived Birr Castle in time for luncheon. Alan and Poppy Pryce-Jones staying for the night. In the afternoon Michael had us driven (he cannot drive himself) to see the Jacobean ruins that belong to the Harewoods, very melancholy but complete. I feel terribly tired.

*Sunday, 25th April*

So far I have not done a stroke of work. I have breakfast in bed, rise at 10.30 and am down at 11.30. I read a certain amount, eat a lot, but carefully, wander into town to buy handkerchiefs and shoes. The weather is superb and the air scented with peat. The shop assistants are polite and send whatever one buys round to the Castle; this never happens in England now. In the Castle are a butler, a footman and four housemaids, besides a cook and kitchenmaids. Michael and Anne leave tomorrow but are allowing me to stay on for a week; and I have simply got to make a beginning of my new book. They are angels of generosity and understanding.

*Sunday, 2nd May*

All this week I have not felt well. Have been without appetite and pursued by attacks of nausea. What is it, if not just Ireland? I do not like Ireland. I do not like the country here. It is horizonless and dead. One cannot see further than one's hand. I wish I could define properly what it is I do not like about the climate, the people and the scenery. My dislike is almost intuitive, certainly temperamental and racial. I fear the native hostility under the mask of deceit. At Mass the church here is so crowded that one cannot worship. Irish Catholicism is like a vice, crushing the congregation like nuts. The Irish God is not loving. He is a tyrant. The people are tight within his grasp. Unlike Latins they are subdued by the Church, not elevated by it. They derive from it no inspiration, recreation or romance. Here it is grey and puritanical. In the church the men herd on the Epistle side, the women on the Gospel side like battery hens. One senses that their appalling mendacity and untrustworthiness are the consequence of their age-long abortive attempts to escape the clutch of the priests. Oh, I do hate the whole island.

Things here strike me forcibly. A cart gallops though Birr town, with a line of three horses, unbridled, following at a trot obediently behind in and out of the traffic through the streets. Why do they follow obediently without a rein? The lodge-keeper never fails to open the big double gates to the drive just at the very moment the car comes into sight, as though by magic, the chauffeur not having hooted. Creepy! The family are treated like royalty, and Michael is indeed like a German princeling. One must realise this before understanding him. The town takes the greatest interest in his coming and going, and Anne knows this and plays up to it. She is respected in consequence. There is too a sanctity about Desmond's memory. If you mention his name there is no respectful hush, but eyes sparkle and he is referred to as if still alive. The Irish are all eyes, and nothing else. No compassion, and I doubt whether there is any love, except for the dead. Much hate for the living.

Since the Rosses left I have got down to my new book – The Classical Revival shall I call it? – and worked about seven hours a day, with short intervals for walking into town and round the demesne. The plunge has been taken but I have hit, and shall hit again, my head against a few hard rocks.

*Tuesday, 4th May*

Harold told me the story of a German friend, a long-distance runner, whom he met in Berlin and who pursued him for ten years with a hopeless passion which very much bored Harold. However, the story had a tragic ending for the young man was finally shot by his own countrymen in a concentration camp. Harold remembers urging him, as a good German, to oppose and resist the Nazis at all costs. Harold said he thought and hoped [his son] Ben was in love with a friend he had met at Oxford.*

*Thursday, 13th May*

Lord Crawford told the Admiral and me of his interview with Sir Stafford Cripps,† who was quite ready to buy the contents of both Harewood and Osterley, and indeed realised he would have to do this sort of thing increasingly in future. He proposed having a list drawn up of the 100 greatest houses with collections. How often have similar lists not been drawn up? Cripps said he recognised the Trust to be the fitting body to hold them. This opens up a vast question as to how the Trust is to administer them. A limitation of great houses, with contents, to 100 is going to cause trouble in future. What is considered bad architecture today may be considered good tomorrow. Besides, how many experts will agree on what is the best today?

*Friday, 14th May*

This glorious morning I motored to Rousham.‡ Arrived at one o'clock and met by Mr Cottrell-Dormer,§ a very gentle, intelligent, unassuming man. The house itself is disappointing, for it was added to and spoilt in the last century, and the Kent wings have been interfered with, or rather the connecting colonnades. There are only two rooms by Kent left: the dining-room with painted canvas ceiling in arabesques and great chimneypiece, gilded, and a surprisingly low ceiling; and the saloon, with ribbed ceiling and strikingly deep compartments. The stucco-work of picture frames

---

* See entry for 12 October 1948.

† He had succeeded Dalton as Chancellor of the Exchequer.

‡ In *Another Self*, J.L.-M. claimed that, while an Oxford undergraduate *c.* 1930, he was awakened to the vocation of architectural conservation by attending a dinner party at Rousham (then let to a 'capricious alcoholic') at which the guests vandalised the pictures and statues; but this has been disputed by some, and he makes no mention of the episode when writing about Rousham in his diaries.

§ Thomas Cottrell-Dormer (b. 1894); m. 1936 Elspeth Malcolm (d. 1977), er dau. of Sir James Malcolm, 9th Bt.

and walls done by Roberts of Oxford about 1764. Some of the chairs are by Kent, but their quality is not outstanding.

The gardens are very important as the only Kent layout to survive, apart from the mess left by the urban authorities at Chiswick. There are statues, in a distressing condition, a seven-arched portico (Praeneste), grottoes, glades, a cascade, bath, pools, temples, and straight and serpentine rides. The gardens are miraculously intact after 200 years. We had an al fresco luncheon below Praeneste, close to the Cherwell, and watched the mayfly hatching and flying off the river. Saw the kestrel.

*Thursday, 20th May*

To tea with Lady Mander.* A Pre-Raphaelite tea party – Sir Sydney Cockerell, with whom I had a long talk about Ruskin, Miss Lushington† about Rossetti (she has his willow pattern dinner service to sell), Mrs Angeli, William Rossetti's daughter, and Mrs Joseph, Holman Hunt's daughter. It was fun. Sir Sydney is very spry and on the spot. He said the pity about Dr [G. M.] Trevelyan was that he had no sense of beauty and was totally ignorant of art. These disqualifications prevented him from being a really great historian. Of Kathleen Kennet, whom he had loved, he said she was no artist and knew that he was aware of it.

I told Sir Sydney that because I was more interested in the Classical than in the Gothic it did not make me despise the latter, whereas Ruskin who loved the latter despised the former. He said Ruskin favoured the Gothic because it was the individual expression of man's creative ability, whereas Classical motifs were mechanical and expressions of nothing. 'There is no scope', he said, 'for individual expression in a succession of egg and tongue.'

---

* Rosalie Glynn Grylls (1905–88); author of works on 19th-century literary figures; m. 1930 Sir Geoffrey Mander (1882–1962), sometime MP for Wolverhampton, who had donated Wightwick Manor, his house in Staffordshire, to the N.T.

† Susan Lushington, MBE (1872–1953): her sister Margaret m. Stephen Massingberd of Gunby, brother of Lady Montgomery-Massingberd.

*Wednesday, 26th May*

Tonight [at Long Crichel] Bob [Gathorne-Hardy] talked to me about Logan Pearsall Smith whom he hated at the end. He has finished his life of Logan. I cannot but think he has made a mistake in writing it, and in particular setting out to prove Logan's insanity. It can only do Bob harm, for his readers will assume he is getting his own back on Logan for having cut him out of his will. Bob is a charming person with a thirst for all forms of knowledge, and bald truth. He has quenchless curiosity, disarming frankness, and great volubility. He told me how, before Logan died, he slept in Logan's room on the sofa, kept awake by Logan's coughing; how two nights after his death he slept, no less unhappily, in Logan's bed, Logan lying on the sofa in his coffin. Bob is not exactly fastidious in mind or body.

*Thursday, 27th May*

Today we called for the Anthony Wests* and motored them to Stourhead, Kitty intending to paint in the garden. Anthony West is the natural son of H. G. Wells and Rebecca West. He has the profile of his father; his eyes and the lower part of his face are caricatures of his mother's. He has dark hair and eyes, sallow skin, a heavy, slack chin. Oafish. Is said to be clever; and is quirky, contradictory. Rennie Hoare greeted us at Stourhead with much gush which E. and I received without enthusiasm. In fact E. was very cold. I tried to appear warm but firm. Rennie made several preposterous suggestions regarding furniture arrangement which we could not adopt. I distrust him profoundly. This afternoon we finished arranging all the state rooms on the front. There are three behind which must wait for our next visit.

On our return the Wests took us to Fonthill. Of Beckford's† Abbey there still remains one tower, into which we went. The

* Writer (1914–87), best known for his book on his father H. G. Wells.

† William Beckford (1760–1844); traveller, writer, art collector and builder of Fonthill Abbey (which collapsed soon after he sold it in 1823); J.L.-M. was to move into his Bath library in 1974, and write a biography of him, published by Michael Russell in 1976.

complete Abbey must have been beautiful as well as striking. The quality of the surviving ashlar is good. Situation high and very remote. Tisbury church has good brasses and some stones to the Arundell family in the chancel. Then to Wardour Castle* round which we walked. We were not allowed inside because there is to be a sale of all contents next week. Ted Lister once took me to luncheon before the war. The son and heir† was present and told us how much he adored the place. He became a prisoner-of-war and, being a badly wounded case, was exchanged for a German prisoner. On his way from Liverpool to Wardour he died. The exterior is dignified and clean-cut. Much of the stonework now broken and the cornice of the front perished. The Jesuits have bought it. I bet they won't repair it.

*Tuesday, 1st June*

To Blickling [with Alec Penrose‡] where we had a fairly profitable day. Wyndham Ketton-Cremer lunched at the Buckinghamshire Arms; also Lord Lothian§ whom I allowed to take away some engraved glass, golf clubs, etc., I trust acting correctly. Alec said of Wyndham he is the sort of man who has found contentment by cutting off all limbs that offended him. Alec, I find, has aged mentally. Yet he is a dear man. I admire his taste and I am impressed by his profound faith. He peers bewildered through owlish spectacles in the way, I imagine, Edward Lear did.

I motored after tea to St Paul's Waldenbury to stay with Burnet. We discussed the cussedness of inclinations beyond one's control. Something inside one may whisper futility, and caution against the inevitable backfire of passion. Affairs of the heart mean not a fig

* Georgian mansion built in the vicinity of the original (ruined) castle.

† John Arundell (1907–44); s. father as 16th and last Baron Arundell of Wardour, 1939.

‡ Alexander Penrose (1896–1950) of Bradenham Hall, Norfolk; Honorary Representative of N.T.

§ Peter Francis Walter Kerr, 12th Marquess of Lothian (1922–2004); father of the Conservative politician Michael Ancram (b. 1945), who s. him as 13th Marquess.

more than the grip of momentary drunkenness, rendering one rudderless and unreliable. Civilised beings must rise above the distractions of lust. Pious thoughts which tomorrow may wither beneath the sun of a new love.

*Sunday, 6th June*

Stuart Preston came to stay for a week. I met him at Victoria station. He looks well, is brown, not fat but stalwart, and has become very bald, with a tonsure. I invited the Cyril Connollys to meet him at dinner since Cyril expressed the wish. C. is a lumpish, bad-mannered man and was as bored with me as I was with him. His puny little wife [Lys] is quite sweet and at any rate polite.

*Monday, 7th June*

Went to Covent Garden with Stuart – *Giselle* and *Les Patineurs*. I like Second Empire music. We dined late at the Ritz Grill where Alvilde Chaplin joined us. Stuart said that she grumbled too much. I suspect that he thinks I do too. Grumbling is not at all a bad thing if, like literary criticism, it is constructive.

*Wednesday, 16th June*

Today gave a luncheon party of five and was quite nervous beforehand, my table being very small and my guests very grand. But it was a success. Guests were Michael Godwin, editor of *The Nineteenth Century*, Diane Abdy, Sibyl Colefax and Gerry Wellington. Excellent meal, lots of drink, ending with Cointreau and brandy. Gerry rattled off the names of every marble inlay on my table.

To Hatfield [House, Hertfordshire] as a tourist. Escorted round the house. This palatial mass less fussy than I remembered it to be. The north front quite plain and more austere than Blickling. Brick darker; few fanciful windows. Condition still a little dusty and unkempt from the hospital having been there all the war. It is not the architecture so much as the relics that interest me – Queen

Elizabeth's garden hat and stockings, her jewel case, and those three astonishing portraits.

Stayed the night with Burnet at Bury Farm. After dinner David Bowes-Lyon* walked round from St Paul's. He was alone, his wife being in London. He was wearing a blue collarless shirt under his coat, his neck bare, suede shoes and tight trousers. Has strong, crisp hair and regular white teeth. Very youthful; good complexion in spite of some sharp, haggard lines on one side of his face. He is a charmer. Took us round his garden in the twilight, and into the house.

*Thursday, 17th June*

Drove Bowes-Lyon up to London. Pouring with rain and no windscreen wiper working. His conversation very strange. Did I not think women's thighs ugly? Men's figures more aesthetic? Did I like wearing shorts? He did not disapprove of any sexual practices – and so on. Trying not to be too distant, I did not commit myself to any opinions. He must have found me either a dolt or a prude.

*Saturday, 19th June*

After luncheon motored Dame Una Pope-Hennessy to Petersham. I had a down on this lady today. She talked of nothing but her successes in Paris and how much more intellectual she is than anyone else. Told me she has sold more than 150,000 copies of her *Dickens*, which I can hardly believe, and this year had a capital levy on her earnings. Most gracious to me about the favourable reviews of my own book by the ignorant, and pitying over the bad ones. When I said humbly that it made no pretensions to be a contribution to literature, she snorted, 'Of course it isn't.' Now, she was quite right, but she could have kept her views to herself, or snorted with less

* Hon. (Sir) David Bowes-Lyon (1902–61); 6th son of 14th Earl of Strathmore (and brother of HM Queen Elizabeth, consort of King George VI); horticulturist and director of companies; m. 1929 Rachel Spender-Clay.

vehemence. We joined a party of Richmond Georgian Groupers and went over Montrose House (very rich, very bad taste indeed), Rutland Lodge, Petersham Manor, and other houses, the names of which already escape me. Dame Una inquisitive and caustic. Would not allow me to have tea when offered – I was dying of thirst – because she wanted to return home for tea; and when I dropped her at 5.30 did not invite me in.

*Friday, 25th June*

Our great day at Stourhead. We met Paul Hyslop for luncheon at the Spread Eagle. Then the Eshers, Rennie Hoare and Paul Methuen joined us at the house. Lord E. cordially disliked R.H., thought him a bore and a philistine. He approved wholeheartedly Eardley's and my arrangements – though suggesting a few minor alterations, to appease Hoare and Methuen. We showed Esher the surplus furniture in the basements and attics. He decided that, after Rennie Hoare had made a pick of what he wanted from the Trust, we could take the rest to other houses, when needed, provided it was carefully catalogued as belonging to Stourhead, and sell the indifferent stuff. We shall have to decide what may in future be considered of interest to Stourhead that today we dismiss as rubbish. After tea, Simon Buxton [the N.T. agent] and I walked in the gardens along the lake. All the azaleas now over. Some of the old beeches have got to be felled for they are dangerous. It will be a tragic day when the great tulip trees by the water have to go.

Dining, on my way home, at the King's Head, Cirencester, I was overcome by an attack of unaccountable melancholy in the dining-room. I could scarcely finish my meal for longing to get outside, and away. At Wickhamford I sat in Mama's bedroom, telling her of my strange experience. She explained to me that it was in the King's Head that her mother died in 1896 while waiting for the carriage to drive her home to Coates. Mama, a little girl at the time, was alone with her. My grandmother had been driven nearly mad by the violent ringing of the Abbey church bells opposite. Ever since my mother has loathed church bells.

*Saturday, 26th June*

Away at 9.30 to Hidcote. Walked round the garden with Lawrence Johnston who, apart from absent-mindedness and some loss of memory, is otherwise sane and hale. He said he was incensed by a letter he had received from the Trust and had now decided no longer to 'give' us Hidcote. After much discussion and persuasion he agreed to leave it by will, if I would witness the codicil. The garden is a dream of beauty. The old-fashioned rose garden smelled as fragrant as I have always imagined a garden in a French Gothic tapestry might smell.

I motored to South Wraxall Manor to stay with Lady Glyn.* She is the mother of David Long who was killed in the war and grandmother of the heiress of this beautiful house. David Long came to see me at the beginning of September 1939 in a great hurry for he was drafted abroad with his regiment. He begged me to devise some scheme whereby South Wraxall, which he loved, might be preserved by the National Trust. As far as I remember his solicitors raised difficulties and objections in his absence. The Eshers are staying here and they got me invited to talk over the future of the place. Lady G. is old now with a face like parchment, and old parchment at that. Also staying Lady Marjorie Beckett,† Diana Worthington's‡ mother. She knew I was a friend of Diana and said she had no idea how desperate poor Diana was before her suicide. She was sweet to me because I loved Diana and asked me to stay with her in Yorkshire. She must have been prettier than Diana who had a huge frog-like mouth that was, strangely enough, seductive. When smiling and lowering her eyes she reminded me of Diana.

---

* Sibell (d. 1958), dau. of 2nd Baron Derwent; m. 1st 1910 Brig.-Gen. Hon. Walter Long (killed in action, 1917; their son David [1911–44] s. grandfather as 2nd Viscount Long, 1924, and was killed in action, 1944), 2nd 1921 Ralph Glyn MP (1885–1960; cr. Bt 1935, Baron 1953).

† Lady Margaret Greville, dau. of 5th Earl of Warwick; m. 1st 1904 2nd Earl of Feversham (d. 1916), 2nd 1917 Hon. Sir Gervase Beckett, 1st Bt (d. 1937).

‡ Lady Diana Worthington, dau. of Lady Margaret by her 1st marriage; drowned herself in River Ouse, October 1943, after her husband had left her.

*Sunday, 27th June*

This house is not one I should care to live in. Lady Glyn has furnished it entirely by herself with what she bought from the Thornton Smith sale. The furniture is pretty, but not exactly good. All the floors are covered with rush matting. The various fireplaces of 1598 are interesting, particularly the gigantic Flemish one in the big room which gets uglier the longer you look at it: the loathsome caryatids with cruel boxes round their fat, shapeless bodies.

Lord Esher is restless during weekends. Likes to talk. Never reads. Nevertheless is bubbling with fun and jokes; counting the cakes on the tea-table and calculating how many he may eat, and then gorging. Never walks a yard, saying we should hold Sir Edgar Bonham Carter, who was a rugger blue and is now a cripple, as a warning not on any account to take exercise. Says he would rather remain in England and be atom-bombed into a jelly than emigrate to the colonies, blaze trails through the bushvelt and be eaten by scorpions.

*Friday, 2nd July*

Dined at Kew with Mark Ogilvie-Grant, taking Malcolm Bullock and George Dix. A very hilarious, male, witty-smutty, funny party, at which disclosures and confidences poured out faster than the drink. Even Malcolm was embarrassed by certain idiosyncratic disclosures. The more outrageous they became the more harmless. Nearly choked with laughter. Oh, lust *is* a jest! How *would* we laugh without it?

*Saturday, 3rd July*

With courage opened Papa's letter in reply to mine telling him I was more than £600 overdrawn. He wrote kindly that we must have a financial talk next time I go home. No recriminations, which is very unlike him.

*Wednesday, 7th July*

At 4.30 Lord Crawford, Lord Esher, the Admiral and I went to the Treasury for a discussion with Sir Edward Bridges* and Sir Bernard Gilbert arising from the Treasury's announcement of the Chancellor's intention to set up a Commission to deal with the problem of large country houses with collections. I am much concerned because my memorandum on the problem, drafted before the announcement, is to be circulated to the Executive Committee. In it I have urged very strongly that the Trust ought to come to terms with the Government and indeed ask for, and accept, government subvention, in spite of our hitherto having set our faces against the risk of state interference. The alternative, I submit, is for the Trust to sink, for we cannot compete with Treasury resources. I think I have convinced Crawford and Esher, both clever men, but the Admiral and Hubert Smith [Chief Agent] do not yet see the necessity. The Trust is at a critical juncture and I seem to be playing a backstair role in guiding its affairs. Backstair is the word.

*Sunday, 11th July*

On my way to the bathroom saw Emily's newspaper with large headline, 'Fabulous Lady Cunard dies at 71'. This has indeed made me sad. My day quite overclouded by it. I telephoned Tony Gandarillas to condole with him. He was in tears. Said he was with her while she died; she had no pain at the end, being kept under drugs. I met little Diane [Abdy] in Bennet Street after luncheon. She said Bertie was also with her when she died and feels as though he has lost his mother. Yesterday morning Emerald tried desperately to say something important but was unable to speak. This worries Bertie. Gordon, her maid, became a saint at the end, slept in her room, waited on her hand and foot, and never

* Civil servant (1892–1969); Permanent Secretary to the Treasury, 1945–56; cr. Baron, 1957; son of Poet Laureate Robert Bridges, and first cousin of J.L.-M's future wife Alvilde Chaplin.

left her. Apparently it was cancer that killed her. I remarked to Diane that in walking to Brooks's this morning I kept saying to myself, 'Why do all these ugly and stupid people that I pass live, yet Emerald dies?'

My sorrow for Emerald is different to what I felt when Kathleen Kennet died. That was a dear friend going. Emerald's death means the end of an age, a legend. I regret that I did not see her more often these past two years, but hers was a world not mine. I admired her more than I admire most women, for her lightning perception, her wide reading, her brilliant repartee, her sense of fun, and sparkling, delicious, wonderful nonsense. If only I could have attended her dinner parties as a dumb servitor, the awkwardness of trying and failing to contribute to the conversation would not have arisen. I would have been content to listen to her and watch her deft manipulation of the conversation until eternity. She seemed always to like me and was charming, but I knew I could never entertain her, and so I avoided her too often. Yet I am glad I knew her for no one will ever take her place. No ordinary mortal can afford to be so detached from the chores of everyday life. Hers was entirely artificial, or unreal for these days, uncontaminated by worldly duties. What a loss she will be.

*Friday, 16th July*

Somewhat to my surprise my Memorandum passed through both Committees with hardly a dissentient voice raised. It was agreed that if the Chairman was asked by the Chancellor to accept a grant, it should be taken, provided it was attached to the maintenance of a specific building only, and was not a contribution to general funds.

Charles Fry back from America telephoned that he needed to see me at once. I called this evening. He is unchanged – detestable. He is utterly untrustworthy, without conscience, moral scruple or decency. I shall have to see him once more as my publisher, and that is the end.

*Tuesday, 20th July*

Lunched at Madresfield [Court, Worcestershire]. Lord Beauchamp* is fat, with a great paunch, looking like God knows what, wearing an old blue shirt, open at the frayed neck, and a tight pair of brown Army shorts, baby socks and sandshoes. Lady B. plump, but pretty. The house is not in my eyes beautiful. The situation, however, is made beautiful by the Malvern Hills looming over it. You approach it by a straight drive of more than a mile, but the actual estate is on flat and dull ground. The gardens (there are ten gardeners) are delicious, especially the long avenues and paths, and the arboretum. Busts of Roman Emperors under arches of yew close to the house, which is moated. The contents are marvellous – pictures and sixteenth-century portraits. As for the miniatures, of which there are a great number, they are superlative. Also some good French furniture and many bibelots; snuff boxes, gold, silver, bejewelled, etc. One could spend hours here enjoying these things which by themselves make Madresfield worthy of preservation for all time.

We lunched in the great hall – much altered eighty years ago. It faces a little central court, half-timbered in a Nürnberg manner. Lady Beauchamp is a Dane and her two stepdaughters and old mother, who does not speak and to whom one does not speak, were staying. Lord and Lady B. spent all afternoon conducting and explaining. A picnic tea was had by the swimming pool. Then he took me to see two half-timbered lesser houses on the estate. The rich tenants from the Black Country most obsequious, and apologetic to the Earl for not being in their best clothes, whereas he was dressed as described. Earls with sores on their knees should not parade them exposed to their villeins. In spite of his fatness and unshaven porky face, his manner is patrician and stiff.

* William Lygon, 8th and last Earl Beauchamp (1903–79); undistinguished elder son of 7th Earl (the bisexual statesman and art collector forced into exile); m. 1936 Else 'Mona' de la Cour.

*Sunday, 1st August*

Debo and Andrew [Hartington] drove me to Chatsworth [Derbyshire] this morning. The site of the house, the surroundings unsurpassed. The grass emerald green as in Ireland. The Derwent river, although so far below the house, which it reflects, seems to dominate it. Black and white cattle in great herds. All the hills have trees along their ridges. Neatness and order are the rule although, Andrew says, there are fourteen gardeners instead of forty before the last war. The inordinate length of the house undeniably impressive, and the 6th Duke's extensions do not make it lopsided, as I had been led to suppose. The limitless landscape can absorb it. The uniform yellow sandstone helps link the old block to Wyatville's towered colonnade, which might be taken out of a Claude painting. We wandered through the gardens, greyhounds streaming across the lawns. Andrew turned on the fountain from the willow tree. Water not only drips from the tree but jets from nozzles all round. The cascade not working this morning, but will be turned on for the public this afternoon. At present the great house is empty, under covers and dustsheets. Next year the state rooms are to be shown. We entered the house from the west door, let in by Mr Thompson, the librarian. The state rooms are all on the second floor, reminiscent of Hampton Court, one leading to the next without passages. All pictures taken off the walls. Interior terribly hot and stuffy. Andrew let me look through two volumes of Inigo Jones drawings of masque costumes. Henry VII's prayer book, with illuminations, given by the King to his daughter who was asked to pray for him, inscription in his kingly hand.

The scale of Chatsworth is gigantic, beyond comprehension (like St Peter's, Rome) until experienced. The detail of outside stonework of high quality, notably the antlers over windows, frostwork in the central courtyard, the panels of trophies, by Watson presumably. The Tijou ironwork easily identifiable. The Hartingtons, eager to know their possessions, intend to spend several hours a day systematically looking through papers in the library, like schoolchildren at a holiday task. When it comes to working on Inigo Jones, Andrew says I may have full access to the Chatsworth library papers.

As a couple the Hartingtons seem perfection – both young, handsome, and inspired to accomplish great things. He has a splendid war record and won the MC. Has contested one constituency and is now nursing Chesterfield, a very Socialist seat. Unlikelihood of winning does not deter him. Both full of faith in themselves and their responsibilities. She has all the Mitford virtues and none of the profanity. I admire them very much.

*Tuesday, 3rd August*

This morning it poured [at Chatsworth], but slackened a bit at eleven. Andrew had to write letters, but Debo and I rode – the first time I have ridden for quite ten years. We went through the great Wyatville entrance and into the gardens of Chatsworth below the terrace. The wooden surrounds of the west front windows are still coloured gold, now rather faint, but the sash-bars have not been gilded that one can see. We went up the hill to look at the Cascade Temple and back again, then across the main road to the far side of the valley to see the Russian Lodge, built by the Bachelor Duke.* His spirit at Chatsworth is very prevalent.

*Friday, 6th August*

I am forty today. The shock is not too great because during the past year I have been telling people that I was forty, in anticipation. But I am rather less good-looking and very bald now. My figure is as slender as ever. Only occasionally does my stomach swell, owing to the bad bread, but it soon flattens itself. I have lately found that the skin of my jaw and chest is slacker than formerly. I am less stirred by desire than I used to be. It is the forms of physical falling-off that I most resent: the fact that the life-line only reaches an angle of 89.9 rather than 90 degrees. Oh dear, to say nothing of the decay of teeth,

---

* William George Spencer Cavendish, 6th Duke of Devonshire (1790–1858); Whig statesman and art collector, whose biography by J.L.-M., written at the request of Debo Devonshire, was published by John Murray in 1991.

eyesight and hair. When in another twenty years I am too old to work I shall retire to a monastery and pray, for I shall presumably no longer see to read. This is my one consolation: that when my active life must cease I can still do good by praying. I am sure this should be the occupation of old age. One need never be idle. The prayer wheel when all else fails. At present my mental faculties, never first-rate, are better than they have ever been. All my life I have been a slow developer.

*Sunday, 8th August*

Worked steadily this weekend. My notes swell to enormous proportions. Late this evening Rick [Stewart-Jones] and I walked in Battersea Park in the drizzling rain and looked at the open-air sculpture. The setting very beautiful in Lord Redesdale's lovely garden of umbrageous trees. I told Rick I had hardly any true friends; but this was an untruth. He said I was too fickle to deserve any. I don't believe this is true either. I now think with affection of James Pope-Hennessy, Ben Nicolson, Mark Ogilvie-Grant, Patrick Kinross, Johnnie Churchill, Michael and Anne Rosse, Bridget Parsons, Harold and Vita, besides A, B and C. I have however no lovers and with folded hands await some devastating romance.

*Saturday, 14th August*

Motored to stay the weekend with the Sitwells at Weston [Northamptonshire]. Sachie is like a child in his enthusiasms and impulsiveness, his simple and direct humour and readiness to laugh like a sensitive trigger. He is a voluble talker. His mind flits from houses, paintings, music, poetry, birds, nuns, flowers to jewellery and strawberries within one breath. He is infinitely sympathetic and inspiriting. The sweetest of men. Yet he is outspoken and likes giving advice. He warned me (a) to have more self-confidence in my writing and set aside more time for it, (b) to take steps to save what hair I have left – he recommends some infallible lotion the Duke of Westminster uses – and (c) not to dwell upon cancer. We talked for hours about writing. He has written fifty books, has seven more coming out this year. Yet writing is a terrible effort for him and for weeks he cannot put pen to paper. Georgia is charming in her own home. She is also very pretty. Reresby a nice, good-natured boy, lively and intelligent.

*Tuesday, 17th August*

Motored to Polesden, picking up Robin Fedden. On to Rye where we found Mrs Henry James,* her niece and solicitor at the Mermaid Inn. Walked round to Lamb House, which she offers with the garden to the National Trust. A delightful George I house in a narrow back street, on a corner. A great tragedy is the complete destruction of the garden house where Henry James wrote from 1898 to 1916. It was a simple structure judging from photographs and I would have it rebuilt. E. F. Benson rented Lamb House after Henry James's death until he died in 1941 or thereabouts. All the windows remain blown out. Hardboard has been temporarily substituted, so the rooms are pitch dark. They are nearly all panelled. The stair balusters are twisted and the treads shallow and broad, beautiful to walk up and down. The house is in bad condition but can be repaired easily. It is fully furnished with much furniture that belonged to the novelist. His pictures still hanging on the walls. Mrs James told me that the most intimate belongings, including writing-table and piano, were destroyed with the garden house. Much of the rest was removed to America by the family on the novelist's death. She is unable to 'give' what furniture remains in the house, but we have the option to buy it. So Robin is going to pick out what he thinks ought to remain, with the assistance of Henry James's old secretary who is still alive.†

*Friday, 27th August*

A lovely day rinsed in autumn melancholy, the early sun slanting through the Iford trees upon the dew and the tranquil doves' notes

* Daughter-in-law of the philosopher William James (1842–1910), elder brother of the novelist Henry James (1843–1916).

† Miss Theodora Bosanquet (d. 1961).

soothing. We [J.L.-M. and Esher] drove without stop to Hidcote. Found Lawrence Johnston and lawyer, and Nancy Lindsay.* Laurie J. signed the deed of gift like a lamb so, since he leaves for abroad in a fortnight, the place may be said to be saved. This has been a struggle but it is accomplished. We were conducted round the gardens by the usual route. How often must the old man have done this tour? I think it was a sad occasion for him and I wondered how far he understood that he was giving away his precious treasure of a garden. 'I have another Hidcote,' he murmured, presumably referring to his garden at Mentone. Miss Lindsay is like an old witch, very predatory and interfering. She maintains that she has been deputed by L.J. to supervise these gardens in his absence abroad. We were not overcome with gratitude. Anyway no mention of this condition was made either by L.J. or his solicitors before the signing. Sibyl Colefax will be delighted that the deed she worked so hard to bring about has been done.

*Wednesday, 1st September*

Sibyl said to me, 'You and I are happy.' I said, 'I am not happy, Sibyl. Are you really?' She went on, 'I haven't finished my sentence – I was going to say, happy in having been born with no possessions. No, I am not happy. Old people are never happy. But I *was* happy. Now I am only interested in the young.' This is the only occasion when I have heard her speak of her inmost self. Now as to possessions, the fewer one possesses, and of course I have very few, the more one loves them. People like the Hartingtons who own priceless works of art are not so fond of their Inigo Jones drawings, their Rembrandts and William Kent furniture as I am of my one little water-colour by Ethel Walker.

*On 4 September, J.L.-M. left with Desmond Shawe-Taylor for a month's holiday in Italy.*

---

* Spinster daughter of Norah Lindsay, gardening mentor of Lawrence Johnston. In a fit of rage against the N.T., she later destroyed all papers relating to the garden's creation – a fact lamented in 2005 when an anonymous donor gave £1.6 million to restore Hidcote to its former glory.

*Monday, 6th September*

My first impression of Rome is that the whole city, and certainly the hotel, are slightly shabbier than last year; also the inhabitants. That bloom of expectancy has gone; a faint disillusion prevails. Is it because the Romans expected an eldorado before the elections last year, and now they are over and the same Government is in power, they are bored and disappointed? On leaving the hotel my steps automatically take me past the Villa Medici to the Pincio. I then sit on the balustrade overlooking the Piazza del Popolo. It is a bright, cool day, ideal for sightseeing, with a breeze. I descend and look at both sides, Vignola's and Bernini's, of the great arch. Then immerse myself in the church of Santa Maria with its superb collection of Florentine sculptural tombs and screens. Then cash a cheque at the American Express for nearly 2,000 lire for each £1, and walk to lunch at a favourite *trattoria* close to the Piazza Navona.

Desmond calls for me at 5 o'clock and we walk to the Vatican City. I notice how much Bramante's Palazzo Giraud evolves from Alberti's Palazzo Ruccellai in Florence; the same thin pilaster strips to each floor. The approach to St Peter's very squalid at present with barricades everywhere, and the Borgo up and cranes working. I hope they do not mean to fill up the vista that Mussolini cleared. Rome is crammed with Catholic girls from all over Italy wearing red berets, who smell very strong and acrid. 'What we now want', said Desmond, 'is some Protestant boys.' More impressed than ever by the unassertive splendour of the interior of the basilica, so vast and clear of all pews and seats. People complain of the arrogance and coldness of St Peter's. I do not agree. I find the interior, when empty, humbly offering shelter, asking to be filled and loved, offering faith and understanding. The predominant blue-grey is restful and effuses a misty tone through which the sharper colours of mosaic and gilding glow. Walked up to San Onofrio but could not enter the church. Enjoyed the western view in the sunset.

In the evening Guido Ferrari* called at the hotel. Has improved in mind and body. Is now very beautiful with raven hair and white

* Italian architecture student, English on his mother's side.

teeth and eyes of bear-like brown, a Michelangelo ephebe. Is less discontented with his lot, no longer wishing to adopt British nationality. I expect he has a girl, but do not enquire. Italians don't like familiarity. He says my Italian is worse than ever and it is a waste of time giving me lessons.

*Through the good offices of Sir D'Arcy Osborne, British Minister to the Vatican, J.L.-M. was granted an audience with Pope Pius XII at the papal summer residence near Rome, Castel Gandolfo.*

*Tuesday, 14th September*

My cold very much worse. Am feverish and my nose pours. All day without any intermission the rain pours and pours. After a bad night I get up early and catch a tram – over one hour – to Castel Gandolfo. Am feeling very nervous because I can think of nothing special to say to the Pontiff. Arrive at the village at 10 and first look at the lake in a crater below and, over its bank, more extraordinary, at the Roman Campagna at a still lower level. A very classical situation. There are no buildings on the shore of the lake except on the Castel Gandolfo side. I go to Bernini's round church in the village to shelter from the rain, and to compose and prepare myself. A Mass is in progress. Then at 10.30 I walk to the Palace, a shapeless building of yellow wash towering over the village. At the gate are a crowd of Boy Scouts and Catholic Youth. I edge my way through and wave my official invitation to the handsome Swiss Guard in his fantastic Michelangelo uniform of yellow and blue stripes. I am passed from one guard to another, from one officer with a red plume to another, from a gentleman usher to a cosy major-domo, and left in the fourth chamber hung with crimson brocade and, over a table, a large crucifix. The green marble doorheads have 'Pius XI Pont. Max A.V.' carved on them. So this suite is fairly contemporary. It is all right but not outstandingly opulent. I sit on one of the gold chairs with crimson brocade upholstery, and wait. Presently a very distinguished old lady in black, with black veil, and wearing pearls and a few good jewels, comes in. She has what was once a beautiful face with deep black shadows under her eyes. I rise from my seat and make a gesture of politeness. She does not recognise my presence but, grasping her rosary and muttering prayers, prostrates herself with utmost reverence before the crucifix. When I next look up I hear her say, '*Giovan signore, ho grand fame*', which surprises me. She dives into a capacious bag, extracts a biscuit and nibbles it. She tells me that the Pope has suddenly had to see several cardinals just arrived from South America, and our audience will be postponed indefinitely. She draws me to the window and looks out upon the lake which she supposes is the sea. She is Brazilian and says, 'An English Catholic, what a contradictory thing to be.' She speaks with great volubility about the splendid qualities and strength of the English. Then she discourses very knowledgeably on religion. All our troubles today are due to our divorcing religion from everyday life, and even the pious only give lip-service to God. She directs me never to neglect the Holy Ghost in my prayers and thoughts, admitting that it is difficult to distinguish Him from the other Two. She assures me that through years of unhappiness she has reached absolute contentment through her religion. I admire and like her, but wish she would offer me a biscuit. We are then joined by a superior young Italian Monsignore carrying a precious parcel wrapped in tissue paper, and an uncouth young American from Texas. For one hour we four are together, shunted by the major-domo from room to room in a sort of silent musical chairs. It is I suppose what the immediate after-life may be, namely thrown among the same people who have died at the very moment as oneself, and moving through the mansions of Purgatory towards Heaven. We pass other people without making any contact. However a young priest in a wheelchair, in a deathlike apathy and presumably the last stages of consumption, is pushed past us. I saw his face on returning from his audience wreathed in ghastly smiles. It was an expression of resigned beatitude.

The Texan, much to my surprise, produced from his trouser pocket a gold wristwatch, a gold pocket-watch, a gold pencil and chain, and a gold cigarette case. He asked me if I supposed the Holy Father would accept them as a souvenir. I said I was sure he would not, but advised him to consult the Brazilian lady whose fourth audience with a different Pope this was to be. The American said, 'I don't think a cheque would be quite the same thing. I could not afford 100,000 dollars and I daresay he has enough money to go on with.' After a pause he said, 'I am going to be quite homely with the Pope. What are you?' And finally when we had reached the last state room and the Brazilian had complained of hunger pains and asked him for a biscuit, the Texan produced a Chesterfield cigarette and invited her to smoke.

By this time purple Monsignores were running in all directions. Whenever His Holiness was ready for the audience a vicious little bell rang and cassocked liverymen fairly scampered to open and shut doors. We were constantly moved along, now from chair to chair, the pace gradually slackening. The drill was very effective. First the Brazilian lady disappeared, and returned radiant, her hands full of parcels, saying, 'He is wonderful. He is so good and kind. May you all have every happiness and blessing from this visit. *Arrivederci*.' Suddenly, instead of the three of us who remained being called singly into the next room, the door opened and in stepped swiftly a tall, erect, brisk figure, all in white, wearing a white biretta. Until I saw an attendant Cardinal genuflect I did not realise it was the Pope. He went straight to the Texan ahead of me – this was prearranged for the three of us were spaced on our chairs at intervals. The Pope without wasting a second talked to him with much affability. With one nervous movement the Texan fumbled in his trouser pocket, but mercifully thought better of it. The Pope turned, the Texan left, and the Holy Father approached me. I walked towards him and fell on both knees. The next one and a half minutes remain but vaguely registered. He held out his hand for me to take and I just noticed the ring, as I kissed it, to have a large dark stone encircled with lesser gems, not diamonds. His presence radiated a benignity, calm and sanctity that I have certainly never before sensed in any human being. All the while he smiled in the sweetest, kindliest way so that I immediately fell head over heels in love with him. I was so affected I could scarcely speak without tears and was conscious that my legs were trembling. His face was strong and healthy, not handsome, but made beautiful by his extraordinary charm. I noticed his nice strong teeth like old ivory. He spoke a gentle, hesitating English. Asked me where I lived and when I said London, said something of it being a 'dear place'. I told him I had witnessed the ceremony at St Peter's with Sir D'Arcy Osborne and had been immensely impressed by the crowd of Catholic Youth.* He said, 'Did you see how beautiful it was. I am so glad. I want to bless you and all those dear to you', and beyond a few other polite, but trite, remarks, I can recollect nothing. He then handed me a little blue envelope embossed with the papal arms. It contained a not very expensive medal with his head on one side and his arms (heraldic) on the other. I knelt for his blessing and he passed on. In turning to leave I noticed a cardinal slip into his hand, held out behind with desperately wagging fingers, another little envelope for the next guest. I walked back through the state rooms, now filled with groups of young men carrying some large images and awaiting their turn for the papal audience.

*J.L.-M. returned to England in early October.*

*Tuesday, 12th October*

Anthony Blunt† lunched. He now asks to be appointed to the Historic Buildings Committee and says that where he is deficient, e.g. in English portraiture, he will get young Oliver Millar‡ to deputise for him. My fear is that he will be too busy and not answer letters. But he has an agreeable manner, though distant. He told me in confidence that Ben [Nicolson] is 'no good at pictures'. One must discount this a little. All art experts are notoriously uncharitable about each other, especially if they are friends. He says someone must warn Ben who has made himself the laughing stock of Europe over [David] Carritt, with whom he is madly in love.

---

* J.L.-M. had witnessed this spectacle the previous Sunday, writing in his diary that he was 'slightly disturbed' by its 'Fascist tinge'.

† (Sir) Anthony Blunt (1907–83); Surveyor of the Royal Pictures, 1945–72; officially disgraced in 1979, when it was revealed that he had been a Soviet agent.

‡ (Sir) Oliver Millar (b. 1923); Deputy Surveyor of the Royal Pictures, 1945–72 (Surveyor, 1972–88).

*Wednesday, 13th October*

This evening dined with the John Wyndhams.* A young marrieds' party. I sat next to Mrs Alaric Russell and Miss Elizabeth Winn,† a niece of Nostell. Venetia Montagu's‡ daughter there – a tall, rather plain but commanding girl, with her mother's sharp Stanley intellect. Jock Colville§ greeted me by my Christian name as an old friend, but I scarcely know him. He is Princess Elizabeth's secretary and is marrying her lady-in-waiting next week. He worked under Churchill during the war. Very intelligent. Much charm. I liked him. Royal servants are trained to be come-hitherish. It must be a ghastly effort at times. After dinner, when the women left, talk was about how little we know of the everyday life of our ancestors in spite of George Trevelyan's history. Jock Colville suggested we ought to go home tonight and write down in minute detail how we drove to the Wyndhams' door, left our car at the kerb, its doors firmly locked, rang the bell, were kept waiting on the doorstep, how we were received by a butler wearing black bow tie instead of white, what the hall smelt like, how the man took our coats and hats, putting them on the chest downstairs, and how he preceded us upstairs, one step at a time, etc., etc. He said that Princess Elizabeth's child would be the first heir to the throne born without a Home Secretary being in the room; that Chuter Ede¶ was to stand in the passage. Said there is no record left of how Asquith treated George V when threatening him with the creation

---

* Hon. John Wyndham (1920–72); son of 5th Baron Leconfield; Conservative Party official (later Private Secretary to Harold Macmillan, Prime Minister); cr. Baron Egremont, 1963, prior to succeeding father as 6th Baron Leconfield, 1967; m. 1947 Pamela Wyndham-Quin.

† Niece (b. 1925) of Rowland Winn, 3rd Baron St Oswald, of Nostell Priory, Yorkshire; later renowned as a mimic.

‡ Judith Montagu (b. 1923); dau. of Rt Hon. Edwin Mongagu (1879–1924) and Hon. Venetia Stanley (d. 1948; sometime love object of H. H. Asquith, Prime Minister).

§ (Sir) John Colville (1915–87); civil servant, wartime (and future) aide to Winston Churchill; then Private Secretary to HRH Princess Elizabeth; m. 1948 Lady Margaret Egerton, dau. of 4th Earl of Ellesmere.

¶ James Chuter Ede (1882–1965); Home Secretary, 1945–51.

of 500 peers in 1911; but that the King told his mother, Lady Cynthia Colville,* at 9 o'clock one morning, when she felt too ill with a splitting headache to record a story she has now forgotten. Thus does history pass into the shadows. He spoke of Churchill with great affection. I left at a quarter to one o'clock, having drunk too much champagne and port. A fatal mistake.

*Friday, 15th October*

Committee meetings today and the Trust's Annual Meeting at Goldsmiths' Hall at 4.30. The Bishop of London the chief speaker. He said that the social revolution we were going through would prove disastrous if this country did not preserve for the masses the culture which had been lost to France during the French Revolution. Mrs Hugh Dalton was present, smiling blandly like a crocodile, and I hope took it all in.

*Tuesday, 19th October*

On leaving Alcester I drove to Ragley [Hall, Warwickshire] up the Worcester drive, not the Arrow drive. Arrived 3 o'clock. The house stands on an eminence and the ground slopes from all four sides. This is unusual. Consequently there are distant views from each front. Moreover there are no modern annexes to mar the house, which was built in 1683 by a Seymour. My hostess told me the architect is thought to be Robert Hooke.† I should have guessed Talman‡ or Francis Smith§ for it has affinities with Dyrham and Sutton Scarsdale. The material is blue lias stone, of the off-Cotswold, Bidford-on-Avon variety, and some sandstone, which

* Lady Cynthia Crewe-Milnes (1884–1968), dau. of 1st Marquess of Crewe; a Woman of the Bedchamber to HM Queen Mary, 1923–53; m. 1908 Hon. George Colville (1867–1943).

† Architect (1635–1703); worked at Ragley, 1679–83, revising design of a previous architect.

‡ William Talman (1650–1719).

§ Francis Smith of Warwick (1672–1738).

has perished, notably the dentils of the cornice. The great columned portico may be of later date than the house. You enter by an opening below the perron (added by Wyatt) and, as at Kedleston, pass into an undercroft.

Lady Helen Seymour* was awaiting me in the library. She is tall, about fifty-eight, with lovely blue eyes, and must have been a beauty. *Très grande dame.* Was the youngest daughter of the 1st Duke of Westminster. Her son, Lord Hertford,† the owner of Ragley, is only eighteen, and has just left Eton. She showed me over house and grounds. The great hall magnificent, now quite empty. The stucco-work might be by Gibbs's Italians, or even the Italian who worked at Ragley, called Vassali. The other rooms on this floor have Rococo ceilings of 1740 or thereabouts, which Lady H. believes to be original, and later ceilings in a thin Adamish style with small round grisaille cameos, perhaps by Holland, but this is all guesswork. I have as yet read nothing about the house. In the library is a large Reynolds of Horace Walpole as a young man. He was a cousin of Marshal Conway, a Seymour,‡ to whom he was devoted. There is a Reynolds of him too. Altogether some eight Reynoldses. There are magnificent Chippendale hall benches, the finest I have seen; two panels of carved fruit in the library which might be by Gibbons; some Louis XV marquetry commodes; a huge bed under a dust sheet or, rather, very pretty chintz curtain, so that I could not see it, in the Royal Bedroom that once had lacquer wallpaper. The woodwork is still painted black and gold. Doorcases and dados are nearly all 1683. There are excellent Morlands§ and a huge Wootton¶ of three packs of hounds meeting at Ragley. I think it is one of the most interesting great houses

* Lady Helen Grosvenor, dau. of 1st Duke of Westminster; m. 1915 Brig.-Gen. Lord Henry Charles Seymour (d. 1939).

† Hugh Seymour, 8th Marquess of Hertford (1930–1997).

‡ Henry Seymour Conway (1721–95); field marshal.

§ George Morland (1762–1804); painter specialising in scenes from English rural life.

¶ John Wootton (*c.* 1682–1764); landscape and sporting painter specialising in horse subjects.

I have seen. The stables are enchanting, built round two courtyards. The laundry yard has a colonnade. The lower courtyard is elliptical. Lady Helen fears they will have to leave the house and move to a smaller one on the estate. Heating is a great problem and they have only two servants, one Swiss. I liked her much.

I dined at Bretforton Manor with Harry Ashwin who showed me photographs of the Ashwin family and us children when we played Red Indians, which we did in the shrubbery there for days on end.

*Friday, 22nd October*

This morning Papa and I motored to Ombersley, the first time I have ever been inside the house. We were asked to go there by Lord Sandys,* who has just succeeded his cousin, dead at the age of ninety. The present lord is seventy-two and as Colonel Hill was a friend of my father. He and his wife charming and hospitable. In return for asking me to wander round the house and assess the contents (a curious request) he gave me a present of four pots of honey, some pears and a box of cigars. The front of the house facing the road is dull Grecian *c.* 1810, with plain portico, added in stone by the Marchioness of Downshire, the last Sandys in her own right, to a William and Mary house behind. The old house consists of a central hall comprising two storeys, a gallery connecting the upstairs bedrooms, and a ponderous ceiling of the 1810 period. The bedrooms all wainscoted in oak of William and Mary time with nice panelled doors and brass locks and handles. Handsome staircase of three balusters to each tread. One corner room contains elaborately raised door-cases with small pediments. It is a treasure house, full of good, but not exceptional, and some junky, things. Many portraits of Sandyses, one mid-sixteenth-century portrait of

---

* Arthur Hill, 6th Baron Sandys (1876–1961); m. 1924 Cynthia Trench-Gascoigne. The Sandys family (from which the Hills descend in the female line via Mary Sandys, Marchioness of Downshire – only child of the last Baron Sandys of the first creation – who succeeded in getting the barony recreated in 1802 for the benefit of herself and her younger son) was of particular interest to the Lees-Milnes as they had once owned Wickhamford, where the church contains their splendid memorials.

Sir John Cheek, a good Jansens of George Sandys, poet and traveller, a charming Dobson of a Sandys and Prince Rupert at a junketing, Sandys dipping the ribbon of a third disaffected friend's hat in the Prince's glass of claret. A delightful portrait of Lady Downshire, her little foot peeping out of her skirts and resting on a footstool. There is some nice Regency furniture in the bedrooms, the remains of a George II state bed, of splendid red Genoa velvet, but mutilated. Several gilt gesso mirrors and gilt gesso tables of Queen Anne date, very good indeed.

We were given a picnic luncheon with sherry and white wine. Lord and Lady S. have not moved in yet.

*Tuesday, 26th October*

Rather ghastly meeting of the Keats–Shelley committee at Lady Crewe's house. She makes acid remarks which she instantly corrects with something worse in a low voice which mercifully can seldom be heard by the victim. Has a great sense of malice, which is entertaining.

*Friday, 5th November*

Sibyl Colefax lunched with me alone. She has a slight grievance against the Nicolsons. She says Vita is selfish and neither she nor Harold does anything to get the boys married. It was bad for them to live with their father all the week and both parents every weekend. Then she discussed Ben's new love, Carritt, so I thought it better to change the subject. She also wants to join the Keats–Shelley Committee, but James says Lady Crewe will not hear of this.

*Saturday, 13th November*

This morning paid my first visit to the Public Record Office reading room. After a long wait I was brought several long parchment rolls of accounts of royal building works, dated 1585. When I had unrolled them I endeavoured to anchor them with a heavy book. But they have a habit of releasing themselves, rolling themselves smartly up again and covering one with a shower of Tudor dust. The separate sheets also get entangled. Both sides are written upon. They are devilish things. Noël Blakiston came and read through some of them for me. With his help I became almost expert. With practice one's eye becomes accustomed to the script. The Elizabethan scribe abbreviated his script far more than we do ours. Hence *Ye* for *the*, and a squirl for *ion*.

*Sunday, 14th November*

Newman, the hall porter at Brooks's, told me I would be surprised if I knew which members, to his knowledge, stole newspapers out of the Club. I said, 'You must not tell me,' so he promptly did. Queen Mary's equerry, Coke,* he says, an old member, steals the *Sporting and Dramatic* the very morning it comes out. He does it every week and Newman has often watched him.

Soaking in my bath this morning I decided I should not have such hot baths for my body is becoming horribly soft. Of course if one has no features or bone structure one cannot remain handsome after forty. So is it worth bothering about?

*Tuesday, 16th November*

Terrible meeting at the SPAB when it was revealed that poor old Mr Horne had spent £10,000 on restoring one of their lesser houses at Goudhurst and still wanted to spend a further £1,000. No one on the committee had an inkling of this. I suggested a subcommittee of inquiry should be set up, and so they put Rick and me onto this. Horne was sent out of the room like a disgraced schoolboy and much embarrassment ensued. I notice that although decent people profess to be saddened by another's discomfiture on such occasions, they derive a nasty kick out of it. *Schadenfreude*.

* Major Hon. Sir John Coke (1880–1957); 7th son of 2nd Earl of Leicester; equerry to HM Queen Mary, 1938–53.

*Monday, 22nd November*

This evening called on Doreen Baynes, looking very delicate and frail. She thinks all laws against sexual offences should be abolished. I said, 'Even if cruelty to children is involved?' Her head shook and she said after a pause, 'Yes.' She wanted a detailed account of my Saturday in London from dawn till bedtime, in detail, nothing omitted. I said, 'Nothing, Doreen darling?' 'Oh well, you know what I don't want to hear.' She has the novelist's curiosity. She writes in bed every day till 1 o'clock, lunches alone, then walks at breakneck speed, she says often running; returns for tea to receive some friend or other; reads at dinner alone and retires to bed immediately. She says happiness consists in finding the right rut and never leaving it.

*Tuesday, 23rd November*

Lunched with Sibyl Colefax. Oriental incense from joss-sticks in the hall. Rather highbrow party consisting of the Ronald Trees* (perhaps not very highbrow), Vita Sackville-West, Willie Maugham,† Desmond MacCarthy, Ruth Draper‡ and me. I sat between pretty Mrs Tree and Ruth Draper. Latter is an enchanting woman, with great perception. She misses no nuances, has a low, modulated, seductive voice, like her sister, Mrs James. They belong to the aristocracy of American women who are exceedingly gentle in manner. She told me that her performances tire her, but she loves them. She thinks she ought to stop acting soon or she will make the mistake of most actors and actresses who do not know when to retire from the stage. She senses the kind of audience she has in front of her at once and always knows whether they have seen her before or not. She loves England. Towards the end

* Ronald Tree (1897–1976), American-born Conservative politician and society figure; m. 1st 1921 Nancy Field (for whom he had bought Sibyl Colefax's decorating business in 1944), 2nd 1947 Mary FitzGerald.

† William Somerset Maugham (1874–1965); novelist, playwright and short story writer.

‡ American-born actress and impersonator (1884–1956).

of luncheon conversation turned to the Russian temperament. MacCarthy said all Russians were children, with children's sense of fun and cruelty. He is very entertaining and laughs a lot himself like a child for the sheer fun of being alive.

*Wednesday, 24th November*

The new Lord Bearsted* came to see me. He said that several of the pictures his father gave us at Upton were not his to give. Would we please strike them off our list. I am always willing to oblige donors but I can't very well do this without my committee's consent. I have had a victory in getting authority for Lady Berwick to be paid £5 10*s*. a week for her servant's wages [at Attingham] as from the date of her husband's death [in 1947].

*Thursday, 25th November*

Having met Ruth Draper I thought I should see her on the stage. So went this evening by myself. Her monologues may not be, are not, I think, great art, but they amount to great virtuosity. It is a remarkable physical and mental feat for one woman to hold crowded audiences night after night, with matinées too. She is amusing as well as moving in the role of the Irish mother of a son killed in the 1914 War, and that of the village postmistress in 'The Return of the Soldier' in 1945, a role astonishingly evocative of a poignant subject.

*Friday, 26th November*

Dined with Sheila Plunkett [formerly de Rutzen] in the little house she has taken in Montpelier Walk. We talked of her brother Johnnie Philipps, who Sheila said was settling down and becoming more serious, working at his film and drinking less. Laughed over a story of him play-acting with their father, who when dying imagined he

* Marcus Samuel, 3rd Viscount Bearsted (1909–86); Eton contemporary of J.L.-M.

was in a railway carriage. Johnnie had to coax him back to bed on the pretence that the train was about to leave the station. Now, while we were sitting and laughing about Johnnie he was dying in his bath in Albany a mile away. He was found drowned early next morning by the night watchman who had heard the overflow of his bath water. The papers say he had a heart attack. He was thirty-three. An erratic, whizzy creature, he had charm. He led a pre-war sort of life of dotty irresponsibility which was rare and only fairly acceptable. This death has upset me without moving me to tears. I am terribly sorry for poor Sheila who loved him dearly.

*Wednesday, 1st December*

Loelia [Westminster] took me to a picture-framer in Blue Boar Yard. Wearing extremely chic clothes and wrapped in furs. Not once or twice but three times she asked for my picture to be framed in the *very cheapest possible* manner. Kind of her, but I caught the old aproned craftsman casting a glance of amazement at her expensive presence.

*Thursday, 2nd December*

Harold having dined with me at Brooks's took me across the way to Pratt's. Talk was of the appointment of the new National Trust secretary and the pains the small committee were taking to choose a man who would not interfere with Hubert Smith's and my work. Harold observed that all scandals derived from written indiscretions. He spoke too openly at Pratt's of his being ignored by the Socialist party who persistently overlook his very existence except when they make him stand for Croydon,* and then do not thank him afterwards.

* Following an election campaign during which Harold Nicolson had made little attempt to disguise his disdain for North Croydon and its residents, he had lost to the Conservative candidate by a margin of twelve thousand votes.

*Wednesday, 8th December*

I went to Belgrave Square at Lady Crewe's invitation to attend a concert given for the Keats–Shelley Committee, of which the Queen is patron. Those of us on the committee were aligned in a small room. Lady Crewe said to Jamesey in her sepulchral voice, 'I shall pass the Queen round from left to right like the port.' The Queen arrived dressed in red velvet. When my turn came to be presented Lady Crewe said, 'And you won't know Mr L.-M., of course,' which was not calculated to put either of us at ease. But the Queen replied, 'Yes *indeed*,' with marked emphasis on the last syllable. For this I give her the highest marks for she did not know me from Adam. She speaks in a clear, soft voice, is sweet and abounds in charm. Her voice is her secret weapon. It could disarm the most hostile adversary. She looked pale and would, I thought, have been improved by a little colour or rouge. We followed her upstairs to our seats. I was close to Quentin Crewe* and just behind Midi [Gascoigne]. Vita recited two odes of Keats but was nervous and a little halting. Silveri† sang Neapolitan songs in a huge, resonant voice far too big for the room. Finally Cecil Day-Lewis‡ recited the last seventeen stanzas from *Adonais* in a measured, rhythmical voice, emotional enough and yet so firm that I don't remember being more moved by a poetry reading in my life.

This evening Sarah Churchill invited me to a party given by her sister Diana Sandys, that sweet, chirpy little creature. Two men, one called Bunny Austin (not the tennis player), and Anthony Beauchamp,§ a dark gigolo with a scar (I take it he is going to marry Sarah), and Mrs Winston Churchill. I sat next to Mrs Winston at the theatre, a new revue called *Oranges and Lemons*. I don't really like her, and never did in the old days. She is jerky and precise in manner, and yet miauly; laughs and speaks as though she feared to

---

* Journalist, traveller and writer (1926–2001), who waged a lifelong battle against an incurable muscular disease; half-brother of J.L.-M's friend 'Midi' Gascoigne.

† Paolo Silveri; Italian singer.

‡ Poet (1904–72; Poet Laureate, 1968–72).

§ Photographer; m. 1949 (as her 2nd husband; diss. 1957) Sarah Churchill.

touch or swallow dirt. She is, I suspect, *au fond* snobbish, exclusive and disapproving. With her white hair she is still a beautiful woman. We had nothing to say to each other and at dinner at Sarah's flat later, all perching on chairs and sofas, I avoided her. I was very tired this evening and did not like the company at all. Don't suppose they cared for me.

*Sunday, 12th December*

Last night Henry Henry dined. He is like some big, floppy sunflower with a radiant face which one watches slowly unfold when recognition of what one is endeavouring to impart slowly dawns on him. A gentle child. Tells me he is extremely in love with someone who inadequately requites his sad passion; that he is very undersexed, is seldom aroused, and when he has his pleasure takes two whole days to recover his senses. A poor look-out.

Had a dinner party tonight of Riette Lamington and Johnnie and Mary Churchill. Johnnie unchanged, also (like H.H.) a child in his approach to life, sweet and funny. Every person and thing is a rollicking joke to him. He loves giggling with me as we used to do at our crammers in Stanway. Mary seems a perfect wife whom I hope the volatile Johnnie will retain.

*Monday, 13th December*

Charlotte Bonham Carter* gave what she calls a fork dinner at 7 o'clock and then took me to the Albert Hall. She is an extraordinary character, flitting to and fro, from one idea and one place to another. Clever, charitable and engaging. The Vere Pilkingtons,† Patrick Kinross and the Lennox Berkeleys there. Lennox had his new concerto for two pianos and orchestra played for the first time,

---

* Charlotte Ogilvy (1893–1989); idiosyncratic social figure; m. 1926 Sir Edgar Bonham Carter, colonial civil servant and member of N.T. committees.

† Charles Vere Pilkington (1905–84); director of Sotheby's, 1927–58 (Chairman, 1953–8); harpsichordist, pupil of Violet Woodhouse; m. 1936 (as her 2nd husband) Hon. Honor Philipps (1908–61), yst dau. of 1st and last Baron Kylsant.

Malcolm Sargent conducting. It was enjoyable, full of melodies and vigour. I watched Lennox sitting in profile with his long nose turned to the orchestra like a serious salmon, in his tense, shy, modest manner. At the end there was much applause. He appeared on the platform three times and bowed sweetly as though wondering why he was there. He is another childlike person. Charlotte insisted on dragging reluctant Patrick and me behind the stage to shake hands with Malcolm Sargent. Such visits to green rooms always embarrass me. I dislike seeming to be on the lion prowl.

*Thursday, 23rd December*

Today worked slackly for there is a distinct Christmas feeling in the air. All the girls and women in the office are agog. Women revel in Christmas, my Mama a genuine exception. I gave the girls some chocolates, but am cutting down on presents this year because I am so very poor.

*Friday, 24th December*

Motored to Wickhamford and stopped at Oxford to look at the Merton, Wadham and Bodleian frontispieces. At home this evening wondered how I could possibly survive Christmas: my father's thin jokes, my mother's fuss about the cooking, Deenie's fuss lest the robin might not return to its bird-bath and her radiators freeze during her absence from home. Of course I am an absolute beast.

*Christmas Day*

At least I was devout at Mass in Broadway. It was a bright sunny day and after church I motored up Willersey Hill and walked to Dover's Hill along the edge of the Costwolds overlooking the Vale. It is a fine sweep of a hemi-cycle, like a Greek amphitheatre in terraces, a curious, primitive isolated formation with distant views towards the Malvern, Bredon and Dumbleton hills. This Christmas I have visited Campden Market Hall, Hidcote, Charlecote,

Packwood and the Dial House at Knowle, which a solicitor named Parr wants to leave to the Trust.

*Friday, 31st December*

So soon after my return from several days' rest I find my nerves ajangle in the office, with nothing to account for it. It is in the mornings that I feel so ill. This evening Alvilde took me to *Scott of the Antarctic*. John Mills as Scott looked very like Peter [Scott]. Diana Churchill played the young wife, Kathleen. How strange to see featured in a film a woman whom I had known so intimately as K. She played the part quite well and K. would not have objected, I fancy. No sentiment she would have been ashamed of. It is a good film and the frostbitten heroes in their tent just as I imagined. The horror of it. How foolish I was not to have learned more about this epic story from Kathleen when she was alive. Returned and changed, and went to the Savoy with Alvilde and her child Clarissa* to join the Kenneth Clarks' party for New Year's Eve. It was horrid. Such a noise, with people whistling, pulling crackers and blowing streamers, that I could not hear a word anyone spoke. How can people enjoy this form of entertainment? I hate the New Year anyway.

* J.L.-M's future stepdaughter (b. 1934), o.c. of Anthony and Alvilde Chaplin; m. 1957 Michael Luke.

# 1949

# 1949

*This year saw two emotional upheavals in J.L.-M's life: his falling in love with his future wife Alvilde Chaplin; and his father's death from cancer at the age of sixty-nine.*

*Sunday, 2nd January*

Helen and Johnnie Dashwood and Alvilde Chaplin dined. Johnnie embarrassed Helen by *risqué*, schoolboy stories, and Alvilde looked unamused. Yet next day I received from Alvilde a note of warm thanks and invitation to dine Monday week. I began, with the New Year, writing my Renaissance book this weekend, but was disconsolate.

*Monday, 3rd January*

Called on Sibyl Colefax who was lying in her bed, coughing. Yet she talked and made plans for the future and was interested in everything. She is a courageous woman. She looked like a tiny dried leaf that is always crumpling at both ends. I asked her about Kathleen Kennet who always told me that she disliked Sibyl for her lion-hunting. Just a slight case of pot and kettle. Sibyl told me that she knew K. very well when she was engaged to Scott who was always unhappy with K. on account of her 'cheapness'. Said Sibyl, 'She was a self-advertiser. She dramatised her widowhood, seeking publicity at all turns.' Sibyl also told me that K. was a snob who tried to vamp all distinguished men. How odd it is to hear conflicting explanations of mutual dislike from two women at different times, both women of more than normal intelligence and integrity.

*Friday, 7th January*

This morning went to the dentist who gave my swollen face one look and said in his heartiest manner that the old tooth was on its last legs and must come out. *His* face was wreathed in sadistic jubilation. When I begged not to have gas he said I could have an injection. He accordingly telephoned the anaesthetist who came into the room as though he had been waiting next door at the keyhole. What a strange experience to be awake and alive, and within sixty seconds, as it were, dead to the world. Scarcely had the needle come out of my arm than I was off, but not before they put a sponge of gas before my mouth, which was cruel and deceitful of them. I was under for thirty minutes and the first thing I remember on coming round was a sensation of acute regret at leaving an elysium and returning to a real and less agreeable world. It was proof that time does not exist and is a figment of the imagination.

I talked this over with Doreen Baynes this evening. She was convinced that my experience had been of the other world and the fact that I recall it as elysium proved her point. Of course I was not actually dead, because my heart was beating. So in what world was I? On the threshold of another? Doreen could give no satisfactory answer. No one ever can.

*Monday, 10th January*

Dined with the Chaplins who have rented Cecil Beaton's house in Pelham Place. Amongst others were Paz Subercaseaux,* Eddie Marsh, and a new young man called Christopher Warner, who is tall, dark and handsome, a tea-leaf-fortune-teller's delight. Eddie tells countless stories of people he has known in the dim past and recites reams of poetry whenever the conversation touches one hair's breadth upon a quotation. He must have been the perfect Edwardian house party guest. He told us how he saw Sarah Bernhardt† act in 1887, an experience he can never forget. Anthony

---

* Wife of Léon Subercaseaux, Chilean Minister to the Court of St James.

† French actress (1844–1923).

Chaplin teased me a lot in pretending to be pro-Russian. He asked, who would prefer not to live under Bolshevism than not live at all? I said I would.

*Thursday, 13th January*

Dined with Cyril Connolly and Lys.* Alan Pryce-Jones and Alan Ross† there. Alan [P.-J.] likes to pretend that he is sodden with middle-aged defeatism and gloom whereas he is the soul of youthful gaiety and charm. Cyril is the most brilliant talker I have listened to. He surprised me by saying he had read no Trollope, no Dickens and only one Jane Austen novel. After dinner a lot of people dribbled in for champagne. I believe Cyril and Lys often entertain like this. I left at 12.30 without saying goodbye. Must write.

*Sunday, 16th January*

Eardley, Alvilde Chaplin and Loelia Westminster dined. Eardley pronounced Loelia 'brave' in the French sense, and Alvilde beautiful.

*Wednesday, 19th January*

Dined with Alvilde and Anthony Chaplin; the Sachie Sitwells there. Anthony, who is sensitive about such things, was furious with Georgia for scolding him for not wearing a dinner jacket. Anthony claimed that he had worthier things to spend his money on, and I agreed with him, having no money of my own to spend on anything.

*Thursday, 20th January*

To the theatre with Alvilde, Ibsen's *Wild Duck*, most lugubrious but excellent.

---

* Lys Lubbock; editorial assistant of Cyril Connolly on *Horizon* who was effectively his common-law wife at this time.

† Poet and editor (1922–2001).

*Friday, 21st January*

Dined with Sibyl Colefax in her house. She was dressed and up, and though more bent than ever, quite bright. A most excellent meal, the best I have had in England for years. I knew everyone there but the Angleseys, and sat next to her.* Nigel [Nicolson], who is devoted and wished to marry her, and Diane Abdy present. Also John Sparrow,† Paz Subercaseaux and Alvilde, with whom I went. Sitting with Sibyl after dinner we discussed sanctity and S. said quite seriously that I was probably a saint. Felt obliged to disabuse her.

*Saturday, 22nd January*

At 11 went to Peter Derwent's memorial service at St Mark's, North Audley Street. The choir sang well and the music was beautifully chosen. Alvilde was present, wearing a snood over her hair, looking very romantic like a nun. We walked away from the service together and there, ahead of us, was Nancy, not walking but running along the pavement to Heywood Hill's shop. We took a taxi to [Thomas] Cook's to inquire about fares to Portofino where she has asked me to stay in mid February. I fear I cannot afford to go.

*Sunday, 30th January*

Finished chapter on the French Renaissance. This evening dined at Alex Beattie's‡ studio in Fulham very late, with Alan Lennox-Boyd and Gerald de Gaury.§ The last told me he is writing the history of the Meccan pilgrimages. Says he can only be happy in the East. I can't make out whether he is a second Lawrence of Arabia or a complete fraud. Beattie is a good-looking and amiable ass. He asked me if I had ever been in love, and when I said 'Yes, of course', seemed surprised. He vouchsafed that he liked sleeping

---

* Shirley Morgan; m. 1948 Henry Paget, 7th Marquess of Anglesey (b. 1922).

† Barrister (1906–92); Warden of All Souls, 1953–76; friend of Harold Nicolson.

‡ Friend of Alan Lennox-Boyd referred to in entry for 20 April 1948.

§ English army officer and Arabist; intimate friend of the Regent of Iraq.

in bed with people he is fond of, but did not care much for sex. It left him cold. He is, I suspect, a Narcissus. 'As for women,' he said, 'they are so damned soft. Their bodies have no firmness.'

*Wednesday, 2nd February*

X.* dined with me here and we drank Beaujolais over the fire. Became very tipsy. I had the greatest difficulty getting her away for she wished to stay the night – a thing obviously out of the question. This sounds as though I were as virtuous as St Antony and like him desired by every female I encounter. Both assumptions are very far from being the case. When one is a foot away from X. her cat-grey eyes dilate like those of a film star in a close-up. She is very bewitching and seductive, is always gay, loves the ludicrous and makes me laugh.

*Friday, 4th February*

Stayed last night at Long Crichel with my dear Eardley. Thank God, with him my relations are absolutely straightforward. The relief of it. We like to believe we make a perfect combination for we criticise each other mercilessly, usually laughing like mad, for alone we are very funny. A third person overhearing us might not think so.

*Tuesday, 8th February*

A long special meeting of the Finance Committee to discuss the Memorandum to be submitted to the Gowers Committee.† It is agreed that our points are of the utmost importance. We have

* Identified in original typescript as Anne Rosse.

† Committee set up by Sir Stafford Cripps, chaired by the civil servant Sir Ernest Gowers, to consider the Government's role in architectural conservation. It reported in June 1950 to the effect that country houses were an important part of the national heritage, and the state ought to provide grants and tax exemptions to enable their owners to carry on living in them. This eventually resulted in the setting up (1953) of Historic Buildings Councils, to provide endowment grants to both the N.T. and (under stringent conditions) private owners.

reached a crisis in the Trust's affairs. I strongly deprecated a proposal that we should surrender to the Government all 'museum' houses, *i.e.*, those which the families have left and which may not be inhabited again, because I foresee all families leaving these anachronistic white elephants in time. And then what will be left to us?

Dinner party given by Y. When the other guests left I stayed behind, thinking no evil, fearing no evil. Silly fool. I had put my head in a noose, and soon scented danger, too late. My hostess expected me to make love to her. How insatiable these women are. Any youngish man in a calm, it seems. Inventing an urgent excuse – one cannot have a committee meeting at midnight – I bolted, and heard the clang of the front door behind me. It made a terrible sound which echoed down the street. 'Heaven has no rage like love to hatred turned, Nor hell a fury like a woman scorned,' it seemed to shout at me. Passionless friendship is all I seek these days.

*Tuesday, 15th February*

On Sunday Alvilde telephoned me from Amalfi urging me to join them in Rome. This evening I consulted Rick [Stewart-Jones] who instantly offered to pay for my ticket there and back, which is angelic and typical of him. He said he preferred it to be a gift than a loan. So now I shall fly to Rome on Saturday. I dined with Paz Subercaseaux who gave me 7,000 lire for my journey which was equally angelic. Jamesey, who was present, talked in raptures about Norway. Of course he is in love with a Norwegian, as he confessed to me after dinner.

*Wednesday, 16th February*

Dined with the Aberconways* in their new house left to Christabel by Samuel Courtauld,† in North Audley Street. A splendid house

* Henry Duncan McLaren, 2nd Baron Aberconway (1879–1953); m. 1910 Christabel Macnaghten.

† Industrialist and art collector (1876–1947).

of Burlington date and style, with gallery on the grand-miniature scale; a central coffered dome. Many well-known French impressionist painters (Courtauld). Opposite my place at dinner a ravishing Renoir of women with parasols in a punt on blue, sunlit water. I sat next to Betty Hussey, to whom I am devoted for she is gay and buxom, natural and forthright, and Lady Elizabeth Hofmannsthal, who is a great beauty with the soft, peony skin of all Pagets. The David Bowes-Lyons, he insinuating all sorts of forbidden things in veiled terms and proposing a trip with me in the spring. He is an extraordinary, complicated, perhaps not-so-buttoned-up man who cannot call a spade a spade and is a walking riddle. Anthony Blunt and Christopher Hussey with whom I had Tudor talk. Hussey is sure that Longleat is of French inspiration. Lady Aberconway, with her milk complexion, wants to appear a pretty goose, but is as clever and calculating as a monkey. He, all affability and big business. He holds up a hand as a dog holds up a paw to be taken. But one is not disposed to stroke him.

*Saturday, 19th February*

It is heaven being in Rome again after so short an interval. I drove in an old *carozza* round the Pincio to the Hotel de Ville where I supposed the Chaplins to be staying. But no, they were at the Inghilterra. Went at 7 o'clock to their room there which is Henry Jamesean, not unlike Brown's Hotel, Dover Street. Alvilde has a white pekinese called Foo. Anthony asked if I wished to see his toad found at Paestum. Whereupon he fetched a chamber pot covered with a face towel. In it lives the toad which he says is over sixty years old, possibly eighty, and has all its life been in the same garden avoiding the peasants and death, since all primitive people kill toads for being evil, which they are not. Anthony also has several lizards and frogs in cardboard boxes. They seem to be given nothing to eat yet thrive. Toads can live for months without food. We dined sumptuously at Alberotti's restaurant where D'Arcy Osborne once took me. I am so happy to be here – lovely Frascati wine, scampi and chocolate cake. It is warm tonight. No topcoat needed.

*Tuesday, 22nd February*

This morning Alvilde and I motored to the Vatican Museum and walked down the long galleries to the Sistine Chapel, straining our necks and eyes towards the ceiling which she assured me had faded since she last saw it twenty years ago. Again I thought the marble screen as fine as anything there. We were horrified by the damage done to the Loggie walls by pencilled and incised names within recent years. The lower part of these famous arabesques is totally obliterated, both paint and plaster work. Even the Raphael walls of the Stanze have been mutilated. They could easily be protected by glass panels. These Stanze always leave something to be desired. True, they are much faded and cracked. But the scale of the murals is too big for the low rooms. We went into St Peter's. The overall grey marble makes a peculiarly fitting background to the opulent golds and reds and greens. I made her kiss St Peter's toe which she did with a reluctant grace, not to mention a positive grimace.

*Wednesday, 23rd February*

At 9.30 we left for Florence. I got awful sciatica in the tiny motor. Alvilde is the perfect travelling companion. Anthony is fun but one has to play up to him continuously. Sun dazzling, slightly cold, with wind on the hills. An exhausting drive for the road winds and winds and the hills are very steep. Stopped in Siena for coffee. A. and I visited the cathedral and admired the floor paving, or what we could see of it. Anthony refuses to look at buildings or pictures. He will only stop to look for frogs in ponds. This affectation is silly for a cultivated man, and maddening for A. The road between Siena and Florence covers beautiful country. Tuscany with its gentle hills and little towns, large villas, vine terraces and cypresses, is Paradise, Classical not Picturesque like the country round Assisi and Perugia. We stay at the Grand Hotel, Florence, in great comfort, overlooking the Arno. The view from our bedrooms, each with a terrace, on the top floor, is exquisite, a rushing fall of Arno water below, the campanile and cupola of Santo Spirito and the bulk of the Carmine opposite us; and the cypress-clad rise of Bellosguardo beyond.

*Thursday, 24th February*

What a day! The sun so hot that I sat on my terrace without a coat, yet inside the churches icy cold. Alvilde and I sightsaw this morning, first the Botticelli of St Augustine in the Ognissanti church next door, then to the Uffizi to feast on Lorenzo Credi and Bronzino. In the entrance there is an Etruscan torso of a man two centuries BC, massive and powerful just like one of the rowers of a skiff on the Arno this afternoon. We ate *zabaione* in the piazza before plunging into the sombre Duomo.

Harold Acton lunched with us at the hotel. Was wickedly funny reviling the English literati whom he dislikes, including poor Raymond Mortimer who gave his book a filthy review. He said he was a Jew, which R. hotly denies, being connected with Meyer and Mortimer, the military outfitters; that as a young Bohemian in Paris he sported a cloak and broad-brimmed floppy hat, and was shouted at by a passer-by, '*Va-t-en, folle bergère!*'

I admire Anthony for the independence of his views, if I do not admire all his views. He dresses well and is always spruce. When at luncheon the waiters made A. take her Pekinese out of the dining-room, Anthony said to me, 'I wonder what they would say if they knew I had two toads in my pockets.' This afternoon instead of going out he sat on his terrace reading Shakespeare's sonnets.

We dined at the Buca Lapi restaurant in the basement of an ancient palace, drinking delicious Orvieto white wine. A guitarist and violinist were playing Cimarosa, who was Napoleon's favourite composer, Anthony says.

*From Florence they travelled via Pisa to Portofino, where they stayed for a week, first at a hotel, then at a 'castelletto' lent by the Chaplins' friends the Cliffords. This visit was 'divine' and 'romantic', despite Alvilde's pekinese falling ill and Jim suffering from toothache. 'Such laughter we have. They say I must come and live with them in Paris. Alvilde is incredibly generous and pays for everything.' On 5 March J.L.-M. parted from them at Genoa, taking the night train to Paris.*

*Sunday, 6th March*

How rude the French are after the outgiving Italians. I found myself sitting next to the Duke of St Albans* in the train from Paris. He is a non-stop talker, but very funny. Hitherto I had only met him casually at Brooks's. I was furious that at Dover he paid no duty on two bottles of brandy and six of champagne whereas I had to pay 32 shillings on one bottle of liqueur. He was delighted and said it was because he was wearing a hat and I was not, but I believe it was because he is a Duke and I am not. In the carriage to London he spoke about King Edward VII's petty nature and his awful behaviour with women, as though his own was impeccable. He said that whenever the King saw a pretty woman he sent his equerries to fetch and present her to him, then would invite her to tea while commanding her not to come wearing a hat, or veiled. He said, quite irrelevantly, 'Oliver Messel is a pervert, isn't he?' I said, 'I don't think so.' I will not subscribe to the notion that homosexuality is wicked or disgraceful.

*Monday, 14th March*

I have been back a week. My mind is in turmoil. A fire has been lit. How absurdly coy and genteel one is, even to oneself, about one's emotions, when they are serious. Here the weather has been bitterly cold, unrelieved by sun. A sore throat has turned into a cold, so I retired to bed on Saturday until today.

Jack Rathbone,† our new Secretary, has started work. We were friends at Oxford. He is going to be a success with my colleagues. Have received several post cards from Alvilde who arrives in London tomorrow.

---

* Osborne 'Obby' de Vere Beauclerk, 12th Duke of St Albans (1874–1964).

† John Francis Warre Rathbone (1909–95); solicitor, member of Liverpool shipping family; Secretary of N.T., 1949–68.

*Tuesday, 15th March*

I lunched with Harold at the Travellers. He ordered a bottle of wine of which I foolishly partook, for I had vowed on my return from Italy never to drink in the middle of the day. The old men at the Travellers looked askance at Harold, the Socialist, surrounded by young men whom he corrupts with wine and seditious talk, the fools. But Harold is as dear as ever and enhances the lives of his friends, young and old. I drove him to Knole and we looked at the garden wall. He was deeply shocked. He thought it had been repaired in a way an urban corporation would have done it and is going to complain to the Committee.

Back in London, I told Harold I was going to meet Alvilde on the Golden Arrow and wanted to buy flowers for her. He dissuaded me, saying it was a Continental and bedint thing to do. I met her and she dined here, bringing me some ham and liqueur as a present – not bedint.

*Thursday, 17th March*

Lunched with Sibyl Colefax at the Dorchester in a fearfully over-heated room. I thought I should die and sweated like those spongy water ferns met with in Italian grottoes. My cold is now feverish. Sat next to Juliet Duff* and Lys Connolly. Alvilde there but we could not speak. Walked away with James who told me his mother is to have a serious abdominal operation. Tonight Alvilde took me to the French ballet – *Carmen*, vigorous and sexy – and we dined at the Dorchester. Her beauty is proud, guarded, even shrouded. Rather Pre-Raphaelite in manner, not in substance. She has had a sad married life, if it can be called married. Cecil Beaton invited us both to meet Nancy for dinner, but we decided we would be happier alone.

---

* Lady Juliet Lowther (1881–1965); o.c. of 4th Earl of Lonsdale; m. 1903 Sir Robert Duff, 2nd Bt; mother of J.L.-M's friend Sir Michael Duff, 3rd Bt (1907–80).

*Saturday, 19th March*

Stayed in all day on account of my cold. Alvilde sent a car for me and we went to *The Heiress*, an absolutely splendid production with Ralph Richardson and Peggy Ashcroft. We dined at home over her champagne. I took her back to the Dorchester and left her there. My cold is still very bad. I am in a daze. I do not quite realise what has happened to me. This is the first time that a woman I have loved has loved me. I say 'loved' which is totally different to 'lusted after'. I have had plenty of reciprocal lust of one kind and another. I want to be with her all the time. My cold makes the situation more unreal, and me surely unappetising. Which goes to show . . . What? Her nobility and sincerity.

*Sunday, 20th March*

Stay indoors all day except to go to Mass. Still feel ill. Try to write fitfully. The reality of this love dawns on me slowly like a creeping paralysis. One becomes a victim to a great power that is irresistible. How selfish I have been hitherto, all the stony way to middle age, in full control of my emotions, and probably cruel at times. I met A. this evening. We tried Soho and could get in nowhere, so ended at the Mirabelle where we had a very expensive and perfectly filthy meal. Then returned home and talked and made plans for the summer. We are very happy.

*Monday, 21st March*

A. and I lunched at the oyster bar, Wilton's. This evening she came round here and we ate honey sandwiches and drank tea, sitting on the floor in front of the fire. She left to dine with Anthony who came over from Paris this evening.

*Tuesday, 22nd March*

Motored Alvilde from the Dorchester to Victoria. Put her into the Golden Arrow, and left. She gave me a letter and I gave her one, which we agreed not to open until we had parted. Then went to the ballet, Danilova in *Coppélia*, with Sheila Plunkett. Very enjoyable. Dined at the Lyric. S. is a dear, so gay and laughing, and very pretty and distinguished.

*Wednesday, 23rd March*

Jack Rathbone is very sensible and understanding, and grasps the situation of our peculiar, sensitive, dedicated staff, which must be totally unlike the staff of most organisations, and maddening to an outsider.

*Thursday, 24th March*

Depressed because no letter from A. today and as yet – 9 p.m. – no telephone call.

This morning I went on a small deputation to give evidence before the Gowers Committee, in a fine early Georgian room at the Treasury. It was an interesting and enjoyable experience. I sat between Esher and Anthony Blunt. Dear Lord Esher, who never lets one down, contributed wise and weighty interpolations. How excellent he is dealing with civil service minds. I found myself speaking up rather a lot. After all, I know a good deal about this subject. The issue lies between us and the Ministry of Works. I felt that general sympathy was with us, and believed we made a good case.

Jamesey came at 6 o'clock. I told him about Alvilde. At first he made wild and preposterous guesses. When I disclosed, he was amazed and delighted, and encouraged unreservedly. When he left I got worried, but at 11 o'clock she rang up. Line as clear as though she were in the next room. Her usual firm, take-it-or-leave-it, fierce little voice. I knew she was pleased really, and I went to bed happy.

*Wednesday, 30th March*

Got home before 6 o'clock to find a note from my father. He has seen a specialist who reports a growth on his bladder. He is to go to a home in Queen's Gate next Monday to have bladder opened up and diagnosed lest it be malignant. This worries me a good deal. Mama is to stay here for a week at least. A. telephoned as arranged at 6 o'clock. She writes every day, as do I.

Went to *Coppélia* again, with Lady Anderson in the Royal Box. Danilova ill and Swanilda taken by Moira Shearer* who is far better, with beautiful arms and hands. We ate, in a little room behind the box, a course during each interval, most civilised. The box and room so elegant and Edwardian. I sat next to a very young Princess Murat who is in London to learn typewriting, and Susan Lowndes that was, now married to a Portuguese and living in Lisbon, charming. Was driven back to Belgrave Square in Chips Channon's Rolls. Had a drink with him and Peter Coats in Peter's bedroom, he being ill in bed. Chips told me astounding news that he and Peter go dressed up to fancy dress balls. There are two or three a week, entirely homosexual, where the boys masquerade as women, and he and Peter dance. The boys are gents, many in the Brigade of Guards.

*Saturday, 2nd April*

Felt quite calm and content this morning having spoken to A. last night. By the first post received two letters from her. While reading them I was handed a telegram by Emily asking me to ring again tonight because she is anxious. Goodness, the absurdities of love!

Just before luncheon came a letter from Dr Astley, my father's doctor at Wickhamford, announcing that he had received a report from the London specialist of 'exceedingly grave' news. The tumour on the bladder was almost certainly malignant. I telephoned the nursing clinic where Papa is to go on Monday and spoke to the matron. She advised that we should await the chemical examination of the piece of tumour to be extracted on Monday before telling Mama, who as yet knows nothing; not till then will they be sure they can operate and remove the whole

* Ballerina and actress (1926–2006), whom J.L.-M. later got to know in South of France; m. 1950 (Sir) Ludovic Kennedy.

tumour. If bad, I gather nothing can be done. I telephoned Dick* at Shaw. He is a great comfort and help and strongly advised against telling any member of the family until the diagnosis is known.

I telephoned Wickhamford this evening and both parents spoke to me from their beds, sounding quite cheerful and cosy, which made me feel how pathetic they were in their ignorance. I telephoned Paris and spoke to A., who is unhappy because she received no letter today. Heavens, what mixed emotions!

*Monday, 4th April*

Met Mama and Papa at Paddington at 11.30 and motored him to the Queen's Gate Clinic. Took her to lunch at the Allies Club. At 4.30 she and I went back to the Clinic and found him coming round after the operation. The specialist removed two small growths in the bladder through the penis, which is almost unbelievable. Mama is staying with me in the flat, she having my room, I sleeping in the back of Geoffrey's drawing-room. She insisted on meeting, with me, the specialist's assistant, who told her Papa would have to return every three to six months for observation, which alarmed her. I made an appointment to meet the specialist.

*Tuesday, 5th April*

At 6 o'clock I saw the specialist who told me that he had indeed removed two malignant growths. He assured me my father could only live two years at most, as the growths were bound to return. He advised against telling either him or my mother the truth unless the analysis next week reveals something even more serious than what he has already discovered.

*Monday, 11th April*

Papa and Mama went home today. They seemed so pleased and I pray that by some miracle he may be all right. Mama very sweet

* J.L.-M's yr bro. Richard Crompton Lees-Milne (1910–84); managed family cotton mill at Shaw nr Oldham; m. 1935 (as her 2nd husband) Elaine *née* Brigstocke.

and considerate yet I find her a little tiring because she cannot concentrate on one topic at a time. She says she will not come to London this summer to meet Hugh MacDonnell [Canadian admirer] because she is now determined to do nothing to distress Papa. Evidently at the age of sixty-five she is still moved to love. She advised me to love Alvilde while I could, adding that this was perhaps not the advice a mother should give a son. James called last night while I was with Papa. They got on like a house on fire.

*Wednesday, 13th April*

Dined tonight with John Lehmann* at his covetable house in Egerton Crescent. Guests were Sibyl Colefax, Ethel Sands, Peter Quennell and an unknown woman. Much Sibyl talk of famous people she had known, such as Robbie Ross.† John Lehmann and Peter Q. complained that there were in England no young authors with any style; that in their day their elders, like Lytton Strachey, kept them up to the mark. How often have not these sorts of complaint been exchanged by the middle-aged? Peter's wit and brilliance always impress me but his malice is without limit. I relish it because, so far, it has not been directed at my face, and what is directed at my back I cannot mind, so long as a kind friend does not repeat it.

*Thursday, 14th April*

The office shut at noon for the holidays. I, who had decided after all to go to Jouy, collected my ticket and, having worked in the afternoon, bought A. an Easter egg made of Sèvres porcelain and another smaller one for Clarissa [Chaplin] and left by the 5 o'clock plane for Paris. A wonderful day but I felt so full of misgivings that I fortified myself with brandy and water. Landed at Le Bourget and was met by A. looking beautiful and radiant at the Invalides. She took me to a restaurant for dinner, I consuming a whole bottle of wine and a liqueur with the result that, although blissfully happy to

* Writer, poet, editor and publisher (1906–87).

† Friend and literary executor of Oscar Wilde (1869–1918).

be with her, I was reduced to a state of nervous idiocy. We drove to Jouy-en-Josas. Her house, Le Mé Chaplin, most picturesquely set on a hill with a Turneresque view over a valley, crossed by a Louis XIV aqueduct in the background. The village of Jouy hidden by misty trees below. The moon was shining in the sky, the nightingales singing like sopranos, everything as romantic as could be desired while, arm-in-arm, we walked into the garden and into the house where Anthony was playing Mozart on the piano.

*Good Friday, 15th April*

The actual house is modern and unbeautiful but filled with A's pretty things. Doors of glass and huge windows open upon a garden of enchantment. It is a summer retreat. We went in the morning to the village. The church all shut and dark and dead, as though God deliberately withholding himself from me. This evening the four of us (Clarissa is here) motored to Dampière and looked at the outside of the Luynes château, most impressive, Mansard's work, with detached wings and forecourt and, on the far side of the road, a stone balustraded 'lay-by' as it is called today in Great West Road jargon. We dined and drank Suze which tastes of gentian. Anthony behaves wonderfully to me. We are a sort of blood brothers. His conversation with Clarissa, aged fifteen, about his love affairs and sex life makes my hair stand on end, but not hers evidently. How much, I wonder, should one believe?

*Tuesday, 19th April*

I return today, A. having motored me to Paris. This visit has exceeded my dreams. Perfect weather, sun shining every day and moon at night. The eyes of God did not blink for one second. The country at its zenith, the hyacinths and tulips out by day, the nightingales and tree frogs by night. Anthony took us to a marsh where on warm nights they congregate and sing in thousands. He says their voices were the first animal voices heard on earth – a very impressive thought. I sat on the terrace of my room writing, or in the garden reading, talking and laughing. Every half hour A. would come to me, or I would look for her. Anthony is delighted because A. is made happy. It is all A's, the house, the money, everything. Was there ever a more topsy-turvy business? They have never lived as man and wife and A. says she hardly knows how Clarissa was born.

One morning we walked about Versailles, round the Trianon and the Temple d'Amour. Another day we took a picnic luncheon and drove to Chartres, never seen by me before. Surely no blue glass like this exists anywhere else in the world. The solemn grey cathedral is untouched by time and accident.

*Thursday, 21st April*

Motored today to Biddlesden Park, close to Stowe, in well-wooded Buckinghamshire country. In 1937 I went to see this house for the National Trust and recommended acceptance. Now the same owner, Colonel Badger and wife, very nice people, entertained me again to luncheon and showed me around. I had forgotten it entirely and after this second visit read my first report made twelve years ago and was surprised at the things I had noticed. I then motored to Wickhamford and stayed the night. It was Papa's sixty-ninth birthday. He is thinner and does not eat much. Deenie and Colonel Sidney, lately widowed, dined and we drank champagne in celebration of this melancholy little event. Colonel Sidney is seventy today and is absolutely miserable.

*Monday, 25th April*

After a National Buildings Record meeting I met Alvilde at Kensington air station and motored her to the Dorchester. The Bearsteds travelled over in the same plane. As I said to A., one can never get away with any secret, however much one tries. Therefore it is better not to try.

*Thursday, 28th April*

A. and I went to Paris by air this afternoon, I having to make untruthful excuses at the office, and feeling guilty and unhappy.

She gave me a little gold toothpick as a present. We dined at Albert's again and motored to Jouy. We stopped at the same corner of the road near the village to listen to the same nightingale. Anthony remains in London and Clarissa away. Terrible black moments of despair are mercifully redeemed by moments of unadulterated bliss. I suppose this is often the case. Neither can be described.

On Friday morning we were taken round Versailles by the curator, a young man called Van der Kemp,* previously arranged by A. I was so shy about my bad French that I could not converse intelligently. I feel desperately ashamed because when I left Grenoble University in 1927 I spoke like a bird. Van der Kemp took us not only into the state rooms but the *petits appartements* of the Pompadour and du Barry, not seen by the public. *Petits* they are, and enchanting. In Marie Antoinette's boudoir her own clock played tunes for us, little airs specially composed for it by Mozart, Glück and others. The pathos of it. These rooms must be the most exquisite in the world. In my youth I used to despise French architecture for being effeminate and effete. How I dared, contemptible fool that I was. The prejudices of adolescence make one blush in remembrance. We walked upon the lead roof of the palace and admired the formal rides and parterres.

We went to George Chavchavadze's concert of Mozart and Schumann concerti, lovely works which A. said he played badly – he had a horribly inflamed eye; then to a party the Chavchavadzes gave in Noël Coward's flat in the Place Vendôme. Awful, it was. A. says French society is less intellectual and more superficial than English. It is certainly more sophisticated and alarming.

Saturday we went to Chantilly. Had the most excellent luncheon I ever ate, and then round the castle, looking at the pictures – the Clouet drawings and Fouquet illuminations. To tea at the Duff Coopers'†, a delightful Louis XV villa with an English garden lolling down to a lake with weeping willows and a cascade.

---

* Gérald van der Kemp (1912–2002); museum curator and writer.

† They had settled at Chantilly after his retirement as Ambassador in 1947.

The Walter Elliots* staying. She a red-faced, horsey-looking English woman, yet clever and non-horsey, but plain and badly dressed. He speaks with a broad Scotch accent. Lady Diana wearing trousers and cowboy jacket with large silver buttons and cowboy hat. She is very offhand. When I left she was lounging across a chair, did not get up or proffer a hand, so I mumbled goodbye and followed A. out.

We are ecstatically happy alone, and dined at home. All Sunday spent in Jouy in the sun. A. is considered one of the best-dressed women in France, which for an English woman is some compliment.

*Tuesday, 10th May*

Jamie Caffery† dined with me at Brooks's. I drank too much – two glasses of sherry, half bottle burgundy and one glass port – and felt ill next day. When shall I ever learn? Caffery is a handsome-ugly young tough of twenty-nine, with fine straight hair like powdered gold. Face cruel in repose and mouth of no shape. Comes from the American upper crust, whatever that means. He told me he has a great-grandmother alive. His sister has a child of ten, so the old lady is a great-great-grandmother. Unusual.

*Friday, 13th May*

This evening after my committees I met A. at Thurloe Square and we motored off for the weekend. We stayed the night at Harleyford Manor on the Thames. This was the best night's lodging we were to have, for the food was excellent and the beds comfortable. Otherwise a squalid, adulterous place run by peroxide blondes. Nothing dusted, tooth tumblers unwashed. Yet still a country house with Clayton family pictures on the walls, a lovely house

* Rt Hon. Walter Elliot, MP (1888–1958); former Secretary of State for Scotland; m. (2nd) 1934 Katharine (1903–94), dau. of Sir Charles Tennant, 1st Bt, cr. life peeress as Baroness Elliot of Harwood, 1958, known as 'the Happy Hippo'.

† Friend of Stuart Preston.

once, a true riverside villa built by Sir Robert Taylor.* We were told the proprietor was a Clayton, a curious *déclassé* sort of man, as much gone to seed as his house, only less handsome.

*Saturday, 14th May*

Poor A. trying to choke down a bad cold. We motored to Bibury and stayed at the Swan, she spending the day at Hatherop Castle school with Clarissa whose confirmation took place today.

*Sunday, 15th May*

We took Clarissa and Barbara Moray's† daughter Arabella Stuart‡ out from school for the day, starting with a drink before luncheon with David Stuart§ at his house in Coln St Aldwyns. He looks a sweet, pretty boy of eighteen, whereas he is already a widower, for his wife died giving birth to a son. David lives here with the baby and late wife's ten-year-old daughter by former husband. After lunching at Bibury we drove to Newark Park [Gloucestershire] for me to see the house offered to the Trust. It is of little importance and the most desolate and gloomy place imaginable, miles from anywhere. The house, basically a mid-sixteenth-century hunting-box, has one window of that date with pediment over Corinthian columns. Otherwise done over in late eighteenth century, with stucco composition and fake battlements. Interior of simple, classical decoration. The site overlooking a Cotsworld coomb with overgrown view towards the Severn estuary, unsurpassed. We left this Wagnerian haunt for Nether Lypiatt. During tea a sudden storm arose out of a blue sky. Lightning struck the water tank at the top of the house, burst a main pipe and flooded the drawing

---

* Architect (1714–88); built Harleyford Manor *c.* 1755.

† Barbara Murray of New York; m. (2nd) 1924 Francis Stuart (b. 1892), who s. 1930 as 18th Earl of Moray and died 1943; wartime lover of Tom Mitford.

‡ Lady Arabella Stuart (b. 1934); later a cookery writer; m. Mark Boxer, cartoonist (1931–88).

§ Nephew (1924–99) of 18th Earl of Moray; m. (1st) 1945 Grizel Gillilan (d. 1948); s. father as 2nd Viscount Stuart of Findhorn, 1971.

room, ruining the ceiling. Our hosts were desperately searching for buckets and in their panic producing tea cups to stem the devastating tide. What a bore children are! The two girls [Clarissa and Arabella] giggled over the disaster like zanies. I never know how one should treat them. I adopt the jocular attitude until I, and they, grow tired.

*Alvilde, who could only spend a limited time in England owing to her French tax residence, returned to Jouy, where J.L.-M. rejoined her for the first weekend of June. It was something of a* ménage à quatre, *Anthony Chaplin having also invited his young English lover (and eventual second wife) Rosemary Lyttelton.**

*Saturday, 4th June*

We are a curious party *à quatre*, for Anthony's inamorata Rosemary Lyttelton is staying. She sleeps upstairs near him and I on the next floor next to A. Rosemary is very pretty and very slight, too thin perhaps for some tastes, but evidently not for others'. As A. says, she is *racée*. Her little face is dead-white, her hair auburn which glistens in the sunlight. She reminds me of the young Queen Elizabeth. She is musical, talented and extremely intelligent, well read for her age, and much in love with Anthony who pretends to us to be tired of her because she is too clinging. This is nonsense, of course, and a pose. He treats her very sweetly, however. Anthony has breakfast with A. in her bedroom always, plying her with outrageous questions about us.

This afternoon we motored to Fontainebleau where we went round the apartments which display a wonderful sequence of decoration and furnishing from the time of François Premier to that of Napoleon. I find the F. Premier style slightly sickening, like the monarch himself, a bounder, who was also straitlaced and lascivious.

---

* Rosemary Lyttelton (1922–2003), dau. of Oliver Lyttelton (1893–1972; cr. Viscount Chandos, 1954), businessman and Conservative statesman; m. (as his 2nd wife) 3rd Viscount Chaplin, 1950.

At Fontainebleau is the best of the genre to be found anywhere in France. I am possibly mistaken in despising it, for every style that is distinctive and earnest should be respected, if it cannot be liked. An architectural historian must learn to evaluate every style and not allow his judgements to be swayed by fashionable quirks and prejudices.

*Thursday, 9th June*

Met A. at the Ritz at midday. We went to the Burlington Arcade for her to choose a ring for me. I have given her my Trinity ring which is being reduced in size to fit her tiny finger. We realise this exchange is sentimental but believe it to be the best troth plight available. She will wear what I have worn for eleven years. As I cannot wear one of hers she has bought me an old gold one, very pretty, which she put on my finger in the taxi cab. Our love is now established and permanent.

Went to a cocktail party given by the Rosses at Oliver Messel's house. Anne greeted me by throwing her arms round my neck, saying, 'Is it true that you are in love with that hard little thing Alvilde?' And Harold Acton made some reference to it. Thus taken aback I remained dumb and blushing. I won't suffer any criticism of A. to pass. Nor do I want to make a fool of myself, and incidentally her, by showing indignation. So decided the best thing was to turn away and talk to someone else.

*J.L.-M. now faced a month's separation from Alvilde, during which he brooded on the problems facing their relationship.*

I dined with Harold [Nicolson] at the Travellers. Over a bottle of champagne I told him I needed his advice how best I could work half-time for the National Trust in order to spend the other half with A. in France. Harold mumbled that love was a wonderful thing which must not be thrown away. That was not much help. Then he rambled off in talk about Vita who is ill with a weak heart. Consequently I did not press my point, seeing I would get little sympathy if I did.

*Friday, 10th June*

A. has gone. For five weeks I shall not see her, and already the agony has begun. Jamesey, returned from France, came in to talk. His advice is that I should do all in my power to marry by letting A. divorce Anthony, if she wants to. He says it is middle-class to have financial scruples because she has money and I have none, and ridiculous to have religious scruples about divorce; also needless to have moral scruples about Anthony who is a thoroughly selfish, if charming, cad.

*Wednesday, 15th June*

Found my father at Thurloe Square, he having come to stay yesterday. He is a bit thinner but looks extremely fit and feels it, I am glad to say. But he still passes a little blood, which is a worry to him, and to me a horrid prognostication of his fate. He goes to Ascot every day. This evening I went to Jamesey's flat. His new friend, a house painter, was there, wearing a battle-dress and rather grubby. Has a nice open face and laughs in raucous guffaws. I think this sort of association pathetic. What can J. get from it beyond the one thing that is not dispensed because the boy likes girls? Paul Wallraf* who walked away with me says J. is becoming amoral about money and borrows from his mother and poor friends what they cannot afford in order to make frequent trips abroad, taking friend. Silly business.

*Thursday, 16th June*

At Batsford's Sam Carr told me they were sacking Charles Fry who has become quite impossible. Their American branch has suffered badly from him. I am not surprised. Yet I am sorry for this clever and deplorable man losing his livelihood in middle age.

---

* Art dealer.

*Thursday, 23rd June*

A letter from A. saying she cannot make up her mind to divorce Anthony and that anyway she thinks we had better live apart lest I get tired of her. I? Does she mean lest she gets tired of me? This has depressed me somewhat.

*Friday, 24th June*

Gerry Wellington called at Thurloe Square for tea and we motored off to Stratfield Saye. John Steegman,* author of that inimitable *Rule of Taste*, Rupert Gunnis† and Esmond Burton‡ staying, all of us enlisted as guides to the party of National Trust members visiting the house tomorrow.

*Saturday, 25th June*

Everything went well and fortunately no one misbehaved. Each one of us was posted in a different room. Gerry, quite ruthless, would not allow a moment's relief. We were coached what to say and he took infinite pains labelling the exhibits and providing a printed brochure. The usual ignorant, dreary lot of members came. After a high tea we were driven, the five of us, to Bradfield School to see a performance of *Agamemnon* in Greek in the outdoor theatre – a disused chalkpit converted, stone seats *à la grecque*. Trees surrounding. Very picturesque. The boys performed extremely well and Clytemnestra brilliant. I think boys prefer melodrama to less emotional forms of acting. I was a bit bored at times, but the seat was too uncomfortable to allow dozing off. As the night drew on, so lights were turned on to the stage. The beauty of the setting, birds and doves cooing from the trees, the coloured togas, the chorus of boys declaiming, certainly made a picture. The Duke and

* Art historian and poet (1899–1966).
† Author (1899–1965) of *A Dictionary of British Sculptors* (1951).
‡ Artist and craftsman.

Lord Montgomery* were the guests of honour. They walked in with the headmaster, Hills, late of Eton. I sat immediately behind Montgomery, now a bent little man, with small, mean, hatchet face like a weasel's. He has ugly hands with crooked, gnarled fingers. I hated his little brown bald skull a foot below me.

*Sunday, 26th June*

Lady Hudson and Lady Granville† came to tea, and Lady G. suddenly developed St Vitus's dance and jangled the cup in her saucer, spilling scalding tea through a thin silk dress on to her knees, and smashing the saucer to smithereens. Gerry leapt up, seized the table upon which a few drops of the tea had sprinkled and rushed away with it to have the surface repolished. He made not one gesture of help or sympathy to poor Lady Granville who was in considerable pain and distress. Typical Gerry behaviour. I do love him. He never lets one down. His patent anxieties about his possessions bring these catastrophes about. I enjoy teasing him in a subtle way. Oblique references to sex make him bridle with a nasty covert leer. Now that he is a duke he thinks it unbecoming to let himself go.

Motored to Wickhamford. At home found a cocktail party on the lawn – hellish. I showed Mama my photographs of Alvilde. She looked at them very attentively and pronounced A. beautiful – which she is.

*Wednesday, 29th June*

Motored to Sissinghurst to stay the night with Vita. The garden here is almost blowsy with bloom. Surely no other county but Kent can be so lush and rich. I asked Vita why she liked the

---

* Field Marshal Sir Bernard Montgomery (1887–1976); cr. Viscount Montgomery of Alamein, 1946; best-known British commander of Second World War, renowned for his inspirational qualities, short temper and vanity.

† Lady Rose Bowes-Lyon, dau. of 14th Earl of Strathmore (and sister of HM Queen Elizabeth); m. 1916 William Leveson-Gower, 4th Earl Granville (1880–1953).

old-fashioned roses so much. She said because they reminded her of Tudor heraldic roses and Caroline stump-work. The Sissinghurst garden enchants because it is both formal and informal. The straight paths lined with yew and the pleached lime alleys lead to orchards, their fruit trees swathed in ramblers and eglantines.

She and I sat down to dinner at 8 o'clock. A cold meal with white wine which we drank and drank until 12.20 when we left the table. Vita is adorable. I love her romantic disposition, her southern lethargy concealing unfathomable passions, her slow movements of grave dignity, her fund of human kindness, understanding and desire to disentangle other people's perplexities for them. I love her deep plum voice and chortle. We talked of love and religion. She told me that she learnt only at twenty-five that her tastes were homosexual. It was sad that homosexual lovers were considered by the world to be slightly comical. She is worried about Ben's love for Carritt who doesn't reciprocate and is perpetually unfaithful. As for my predicament, her advice was to marry if I had the chance. She protested that it was nonsense for the Catholic Church to discountenance a Catholic marrying a divorced Protestant whose previous marriage it had not regarded as a sacrament. The memory of this evening will be ineradicable.

*Wednesday, 6th July*

John Russell lunched. He has recovered his young Shelley looks and is handsome again; and more mature. He and his wife now live in Essex where they have a farm. I cannot envisage John milking cows or cleaning pig sties or spreading manure. It is splendid how this young man, the son of a bicycle shop proprietor, became rich and established at the age of twenty-three.

Mama came to stay and went out with Hugh MacDonnell, in spite of her previous avowal. This clever man is tremendously dull. I dined with Mark Ogilvie-Grant, and took the Rosses to Kew. It is curious how every human being believes the set he moves among is superior to every other.

*Thursday, 7th July*

Mama and I dined alone. She is exceedingly worried about my father, who is not well: haemorrhage and clots in his urine.

*Wednesday, 13th July*

Had a sebaceous cyst cut out of the ear. No pain at all, but felt ill all day with fits of unconsciousness. Stayed at home.

*On 14 July, J.L.-M. rejoined the Chaplins at Jouy. The following day he and Alvilde set out on a tour of Provence.*

*Friday, 15th July*

A. and I left Jouy at 9.30 and motored to Chalon-sur-Saône, staying at the Royal Hotel. After dinner we walked in the moonlight. On the bridge I made a confession which greatly disconcerted A. Slept in a large double bed, if sleep is the right word, for some demon kicked a tin can in the street below our window all night long.

*Saturday, 16th July*

A. is a fussing car owner who shouts directions all the time and gets rather impatient with me. In fact she is impatient with inefficiency, hesitancy and hopelessness, which are among my many failings. We arrived in the Riviera Hotel in Aix in time for the first of the Festival's concerts, chiefly Mozart, given by Casadesus in the Bishop's Palace. Rory Cameron, George Chavchavadze and a large party all in rich, huge, American limousines, with chauffeurs and valets, arrived from Paris last night. Rory guessed all and in fact everyone now knows. A. doesn't care at all – so why should I? The hotel very comfortable and food excellent.

*Sunday, 17th July*

Aix is a ravishing little town set like a jewel in open country. It has rows of very old palaces in a sort of Florentine late Renaissance style, but with a character Provençal rather than provincial. A. adores Provence and is determined to buy a house here or nearby, but I am a little depressed by this thought for I would prefer to live in Italy.* Our idea is to live together, married or not, dependent upon whether she and Anthony divorce and upon money arrangements, for I could not have a job in England if we were married owing to her domicile abroad.

*Tuesday, 19th July*

Motored to the aqueduct of Roquefavour and lunched there. Then lay in the sun a little beyond. A. is determined to make me brown and fatter, for she says I am a white Gandhi-like skeleton.

*Thursday, 21st July*

This morning stayed late in my room trying to burn myself for A's sake at my window. I don't really like it. Sunbathing is a modern craze. The Ancients would never have done it.

*Friday, 22nd July*

A. is more keen than ever to buy a house in these parts. She says she could not live in Italy because of the Italians' cruelty to their animals. It is so frequently the case that people who care so vehemently for animals do not care for humans. Both Chaplins and my mother are like this.

*Saturday, 23rd July*

Terribly hot driving. We covered nearly 300 miles, arriving at Jouy for dinner. Then sat up late with Anthony discussing our affairs. It was settled that in September he and A. would consult a lawyer in London as to whether it would be advantageous for them to

* They later compromised by living at Roquebrune near the Italian frontier.

divorce, or have a legal separation. Anthony says he wants a job in London where Rosemary will be, but doesn't want to marry her, which I doubt being true. A. does not necessarily wish to marry me but wants me to leave the National Trust if they will not give me a half-time job. If they will, I can live half the year in England and half with her in Provence. She will definitely not surrender her French domicile. With this decision I sympathise. It is difficult for me to know what to do. I am in great confusion.

*Monday, 25th July*

I am back in the London office. Eardley dined and I told him all. He is so patient with me and listens to all my problems. E., who is incurably romantic, said that he would chuck Long Crichel and his perfect life there for love and give all he possessed to the loved one. And he would too.*

*Thursday, 28th July*

Dined at Alan Lennox-Boyd's punctually at 8.30 to meet the Regent of Iraq and his new wife.† They came at 9.15. Then dinner at separate tables. I hated the evening and talked to Gerald de Gaury and Alex Beattie and Svelode of Russia and Mamie Pavlovsky. The party did not break up until 1.30 so I was obliged to stay on, drinking more and more and getting more and more tired. Mamie resolutely refused to go on to a night club with the silly Iraqis, and I did too. Mrs Iraqi only interested in film stars, horses and night clubs, so I was not a great success with her. She is a pretty little thing, plastered with jewels. How people like Gerald can be bothered with them I can't understand. Is he a spy, and if so for whom?

---

* And he did, leaving Long Crichel in 1957 to live with his Bulgarian lover.

† Prince Abd al-Ilah (1914–58); uncle of King Feisal II of Iraq (1934–58), during whose minority (1939–53) he acted as Regent; known for his anglophile sympathies and homosexual inclinations; married three times; murdered together with the King in Iraqi Revolution, 1958.

*Sunday, 31st July*

I took Papa to Paddington station this morning. He had had no operation. They looked at his growth and cauterised it a little, although he declared they did not touch it for he felt no pain. The doctor told me there was nothing they could possibly do and that he might live eighteen months.

A. keeps writing me letters nobly offering to do anything I ask, even to live with me in England in spite of losing money. I am in a quandary.

*Monday, 8th August*

At Mass yesterday at the Oratory, while kneeling before the Gospel at one of my favourite stances in the west transept, it came to me in a flash that of course God alone was worth while because enduring; that nothing human, animal or vegetable endures, neither love, sex, friendship, hatred, oneself, one's ideas, ideals, nor anything else man-made, even by Phidias,* Michelangelo, Shakespeare or Mozart. Only God remains immutable, unchangeable. Then I qualified the satisfaction the revelation gave me by asking myself if God was not merely a fiction, made by each man in his own image. I decided perhaps not, because in thinking of or worshipping God I do not picture him as possessing all the particular virtues which I venerate. Instead I purposely keep him rather vague, wholly beneficent, and of course omnipotent. I don't investigate his ingredients. I don't enquire of myself if he is handsome, ugly, has a sense of fun (this would be a surprise), is gloomy, likes art or horse-racing, is normal or queer, nice or nasty. In fact I don't believe in a personal God the Father. I do believe in the divinitiy of Christ, a human being wholly possessed of God. So I accept the Father and the Son. The Holy Ghost perplexes me.

A. and I write each other rather depressed letters nowadays: what is the use, etc.? She says bravely that she knows she won't live in England and that I won't leave the National Trust. She is probably

---

* Greek sculptor (born *c.* 500 BC).

right. So what? She says she has become bad-tempered but would not be so if married to me. I don't believe this because she was cross when we were together. I am extremely cross now too, always on edge, and I fear it would be so with her after we were married, though not at first.

*Wednesday, 10th August*

Dined at Colin Agnew's.* Bogey Harris there, talking of Edwardian days, said that when he stayed at great houses he always took, in addition to his valet, a man to shave him and nothing else. He and Colin told me Berenson was an old pansy in spite of kissing in the garden every pretty woman who came to the place.

*Thursday, 11th August*

Dined alone with Jack Rathbone. Before and after dinner Raymond Mortimer, Paul Hyslop and Desmond Shawe-Taylor came in. A good deal of puppyish embracing which I take in good part but don't really care for. Like Berenson I prefer to kiss women and even in amity or affection don't relish kissing men as a form of salutation, though it is becoming common. The embracing of women has even got out of hand. Once you give way you can never stop it. And there are times when I sense that women friends, however intimate, are not in the mood to be mauled. Nor can one always be in the mood to maul them, poor things.

*Saturday, 13th August*

We [J.L.-M. and the Eshers] drove in slow stages to Attingham.† My car was simply packed with the Eshers' luggage, he squashed on the back seat, she in front with me. Dined at Lady Berwick's.

---

* Art dealer.

† It had become the N.T's property on Lord Berwick's death in 1947. The state apartments were about to be opened to the public; much of the rest of the enormous house was let to Shropshire County Council for use as an adult education

Delicious dinner with champagne from her cellar, the Eshers drinking nothing. Lady B's sighs and tragedy queen gestures irritated him, and in consequence he talked to me on his other side throughout the meal, which was rather rude.

During the drive I told him that I wanted to retire from the Trust, or work part-time. This announcement caused him quite extraordinary concern. He said that nobody else could do my job but me, whereas hundreds of people could write books better than me. I said, yes, I was sure of that, but my health was not so good and I was tired. His last comment was, 'Well, we must find you a very rich deputy', presumably so that he needn't be paid. Alvilde's fortieth birthday and she away from Jouy, somewhere in mid-France, I don't know where. Oh, lack-a-day.

*Sunday, 14th August*

Rather a ghastly day motoring Lord Esher round the estate and showing him the house. In the afternoon the opening ceremony took place and he delivered the speech I had drafted for him. Of course, he altered and embellished it so that it turned out inimitably his. Tiring, hanging about, talking to people unknown. I left at 5.30 and arrived at Wickhamford at 7.30. Found my mother in the kitchen worn to death and my father looking, at first sight, well. But his haemorrhage worse than ever. In fact he is not at all well. He is languid, gets up late, goes to bed at 5.30 and when up lies on his sofa. I saw his doctor who is much worried; gives him six months at most and told me he is probably now dying.

*Monday, 15th August*

Mama terribly worried. It is awful leaving her in this predicament. I had to tell her that everything depended on her. Until he becomes

college, eventually becoming the N.T's regional office when the lease expired in 1986. Lady Berwick, somewhat critical of both the N.T. and its institutional tenant, continued to live in the house until her death in 1972.

bedridden I don't think we should tell her the truth, or go there too often, or do anything to arouse suspicion. Haines [the old chauffeur] took me aside this morning to say he was certain Papa is failing and moved me greatly by saying he could think of little else. 'When he does not come to talk to me in the morning then I knows how ill he is.'

*Saturday, 20th August*

At 6 o'clock went to Carmen Gandarillas's house to meet Jamesey who is broken-hearted, Dame Una having died. James admirably brave and sensible. He says his mother had a fulfilled life, had written many good books and several first-rate ones. More important than that were her astringent mind and capacious intellect. She was one of the most important women of her day. I told him she was the best debunker of the second-rate. On Tuesday evening she was remarkably collected, and seemed filled with renewed energy. She gave him detailed instructions how he was to finish her book on Lamartine and how to put her collated notes together. Having settled these and other matters she announced that she was going to die the following afternoon. But at 7 the following morning she failed and J. said the ten minutes of her death were an experience he would never free his memory from. It was awful. He never thought such a noise could be emitted from a human frame. Her face became a skull with a veil of torment drawn across it. She was unrecognisable except for her hair. He held both her hands and helped her to die. Meanwhile she was kept conscious while extreme unction was administered by a clumsy, fumbling priest. Otherwise there was nothing terrifying about her death, James said. What he described sounded terrifying enough to me.

*Tuesday, 23rd August*

I drove to Midi's for dinner. In discussing my problems, she declined to give advice. She has never met A. She merely said, 'You have to bear in mind that you may be sacrificing your country, your religion, your career and your independence.' That was food enough for thought.

*Monday, 19th September*

I got back from my three weeks' holiday in Italy today.

On 26 August I flew to Paris, stayed the night at Jouy and next day motored alone with Alvilde in her new car, a Plymouth, which is a treat to drive. We stayed the night at the Grand Hotel, Nancy, that wonderful city. Next day we stayed in Zurich at the Belle Rive au Lac, clean and well-appointed after the French hotels. On the 29th we reached San Vigilio on Lake Garda, staying at the Locanda. Some embarrassment caused by Sir Eric de Normann and wife staying. He is head of the Ministry of Works and knows me. Since A. and I were sharing a room we had to be on our guard and pretend we were not together.

Thereafter Verona and Milan. On the 7th to Venice, staying at the Danieli (two rooms with a bathroom between). Too many English people about. To my amazement Cyril Connolly, meeting us in the Piazza, solemnly congratulated A. on becoming a Viscountess on the death of her father-in-law.* He should have known better. K. Clark accompanied us one day to Padua, conducting us to his chosen monuments, a signal honour. Bergamo and Vicenza visited. In Venice we visited all Palladian churches with Hiram Winterbotham,† a great Palladio enthusiast.

Our Italian tour was punctuated by some unforgettable little scenes and incidents. 1. The small urchins, to one of whom we gave a few lire for guarding the car while we visited the Villa Capra, waving and cheering us as we drove away. 2. The lift boy kept lighting Hiram's cigarette which for some reason refused to take flame, while bubbling with laughter. 3. Three extremely well-bred old ladies drifting in a superbly groomed gondola to the steps of the Danieli and being helped to land by a pair of gorgeously liveried

* Eric, 2nd Viscount Chaplin (1877–1949), had died on 12 September.

† Businessman, philanthropist and connoisseur resident in Gloucestershire (1908–90).

gondoliers. 4. At a restaurant a mother and daughter licking their handkerchiefs and scrubbing with all their might the lapel of a man's coat which had been stained by food. 5. Women and men with their hands on St Antony's tomb in Padua cathedral, wishing as they prayed with the utmost fervour – for what? A new pair of shoes? A new carpet-sweeper? Renewed faith? New lovers?

Now my relations with A. have entered a new phase, undergone a sea change from the first fine careless rapture into something certainly richer and possibly stranger. It is part of the inevitable process of love. At times we had rows, mostly slight, but some of them deep. Since I do not know which of my tiresome habits rile her I cannot enumerate them. No doubt there are plenty, for she gets cross and snaps at me and grouses like a spoiled child. This conduct has a most unfortunate effect on me, makes me want to escape, turns me in on myself, makes my love grow tepid. A. instantly recovers from these bouts which leave me unhappy and disturbed. Dwelling on them I say that I do not think after all I can live with her permanently. She says I have changed and gone back on what I repeatedly wrote to her during the summer. There is some truth in this. I am very worried. I still believe I can live forever with the Alvilde I knew before we went to Aix; whereas the other Alvilde I could not live with, the Alvilde that fusses over inessentials and takes things badly. There was a night on Lake Garda when I left her in the garden in anger, and walked by myself under the moon along the shore, and sat on the shingle praying for help from the lapping waves. When I returned A. was in tears. Then I was all penitence. There were other moments when she taxed me angrily with no longer loving her. I could give no honest answer for during those moments I had temporarily ceased to love her.

*Tuesday, 20th September*

We returned by the ferry boat on Sunday night. I am glad to be out of France. I hate the beastly country with its ferocious, mean, cruel inhabitants. This evening A. left for Scotland with Anthony and her mother-in-law to attend Lord Chaplin's memorial service at Dornoch.

*Wednesday, 21st September*

Trained to Manchester and stayed the night with Dick and Elaine at Park Cottage [near Oldham]. We deliberated how best to tell Mama the truth about Papa's illness and agreed that on the next occasion when he was taken worse, whichever one of us was present should tell her, with Astley the doctor present. D. and E. are devoted to each other. Their little house is bright and comfortable. But oh! what a district of soiled rain like stair rods, black tearing clouds across the blackest moors and scarlet cottages, and tall chimneys like prison warders at every corner one tries to escape from.

*Friday, 23rd September*

Lunched A. and Anthony and Mr Harry Batsford, upon whom Anthony exercised all his charm. We want him to write a book on reptiles for Batsford's. On leaving I walked with Anthony who said he could not think why I hesitated to live permanently with A. A. tells me that Anthony says to her that she is a fool to be cross with me. She dined with me at Thurloe Square and is sad that we separate tomorrow.

*Saturday, 24th September*

I took Mama for a stroll along 'the donkey patch' in the sun and said that Astley took the gravest view and wished to speak to us both at a convenient moment. She said at once that she did not wish to be told by the doctor. She wanted him to tell me so that I could pass it on to her. Her courage was wonderful. She did not weep. At one moment only I thought she might break down, when she said she could not imagine life without him after forty-five years. (I marvelled that she seemed to have forgotten those long wretched years when they were on the worst possible terms. God is sometimes merciful to the afflicted.) Then she pulled herself together and said he must have no suspicions of what we knew. While we were talking old Mason called to speak to her from the road. She called back to him cheerfully, answering his inquiries about Papa as though nothing were the matter. In the house Papa was up and dressed and she joined him and laughed and joked with him. When I confirmed later in the day that Astley pronounced the bladder growth to be malignant and gave him three months to live at longest, she took it calmly. How I admired her.

*Saturday, 1st October*

Jamesey amused me by telephoning: 'You know the picture of an eighteenth-century house which I am leaving to you in my will?' 'Yes,' I answered. 'I can't wait for it.' 'Well, I am ringing you up to say that I have sold it and it is in Appleby's shop window if you want to buy it.'

*Sunday, 2nd October*

Ivy [Compton-Burnett] and Margaret [Jourdain] lunched with me in the Cromwell Road and Margaret returned to me the second half of my book with her corrections. Then I met A. and Anthony off the Golden Arrow and brought her to dine here. On the way there was trouble for she thought I was not pleased enough to see her, and at the door she said she had been a fool to come. My reprehensible fault for not being demonstrative enough.

*Tuesday, 4th October*

A. and I went to the Cimarosa opera *Il Matrimonio Segreto*. Very pretty Mozartian music never rising to great heights. Had a reconciliation with A. and stayed the whole night with her at the Dorchester, slinking out in the morning like a thief in the dawn, which I don't like. Nevertheless the pledge has been re-sealed for all time.

Inspired by A., I have begun to study wild flowers. This is a new fascination which promises to be more dangerous to motoring than architecture in so far as turning the eye from the wheel is concerned. How shocking that I, country bred, never learned about wild flowers in childhood.

A. and I have reached a happier and even high plane but she wants to be with me all the time. This is where I fail for I cannot be with anyone all the time. It is just not in my nature. I console myself with the certitude that no true and enduring love affair ever runs entirely smoothly. How can two individuals, who choose to coalesce, not clash fairly frequently? The triumph of love consists, not in winning, but enduring. Marriage is a very unnatural state. But then so are logic and art unnatural. All the most worthwhile and glorious things achieved by mankind are unnatural. To be natural is to be animal. Only fly-by-night lovers expect to have no ups and downs – for six weeks at most.

*Sunday, 9th October*

A. told me that Caroline Paget married Michael Duff* hurriedly because she was going to have a baby by Duff Cooper, her aunt's husband, who for years has loved her. Michael does not mind and has always been devoted to Caroline, who is anyway not interested in gentlemen. Nor is Michael interested in ladies. It all sounds so queer yet is simple and satisfactory enough.

It amused me that Anthony Chaplin should telephone asking me to ring up Rosemary Lyttelton on his behalf.

*Tuesday, 11th October*

Tonight Rose Macaulay dined for Anthony Chaplin particularly wanted to meet her. I invited James thinking it would improve the party, but James talked incessant 'shop' to her and Anthony did not like this. However after dinner he found that she knew about green tree frogs and was delighted. Talking of religion Rose said she was an Anglo-Agnostic, explaining that she had great affection for the C. of E., in which faith she was brought up, yet was a non-believer.

---

* Lady Caroline Paget, dau. of 6th Marquess of Anglesey; m. 1949 Sir Michael Duff, 3rd Bt. (The child was stillborn, though the couple did subsequently adopt a boy.)

*Friday, 14th October*

A. and I went to Marlow, staying at the Compleat Angler. Over dinner there was a crisis caused by my saying that I saw no prospect whatever of my being able to leave England and the National Trust for half the year. Coldness and hurtness and tears; but all made up in the morning. I am rather tormented by this problem.

*Sunday, 16th October*

Trouble again today for after breakfast I telephoned A., rather too abruptly I confess, that I must be left to work. The consequence was distress, and she did not turn up for lunch at the Allies Club. Tonight there was a passionate reconciliation. A woman's love is very fearful, for her whole life can be subordinated to it to the exclusion of every other interest.

*Tuesday, 18th October*

Alvilde left this morning. My family arrived after a terrible journey, Papa suffering agonies. I had a glimpse of him lying in bed in the nursing home looking like a corpse. To me it is inconceivable that he can survive another operation, now fixed for Friday. The prolongation of life is a cruel and unnecessary business.

*Wednesday, 19th October*

I have put off my plans for going away this week. Audrey [J.L.-M's sister, Mrs Cecil Stevens] has come up from the country to join us. We all sit around doing and saying nothing but the same fatuous things. It is a great strain. It is terrible how far I feel from them all. A bad day, this. Dentist in the morning. In the afternoon an X-ray at St Thomas's Hospital of my back. Worst of all, Margaret Jourdain returned the first part of my book with a letter that has properly put me in my place. She says that the book does not hang together, a third of it must be cut, and my style is atrocious.

I am not being as nice to Mama as I should be, and it is wicked to allow her to get on my nerves at a time like this.

*Thursday, 20th October*

I say to myself this morning that all this moaning and groaning and self-pity must cease. Circumstances may be bad at the moment but the world is not wholly unendurable, and the sun is shining.

I asked Jack Rathbone (who is always sympathetic and patient) if he thought it feasible for me to have a half-time job with the National Trust. He counselled me to wait until the Gowers Committee Report comes out at the end of the year, for it would affect the composition of the Nat. Trust and my job in particular.

I called at the nursing home in Queen's Gate at 7.10, ten minutes later than arranged. Went to Papa's room, he up and eating and very cross that I was late. He said he had seen enough people and I had better go back to the others in the flat. I felt like a whipped puppy and slunk away, tail between legs.

*Friday, 21st October*

Papa had his operation this evening and it passed successfully.

*Saturday, 22nd October*

I telephoned A. who at once enquired whether I had seen Lord Esher. I said No, but I had talked to Jack who advised my coming to no decision until Gowers Report was published. Reaction – instantaneous disappointment. So there and then I wrote her a letter begging her to try and enjoy life when we were not together since we must inevitably be separated for much of our lives. This provoked from her a letter which she regretted the moment she had posted it and followed with a telegram begging me not to open it. Oh God, the suffering one inflicts.

*Thursday, 27th October*

I motored to Buscot [Oxfordshire]. A most lovely autumnal day. Along the road verges I noticed toad-flax, dandelions and vetch still in flower. Am glad to get away from poor Mama, whom I have told to stay on until the end of next week. At close quarters she gets fearfully on my nerves. She is interested in nothing I say and her insincerity amounts to positive dishonesty and an inability to be straightforward and even truthful. Yet I am so deeply sorry for her and filled with admiration of her bravery. Why can't I be demonstrative? What a stinking beast I am.

*Monday, 31st October*

I am terribly disheartened by my new book. Am still carefully pruning and rewriting and improving (I hope), but realise that it is definitely bad – damn M. Jourdain. If ever I write another I must put it aside for two months at least, then re-read it with a fresh and critical eye. I think the failure of this Tudor book is depressing me more than Papa's illness, a wicked thing to say and proof of my irredeemable self-centredness.

*Tuesday, 1st November*

My poor mother. All her tiresomenesses are dissipated by her abundant sweetness and charm. I said goodbye to her for she is taking Papa home to Worcestershire in an ambulance on Friday. Doctors can do no more for him. I would definitely do anything within my power and deprive myself of what I hold most dear (which is A.) if I could thus prolong his life free from pain and distress. But this is not saying I would want to. One must be honest with oneself.

*Wednesday, 2nd November*

A filthy wet November day. George Howard* is stout and uncouth, sometimes forthright to rudeness. Perhaps his heart is kind. How can one tell? Talks a good deal about antiques but is alarmingly

* George Howard (1920–84); Hon. N.T. Representative for N.E. England, 1948–58; later President of Historic Houses Association and Chairman of BBC; m. 1949 Lady Cecilia FitzRoy; cr. life peer, 1980.

ignorant for a National Trust representative and, worse still, without taste. He took me over Castle Howard [near York], now empty, the school having gone. Its aspect is exceedingly forlorn. It is not in bad condition, but very unkempt. It looks sad with the dome and the best rooms burnt out, but there is enough space left for a country house these days, in all conscience. The lack of symmetry in Castle Howard has always worried me. The sculpture of the stonework, cornices, columns, etc., is crisp. George intends to move himself into the East Wing and open the rest to the public. We drove to the Temple of the Four Winds, now in a state of dereliction, but a very elegant building, more Palladian than Baroque. The monopteral, Doric mausoleum is a splendid affair and the bastioned retaining wall forms an impressively massive base. In fact it is a composition of grandeur and genius. We went into the vaults where are many gaping niches unused. George intends to be buried there, the first to be so since the eighteenth century. And so he should be, for he will be the re-creator of Castle Howard. The rotunda chapel above is faultless. The English Georgians were better craftsmen than Palladio's men. George much distressed because hooligans have thrown bricks through the windows, breaking panels of original glass.

*Wednesday, 9th November*

Alvilde left for Paris this morning [after a five-day visit]. Every evening we met and dined and nearly every day lunched together. This visit was a great success. There were no crises or difficulties, and all was sunshine. I am happy and at ease.

I left early this morning for Newport, Monmouthshire. Was met at the station by John Morgan* flying his personal flag on the radiator of his motor, and driven to Tredegar. He is absurdly pompous and puffed up with self-importance, yet has a genuine sense of duty, and his religion means everything to him. We spent the afternoon

* Hon. John Morgan (1908–62); s. father 1954 as 6th and last Baron Tredegar; Eton contemporary of J.L.-M.; m. 1954 Mrs Joanna Russell.

going round the house. Now it *is* important, and probably the best in Wales. Nevertheless I was a trifle disappointed by the coarse, unrefined quality of the craftsmanship. Some of the contents are superb, notably the French furniture and in particular the Adam bureau-cum-harpsichord all in one, with a clock in the pediment. John showed me the figures of his estimated income after he has paid death duties, which amount to 80 per cent. His gross income is £40,000. After paying tax it will be reduced to £3,700, and he cannot spend his capital because it is all in trust. I slept in the panelled room in the bed said to be Mary Queen of Scots', but I wonder. John is very dogmatic about his possessions and at the same time ignorant, like many owners. He told me that on clearing his cousin Evan's* bedroom cupboard he came upon 'instruments of the most bloodcurdling nature'. He took them gingerly between finger and thumb and threw them in the dustbin. I said that in doing this he gave the dustmen ample opportunity of circulating scandalous gossip about the family. John forebore to tell me what the 'instruments' were.

*Saturday, 12th November*

Patrick Kinross dined. He is back from Cyprus, Turkey and Greece. He says Greece and the Greeks are heaven. They are warm-hearted, human and more intelligent than other Europeans. They are all sensual without being sentimental, and every Greek man is homosexual. They go to bed just as they would sneeze or laugh. I said I would not care to go to bed with anyone who sneezed and laughed. Patrick in his funny pontifical manner which I love says that true love can only exist between man and woman, true sex between man and man; that women know and hate this without understanding it, just as Ancient Greek women did. Accordingly they resent all men's relationships, fearing them to be such that they can never attain. I think the notion is probably far-fetched.

---

* Evan Morgan, 2nd Viscount and 4th Baron Tredegar (1893–1949); m. 1st 1928 Hon. Lois Sturt (d. 1937), 2nd 1939–43 Princess Olga Dolgorouky.

*Monday, 21st November*

I stayed the weekend with Deenie at Stow, very comfortable. She is easier to be with than my mother. Twice I went to Wickhamford, yesterday and today, and saw my father, the first day sitting in his chair, this morning in bed. He is pitiably thin, but his colour good. He gets extremely tired after twenty minutes of talk. Elaine says that he cannot live two months and that the cancer in his bladder has grown to the size of a grapefruit. In fact this terrible thing literally eats its victim who appreciably diminishes as it increases in bulk. There is something evil and damnable about it. Yet here is my poor father talking about his plans for next spring, how he intends to buy a racehorse if he can afford it, and go to Deauville or somewhere abroad in order to gamble. Is this put on in order to deceive us, or himself? Perhaps God is good to one in such condition in allowing one not to despair.

*Wednesday, 23rd November*

Motored Johnnie Churchill to Chartwell [Kent] this morning. Mr and Mrs Winston were in London so we were able to go where we wanted. It must once have been a nice Queen Anne house, but Mr C. has altered it out of all recognition, and it is now quite ugly; but of course bears his strong impress. We saw his study and adjoining bedroom. If all the photographs and pictures and framed letters from Marlborough, and from himself to General Alexander and others, remain, Chartwell will be interesting to posterity. His bedroom is rather austere in spite of windows on all sides and three telephones by the bed. The view from it is splendid – the great lake made by him and the dam, which I remember him constructing when I stayed here twenty years ago, and the chain of pools in the topmost of which water is pumped by machine from the bottom lake. What a to-do went on during these operations, Mr C., clad in waders, standing up to his chest in mud and shouting directions like Napoleon before Austerlitz. The long downstairs room is now full of his paintings, of which the earlier ones in the style of Sickert, without the later ubiquitous blue, are not too bad. We looked at Johnnie's slate frieze [of the Battle of Blenheim] being installed in the loggia. Johnnie is a dear old friend and we had a great gossip about his family. He says he doesn't care for Christopher Soames but does like Duncan Sandys. Mr C. has cultivated a deafness which he turns on like a tap when he is bored: an excellent form of defence and one adopted by many old people to whom time is precious. Chartwell is fascinating as the shrine of a great man, just as Hughenden is. The moment I set foot in the house I said to Johnnie, 'I have not been here since Oxford days and I vividly remember the smell of the house. What is it?' 'Cigars and brandy,' he said. Of course. It is far from disagreeable, rather like cedar wood. Agreeable, I suppose, because his cigars are expensive ones.

*Tuesday, 29th November*

This morning I was woken by Emily telling me Mrs Dick wanted me on the telephone. I guessed what it meant. She said my father was worse, was almost certainly dying. I said I would leave at once. Within one and a half hours I had packed, put off arrangements and left in the car. Arrived at Wickhamford at 12 o'clock. Found Mama walking in the garden, very quiet and composed. Papa unconscious. Deenie was there and before luncheon Dick arrived from Lancashire. The nurse was with my father all day and Mama went up at intervals but was so overcome that she couldn't bear it and came downstairs. Elaine also sat with him. By the evening I steeled myself and went upstairs and into his room. He was lying on Mama's bed, curled up on his side, his head twisted, almost unrecognisable. His head was wizened to a skull with skin stretched tightly across it, so shrunk and taut it was. His mouth seemed to have slipped to one side of his face and his tongue lolled out. The breathing was deep, wracked and intermittent. How he would have hated me seeing him in that condition. I felt a trespasser, uncomfortable, apologetic. I felt infinite compassion because of the indignity he was put to. Perhaps for the first time I loved him unreservedly.

*Wednesday, 30th November*

When I got back at 9 he was in precisely the same condition. At 10 o'clock the nurse ran downstairs and told us to telephone Dr Astley at the surgery. I went up with Mama. The breathing seemed to me louder and more laboured. Otherwise I noticed little change. There ensued a terrible hour, poor Mama on her knees at his bedside, talking to him who understood not a word and beseeching him to give up the struggle. This he did a little before 11 o'clock. The nurse, Mama and I were present. The breathing became a little easier, stopped, his mouth moved, then his throat, and then nothing. Swiftly the nurse with great dexterity, her hand over his heart, pulled the sheet over his head, and I led Mama away, prostrate with grief. It was a terrible, harrowing experience, yet one which nearly every human being has to undergo, once if not twice a lifetime. I hope never again to go through another like it. The very worst things about death are the disrespect, the vulgarity, the meanness. God should have arranged for dying people to disintegrate and disappear like a puff of smoke into the air. There are many other scraps of advice I could have given him.

*Friday, 2nd December*

Dick and I motored to Cheltenham, to the cremation ceremony at the crematorium just outside the town. We were punctual to the minute, 3.45, for we had been warned not to be early or we would run into the previous funeral service. Behind the chapel was a round building with a large central chimney. I pointed out to Dick that it was belching black smoke. We giggled. Dick and I sat alone in a hideous late Victorian chapel without ornamentation, strictly non-denominational. Behind us the black mutes of the undertakers' party. The coffin on a slab in front of us. Sympathetic C. of E. clergyman officiating, but the service short and devoid of the devotional and spiritual. We were completely unmoved even when he pressed a button and the coffin slid away and the tiny velvet curtains opened, and a cheap, cracked gramophone record struck up *Abide with Me*, and faded out. I believe the coffin is taken off the conveyor belt and does not go to the crematorium until a number of others have been collected. And oh, the unctuousness of the chief undertaker, with his faultless manner, greased hair and black kid gloves! Enough to make one sick.

*Saturday, 3rd December*

Yet the memorial service in Wickhamford church was far worse. All morning the villagers were decorating the church with chrysanthemums and taking infinite pains. Mama remained in the house with Clara Mitchell. Deenie, Elaine, Dick and I went. The church was packed. We went to our pew, the manor pew, and I sat in Papa's place beside the pew door. Felt an interloper. I managed somehow to get through without making a fool of myself, not without effort. Dick, who sat next to me, and was far closer to my father than I was, sang throughout most loudly. The parson gave an excellent address, not embarrassing in any sense. He praised Papa's wisdom, courtesy and charm. Said he never refused to respond to a good village cause and was a typical country gentleman. It was rather strange that the first service at which the choir gallery (which my father gave and which it was his great ambition to see finished) should be used was his own memorial service. I noticed no one in the church. One is made insensate on such occasions, luckily. Was upset when all was over, full of remorse for not having been more understanding and kinder, for until recently my father and I did not get on. He never liked me from the start, for which I do not blame him, although I think he should have tried to be nice to me first. Ours was a case of biological incompatibility. Our hackles rose on the mere approach of the other. Yet within his limitations he was a good man, respected by strangers and loved by his friends and other people's children.

*Wednesday, 7th December*

Went to see Father D'Arcy* to ask him if it would be appropriate to have a Mass said for my father's soul. I explained it was a thing

* Martin D'Arcy (1888–1976); Jesuit and Oxford theologian.

which I would never have dared mention to him while he was alive, for he hated Catholicism and all it stood for. I didn't want to take unfair advantage of him, so to speak, he being in no position to answer back. Father D'Arcy's reply was, 'Certainly, yes. If your father is now in heaven, it can do no harm; if in purgatory, he will now be glad of it.' I doubted that. Then I asked if I might be cremated, please. His answer unsatisfactory. He said it was a difficult concession and I must regard the Church's dislike of cremation as an etiquette, not a dogma, to be respected. I said it seemed to me good manners and socially considerate in view of the appalling increase in the population. If everyone insisted upon having a grave there would before long be little room left for any other purpose. To this remark Father D'Arcy turned a deaf ear in the way of priests who have been floored. Then I told him I wanted to marry. He said that if Alvilde and Anthony could establish that their marriage had never been taken seriously, an annulment was possible, notwithstanding that a child had been born to their union. I don't like Father D'Arcy very much. He is artful, as one would expect a Provincial of the Jesuits to be.

*Tuesday, 13th December*

Lunched with Midi at her club to meet George Chavchavadze who turned up with Malcolm Sargent. The meal was the most hilarious I ever sat through. Conversation was sheer nonsense from beginning to end so that I laughed till it hurt. None of the talk bears recording. In fact it was inconsecutive and quite unrecordable. Malcolm is a splendid foil to George. Each eggs the other on to inconceivable follies.

*Thursday, 15th December*

Alvilde has come back. I met her at Victoria and took her to the Dorchester and spent the night with her there.

*Thursday, 22nd December*

At Ethel Sands's this evening Prince Antoine Bibesco* came in. He is oldish, with straight, thick grey hair. He is the man Proust loved and the widower of Elizabeth Asquith. Abounding in charm and I would guess the cause of havoc in many hearts of yore.

*Sunday, 25th December*

Christmas Day spent at Stow-on-the-Wold with darling old Deenie and Mama. No one else. Dick telephoned from Lancashire and Audrey sent a telegram from Nassau. Alone with D. it would have been easy and restful, but with Mama present it was not. She became vague, argumentative and cantankerous. Abused Elaine until I could hardly bear it and not too nice about Dick. I wrote to Dick and begged him not to pay too much heed to what she might repeat about me, for I should not pay any to what she says about him.

I walked in the afternoon down to Swell, looked in at the little Norman church and at the manor with its Tuscan-Jacobean porch; then across to Nether Swell and on to Lower Slaughter and back to Stow. Very northern, dark, cloudy afternoon, the distant hills cold and watercolourful. How snug England is in the winter, with the cottage windows lit up, warm fires blazing and Christmas decorations hanging from the beams. So pretty all the rooms were, while outside grim and dusky. This is England in the distant heart of the sweeping Cotswolds, with the sweet aromatic smell of log fires unchanged since my childhood.

I now know what made me hesitate after A's slight irritations with me when abroad this summer. It was fear that if I married her she might nag me as Mama has nagged my father ever since I can remember anything. Now I must never forget that until I was about thirty my mother meant everything to me. We were as one. All things change and relationships turn topsy-turvy. Perhaps in the

---

* Romanian socialite, writer and diplomatist (1878–1951); m. 1919 Lady Elizabeth Asquith (1897–1945), dau. of H. H. Asquith, Prime Minister.

next world they right themselves, I mean the good ones become good again and the bad ones are totally forgotten, as they can become partially forgotten in this.

*Thursday, 29th December*

Went to see Sibyl Colefax in bed, looking bright-eyed but slighter than ever. This woman who has known thousands of people in her time is now near death* and is content, or should I say compelled for lack of anyone better, to call upon me, who am younger than she and outside her intimate circle, to her bedside. We talked of the wickedness of mothers for being possessive, something I can never accuse my poor mother of.

*Saturday, 31st December*

Such an odd luncheon alone with Anthony Chaplin at the Berkeley to discuss our mutual plans. A. wanted me to talk to him to find out what precisely is in his mind. The occasion was as happy as could be. Anthony definitely wants A. to divorce him, but he will not marry Rosemary, he assures me. He merely wants to be free. Of what, I asked him? Not of A., for he has been free from her ever since he married her. He agrees with me that I would make a great mistake to abandon the National Trust altogether. I told him that A. was depressed by the thought of a divorce. He said this was pure sentiment for, once the divorce was over, he would see as much of A. as before; and that I must try to make her happy. This should be the first objective of the years that remain to me. We parted in mutual piety.

In the evening she and I went to the theatre and the Savoy. I promised her that if Anthony goes I will live with her and marry her when I get the Church's consent. We went home to her flat before midnight and were together when the New Year came in.

---

* She died on 22 September 1950.

*After 1949, J.L.-M. ceased keeping a regular diary. (One reason for discontinuing was that he was describing his daily doings in letters to Alvilde – but these do not, unfortunately, seem to have survived.)*

*At the end of 1950, he gave up full-time work for the National Trust, being succeeded as Historic Buildings Secretary by Robin Fedden. His offer of part-time services was accepted, and he was appointed the Trust's Architectural Adviser, a job which henceforth kept him busy in England from Easter until Christmas, with breaks during the late summer and autumn during which he travelled on the Continent and researched his architectural books.*

*In 1950 Alvilde divorced Anthony Chaplin, sold her house at Jouy, and bought La Meridienne, a small villa overlooking the Mediterranean at Roquebrune, an ancient mountainside village situated between Monte Carlo and Mentone, a few miles from the Italian frontier. It was here that she and J.L.-M. wintered together throughout the 1950s.*

*In November 1951 J.L.-M. married Alvilde at a London registry office, without having succeeded in obtaining a papal decree recognising the nullity of the Chaplin marriage which would have legitimised the union in the eyes of the Church. The top three floors of 20 Thurloe Square, where he had formerly kept a bachelor flat, became their London home. In order to preserve her French tax residence, she could only join him for three of the six months he spent annually working in England – an arrangement which gave him a welcome measure of independence.*

*Although J.L.-M. was not to resume a day-to-day journal until 1971, he did keep a sporadic diary during 1953 and 1954, which gives a snapshot of his early married life. It begins with scenes from his second conjugal winter at Roquebrune, where he was revising the manuscript of his book on the architect Inigo Jones (his* Tudor Renaissance *having appeared in 1951 to mixed reviews).*

# 1953

# 1953

*Saturday, 24th January*

Willie [Somerset] Maugham who dined with Alvilde and me tonight in Monte Carlo talked of Rudyard Kipling* 'not being quite a gent'. Kipling once lunched with Willie in the Villa Mauresque at Cap Ferrat and the name of a mutual friend was mentioned. 'He's a white man,' exclaimed Kipling. Willie thought, 'How I wish, in order to fulfil my preconceptions of him, he would say he was a pukka sahib.' 'He's a pukka sahib all right,' continued Kipling. We took Willie and Alan Searle† to the Dutch Ballet which was pretty bad. They were like cheeses rolling around, A. observed. Between the acts Willie went to be photographed with the *corps de ballet*. Alan then said he noticed great changes in Willie. He was ageing. 'He is no longer very happy, hates being alone, sleeps little and is inclined to weep.' But he *is* old and will be 79 tomorrow, and his face is like a nutcracker, carelessly wrapped in parchment.

*Tuesday, 27th January*

The Graham Sutherlands‡ to dine. A. finds he too has aged since last year. He is 50, but very good-looking and still youthful in figure. He has a slow, deliberate way of speaking and never says a foolish thing. She has raven black hair as smooth as a gramophone record, and is pretty, foolish, catty but fanatically devoted to him

---

* Writer and poet (1865–1936).
† Maugham's companion (1903–85).
‡ Artist (1903–80); m. 1927 Kathleen Barry.

and jealous of his reputation. She is quite satisfied that he is the world's greatest painter. I said to Graham that I did not understand why so many artists today bothered to travel miles from England to, say, Naples or Marrakesh in order to paint a petrol pump which they could have painted as easily in the Fulham Road. He said this was a point of view which had not occurred to him and he could not share. Delightful though he is, conversation is made difficult by her always wanting to assert herself.

It is strange, in correcting the typescript of my [Inigo Jones] book, to see Eddie Marsh's astringent pencil marks and notes in the first two chapters, and realise that his mind, so active a month ago, has disappeared overnight. I never cared deeply for Eddie. Intellectually he was aloof and dismissive; had favourites; also was inaudible, talked through his teeth. I never felt comfortable with him. He dined with us [in London] on Christmas Day and we thought then we might not see him again. That was an awful day for me. I had received a letter from him that he could not continue correcting my book; the type was so faint it hurt his eyes; besides I was a *bad* writer. My use of words was odd. I could not express myself. For two days I was miserable; then on reading through his corrections again I realised he was absolutely right. Apart from having made a fool of myself – this worried me because he must have told many people – I was no longer the least hurt. I truly believe I can improve my style along the lines he showed me, i.e., to be natural. So I am grateful to the poor old deceased to that very real extent.

*Monday, 9th February*

Last week the bell at the gate pealed loudly and a very chic motor-cyclist, wearing a white helmet and armed *cap-à-pie* appeared, saluted smartly and handed me two letters in heavily embossed envelopes. Alvilde had warned me that Pierre [de Monaco]*

* Count Pierre de Polignac (1895–1964); nephew by marriage of A.L.-M's late friend Princess Edmond de Polignac (whose musical interests he shared); m. 1920 (separated 1930) Princess Charlotte of Monaco; Prince Rainier's father, who was

mentioned that we were to be invited to luncheon at the Palace to meet the Duff Coopers. At first I resolutely refused to go, but seeing how much she wanted to accept, relented. Also agreed that perhaps the Ruritanian experience ought not to be missed.

Today was the occasion. I wore my dark grey flannel suit, and A. put on her best dress. We went to the Hôtel de Paris where we left Mama. There we joined Duff and Diana. Today I liked both more than hitherto. He is not easy to talk to. She says whatever comes into her head and is very funny. The four of us then packed into the Topolino, our tiny 3-horsepower Fiat, and went roaring up to Monaco. The Palace guards in their striped sentry boxes were so surprised and shocked by the insignificance of the vehicle that they stopped us before allowing us to enter the courtyard. This compelled me to go into bottom gear before starting off again. So we passed uphill through the gatehouse making a deafening din. Duff clambered out, crumpled and creased, and shut the door on Diana who yelled at him, 'Papa, let me out!' By this time servants and soldiers ranged on the steps were bewildered. There seemed to be hundreds of them, soldiers in medieval helmets and soldiers holding pikes, major-domos in chains, on every step of the hotel-like marble staircase. We were given table-cards and ushered into a pretty Louis XV room of gilded *boiserie* overlooking the outer court. We were received by aides-de-camp and an American Monsignore. The British Consul was the next to arrive. Then the Monégasque Minister of Finance. No one else. The other guests we were told had succumbed to influenza.

We stood on one foot and then another until a far door opened, and in walked shyly a good-looking young man, plump but not gross, in a dark serge suit and monk's shoes with buckles in place of straps. He [Prince Rainier*] has a head somewhat like Napoleon's, an olive complexion and dark hair with one streak of grey in the front. I liked his face. Each was presented in turn.

---

exiled from the Principality on separation from his wife, but returned to live there on his son's accession to the throne, 1949.

* Prince Rainier III (1923–2005); succeeded grandfather, Prince Louis II, as reigning Prince of Monaco, 1949; m. 1956 Grace Kelly.

Alvilde curtsied and I bowed. He then led the way to the large dining-room after we had been handed cocktails. Since there were more men than women I sat with an aide-de-camp on my left, the dull old Dame de Palais on my right, between me and the Prince, to whom I didn't pass a word the whole afternoon. Although the Palace was quite cold I didn't dare drink the several wines which A. said afterwards were better than the food. This was not good and looked and tasted as if it had been brought in from outside. I believe the Prince does not live in the Palace but with a film star in a villa in Beaulieu. What a suitable young man, we thought, for Clarissa [Chaplin, now J.L.-M's stepdaughter] to marry. His sister Princess Antoinette* was there too. Rather pretty and has recently married a tennis professional with whom she has lived for several years and by whom she has several illegitimate children.

Duff and Diana came back with us to La Meridienne afterwards. She is still extremely beautiful; melting ice-blue eyes. Manner warmer than appearance. I wish I could see more of her to know her better. Her appeal is in the open way of saying exactly what she is thinking: and sometimes even before she has properly thought.

*Friday, 13th February*

Mama stayed with us for ten days and the visit was not a success. Alvilde was intensely irritated and although correct in her manner never friendly and at times snubbing. I too have been intensely irritated and yet sad indeed that I could not be nicer. For me the visit was a conflict of emotions. It is the first time for years that I have been with Mama for a comparatively long period. She has become extremely affected, gushing and unnatural. Her conversation is confined to the Haineses, Lottie her maid, and herself. Nothing, nothing else interests her. She brings every sentence round to

---

* Princess Antoinette de Monaco (1920–2011); known from 1951 as Baronne de Massy; m. 1st 1951 (diss. 1954) Aleco Noghès, 2nd 1961 Jean-Charles Rey (diss. 1973), 3rd 1983 John Gilpin, ballet dancer (who died same year).

herself. 'Don't you think I am wonderful to walk up all these steps?' 'Of course I had a bad headache this morning, but I managed to conceal it from you.' 'Don't bother about me. I don't need any dinner.' Then abuse of her children and children-in-law. A. says she has never in her born days met anyone so difficult, unless it was her first mother-in-law.* I have to face up to the terrible truth that I have grown miles and miles apart from her. I dare not look at her for fear she will say something so silly that I shall be driven to snap. Then I feel miserably, bitterly penitent. And who the hell am I to dare judge her, my mother? And why do I fail every time to give her what she wants, confidence, flattery and oceans of sympathy, since deeply, deeply down I do love her? I cannot, however hard I try. O glory!

*Friday, 27th February*

This evening before dark went for a short walk along the Gorbio mountain path and on my return heard the familiar tinkle-clang of the goats being folded. They were all on the path returning home to bed. The little black dog came bounding up to me, then resumed his duty. The old goats are so wise and patient, but irritable at times and snap silently at the black dog, who wags his tail. There seems to be an instinctive understanding between them. As the path is narrow and precipitous I couldn't pass the goats for a long time so I walked with the sullen young goatherd and was determined to talk to him. Although his clothes are unromantic – he wears old tweed trousers, a slouch hat and carries a long stick but no flute – he nevertheless cuts a pastoral or rather bucolic figure. He has that quiet, philosophic, almost cynical, unsurprised air of the real peasant. Tells me that in May he goes off to the mountains with his goats until November. In the winter he sleeps in Roquebrune village, God knows where – in a barn? – but in the summer on the bare hills, as far as I can make out. Says he is

---

* Hon. Gwladys Wilson (1881–1971), dau. of 1st Baron Nunburnholme; m. 1905 2nd Viscount Chaplin (d. 1949).

Italian, but speaks better French than most of the inhabitants of the village. Says this place – quietly waving his stick around – was Italy and is now France. You don't know where you are from one moment to the next. I much admire the detached, indifferent but infinitely courteous way in which he says goodnight. He is very well bred.

*Friday, 6th March*

Stalin is dead, thank God!

I have finished my Inigo Jones book after very hard work on it since 23 January and reduced its length by 16,000 words. I pray Batsford won't tell me to cut it down still further, for I am sick of it. Whenever I believe I have come to the end of a book I never have; there is always something extra to be done. If not returned for further cutting there are still the preface, the bibliography and the index to be tackled. I like to think this book is the best I have so far written. But it is less readable than the others.

After luncheon I changed into my dirtiest shirt and went for a mammoth walk to Castellare, the village I have long seen as a mirage floating above Mentone. Soon got away from the civilised strip and was among the peasant women carrying long sheaves of silver olive branches on their shoulders, and peasant men with baggy trousers, patched and filthy. The *vallons* or coombes behind Mentone are crammed with disused mills with vast wooden water-wheels. (In one of the mill-houses which had been nastily modernised and concreted Alvilde found a dwelling for the Sutherlands, who are delighted with it.) Castellare is so embowered in olives that from a distance it can be seen only on its own level. I clambered through terraced groves. Under the gnarled old trees grew thin green grass or wheat, interspersed with violets and grape hyacinths. The village is quite unspoilt. At the end of the narrow main street, cobbled, a little domed building has a wrought-iron balcony with book-rest to enable a preacher to read from it in the open air. I drank lemon water seated in the sun behind the café overlooking the distant sea. In spite of the natural beauty on all sides my attention was distracted by the oratory of a bourgeois French shopkeeper at the next table with only his frowsty wife and obsequious daughter for audience. The substance of his talk mere gossip about their relations, *Oncle* Josef, *Tante* Marianne, *Cousine* Bette. Entered the tiny shrine at Castellare and was glad to be a Papist, a participant in the universality, I suppose.

*Saturday, 14th March*

A. and I set out for Italy at 8 o'clock. We changed cars at Mentone and travelled in the Plymouth. Stopped at Albenga on the Riviera where indeed few of the old towns are worth visiting. Here we looked at the octagonal baptistry of very early date. The most remarkable feature the windows with fairly delicate stone tracery, too small for alabaster fillings, and I suppose always unglazed.

We were asked by Quentin Crewe to stay the night at Gli Scaffari near Lerici. He is companion and reader to Percy Lubbock,* the owner. It is exactly twenty years since I stayed in this villa with the George Lloyds who rented it. It was August or September and I had arrived from Corsica where I had ridden across the island on mule-back. I was dressed as near as I dared be to a Corsican bandit in sky-blue trousers and a wide red bandanna round my waist and a striped sailor jersey.† Absurdly pretentious and silly I must have appeared to the staid Lloyds.

Mr Lubbock is 73, purblind and groping about; charming, gentle, with a sort of sardonic, deprecatory chuckle. Deeply read and academic. We instantly liked him; and he was very welcoming. His sympathies are wholly left-wing. Dismisses all social standards and gossip. He and Quentin make a rather touching couple, each with his physical disability. Quentin aged 28 is crippled with an incurable muscular disease and moves in a stiff, ungainly gait, ugly to watch. A very intelligent young man. The garden is divine; a grove of terraced olives above a rocky escarpment on the sea,

---

* Writer (1879–1965); m. 1926 (as her 2nd husband) Lady Sybil Cutting (d. 1943), dau. of 5th Earl of Desart, mother of the writer Iris Origo.

† As related in *Another Self*.

jonquils, irises and hyacinths growing under the olives among the dry grass.

*Sunday, 15th March*

Poor A. very bored (but good) with my desire to see the duomo and piazza at Leghorn. The cathedral destroyed in the war is being rebuilt on the old lines, for what that is worth; the piazza on modernistic lines mostly, but one side on the recognisable lines of round-headed arcades and *piano nobile* and attic storey above. What Inigo Jones presumably saw, and what influenced his Covent Garden piazza.

Our visit to Rome was on account of the next book on my agenda. I have chosen the subject: essays on Ancient Roman, Early Christian, Medieval, Renaissance, Baroque and Rococo monuments of each period. I mean them to be poetical and free, not to be guide-booky or too factual, but representative of each historical and architectural context. I mean to explain what great buildings signify aesthetically and associatively. This will be a test of my limited powers. Maybe I shall fail. Goodness knows who will publish them.

We saw a lot of the Beits in Rome. I am extremely fond of both. Alfred highly intelligent, determined, has broad interests. Clementine always sunshine, is likewise very well informed. She takes immense pains to see all she can and as thoroughly as possible. Won't waste a moment when sight-seeing. What I like.

*Sunday, 29th March*

Pierre de Monaco, pompous and correct, pays us an unexpected call. Peals the bell at the gate. From an upstairs window Walterine [the maid] screams, '*J'arrive! J'arrive!*' And then as though that were not enough, '*Madame est au water!*' Pierre vastly amused. But A. obliged later to instruct W. in more delicate ways of excusing her mistress's dilatoriness in receiving a guest.

I haven't yet heard from Batsford whether my Inigo Jones manuscript is definitely accepted. There is much I want to get down to now. First, the Rome book; then the Jacobean book of essays on three or four characters, Anne of Denmark or James I, Lord Pembroke and Francis Bacon. Then a life of Lord Burlington;* then a dictionary of country houses.

*Good Friday, 3rd April*

Roquebrune village still observes a long-cherished tradition on Good Friday evenings. At 8.30 there are Stations of the Cross in the church of which the interior is draped with black curtains, a valance of white stars at the top and silver tears falling below; altar covered with arum lilies. At 9.30 takes place the procession. This consists of villagers only. First come four Roman centurions wearing helmets and breastplates over yellow tunics, breeches and laced boots. They carry spears. Four bearers wearing white surplices and oriental turbans carry on a bier a figure of the dead Christ covered with a fine net sheet. Two male figures carry a long shroud. A veiled woman carries St Veronica's towel with the face of Our Lord imprinted on it. More Roman soldiers, not so important, mere boys. Then a long trail of women wearing orange garments and black shawls, or black dresses and orange shawls, their faces almost covered, holding candles in parchment lanterns. A man with a drum which he beats at intervals. Behind them all the nice quizzical *curé* hugging a monstrance. The procession begins at the high altar, preceded by a surpliced figure bearing a high wooden crucifix. He is followed by those visitors come to watch, on a circuit of the village. The Roman centurions, who include the electrician, the plumber and the man at the *épicerie*, bear flaming torches. The procession takes place in great earnestness. There is no giggling or sniggering. The performers never recognise their friends in passing. The veiled women recite the Rosary and the men intone on the march.

The village is lit up for the occasion. Each house puts out snail shells filled with oil round doors and windows and up steps and

* Richard Boyle, 3rd Earl of Burlington (1674–1753); architect, exponent of neo-Palladian school, whose life and work J.L.-M. dealt with in *Earls of Creation* (1962).

staircases. This is charming and pretty. Princess Ottoboni who lives in a large villa outside the village gives prizes for the best illuminated houses which some people deplore because it makes the villagers mercenary. On the other hand this tradition might die out altogether. In spite of the sightseers the whole affair is quite unsophisticated and thoroughly bucolic. The participants bump into each other, trip up, drop their torches and look for all the world what they are – peasants.

Lennox [Berkeley] who is staying with us accompanied me into the church and followed the stations with a sort of dumb reverence. He is come to finish a concerto to be performed on the Third Programme in Coronation week, and from his pavilion piano I hear emerge occasional dissonant noises, but nothing consecutive. I much wonder how good a composer he is. I am incapable of judging. I admire his exceptionally good and utterly childlike nature. Deeply earnest and remote in his own world, which is not mine and into which I cannot penetrate. He has much humility and simplicity of heart. The little I have heard of his music strikes me as chill. He doesn't play the piano very well and it is odd to hear him say he cannot perform his own compositions because he hasn't got the score with him. When he has got it he stumbles, goes back again and says such and such passages are too difficult for him.

*Monday, 6th April*

I go back to England this evening by the Blue Train from Monte Carlo. We came out here on a Monday, exactly three months ago. I have been happier here this winter than last. Yet I am glad to be leaving. I have been long enough away from England and my interests. Yet I somewhat dread returning to the National Trust. I know I ought to leave it altogether for my presence there is redundant, even embarrassing. Robin [Fedden] doesn't now need me. In many ways he is better at the job than I was. It is awkward for him when I am about. It is always a mistake to hang about when one has resigned from a post. Yet what am I to do? I can't leave England altogether and give up the £700 a year which the Trust still pays me. Without it I have no regular income at all.

I am fond of my little pavilion in the garden at Roquebrune where I am writing at the moon-shaped table in the window. Beside me my lamp with blue shade and at its foot three blue mustard-liner glasses in Ritzy-Louis Quinze containers of ormolu, and the bronze hand letter-weight and the paper-clip of a duck's head in pewter in which I keep my letters. On a corner shelf the figure of Our Lady with Child, all in white biscuit, once belonging to a church no doubt, on a plinth of angel heads, bought by me in the Nice flea market. My Jump & Vuillamy travelling clock which strikes the hours and quarters, tells the date, day of the week, and phases of the moon. I have to take it with me because if it runs down how can I ever set it properly again? Alas I have the minimum of reference books; there is no room. The pavilion is the size of a *wagon-lit*, just large enough to contain emergency bed, chest of drawers, two chairs and a niche for clothes, plus minute wash-basin.

*Friday, 10th April*

This is the story of Mr Rapton. It has made me curse myself for a fool and incurable waster of heaven-sent opportunities. On Monday I boarded the Blue Train at Monte Carlo at 7 p.m. All my life I have hankered for an adventure in a sleeper but none had ever come my way. At 7.45 I went to the restaurant car for the first dinner. I sat by the window at a table for four. Presently the seat next to me and the one opposite were taken by a dull, middle-aged American couple, business man and wife. I began to read Goodhart-Rendel's book on post-Regency architecture between courses. Presently someone was put into the seat opposite mine. He was an extremely good-looking young man of about 25 to 30. He spoke beautiful French but was reading a novel by Sinclair Lewis in English. Like me he seemed immersed in his book and neither addressed a word nor cast a glance at the Americans and me. But owing to the close quarters our feet and legs touched. After cautious and as it were accidental and occasional light pressures the game was evidently on. Soon there was no mistaking. Every show of eagerness went on below while above we solemnly read our books without a flicker of muscle or betrayal of feeling. Not a word was spoken. During this time I experienced a *coup de foudre*. He was everything I had desired in my most sanguine daydreams – tall, delicate, strong, sensitive, masculine, mature, young, arrogant, well-bred, mysterious, discreet, radiant, beautiful. What a lot of qualities to be made so self-evident within half an hour's silence. He drank nothing but Vichy water. I drank half a bottle of white wine. The Americans ordered no liqueurs or coffee. I ordered coffee to prolong things. He too ordered coffee. We were given our bills. We all paid: then the Americans got up and left the dining car with everyone else. They wanted to clear us out for second dinner. I was debating whether to start a conversation when he, with rather portentous assurance, scribbled in pencil on his bill, 'What car no.? If car?', and shoved it under my nose. He evidently was taking great care that we should not be seen talking. So I took out my pencil and wrote, 'Carriage 1, No.17', and then added, 'I am not alone, there is a stranger with me, and you?' – for I was travelling 2nd class and shared a compartment with an Italian bank manager from Alassio. He then wrote with the same maddening caution, 'The conductor knows me well. Your stay a short time?' This bewildered me. I didn't quite understand. So, still playing his game, and the attendants now hustling us to leave, I wrote, 'I am going to London.' Then he wrote very clearly and distinctly, 'Telephone WHI 3227 Mr Rapton', and got up. As I went he smiled in a manner intoxicating, showing glistening, strong white teeth, and spoke his first words to me. 'You have my telephone number all right?' 'Yes,' I answered, and rushed away. I returned to my carriage, undressed and climbed into my bunk, then my companion did the same and climbed into his bunk. In bed I then took out the bill with our notes on it and started to gloat. To my intense distress I saw that I had misread his note about the conductor, for he had written after 'but' the words 'OK if you stay short time'. Oh God, I thought, the fool I am. I have missed it. I cannot get up, dress, and go to him. And here I was again a fool. My ridiculous bloody stupid temperament (which is not to eat my cake at once but hold it at arm's length and gloat over it) may have led me to think – Well, I may have spurned the experience I have always hankered for. Nevertheless this person is beyond a fly-by-night. He is perfection. He has come into my life to stay for ever and we shall meet tomorrow evening in London.

Next morning, not seeing him at breakfast, I wrote him a hurried note giving my name and telephone number and repeating my great wish that we should meet again, meaning to hand it to him personally or give it to the attendant of his coach. But on walking back to my compartment when we had suddenly arrived in Paris, I saw him in an overcoat, carrying a tennis racquet, standing at the door about to get out. Rather he noticed me first, for he smiled, shook me by the hand, and said good-morning. 'Oh,' I said, 'are you getting out here?' He replied, 'Just for a day', or 'one night' I think he said. So I thrust my note into his hand, saying rather foolishly, 'Here is something you left behind last night at dinner.' That is the last I saw of him.

I got to London Tuesday evening. I did not ring him up on Wednesday evening, but on Thursday morning I could not resist longer. I telephoned the number he gave me. A woman answered. This is So-and-So's office, she said. There is no one here of the name of Rapton. You are quite mistaken. Repeatedly since I have rung up in the evenings, for he said any time after 7.30 he would be there, and never has there been an answer, because it is an office. Did he give me a false name and number on purpose? Or did he make a mistake? Anyway he has not telephoned me and I now know he never will and I shall never see him. This is an absurd little incident, but it has thrown me into a state bordering on hysteria. Oh *God* what an absolute ass I am, what a bloody silly ass.

*Thursday, 16th April*

At Brooks's I overhear Sir John Coke, Queen Mary's Comptroller, telling another member how sad he is made by her death.* He said she never altered her mind once it had been made up; that she had

* On 24 March.

never been known to be late once in her life; that now she was gone there was no member of the Royal family to keep the rest of them up to the mark, no one now to prevent the Queen from having meals with people like Douglas Fairbanks, from motoring in a jeep without wearing a hat, etc. Only once I met her, when I conducted her around an exhibition I organised in Cheyne Walk in 1940, in aid of the Finns. She was extremely stiff and formal, and rather ungracious. Very knowledgeable and informative about furniture and bibelots of a royal sort; contradictory, splendid and awful. Her death truly the end of a spent era.

Yesterday I was at Petworth with Robin putting finishing touches to the house which is to be opened in May. The furniture is poor; the pictures on the other hand outstanding. Sculpture not up to much; and the architecture highly esteemed by the academic, because of the seventeenth-century French flavour. Whiffs of the Sun King. Some truly wonderful rooms of a rare period. And the carvings. And Turner.

*Monday, 20th April*

One of the strange things of the present age is listening to voices of dead friends. This evening at the end of the first act of an opera the Third Programme announcer said we were about to hear a conversation recorded in the Forties between Margaret Jourdain and Ivy Compton-Burnett about Ivy's novels. Margaret's familiar, governessy voice was as natural as if she were in the room, talking to Ivy who is still alive. A still stranger thing perhaps was my turning off the wireless in the middle of the talk because I had something else to do. Now if any of us had been told in 1923 that we could hear a friend who had died two years previously conversing with another friend he would have hung on every word, marvelling.

When Rosamond Lehmann* dined with me last week she said I was unusual in my blending of the masculine and the feminine;

* Novelist (1901–90); sister of John Lehmann; old friend of A.L.-M. who had become a good friend of J.L.-M.

that for a male man I had a very female sensibility. She said she had as many women as men friends and, if anything, preferred their society, yet she admitted there were few women with whom she could talk about fundamental things. Ros has a strong femininity with which I feel at times impatient. I am sure she does not expect or want a gesture of love from me, but I am occasionally made uncomfortable in suspecting that she would welcome the pretence of one. In other words, a very close friendship with a woman, not so much older than oneself, can seldom be quite as straightforward as with a man.

After I wrote to Paul Latham inviting myself to stay at Herstmonceux last Friday he telephoned while I was out. I was rather touched that, even ten years after he left prison, he would not give his name to Emily, who I am sure is totally unaware of his past misdemeanours. Somewhat amused, she told me that a friend had telephoned, 'Tell him that Paul expects him to dinner on Friday.' Poor Paul has become a worse bore than ever. Incessant, absolutely inarticulate talk about himself. He said that he had nearly died so often, once when he tried to commit suicide on a motor-bike, that he had no fear of death and rather longed for it.

*Friday, 8th May*

I love my country house tours more and more as I grow older and become more and more fascinated by persons, places and things. I am a late developer more than most men of my generation and in some respects still quite adolescent, an opsimath indeed.

*Sunday, 24th May*

All last week I spent with Eardley motoring around Cornwall and Devon. It is our West Country spring week which we always contrive to take together at this glorious time of year. It poured with rain every day but one, yet it didn't altogether matter. Devon has a character quite its own – the most lush of our counties, its valleys more verdant, its beech trees more glossy green, its lanes more flowery than any other's.* We motored down miles of tunnelled lanes indecently clothed with bluebells, mauve campions and white starry stitchwort. Cornwall has its special character which I don't quite capture, but felt this time a little. The bit between Penzance and St Ives is, I suspect, the real Cornwall of Tristan and Isolde – a country wild and wide under a cloudy, swiftly flying sky; fields divided by walls so overgrown with grass and turf that they become banks; gorse in full curry bloom, boggy weedy pools and weird rock formations, primeval and whether natural or prehistoric man-made one can't determine.

The eccentricity of people living in large English country houses is almost certain. But the houses must be large enough to sustain the eccentricity and the owners – they must be owners – must live in them all the year round. Evidently the owners need not necessarily be the representatives of old families, or even county families, for eccentricity catches on like burrs. Another book I have long had in mind is about eccentric owners. This I hope soon to start collecting notes for.

John Betjeman said that he and Penelope had to leave their pretty house in Farnborough for their present plain one in Wantage because he suffered persecution mania in the village. In the end he couldn't go down the village street for anxiety lest he forgot the names of neighbours and thereby caused hurt feelings. Wantage town is big enough for it not to matter whom he forgets by name. I can well understand this and in a lesser way suffer the same worry in Roquebrune village.

*At the end of May, Alvilde and Clarissa joined J.L.-M. in London for eight weeks.*

*Sunday, 31st May*

I am at Wickhamford with my mother who has confided in me that she is contemplating marrying a country neighbour, Harry

* J.L.-M's feelings about the county had changed in the course of a decade: see entry for 28 October 1943.

Horsfield.* I tell her that on the whole I favour it because she will have companionship with a man who is eminently decent and intelligent. But – she protests – he is middle-class. I tell her that it doesn't matter in the least so long as he hasn't got habits that irritate. She says he has not, beyond saying 'phone' and 'going to town', which strike me as fairly venial, and I tell her she can train him to drop them. The worst disadvantage however is his children. Mama will have four or five stepchildren, to say nothing of step-grandchildren, in addition to her own. This I agree with her is enough to kill anyone stone dead. I have one stepdaughter and she gets horribly on my nerves. Horsfield is an intelligent, well-read man of some intellect and how he can put up with my mother's silliness and repetitions I don't know.

On Friday, Alvilde, Clarissa and I went to the Abbey dress rehearsal of the Coronation. We were in our seats by 8 a.m. They were in the first range built over the entrance to the North Transept. Thus we looked across to Poet's Corner and over the theatre in the middle of which was set the Queen's throne on steps. The seats are hung with sky-blue damask hangings embroidered with crown and insignia. The floor is covered with golden yellow carpet, plain. I could just see King Edward's chair on my left but not the Throne of State or the altar. A magnificent spectacle. Proceedings lasted until 1 o'clock. The ushers were dressed in black velvet Court dress with silver buckles and silver-hilted swords, and knee breeches. Their uniform handsomer than the scarlet dress uniform of the Brigade of Guards, or the overdressed Highland uniforms with too much jabot and too many daggers and horn bugles. Our usher was George Howard of Castle Howard whose scarlet uniform was very bedraggled. His belt kept slipping down.

* Widower, who had served in Royal Flying Corps during First World War. The marriage took place, but lasted only a few months. Horsfield was still alive on 16 November 1973, when J.L.-M. asked him whether it had been 'unadulterated hell'. He replied: 'Not unadulterated . . . at times she became possessed by demons . . .' J.L.-M. concluded, 'The truth is that Mama was not made to live with others. She could not bear to have the same person about her for more than a few hours. Like me she was a recluse, or more accurately a solitary.' (*Ancient as the Hills*.)

He is an uncouth creature. The music was only rather beautiful. I thought Walton's *Te Deum* had vigour, but Vaughan Williams's *Credo* boring. The Duchess of Norfolk* deputised for the Queen and was excellent. She wore the Queen's robes and carried her regalia. Her cloth-of-gold robe and rich Imperial crown unforgettable. The weight of orb and sceptre carried in either hand called for much balancing and physical strength. The little pages' silk coats were of sky-blue, saffron and maroon; their breeches of white satin. Each followed closely behind his peer. The peers' coronets were very absurd and looked like washstand basins with feet sticking up in the air. I saw Gerry Wellington under his, worn at a scornful tilt like an old dowager's toque. David Crawford looked roguish in his. In truth the robes and uniforms with their depth of colour and glitter of gold were far too splendid for most of the wearers. Nearly all the males were bald. The strong arc lights were unkind to faces and pates, though flattering to the robes. The most striking figure was the Dowager Duchess of Devonshire† in red velvet, wearing an enormous diamond tiara and small coronet, a heavy train of infinite length, and long white gloves. Fortune Euston‡ was one of the Queen's Ladies, dressed like Rhine maidens. The history of England epitomised in this glamorous ceremony.

*Tuesday, 2nd June (Coronation Day)*

A. called me at 5 this morning, which seemed unnecessarily early. Did not put on morning dress but my best blue suit. Clarissa had already gone to her seat with her young man by the time I was drinking coffee in the kitchen. A. dressed in black with her

---

* Hon. Lavinia Strutt, dau. of 3rd Baron Belper; m. 1937 Bernard FitzAlan Howard, 16th Duke of Norfolk, Earl Marshal of England.

† Presumably Lady Mary Cecil (1895–1988), dau. of 4th Marquess of Salisbury, m. 1917 10th Duke of Devonshire (d. 1950), who had been appointed Mistress of the Robes to the new Queen, and not her mother-in-law, dowager of the 9th Duke, who was still alive.

‡ Fortune Smith; m. 1946 Hugh, Earl of Euston (b. 1919), N.T. Representative for East of England, who s. 1970 as 11th Duke of Grafton; she succeeded the Dowager Duchess of Devonshire as Mistress of the Robes in 1967.

diamonds and the prettiest striped turban hat. There was a queue at South Kensington station but we eventually got into a train, jammed like sardines. At Green Park station got out and in our finery had to walk up the escalator which wasn't working. Had no difficulty getting to Brooks's where a vast concourse of members and friends. Hardly a seat to sit on. It was bitterly cold with the windows all out and steps up to balconies erected against the façade. We were perished and sat before a fire in the morning-room wearing overcoats. We read or talked to friends, chiefly the young Meade-Fetherstonhaughs, and watched the Abbey ceremony on the television. It was very moving, the young Queen so calm, grave and sure of every movement, and so palpably serious and intent. Certain scenes specially memorable: her entry to the theatre with arms dropped over her skirt in token of humility; and when the Archbishop walked to the four sides of the Abbey to ask the people if they would accept her as their queen, they replying in the affirmative, and she giving a slow half-curtsey of acknowledgement. It was a gesture on her part of obeisance and yet tremendous majesty – the only occasion she will ever be known to curtsey. Indeed all day I was choking with emotion and unable to speak or cheer. Am neither proud nor ashamed of this.

The weather was damnable. It rained all day. The moment the procession started it positively poured, and the troops were soaked. Yet the procession was magnificent. The colour and pageantry cannot be described. Uniforms superb and resplendent. The most popular figure Queen Salote of Tonga,* a vast, brown, smiling bundle with a tall red knitting-needle in her hat (it having begun as a plume of feathers). Despite the rain she refused to have the hood of her open carriage drawn, and the people were delighted. They roared applause. Extraordinary how the public will take someone to its bosom, especially someone not very exalted who is putting up a good show. All along the route they adored her. Beside her squatted a little man in black and a top hat – her husband. Noël Coward,

* 1900–65; the only ruler of a territory within the British Empire recognised as fully sovereign.

when asked who he was, said, 'Her dinner.'* Public also gave special applause to the Gurkhas and coloured troops, with that unequivocal sense of fair play. As for the carriages the most beautiful was the Queen Mother's, the Irish [State] coach; the most splendid the Queen's. Her gold and glass coach designed for George III's coronation by Sir William Chambers, with vast gold tritons and painted Cipriani panels like something out of a fairy tale, Cinderella's, drawn by six bays with grooms in eighteenth-century livery; and inside the Queen wearing her crown and carrying her orb and sceptre, and the handsome Duke in a cocked hat by her side.

*Friday, 19th June*

On Monday A. and I motored to stay with Elizabeth Herbert† at Tetton Park near Taunton on a strange mission. Long pre-arranged with her, it was to tackle Mr William Esdaile‡ of Cothelstone House near Taunton. He is Shelley's great-grandson through the poet's daughter Ianthe by Harriet Westbrook. Ianthe was married by her aunt Eliza Westbrook to Mr Esdaile of Cothelstone. The present Esdaile owns a notebook of early poems in Shelley's handwriting and/or Harriet's, and probably other undiscovered papers besides. Two years ago, staying at Tetton, I was taken to Cothelstone and shown the precious notebook§ by Mr Esdaile's sister¶ who conducted me round the house, while Elizabeth walked

---

* He was not in fact the Queen's husband but the Sultan of Kelantan, and Coward famously described him as 'her lunch'.

† Elizabeth, daughter of J. E. Willard, United States Ambassador; m. 1921 Hon. Mervyn Herbert.

‡ William Clement Henry Esdaile (b. 1878); gt-gt-grandson of William Esdaile, sometime Lord Mayor of London, who rebuilt Cothelstone House in the Greek style, 1818; grandson of Edward Esdaile (1813–81), who m. 1837 Elizabeth Ianthe (d. 1876), o. dau. of Percy Bysshe Shelley by his 1st wife Harriette.

§ Published 1966 as *The Esdaile MS Notebook*, with Introduction, Commentary and Notes by Neville Rogers. The original notebook is held by the Carl Pforzheimer Collection of Shelley and His Circle at the New York Public Library.

¶ According to *Burke's Landed Gentry*, William Esdaile had no sister. J.L.-M. presumably met his sister-in-law, Dorothy Esdaile, widow of his bro. Percy (1882–1926)

the old boy round the garden. The sister pulled the book out of an old ottoman in the attic and I had opened it only at the first page when she snatched it from my hands and thrust it back into the ottoman because she heard her brother approaching. Mr Esdaile is an eccentric old fellow of over seventy who won't hear any reference to Shelley, either because he is ashamed of the poet for having been an atheist expelled from Oxford or because he married Harriet who came of a non-armigerous family. Neville Rogers and Edmund Blunden* who are editing the complete works of Shelley for the Oxford [University] Press are very anxious to have access to the notebook in order to publish the poems, some of which have never been printed, and were missed by Edward Dowden, Shelley's first biographer [1886]. As a member of the Keats–Shelley committee I offered to help.

So on Wednesday Elizabeth took me over to Cothelstone, an astonishing house. Built about 1810 for the Esdailes as a neo-Greek villa it was added to in Victorian times. Is chock-a-block with good things and absolute trash. A landscape by Gainsborough, some portraits by Reynolds and one by Wilkie, very good, jostle among prints of puppies sheltering under umbrellas, Regency furniture and Edwardian pianolas draped with lace tablecloths and littered with photograph frames. Nothing has been shifted since the turn of the century. There is somewhere a portrait of Ianthe which I saw on my previous visit. We were ushered into Mr Esdaile's study to wait for him. He is slight, thin-lipped, white-faced, rather aquiline and patrician, with a stoop not unlike Shelley's. I dare say when young he resembled the poet in physique. Mrs Herbert explained that we had come early because I wished to talk to him about the notebook. 'I don't know where it is, I believe that I have lost it,' was all he said and instantly changed the subject. After he had blamed the weather, the Government, the Communists, we returned to the attack. 'I believe you have got it,' he exclaimed

and mother of Elizabeth Esdaile (b. 1917; m. 1949 Philip Warmington), heiress to the Cothelstone estate.

* Poet (1896–1974).

sharply to Elizabeth, and again changed the subject. Finally we returned to the subject and I asked him point-blank for permission to have it microfilmed for the Bodleian. I quoted Blunden and Harold Nicolson who attach immense importance to it. 'I don't like Nicolson's voice on the wireless,' was the only answer I got. But he did not positively refuse me. Then he took us both round the garden.

At 4.30 A. and a charming American staying at Tetton, Mrs Fenwick, joined us at a nursery tea of jam, Devonshire cream and cakes in the dining-room. They were all wonderfully flattering and persuasive, played up to the old man and teased him. It was time to leave so Mrs Herbert most cunningly said she was taking the women upstairs. I was left alone with Mr E. who I don't suppose was a bit pleased. But I said to him, pleading, 'I know you won't refuse my request, will you?' And he consented to have the notebook photographed so long as it did not leave the house. I think this was quite a successful visit.

*Wednesday, 1st July*

After a deal of intrigue A. and I met a photographer, sent by the Bodleian, at Taunton station this morning and drove him to Cothelstone by appointment. At last we have succeeded in photographing the Shelley notebook. It amounts to about ninety-five open pages. The poems are certainly in two handwritings, perhaps three. On the first page is inscribed the name, Ianthe Esdaile. I don't know how many poems are in Harriet's hand but I believe several are in Shelley's. I am certain a large number of the poems have never yet been printed. It was thrilling to handle once again, at leisure, the closely packed octavo volume. Mr Esdaile told me he didn't want to sell the book. I advised him to claim a reproduction fee for any poems published. He said to me: 'You must understand that until the last few years Shelley's name was never mentioned in my family. He treated my great-grandmother abominably. He even had the effrontery, while living with another woman, to ask my great-grandmother to join them in their adultery.' He said the notebook was the only relic of Shelley he possessed, apart from his christening robe. I did not ask to see this because I was so worried about getting the photographs taken. Mr E. was in a great hurry to get off for his annual holiday – the old limousine purring at the front door – and would not leave until we had finished. It was a good thing I went, for the photographer was a raw, callow youth, with no manners. Mr E. is a nice old man, old-fashioned, correct and very shy. In the dining room under the Gainsborough landscape is a hideous harmonium with *Hymns Ancient and Modern* on a music stand. Elizabeth Herbert said the squire and his sister played and sang hymns together every Sunday evening.

*Friday, 3rd July*

It was sad walking round Ashburnham House [Sussex] and seeing it half-empied of lovely things, all of which were in place the last time I went there – only two or three years ago on a visit organised by the Georgian Group. Then Lady Catherine Ashburnham* took us round herself, a middle-aged, shy, diffident woman with a gentle smile, fair skin, and rather prominent, strong white teeth. Early this year she died and now every single object is being sold by a distant cousin. Thus ends another immensely long association of an ancient family that took its name from its land. She was the last Ashburnham of Ashburnham.

*Wednesday, 22nd July*

I am alone again, which I enjoy more than anything in the world. Alvilde has returned to France and Clarissa has gone to her father (a rare event) before rejoining her mother. Thank goodness, because in London I have a great deal to do without having to look after her. I get impatient with young girl frivolities, especially when her mother is away. To live with adolescents is quite impracticable and really should not be suffered.

* Daughter (1890–1953) of Thomas, 6th and last Earl of Ashburnham (1855–1924).

*Saturday, 25th July*

Yesterday was a golden day and so hot that I stopped in Oxford for a short half-hour and bathed in Parsons Pleasure. It is always a mysterious little world to me. A masculine world of lush green scythed grass, enclosed by wattle fences from prying eyes, behind which all women are prohibited. Within it the young men strip completely naked. Not a fig leaf is permitted. Secret, shared rites of manhood may be meditated but are not enacted, freed from the shackles of womankind which no doubt envisages all kinds of arcane communion. How disappointed they would be if they gained admittance. The lawn is dappled with light and shadow from shimmering willow trees. The Cherwell leisurely flows alongside. On the opposite bank a meadow of hay and wild flowers forms an impenetrable boundary on the low horizon to the bodies stretched on the scythed grass. I have only seen Parsons Pleasure in idyllic conditions when the summer sun is fully shining. A disagreeable note is struck by the old men with paunches like balloons over scrawny, shrivelled thighs supported by stick-like legs. These satyrs feed on visions of the young men who either play an endless game with a football or lie in abandoned attitudes on the grass plucking at their anatomies or smoothing the golden or brackish flue of their chests. I am always fascinated by their unabashed acceptance of nakedness, yet their pride of body, and at the same time sly interest in their neighbours' – those would-be casual, swift but penetrating glances, measuring up the dimensions of another's figure, and then the relaxed look of self-satisfaction or envy. It is extraordinary how vain the normal man is. I shall never revisit Parsons Pleasure. It must be the preserve of the young. But where else can one bathe in a gently flowing river, which I infinitely prefer to the sea? For on a river one can measure the distance of one's swimming.

*Wednesday, 5th August*

This afternoon we [J.L.-M. and his N.T. colleague Hugh, Earl of Euston] called (I write 'called', but in truth we were trespassing in my old car up the long drive of Ugbrooke [Devon]; to our dismay we had a puncture and had to seek help from our host's chauffeur) on Lord and Lady Clifford of Chudleigh,* who felt obliged to give us tea. Within five minutes they had produced for Hugh the original 'Secret Treaty of Dover' between Charles II and Louis XIV and a letter from Charles's sister Minette† to his ancestor Clifford of the Cabal.‡ Hugh naturally was thrilled because his ancestor Arlington was one of the 'A's' of the Cabal. The Cliffords have fine Lelys of Clifford, Monmouth and Catherine of Braganza. They do not live at Ugbrooke which is empty and decaying, dreary and ugly outside. Lord C. said that when Disraeli stayed he observed as the carriage approached, 'This house must be one of the worst specimens of a bad period,' namely the eighteenth century.

*Thursday, 6th August*

Lord Morley§ succeeded his brother at Saltram [Park, Devon] a year ago. He is 73, permanently drunk, has had to pay enormous death duties, has no children, yet has nobly spent over £10,000, his agent informed us, in decorating the state rooms from top to bottom. It is very well done by Keebles [the decorators], and one of the best Adam interiors I have seen. Lord Morley was away but in the saloon was his butler, wearing his lordship's Brigade uniform, the earl's coronet and Coronation robes at his elbow, sitting to a pretty American female artist.

*Saturday, 8th August*

This afternoon Alex [Moulton] took me in his boat, made of tin, up the River Avon. He attaches a noisy engine to the stern. Standing in the prow I watched the placid brown water ahead

---

* Lewis, 12th Baron Clifford of Chudleigh (1889–1964); m. (2nd) 1934 Mary Knox.

† Princess Henrietta Stuart, Duchess of Orleans (1644–70).

‡ Acronym of Clifford, Ashley, Buckingham, Arlington and Lauderdale, advisers to Charles II.

§ Montagu Parker, 5th Earl of Morley (1878–1962); Boer War veteran.

quiver from the vibration of the approaching engine like the retriever wrinkling its nose. Weather divine at last, no wind, and hot, baking sun. Banks of the river covered with clumps of purple loosestrife, tansies, epilobium, both mauve kinds, and deadly nightshade. We sailed through avenues of tall, bunchy willow trees from which the country boys hang a rope with a stick on the end. They swing on the rope, gathering momentum, then let go and plunge into the water. Scenes of idyllic youths bathing recalled that late Victorian artist, Sir Luke Fildes.* Having passed the bathers Alex and I disembarked, took off our clothes and lay in a field of cut hay. Pricked by stubble and stung by nettles was exhilarating agony not to be long endured.

*Wednesday, 19th August*

This morning, working upstairs in Thurloe Square, I listened to the rag-and-bone man in his cart. His is one of the Cries of London not yet extinct. As he passed my window I looked out. He was young, spivvish, seated on a pile of scrap, holding the reins of an emaciated pony. No one paid any heed, or stopped him. At regular intervals he cried very fast and rhythmically what sounded like, 'Any, any, any knives – or! Any, any, any knives – or!' Alas, the hurdy-gurdy-and-monkey man, along with the muffin man, a large tray on his head and a bell in his right hand, these of my youth have gone for good.

Hilaire Belloc† has died. I used to meet him staying with Mary Herbert at Pixton during the war. He was ailing and querulous. He seemed to exist only on wine, then very difficult to get. But Mary somehow provided it and he sipped it all day long, smacking his lips and complaining how indifferent it was. From time to time he warmed up, and talked and talked and talked. Was sardonic, but brilliant. Was very class-conscious, referring to himself as the

---

* Fildes (1843–1927) is not known for his portrayal of bathing youths, and J.L.-M. may be confusing him with his contemporary, Henry Scott Tuke (1858–1929).

† Writer, poet and Catholic polemicist (1870–1953).

epitome of the middle class and Mary that of the upper. He wasn't wrong. He always wore the same dirty old cloak. One night there was a great noise. Mr Belloc going to the bathroom with a candle set himself ablaze. Mary put him out after filling the bathtub with water. Then she called me for help. There was a smell of burning next morning and the bathroom was full of ash from his rusty old cloak. In similar circumstances he died recently.

*Friday, 21st August*

I have finished my Inigo Jones book and have nothing more to do with it. It will be out in October. I am well on the way with my next book – Rome. I have bought out of my inheritance money from Deenie* and my book a drop-head Rolls coupé, which is frightfully distinguished (second-hand of course and immensely old – 1936). Absurd perhaps; snobbish possibly; aesthetic certainly. On Monday I go to France for six weeks; after this interval I truly desire to be with A. again. I go to Lytes Cary this evening, and hope Giles [Eyre]† will be nice to me.

*Sunday, 23rd August*

Mummy talked for hours into the night about her marriage problems with which I entirely sympathise. She is not in the least in love with H. Horsfield. He is with her – too strange. She doesn't want to marry a bit. Yet does not want to lose him. He crosses himself before meals. She is far better mentally as well as physically: for he takes her on long drives and this broadens her outlook. Ma told me things that she has told no one else about the wooing, and I made her promise she never would tell anyone else for fear of ridicule. I must say I love the eternal child in her which makes men die for love of her, aged 69 and about to become a great-grandmother. When I remember Daddy and Deenie worrying about her health

* J.L.-M's aunt Doreen Cunninghame had died in 1952.

† Art critic and dealer in watercolours (1922–2005), recently installed as tenant of Lytes Cary, N.T. manor house in Somerset.

and happiness and here she is well enough to contemplate remarriage while they are both ashes.

*Monday, 24th August*

This afternoon, in the bus going back to Thurloe Square, I found myself sitting next to a male tart. Rather handsome he was in a Modigliani-like way with a long, oval face and almond eyes. He gave me one of those sidelong looks I know so well, expressionless and full of deep meaning; a second look was of the most languishing and seductive nature, yet one which if seen by a third person would not be noticed. That is so clever of this tribe; it is brought about by aeons of persecution; they know how to elude detection, and the consequence of this subterfuge is a terrible dishonesty. We were not alone in the bus, yet I noticed how he touched my arm without appearing to. I asked him where he lived and he said South Kensington. Then in mincing tones which made me feel a trifle sick, he said, 'Have you done a little shopping?' for I was strung with paper bags. When at my stop I suddenly got off the bus without giving him a glance, I knew he was surprised and affronted. How strange that this Rapton opportunity should again come my way, this time at the very end of my English sojourn. Tonight I fly to Nice.

*Tuesday, 25th August*

Landed at Nice airport at 3.40 a.m., and was driven in a taxi to Monte Carlo. Just before 5 dawn broke. It was a flush of liver red on the sea towards Italy. I left my luggage at the Hôtel de Paris and walked in the early morning light the five or six miles to Roquebrune. As I left the casino *place* it was still almost dark, lamps alight and a man leisurely sweeping up horse dung into a pan. Lights appeared at windows overhead and shutters banged open. When I could glimpse it between the houses the sea appeared mauve. The first smell here, even detected on the asphalt at Nice airport, is a resinous one, of pine and citrus. I walked into the house and up to Alvilde's room where she lay asleep under the mosquito net. I threw off my clothes and jumped in beside her.

*Monday, 31st August*

Last night we dined with the Mosleys at the Hôtel de Paris. The only other guest was Bob Boothby. A. and I deliberated whether we should accept, for, she explained, when David Herbert* brought them unannounced to the villa last summer she was most indignant and would not even offer them a drink. How tenuous are human principles. We agreed that if Bob Boothby, a prominent Conservative MP, was risking it, why therefore should not we who had no stake to imperil. I said that if they were Stalinists I should not go, but I had never felt as opposed to Fascists, much as I detested Hitler whom alas the Mosleys liked and honoured. I sat between Diana and Tom. When her mouth is shut – she has slightly receding gums nowadays – and her face is in repose, she is the most flawlessly beautiful woman I have ever seen: clear, creamy complexion, straight nose, deep blue eyes and grey-gold hair dressed in a Grecian bun swept to one side of her nape. Her figure is tall and slim. She is now as beautiful as she was at 17 and more so than when she first married in her early twenties. Tom Mosley is fatter, rather greyer. A. does not sense his charm. I do. He is well-mannered and attentive. His good manners make me shy. His interests are only political and when he gets talking he is on the verge of delivering a platform speech or rather a benevolent dictator's harangue. I was reminded of 1931 when I canvassed for him and the New Party at Stoke-on-Trent and attended so many of his meetings when chairs were flung at him and furniture was smashed. Now his views are balanced and sane. He talks of England as though it were a foreign country and the English as 'they'. Diana is the first woman I really was in love with.

---

* Hon. David Herbert (1908–95); yr s. of 15th Earl of Pembroke; Eton contemporary of J.L.-M.

A. and I are extremely happy together and it is as though we were having another honeymoon. I am well and interest myself in getting brown. I swim every day at Monte Carlo, for the days are perfect. Swimming develops my chest muscles quite noticeably.

*September*

At dinner the other night, young Lord Hertford, a friend of Clarissa who was staying with us, was saying how much he disliked another of their mutual friends. One of the reasons he gave was that the boy was a pansy. Now Clarissa has told us recently that Hugh Hertford had become a pansy, at least temporarily: she knew this to be true. So I, aware of this, said to Hertford that I never thought this a sound reason for disliking a person. With perfect composure, looking me straight in the eye, he said that he could never like a man whom he knew to be a pansy.

When the Mosleys lunched with us on the terrace the other day I was struck by his moderate views. He is no longer extreme – whether to hoodwink or through resolve, who can tell? He said that only amateur politicians in England harboured bitterness against each other; the professional ones, among whom he included himself, did not. As an example he gave that old fiend Beaverbrook whom he had for a generation opposed on all matters of political principle. Yet they always remained the closest friends. Bridget [Parsons] who stayed with us afterwards said that no consideration of guests for hosts would have made her meet the Mosleys here. She was sure that Diana would as willingly shovel us into a gas oven as smile on us. Peter Quennell on the other hand said he would willingly meet them because they are now rendered utterly innocuous.

*Sunday, 20th September*

Bridget left us yesterday after a ten-day visit. She was a perfect guest and entered into all our fagging, waiting and washing up. I love her, but she is lazy, selfish and insincere. One day Peter [Quennell], Bridget and I walked from the golf course at Mont Agel down to

Roquebrune, having started from La Turbie. The walk took us three hours. They both agreed that the view from the *col* overlooking Italy is as lovely as anything on the Mediterranean to be seen. Both are my match for walking and endurance.

Lately I have had nightmare after nightmare. Three nights ago I had four, of which I remember three. (1) The corpse of my 'first' wife, murdered, was in the *grenier*. I saw its bare legs protruding from a blue skirt. I begged Alvilde to have it moved before it was discovered. But A. wouldn't, saying she must wait until they moved the drawing-room carpet from the *grenier* in the winter. (2) Lord Zetland was making a speech in the House of Commons (not Lords). He was on all fours on a table and he delivered his peroration, laughing, 'The path to the grave is smooth and easy.' (3) I had a bed-sitting room in the House of Lords. It was empty when I went to the bath. On my return the Chamber was packed with peers. I had nothing on but my underpants. Gibbons, the wine waiter at Brooks's, produced a trolley on wheels. As he pushed it in front of me I moved myself out of sight. The fourth dream I forget. But last night I dreamt I was in a church which was about to be blown up, counting the seconds for the fuse to go off. I believe these nightmares may be caused by the mosquito net. Or perhaps it is wine, perhaps my going to bed too soon after dinner, perhaps a bad conscience.

# 1954

# 1954

*Sunday, 17th January*

And here we are, A. and I, back at Roquebrune again. I haven't written a word in my diary since I was here last summer. We arrived ten days ago and shall presumably stay until April. In London my time is so occupied working for the National Trust that I have little time for diary writing. Whereas here I am so occupied writing books that the same thing applies. In November my *Age of Inigo Jones* was published. It is too expensive to be widely bought. Yet so far it has had splendid reviews, far better than my previous ones, and for the first time in my life I have experienced an achievement of success. The *TLS* was frankly laudatory, also the *Spectator*, *Tablet* and *Time & Tide*. Harold Nicolson in the *Observer* gave it a review anyone might covet. No carping notices yet. On Xmas Day, which like the last we spent with the Moores at Parkside, Englefield Green, I was able to compare my state of content with the previous Xmas there, when that very morning I received a terrible letter from Eddie Marsh saying the manuscript was so frankly bad it was a waste of his time trying to correct it. How strange is life.

Now I have begun sketching out my new book – *Roman Mornings*. I asked Rupert Hart-Davis* if he would consider publishing it and he said yes, he would consider. This is a new experiment. I want to write about architecture in a readable manner, that will be informative and literary. Shall I succeed? After which I have in mind

---

* (Sir) Rupert Hart-Davis (1907–99); writer, editor and publisher; Eton friend of J.L.-M. He did not finally take *Roman Mornings*, which was published by Wingate in 1956.

a book on Lord Burlington and the Whig architect peers.* In fact I long to write a biography. I feel inspired with confidence by my good reviews. But I must not indulge in self-satisfaction. O no.

Strange that Duff Cooper is now dead. I did not find him an appealing figure: yet A. loved him.† He was very much a woman's man. He loved women and was indeed an arch-pouncer, which was one reason why I didn't much care for him. He put my hackles up in the way they rise when I see big lecherous dogs make themselves so offensive to Foo [A.L.-M's pekinese]. Duff was lecherous like many physically small men. I am assured he was a poet underneath.

*Sunday, 7th February*

Nancy Mitford got quite cross with Alvilde who was complaining about the pigeon-shooting from the Casino. Fat Italians, Alvilde says in her best *donna inglese* manner, sit on armchairs potting at tame pigeons let out of bags in which they have been kept in total darkness for several days without food. In the sudden sunshine they are blinded and bewildered. They are ruthlessly shot into the sea. It is no worse than shooting hand-fed pheasants in England, says Nancy the anglophobe. I consider all sport revolting. Cruelty does not come into the picture. It is the moral depravity of the killers which I find so distasteful.

How is it that one dislikes a person with whom one shares a secret depravity? The more the depravity is shared, the more one dislikes the person: and when others speak ill of him the more one feels inclined to agree with them.

All last week we were under a cloud. A. truly believed she was going to have a baby. She even telephoned the doctor in London, and sent a specimen to be analysed. On Friday night we telephoned London for the result. I was in such a state of nerves I could hardly speak. When we were told the result showed nothing of the kind,

* Published by Hamish Hamilton in 1962 as *Earls of Creation*.

† She is said to have been one of his innumerable conquests – though her name does not feature in the edition of his diaries published in 2005.

I was so relieved that I forgot to worry over the possible worse consequences for A. Anyhow we go to London in a week for her to be examined in hospital. I know many men are indifferent to children and don't look forward to having any of their own, but when they do a paternal instinct develops in them. Well, I am sure it never would in me, and that on the contrary I might hate mine.

*Thursday, 11th February*

Nancy says that music to her is delicious manure. At a concert this evening at Mentone I realised that to me it is like a drink or a drug. It accentuates the mood of the moment. If one is writing, or in love, it inspires one to write or love better. This afternoon I had been annoyed by two letters from England. Throughout the concert I was inspired with the most devastating retorts, which now an hour later have fled from me.

At luncheon today Willie [Maugham] said after a silence, 'I have just come to a decision. All women ought to be kept in harems.' I said, 'I suppose Alvilde's presence has brought you to this conclusion.' He then watched A. put two lumps of sugar in my coffee for me, and said, 'When my wife was really cross with me she used to say, "I forget whether you like sugar in your coffee."'

*Monday, 15th–Sunday, 21st February*

This week in London, which I very much hated for the anxiety about A. and the pain in my back and because Thurloe Square was let and I had to stay in Eardley's flat, was spent hobbling around in the rain. However I enjoyed the evenings. The Sutherlands dined with E. one night. E. believes Graham is noble and self-sacrificing in coming from abroad to give evidence against John Rothenstein in the Tate Gallery case.* Another evening spent with Edward Le

* Scandal resulting from the art critic Douglas Cooper publically insulting Sir John Rothenstein, Director of the Tate Gallery, at a dinner to inaugurate the Gallery's Diaghilev exhibition, and Sir John responding by knocking off Cooper's spectacles.

Bas* in his studio (very nice man who thinks too much about boys and drinks too much); E. benefits from Edward's tuition at the easel. Another evening with Harold [Nicolson] and Alan Pryce-Jones. Alan in one of his worldly moods. He said there were three women he might marry: 1. Bridget Parsons (little hope); 2. A very rich Rothschild unknown to me; 3. Elizabeth Cavendish† (does she know?). In a disingenuous manner he said, 'But how could I, a person of little position in the world and with an income of a mere £3,000 a year, ask one of these women to share the squalid life I could offer them?' Another evening with Rosamond and Joshua Rowley.‡ Ros said she once had a maid who gave birth to an illegitimate baby which the lover murdered. It all happened in R's house.

*March*

San Satiro at Milan more sophisticated than I remember it. Even A., who dislikes Italian Renaissance architecture, was impressed by it. The fantasy about it is almost Rococo, *viz.*, the round windows set in a halo in the crossing arms; same arrangement appears in Santa Maria della Grazie I think, and in the exquisite chapel at San Eustorgio. There is a jewel-like quality in these Milanese works of Bramante§ and his school which is essentially fifteenth-century, quite unlike B's Roman buildings. They recall Michelozzo who in fact built the Pontonori chapel. When B. got down to Rome he became a different architect altogether, more avant-garde, more strictly Classical. How and why did this happen? Rome more sophisticated – and the court of the Popes. Then at Pavia there is something almost Baroque in B's duomo, in the strange pointed piers of the crossing, like the prows of ships about to collide.

---

* Artist and collector of modern paintings (1904–66).

† Lady Elizabeth Cavendish (b. 1926); dau. of 10th Duke of Devonshire; Lady-in-Waiting to HRH Princess Margaret; intimate friend of John Betjeman from 1951.

‡ Sir Joshua Rowley, 5th Bt (1920–97), of Tendring Hall, Suffolk; Deputy Secretary of N.T., 1952–5.

§ Donato Bramante (1444–1514); Italian architect.

Back to Rococo again. I have said in *Roman Mornings* that Rococo was not an architectural style. No more was it when one considers Bramante's Rococo-isms, and indeed Michelangelo's of the sixteenth century which pundits now call Mannerism – really the same aberration only two hundred years earlier. Again, what more heterodox than the hideous Casa dei Zuccari (1590) in Rome with its portal and window made of monster faces, the one swallowing the visitor, the other the daylight – gobbling up both with their awful jaws.

*Monday, 5th April*

Before A. and I left by the Blue Train for London tonight Graham Sutherland allowed us to have a look at the portrait he is doing of Eddy Sackville-West. We thought it extremely like, sensitive yet un-caricatural. Graham works by a curious system. He paints parts of the figure – head, torso, legs – separately and then copies these parts faithfully onto the final big canvas, sewing the various limbs together, so to speak.

*Thursday, 22nd April*

James Pope-Hennessy dined alone with me [in London] last night. He had come from a meeting with Christopher Hassall,* to whom Eddie Marsh left everything. Jamesey asked him outright if Eddie ever loved anyone physically. H. replied that the farthest Eddie ever went, so far as he knew, was to take his, H's foot, and polish it while holding it against his bosom. Oddly enough Harold Nicolson told me last week that before the First World War Eddie was said to delight in taking off the hunting boots of his young men friends. Hassall suggested that since during puberty Eddie's voice didn't break properly he may never have developed properly in other respects.

Hassall has inherited all the Rupert Brooke correspondence which he proposes to sell to King's College for a hundred pounds,

* Poet, writer, playwright and librettist (1912–63); author of a biography of Rupert Brooke, published posthumously in 1964.

having been offered five thousand by an American university. There is a letter to Eddie, written after Brooke's death, from a New Zealand sergeant, reminding Eddie how he first met Brooke in the Brompton Oratory. He was looking at the statue of St Cecilia,* when a strange voice accosted him. He turned round and saw the most beautiful face in the world. Brooke struck up a warm friendship with him and used to call him 'my St Cecilia' – which is rather off, somehow. A surviving friend of Brooke's told Hassall that no photograph could ever do justice to his good looks and that his complexion was flawless.

Today I went to Nurstead Court near Gravesend [Kent]. It belongs to Major Edmeades† who is a nephew of Lady Baker of Owletts,‡ and is interesting only for its semi-remaining aisled hall of great round columns in timber instead of stone, condition deplorable. The major's old mother lives with him. The whole place terribly down at heel, messy, smelly, in fact squalid beyond the bounds of Alan P.-J's imagination. I went on the roof. It is perished, tiles off, lead rotten, water pouring through in wet weather. No servants. Poor major! How are the gentry fallen. He cannot afford to mend the roof, and has to find thousands of pounds to pay off death duties. Then he showed me some of his trim labourers' cottages, all with television. A good landowner. He works every day as long as the light lasts, like a farm hand, but without holidays, for he never goes away.

I went on to see dear Lady Baker at Owletts. It was in 1937 I first went there when Sir Herbert was alive. I have great admiration for the family, for they are charitable, devoted, dutiful, fruitful and successful. Sir Herbert was a superlative human being, a remarkable artist and architect. I love the ethos of Owletts, this nice old Charles II house with its well-designed-and-made furniture of Sir Herbert's. The house full of grandchildren. The garden ablaze with daffodils, cherry blossom and crown imperial lilies.

---

* Patron saint of church music, represented in mediaeval art as playing the organ; said to have been a Roman matron who refused to sleep with her husband as she believed herself to be 'bethrothed to an angel', subsequently executed (with difficulty) by the Roman authorities.

† Major R. W. Edmeades (b. 1914).

‡ See entry for 27 November 1942.

*Wednesday, 21st July*

Gerry Wellington asked us to luncheon today. A. is away but I accepted. I wanted to see the part of Apsley House he lives in. At the N.T. meeting this morning Gerry whispered that luncheon was at 1.30 and the Prime Minister* and Lady Churchill were coming. We were to be only eight in all. I took a bus and walked into the courtyard of Apsley House just as the PM's motor drove in flying the flag of the Warden of the Cinque Ports. So I made a dash for a small side door before the Churchills should enter. The other guests already assembled. I knew only the American Ambassador and Mrs† by sight and Muriel Warde‡ by more than sight. I sat next to Muriel and the Ambassador's daughter, Muriel between me and Sir Winston.

Sir W. looks like a small, fat and frail doll or baby, with a white and pink face, most unnatural in an adult, and no lines at all. There is a celluloid quality about the skin which is alarming. He shuffles. His back view is funny. He was wearing too short a black jacket exposing a shiny striped seat. The front part of him is different in that it is smartly dressed – an expanse of white, semi-starched shirt and cuffs with links, the habitual white winged collar and spotted bow-tie. The shirt bulges out as he slumps in his seat. He has sparse wispy white hair, and is a very spruce old gentleman – in the front. I suppose he does look old, or rather unreal. It is hard to detect a human being behind the mask. Everyone deferred and played up to him when he did vouchsafe a word, laughed rather too hilariously. When he left Gerry said he was in fine form and splendid humour, which simply means that when he is not, he must be terrifying. The Ambassadress and Muriel kept up a running badinage which he was either relishing or paying no attention to, I couldn't make out which. General conversation did not get far

* Winston Churchill had become Prime Minister again in October 1951 and remained in office until April 1955, despite suffering a stroke in June 1953; he was installed as a Knight of the Garter, 1953.

† Winthrop W. Aldrich, US Ambassador to London, 1954–7.

‡ Daughter of Arthur Wilson of Tranby Croft, Yorkshire; family connection of A.L.-M., whose uncle Graham Menzies had married Muriel's sister.

and yet we were all so determined not to miss a word Sir W. might utter that no one listened to his neighbour. However, all he said that I recollect was that once at the age of twenty-five he had danced a *pas seul* (he explained he could never dance with a partner but by himself danced beautifully). At the end of the performance he thought he had a heart attack and next day he felt very ill. So he went to see a famous heart specialist in France who told him that, if he never drank effervescent liquids or smoked again, he might pull through. Twenty years later he again visited the specialist, who congratulated him on his remarkable recovery and survival. 'So I had the satisfaction', said Sir Winston, 'of telling him that every single day since my last interview I had both drunk effervescent liquids and smoked. Doctors still know very little.'

Before luncheon I overheard him asking Muriel who I was. Then as we went into the dining room he asked, 'Does Oldham mean anything to you?' I knew he referred to his first election* when my grandfather and Papa supported him and had him to stay. He remembered it all vividly and asked if Crompton Hall was still standing. I said it was pulled down last year. Then he asked about the Milne mill and I said we still had it and [J.L.-M's brother] Dick managed it.

Conversation between Gerry and Churchill struck me as Trollopian. 'Now, Prime Minister, will you have one of my cigars?' 'No thank you, Duke, I've got one of my own.'

There is no peasantry left in England, yet very occasionally I see a flash of something which evokes it, or rather a memory of it. While motoring through a narrow lane near King's Lynn [Norfolk] this month I passed a middle-aged countryman leaning against a bicycle talking to a woman. He wore not a hat but a chaplet of hop leaves on his head, absolutely unconcerned as though he might be Bacchus himself.

---

* As a Unionist candidate, Churchill had contested Oldham unsuccessfully at a by-election in 1899 and (after his Boer War exploits) successfully at the general election of 1900. J.L.-M's grandfather, James Henry Lees-Milne of Crompton Hall (see entry for 14 February 1945), was a prominent local Unionist who owned the nearby mill of A. & A. Crompton, producers of cotton thread.

# Index

# Index